SPEAKING
THE LAW

*The Hoover Institution gratefully acknowledges
the following individuals and foundations
for their significant support of the*
JEAN PERKINS TASK FORCE ON
NATIONAL SECURITY AND LAW

James J. Carroll III

Jean Perkins Foundation

JEAN PERKINS TASK FORCE ON NATIONAL SECURITY AND LAW

SPEAKING THE LAW

The Obama Administration's Addresses on National Security Law

Kenneth Anderson
and
Benjamin Wittes

HOOVER INSTITUTION PRESS

Stanford University | *Stanford, California*

www.hoover.org

Hoover Institution Press Publication No. 639

Hoover Institution at Leland Stanford Junior University,
Stanford, California, 94305-6010

First printing 2015
21 20 19 18 17 16 15   9 8 7 6 5 4 3 2 1

Manufactured in the United States of America

The paper used in this publication meets the minimum
Requirements of the American National Standard for
Information Sciences—Permanence of Paper for Printed
Library Materials, ANSI/NISO Z39.48-1992. ∞

Cataloging-in-Publication Data is available from the Library of Congress.

ISBN 978-0-8179-1654-1 (cloth : alk. paper)
ISBN 978-0-8179-1656-5 (epub)
ISBN 978-0-8179-1657-2 (mobi)
ISBN 978-0-8179-1658-9 (PDF)

Contents

Appendixes: Addresses and Remarks by President Obama and Administration Officials on National Security Law 279

Introduction

When Barack Obama came into office in 2009, the strategic landscape facing the United States in its overseas counterterrorism operations was undergoing a shift. The public had not yet noticed the shift. Americans still hotly debated the detention, interrogation, rendition, and trial of terrorist suspects. Congress had busied itself with revamping surveillance authorities the previous year; human rights groups were consumed with the subjects of waterboarding, CIA prisons, and closing Guantánamo.

Yet the fabric of American counterterrorism was quickly rendering these issues, if not quite moot, certainly secondary. Gone were the days when American forces were capturing enemy fighters in large numbers. Gone were the days too when policymakers even dreamed of detaining their way to American safety. While America fought endless legal battles over the authority to detain and try enemy forces outside of Article III courts, the enemy itself no longer fled in bulk into the arms of US forces or their proxies. It increasingly operated, rather, from areas in which the United States had no boots on the ground—and no desire to put boots on the ground. Long gone too were the days of aggressive CIA interrogations. There were legacy issues to fight over, to be sure, but new detainees were coming in what outgoing State Department Legal Adviser John Bellinger called the "onesies and twosies."

The action increasingly lay elsewhere. As quickly became apparent when Obama was sworn in, it lay in drones. It lay in Special Forces operations. It lay in hundreds of micro-wars—in the ability to project force on a highly targeted basis into specific locales where US forces were not deployed. It lay in scalpels, not machetes. It lay in technology, not detention facilities. The shift actually began under President Bush, not under President Obama. But it came to fruition during the Obama administration, and the public certainly caught on to the change only after the new president had taken office. The result was that Obama and his administration faced acutely the question of how to talk about its war on terror. What could it say about the rules and about the law that governed American conduct of this war? What was the framework in which American operations were taking place—both legacy operations Obama had once criticized and these new operations that were suddenly taking center stage?

At least with respect to Obama's most conspicuous innovation—the widespread use of drones—the administration had inherited an awkward silence that became deafening the more it ramped up the use of drones. The locus of American operations had shifted from an area—detention—where litigation demanded a significant degree of public doctrinal articulation to an area in which courts were less willing to tread and which therefore produced no public law. There were good reasons for the silence, to be sure. The CIA operated drones as a covert action; other countries, including the countries on whose soil the operations took place, did not want their cooperation known; acknowledging the hand of the United States, even where it was obvious, would beg questions of those countries' consent and sovereignty. But the more central drones and targeted killing became to American counterterrorism efforts, the less plausible the silence became.

The pressure to say something substantial on the war's legal framework began early—and from politically diverse quarters. By the spring of 2009, one of the present authors was writing, "The United States would be best served if the Obama administration did that exceedingly rare thing in international law and diplomacy: getting the United States out in front of the issue by making plain the American position [on targeted killing], rather than merely reacting in surprise when its sovereign prerogatives are challenged by the international soft-law community."[1] UN Special Rapporteur Philip Alston released a report in May 2009 decrying the US government's lack of accountability.[2] The American Civil Liberties Union, similarly,

---

1. Kenneth Anderson, "Targeted Killing in U.S. Counterterrorism Strategy and Law," Series on Counterterrorism and American Statutory Law, The Brookings Institution, Georgetown University Law center, and the Hoover Institution, May 11, 2009. This paper was later adapted for the book *Legislating the War on Terror: An Agenda for Reform*, Benjamin Wittes, ed. (Washington, DC: Brookings Institution Press, 2009), pp.346–400.

2. "Report of the Special Rapporteur on extrajudicial, summary or arbitrary executions, Philip Alston, on his mission to the United States of America," May 28, 2009, http://www2.ohchr.org/english/bodies/hrcouncildocs/11session/A.H RC.11.2.Add.5.pdf

was calling for greater transparency in the legal theory behind the drone strikes and by January 2010 had filed a Freedom of Information Act request for details about the government's targeted killing program.[3] Over time, these pressures grew, alongside the strategic importance of the strikes.

There were other pressures pushing the administration to articulate the legal framework of its war on Al Qaeda. The administration had a strong instinct to distinguish itself legally from its predecessor, particularly as it adopted positions that struck many observers as largely consistent with the positions of the Bush administration. It also quickly developed poisonous relations with Congress over such questions as the closure of Guantánamo and the use of federal courts as a trial forum. It had the political Right to fend off on its formal abandonment of the CIA interrogation and detention program. And it had to contend also with the political Left's—and the international community's—sense of disappointment, even betrayal, at its unwillingness to abandon the war paradigm altogether. Even before the rise of drones necessitated the articulation of legal doctrine, the Obama administration had to explain itself: What

---

3. See Nahal Zamani, "UN Special Rapporteur Calls for Transparency and Accountability," June 5, 2009, http://www.aclu.org/blog/capital -punishment-human-rights-national-security/un-special-rapporteur-calls -transparency-and and "UN Expert on Extrajudicial Killings Calls for Special Prosecutor," May 29, 2009, http://www.aclu.org/human-rights/un-expert -extrajudicial-killings-calls-special-prosecutor. For more on the ACLU's FOIA request, see Jonathan Manes, "ACLU FOIA Request Seeks Info on President Obama's Use of Drones," January 13, 2010, http://www.aclu.org/ blog/national-security/aclu-foia-request-seeks-info-president-obamas -use-drones. The FOIA request is available at http://www.aclu.org/files/ assets/2010–1-13-PredatorDroneFOIARequest.pdf.

kind of war was it fighting, if indeed it was fighting a war at all? What did it see as its powers within that conflict? What would it do to protect America and go on the offensive against the enemy? What would it never do? Who was the enemy, exactly? And how did the authorities the administration claimed interact with civilian law enforcement powers, international law, and the US Constitution?

The Obama administration surely never made any kind of overarching strategic decision to address these questions in a series of speeches given by a diverse range of officials in a shifting legal and policy landscape over the course of several years. It is, therefore, a little artificial to treat the body of these speeches as reflecting some kind of cohesive Obama doctrine of the conflict. The speeches, rather, just happened as the administration—and the individual officials in question—perceived the need to address certain matters officially and in public.

Yet beginning in the spring of 2009 and throughout the remainder of Obama's first term, the administration's senior officials—from the president himself down to an assistant attorney general, the State Department legal adviser, and the general counsels of several agencies—laid out a huge array of legal policy doctrine in the form of addresses to various bodies. And in May 2013, President Obama gave a speech that sharply shifted the landscape. These speeches and those that followed, many of which were covered extensively in the press at the time of their delivery, cumulatively represent the fullest articulation and explication since September 11, 2001, of the administration's view of the conflict and the legal rules that govern it.

In some areas, the doctrine they reflect is spelled out in more detail in legal briefs; the speeches thus serve as a kind of summary of the government's litigating positions. In some areas, by contrast, the speeches themselves represent the most developed doctrine the administration has officially spelled out in public.

The first key point is that, viewed together, they lay out a broad array of legal and policy positions regarding a large number of principles currently contested at both the domestic and international levels.

The other key point is that the speeches almost never *are* viewed together. While the press has had a sense of the incremental articulation of new ideas through their progressive delivery, nobody has ever lined up the canonical national security speeches of the Obama administration and examined the aggregate legal policy framework they lay out as a body of work. With the president in his second term shifting the ground beneath our feet as we write, that is our purpose in this volume.

The Obama administration has received a great deal of criticism for not saying much about the legal framework that governs its counterterrorism operations.[4] The criticism is largely unfair. The administration has actually said a remarkable amount about a surprisingly wide array of contested legal issues at stake in its operations. Viewed together, the speeches,

---

4. See, for example, Editorial, "Too Much Power for a President," *New York Times*, May 30, 2012, http://www.nytimes.com/2012/05/31/opinion/too-much-power-for-a-president.html?ref=world; Editorial, "The Power to Kill," *New York Times*, March 10, 2012, http://www.nytimes.com/2012/03/11/opinion/sunday/the-power-to-kill.html; Editorial, "The CIA and Drone Strikes," *New York Times*, August 13, 2011, http://www.nytimes.com/2011/08/14/opinion/sunday/the-cia-and-drone-strikes.html; and Editorial, "Lethal Force Under Law," *New York Times*, October 9, 2010, http://www.nytimes.com/2010/10/10/opinion/10sun1.html.

in fact, offer a fairly holistic—if high-altitude and ultimately shifting—account of how the administration views the conflict and its authorities to confront the enemy. While the government has expanded upon some of these positions in briefs, no other body of official statements communicates as thoroughly the scope and range of administration views of its authorities and constraints. In other words, to understand the administration's view of the law of the conflict, the canonical speeches represent the richest and most complete explication we have.

As such, the speeches—at least with respect to international law—represent something else well worth highlighting: in some important parts, they represent the *opinio juris* of the United States. The speeches, in other words, are the considered, publicly articulated legal views of the most important actor in the international community about what it will and will not do with respect to waging war against non-state enemies as a matter of international law. To constitute *opinio juris* in international law, a state must convey that it acts—or refrains from acting—out of a sense of legal obligation, a belief that the act is not merely policy, diplomacy, prudence, or the representation of an aspiration for what the law should be, but an expression of belief in an existing legal obligation. In some matters, the speeches express such a belief in an existing legal obligation; in other matters, the speeches appear to express an aspiration to which the administration believes the law should move, without necessarily claiming that the law has already done so; and in still others, the speeches represent policies that the administration regards as plausible and defensible interpretations of international law. Finally, the speeches also articulate policies of the US government in areas in which international law is silent, as well as the US government's assessment of the strategic landscape that confronts it, as a descriptive condition for determining which fundamental paradigms of law—armed conflict or law enforcement, for example—apply to different issues.

The speeches themselves are not law. They are, however, a mode of articulation of law, much of which has been made neither by courts nor by the legislature but within the executive branch itself. In some of the most contested areas, the speeches represent the *only* mode—other than leaks—of articulation of law that largely takes the form of internal executive memoranda and argumentation that is mostly secret. They thus constitute a significant body of expression not merely of the Obama administration's views, but of the nation's positions more generally. It would be quite unfair to dismiss them merely as clumsy public relations efforts by the administration's lawyers.

One important feature of each speech is that it does not merely represent the views of the individual who gives the speech. As Rebecca Ingber, a veteran of the State Department Legal Adviser's Office, wrote:

> While the speechmaker and her office may hold the pen, this does not necessitate ultimate decisionmaking authority over what is said or revealed publicly. Instead, coordination and consensus are often critical.
>
> . . . Though internal assumptions and norms about coordination and clearance are mutable, the greater the coordination in vetting the speech *ex ante*, the greater the likelihood the speech will create internal precedent going forward. This is true in part because . . . cleared language tends to be recycled in other written product addressing the same issues.

In addition, because speechmaking inherently tends to implicate high-level public officials, coordination of the government's position will necessarily involve the high-level speechmaker and will likely be vetted among colleagues of an equal stature to that official throughout the interagency.[5]

Indeed, one of the features of these speeches that makes them canonical is precisely the degree of interagency clearance that goes into vetting them. With the possible exception of the president's own speeches, all have gone through at least some interagency clearance process that makes them, in some meaningful sense, reflective of the views of the government as a whole.

As such, the speeches should not be understood simply as a statement of the views of a single Democratic administration. It's certainly possible for a subsequent administration to come into office and reverse many—even all—of the doctrinal stands these positions reflect, and Obama himself has pivoted significantly since the outset of his second term. But the inertial quality of government decision-making and desire for institutional stability make it far more likely that the most important decisions on legal doctrine—once taken, announced publicly, and justified in public— become institutional views of the federal government itself, resistant to change by future administrations. The tendency will be toward evolution, both across different administrations and within them. From the stand-

---

5. Rebecca Ingber, "Interpretation Catalysts and Executive Branch Legal Decisionmaking," *Yale Journal of International Law* 38, January 16, 2013, http://papers.ssrn.com/sol3/papers.cfm?abstract_id=2201199.

point of America over the long run, this is a good thing—rather than a sharp see-sawing back and forth as administrations change.

We propose, therefore, to look at these speeches as a major part of the Obama administration's legacy in the national security area, an articulation of what aims to be a lasting framework for aggressive action against non-state enemies of the United States that will likely form the basis of future administrations' approaches.

That approach necessarily raises profound normative questions. If one treats the speeches as cumulatively laying out a legal framework for counterterrorism actions, is the framework a strong one or a weak one? Is it durable or fragile? Does it honor the rule of law or do violence to it? Does it reflect our values domestically and globally or does it amount to an assertion of raw power?

Our modest thesis in these pages is that the Obama administration has gotten a tremendous amount right in this body of work. The framework, we will argue, remains incomplete in certain areas and is in some considerable flux in the second term. Its institutionalization in statutory and case law is erratic and may be, as a consequence, unstable in some respects. There are some things that we believe the administration has gotten wrong. In some areas, moreover, the administration has been less imaginative and forward-looking than in others. But by and large, the speeches lay out in considerable detail a developing legal framework that moves the country considerably and constructively toward institutional settlement of contested questions. As such, we shall argue, while the speeches leave some questions unanswered and while aspects of the framework require more work and development, they constitute a major step forward—a sound platform on which future administrations can build.

The use of speeches to express *opinio juris* or to declare international legal views, interpretations of law, or policies that the government believes fulfill its international law obligations is not new. On the contrary, law and diplomacy have traditionally fused the two together in high-level addresses and statements given by statesmen, diplomats, and government leaders—some of them in the form of statements directly to foreign governments and others as statements by the executive to Congress. The Monroe Doctrine, for example, fused policy and legal views of the United States, consistent with practices of the time, and it was first delivered as part of President James Monroe's Message to Congress in 1823. Secretaries of state have delivered the international legal views of the United States in many forms, ranging from speeches to exchanges of diplomatic letters, since the earliest days of the republic. With the rise of multilateral diplomacy over the last sixty years—and not merely state-to-state bilateral relations—statements or speeches addressed to whole groups of states have become a more important mechanism for conveying the nation's legal views, tending to replace the exchange of bilateral diplomatic notes or letters.

But an administration, over the course of two terms, gives a great many speeches. A project analyzing the doctrine laid out in those speeches thus necessarily faces a problem of selection: which to include, which to leave out. The relevant set of speeches, in our view, includes those given by either White House officials or Senate-confirmed lawyers which articulate the legal authorities claimed by the administration in prosecuting the conflict. Viewed in combination with one another, and supplemented where necessary by more detailed statements in litigation or policy documents, these speeches represent the closest thing to a doctrine of the conflict the administration has given—one that is, in fact, significantly more elaborated than many people seem to imagine.

For purposes of this discussion, we treat the following sixteen speeches as canonical. The relevant portions of each are included as an appendix:

- President Barack Obama, "Remarks by the President on National Security," The National Archives, Washington, D.C., May 21, 2009
- President Barack Obama, "A Just and Lasting Peace," the 2009 Nobel Peace Prize Lecture, Oslo, Norway, December 10, 2009
- President Barack Obama, remarks at the National Defense University, Fort McNair, Washington, D.C., May 23, 2013
- President Barack Obama, "Remarks by the President on Review of Signals Intelligence," Department of Justice, Washington, D.C., January 17, 2014
- Harold H. Koh, legal adviser to the Department of State, "The Obama Administration and International Law," address to the American Society of International Law, Washington, D.C., March 25, 2010
- Harold H. Koh, legal adviser to the Department of State, "International Law in Cyberspace," address to the USCYBERCOM Inter-Agency Legal Conference, Fort Meade, Maryland, September 18, 2012
- David Kris, assistant attorney general for national security, "Law Enforcement as a Counterterrorism Tool,"

address at the Brookings Institution, Washington, D.C., June 11, 2010

- Jeh C. Johnson, general counsel, Department of Defense, "U.S. Terrorist Suspect Detention Policy," speech to the Heritage Foundation, Washington, D.C., October 18, 2011

- Jeh C. Johnson, general counsel, Department of Defense, "National Security Law, Lawyers, and Lawyering in the Obama Administration," address at Yale Law School, New Haven, Connecticut, February 22, 2012

- Jeh C. Johnson, general counsel, Department of Defense, "The Conflict against Al Qaeda and Its Affiliates: How Will It End?" Oxford Union, Oxford University, November 30, 2012

- Eric Holder, attorney general, Department of Justice, address at Northwestern University School of Law, Chicago, Illinois, March 5, 2012

- Stephen W. Preston, general counsel, Central Intelligence Agency, "CIA and the Rule of Law," address at Harvard Law School, Cambridge, Massachusetts, April 10, 2012

- John O. Brennan, assistant to the president for homeland security and counterterrorism, "Strengthening Our Security by Adhering to Our Values and Laws," address at Harvard Law School, Cambridge, Massachusetts, September 16, 2011

- John O. Brennan, assistant to the president for homeland security and counterterrorism, "The Ethics and Efficacy of the President's Counterterrorism Strategy," Woodrow Wilson International Center for Scholars, Washington, D.C., April 30, 2012

- John O. Brennan, assistant to the president for homeland security and counterterrorism, "U.S. Policy toward

Yemen," Council on Foreign Relations, New York City, August 8, 2012

- Robert S. Litt, general counsel with the Office of the Director of National Intelligence, "Privacy, Technology, and National Security: An Overview of Intelligence Collection," address at the Brookings Institution, Washington, D.C., July 19, 2013.

Our examination of the speeches begins with a look at the speeches of Obama's first term. In chapter 1, we give a description of the framework they laid out. In this chapter, we describe—but largely refrain from analyzing—what the Obama administration said in its first four years about the legal framework in which it was operating with respect to such questions as the nature of the conflict, the use of drones and targeted killings, detention, trial by military commission and in federal courts, interrogation, and the end of the conflict. The purpose of this chapter is to synthesize the various speeches into a single doctrinal statement that describes in holistic terms the administration's first-term approach in legal policy to the conflict.

Chapter 2 attempts to analyze this framework and examine the stresses upon it. We ask whether the framework is, in the main, the right one. Where did the administration get matters right and where wrong? Where is the framework underdeveloped? In general, we argue, the administration articulated a strong basis for institutional settlement of contested questions—one that gives future administrations a useful set of doctrinal positions on which to build as the conflict continues to morph. Important questions remain open, however, and the framework will require further refinement by both the administration and the legislature.

Chapter 3 looks at the disruption to this framework presented by the president in his first speech on national security legal issues of his second term. This speech offered virtually no changes in legal view but significant shifts in policy and aspiration for the law. We look at the state of the framework in light of these shifts.

The legal framework laid out by the speeches involves a complex interaction between executive branch lawmaking and lawmaking by both the courts and the Congress. In chapter 4, we examine this interaction—the involvement of the judiciary in defining detention authority, its non-involvement in targeting matters, Congress's involvement in defining the rules for military commissions, its authorization for detention in the National Defense Authorization Act of 2012, and its restrictions on detainee transfers in that legislation. Both congressional actions and judicial involvement in the developing framework, we argue, have shaped the institutional settlement the speeches describe in significant respects—allowing the administration to speak often on behalf of, or with the blessing of, more than one branch of government.

The framework described in the speeches has come under fire from multiple quarters. In chapter 5, we engage—and largely reject—both the critique of the political Right, which sees the framework as weak, overly legalistic, and insufficiently military in character, and the critique of the political Left and much of the international community, which sees it as lawless and violative of both international legal norms and constitutional principles of civil liberties.

Finally, in the Conclusion, we offer concluding thoughts and suggest certain stresses on the framework with which the administration and Congress will have to wrestle in the future.

A brief note is in order regarding the unorthodox manner in which we published this volume. Normally, we know, one waits to publish a book until one has written its constituent chapters. But the speeches of the Obama administration on national security legal issues were a matter of ongoing controversy, dialogue, discussion, and debate. We thought, as a consequence, it might be valuable to publish these essays as we completed them, thus contributing to the debate in something closer to real time and reserving the right to benefit from that debate by making changes to these pages before final publication. These essays are now compiled in this volume. This form of publication was something of an experiment, one which we are grateful that the Hoover Task Force on National Security and the Law agreed to facilitate and support.

CHAPTER 1

An Overview of the Obama Administration's Canonical Speeches of the First Term

L et us begin with a simple effort to summarize and reconstruct what the Obama administration said in its first-term speeches on national security legal policy, ignoring for now President Obama's pivot in his National Defense University speech in May 2013 and the resulting flux in the administration's views of these subjects—a topic we will address in chapter 3. Here we offer, initially without much greater ambition, an overview of official statements on the wide range of issues the administration addressed during the first term. Our aim here is not to offer analysis, praise, or critique. Rather, we strive to weave the speeches together around the topics that seem most important in establishing the administration's national security legal doctrine and to construct a synthetic policy document that brings all of the major policy threads together in one place. In doing so, we necessarily make some editorial decisions about what parts to include and exclude and how to intertwine them as a single statement and voice. We do this knowing that officials gave these speeches at different times and under different circumstances across the first four years of the Obama administration, and we specifically organize the summary thematically, not temporally. The exercise gives a sense of just how comprehensively the administration did, in fact, address a set of issues on which critics often accused it of obfuscation and silence. The goal is to establish and explain the baseline set of policies and legal views on which the administration built in its second term—and which future administrations will inherit, absent changes to the framework. We begin with those issues that frame the nature of the conflict at its deepest level.

The Fundamental Nature of the Conflict and the Law Governing It

The first-term speeches at their most fundamental were an effort to characterize legally the struggle against transnational terrorism by non-state groups and the powers the United States government has deployed to wage this fight. The speakers sought both to declare and to expound upon the US government's exercise of national security powers in counterterrorism operations at home and abroad; at the same time, they sought to establish and maintain the legal and political legitimacy of those operations among the American people and, to the extent possible, in the wider world.

One of the striking features of the speeches is their consistent acknowledgment that international law meaningfully limits the American exercise of these powers. After the Bush administration, which very publicly—at least at first—denied legal constraints in general, and international legal constraints in particular, this was not a foregone conclusion in the construction of the US position. Yet other countries have access, or soon will have access, to the kinds of methods and means of counterterrorism that the United States deploys. And, perhaps with that fact in mind, as a matter of general principle the speeches acknowledge that the principles we apply to ourselves—principles of both permission and limitation in confronting transnational terrorist adversaries—we must grant to other sovereign states in similar situations. President Obama acknowledged this point directly in his December 10, 2009, Nobel Peace Prize Lecture in Oslo (see Appendix: Obama—B):

> [A]ll nations—strong and weak alike—must adhere to standards that govern the use of force. I—like any head of state—reserve the right to act unilaterally if necessary to defend my nation. Nevertheless, I am convinced that adhering to standards, international standards, strengthens those who do and isolates and weakens those who don't. . . . Furthermore, America [cannot insist] . . . that others follow the rules of the road if we refuse to follow them ourselves. For when we don't, our actions appear arbitrary and undercut the legitimacy of future interventions, no matter how justified.

This high-altitude principle infuses a great deal of the rhetoric and persuasive ambition of many of the first-term speeches. And its acknowledgment represents an important starting place. It's also a comforting one for many who ache to see the United States embrace international legal standards. But it leaves open the question of what fundamental paradigm of international law actually governs the activities that constitute the American

confrontation with international terrorists. Is the fundamental
legal paradigm one of the laws of war and armed conflict, on the
one hand, or is it extraterritorial law enforcement as limited by
international human rights law, on the other—or perhaps some
mixture of these distinct legal authorities? The differences here
are not academic; they can yield radically different answers to
questions concerning the use of force and its conduct, starting
with whether there is an obligation to seek to arrest and detain
someone before striking with lethal force. They also guide questions of how one detains and tries suspects for crimes.

The Obama administration's first-term answer to this fundamental question was far less comforting to those who seek a
kinder, gentler American counterterrorism. The administration
decisively rejected the widespread expectation that Obama's
election heralded a return to a purely—or more purely—law
enforcement approach, at least insofar as that expectation
included in the short term a law enforcement-dominated
approach outside of the United States itself. From the beginning, the administration emphasized a kind of bifurcated nature
of the conflict, in which law enforcement dominated domestically while war dominated beyond US shores. The first-term
speeches disclaim, at least as a policy matter, any intention to
use law-of-war powers here at home and fiercely defend the
criminal justice apparatus as a means of dealing with both US
citizens captured abroad and anyone captured state-side. On
the other hand, they also emphasize that the fundamental relationship between the United States and the enemy groups it
confronts is one of armed conflict, as a matter of international
as well as domestic law. Let's consider these points in turn.

As early as May 21, 2009 (see Appendix: Obama—A),
President Obama himself insisted that warfare lay at the heart

of the relationship in his address at the National Archives in Washington, D.C., saying, "Now let me be clear: we are indeed at war with Al Qaeda and its affiliates." The administration throughout the first term consistently maintained both that the current conflict is authorized by domestic law—specifically by the Authorization for the Use of Military Force (AUMF)[1] and by the president's inherent constitutional power to defend the nation—and that these authorities are consistent with international law. As Attorney General Eric Holder put it on March 5, 2012 (see Appendix: Holder—A), in his address at Northwestern University School of Law:

> [T]here are instances where our government has the clear authority—and, I would argue, the responsibility—to defend the United States through the appropriate and lawful use of lethal force.
>
> This principle has long been established under both US and international law. In response to the attacks perpetrated—and the continuing threat posed—by Al Qaeda, the Taliban, and associated forces, Congress has authorized the president to use all necessary and appropriate force against those groups. Because the United States is in an armed conflict, we are authorized to take action against enemy belligerents under international law. The Constitution empowers the president to protect the nation from any imminent threat of violent attack. And international law recognizes the inherent right of national self-defense. None

---

1. Joint Resolution to Authorize the Use of United States Armed Forces Against Those Responsible for the Recent Attacks Launched Against the United States, Public Law 107-40, September 18, 2001.

of this is changed by the fact that we are not in a conventional war.

The insistence that the United States is in an armed conflict with Al Qaeda and its affiliates, or associated forces, is unwavering across all the first-term speeches. The nature of this conflict, it bears emphasis, involves *actual* war—not war as a metaphor for policy seriousness, but armed conflict in the strict legal sense. This is the US government's position even though the enemy is not a state. In the parlance of international law, the United States considers itself as fighting a "non-international armed conflict"—that is, an armed conflict against something other than another sovereign state.

Since many US actions using lethal force would constitute murder or other crimes during peacetime, establishing the legal propriety of a state of armed conflict is actually an important point. And the speeches offer a firm and consistent position on this basic issue. As John Brennan, Obama's counterterrorism adviser, put it September 16, 2011 (see Appendix: Brennan—A), at Harvard Law School: "[T]he president has said many times [that] we are at war with Al Qaeda. In an indisputable act of aggression, Al Qaeda attacked our nation and killed nearly 3,000 innocent people. . . . Our ongoing armed conflict with Al Qaeda stems from our right—recognized under international law—to self-defense."

The administration, in fact, reserved the point that America is legally at war even when defending the use—as it has done assiduously—of the domestic criminal justice system as a tool of counterterrorism. That is, the first-term speeches describe the criminal justice system as one instrument available to it in the array of national powers deployable against the enemy in this armed conflict. Speaking at the Brookings Institution in Washington on June 11, 2010 (see Appendix: Kris—A), Assistant Attorney General David Kris explicitly rejected the notion that a war paradigm disfavored the use of criminal justice tools:

> The argument [of those who oppose the use of the criminal justice system], as I understand it, is basically the following:
> (1) We are at war.
> (2) Our enemies in this war are not common criminals.
> (3) Therefore, we should fight them using military and intelligence methods, not law enforcement methods.
>
> This is a simple and rhetorically powerful argument and, precisely for that reason, it may be attractive.
>
> In my view, however, and with all due respect, it is not correct. And it will, if adopted, make us less safe. Of course, it's not that law enforcement is always the right tool for combating terrorism. But it's also not the case that it's never the right tool. The reality, I think, is that it's sometimes the right tool. And whether it's the right tool in any given case depends on the specific facts of that case.
>
> Here's my version of the argument:
>
> (1) We're at war. The president has said this many times, as has the attorney general.
> (2) In war you must try to win—no other goal is acceptable.
> (3) To win the war, we need to use all available tools that are consistent with the law and our values, selecting in any case the tool that is best under the circumstances.

Yet at the same time as these speeches situate law enforcement as one of the available tools with which to win a war, they also consistently emphasize law enforcement as the chief—even exclusive—tool for use at home and against Americans captured anywhere in the conflict. In his Harvard speech, for example, Brennan, even while stressing that the conflict was legitimate warfare, disclaimed any interest in using war powers domestically:

> [I]t is the firm position of the Obama administration that suspected terrorists arrested inside the United States will, in keeping with long-standing tradition, be processed through our Article III courts—as they should be. Our military does not patrol our streets or enforce our laws—nor should it. . . . Similarly, when it comes to US citizens involved in terrorist-related activity, whether they are captured overseas or at home, we will prosecute them in our criminal justice system.

This idea that the legal state of war involves all aspects of American national power recurs often in the first-term speeches. Speaking at the Woodrow Wilson International Center for Scholars in Washington, D.C., on April 30, 2012 (see Appendix: Brennan—B), for example, Brennan declared that in "this fight, we are harnessing every element of American power—intelligence, military, diplomatic, development, economic, financial, law enforcement, homeland security, and the power of our values, including our commitment to the rule of law." To put the matter simply, the war to which Brennan refers is one that authorizes the use of war powers *but does not in any sense preclude the use of other powers.* And at home, he suggests, the chief mechanism for furthering America's war aims lies in aggressive law enforcement.

The result for the United States of the legal state of armed conflict is that its conduct of hostilities against Al Qaeda and those affiliated or associated with it abroad is necessarily governed by the laws of war, rather than by the international law of human rights or by law enforcement legal rules. As State Department Legal Adviser Harold H. Koh said in his March 25, 2010, address to the American Society of International Law in Washington, D.C. (see Appendix: Koh—A):

> [T]he Obama administration is firmly committed to complying with all applicable law, including the laws of war, in all aspects of these ongoing armed conflicts. . . . We in the Obama administration have worked hard since we entered office to ensure that we conduct all aspects of these armed conflicts—in particular, detention operations, targeting, and prosecution of terrorist suspects—in a manner consistent not just with the applicable laws of war, but also with the Constitution and laws of the United States.

These speeches leave some ambiguity at the margins concerning what the administration is promising in terms of compliance with international law. On the one hand, the speeches refer to complying with the laws of war. On the other hand, the administration sometimes emphasizes honoring "laws-of-war principles"—which arguably stops short of promising full compliance. Koh, in his ASIL speech, for example, emphasized that targeting operations complied with the "law-of-war principles" of distinction and proportionality. And Holder, in his Northwestern University School of Law speech, stated that "any such use of lethal force by the United States will comply with the four fundamental laws-of-war principles governing the use of force."

Most notably, Stephen Preston, general counsel of the CIA, in his April 10, 2012, speech at Harvard Law School (see Appendix: Preston—A), conspicuously did not assert that the agency would comply with international law in covert uses of force, but stated instead only that it honored "international law principles." As he put it, "The agency would implement its authorities in a manner consistent with the four basic principles in the law of armed conflict governing the use of force: necessity, distinction, proportionality, and humanity. Great care would be taken in the planning and execution of actions to satisfy these four principles and, in the process, to minimize civilian casualties."

Was this a relaxation of an obligation to comply strictly with the "law of war"? It certainly can be read that way—as a careful hedge against a promise of strict compliance for those situations in which one might, in covert actions, have to bend the rules in the name of necessity. It might also be read, however, in the opposite direction—as a broadening of the commitment of the US government to adhere to law-of-war principles even in circumstances in which the United States uses force outside of formal armed conflicts but where it does not acknowledge the applicability of human rights law. This might include, for example, self-defense operations in belligerencies short of formal armed conflict.

Indeed, the first-term speeches carefully preserve the legal possibility of using force against non-state actors that might not be covered by the existing conflict in circumstances which, while legitimate acts of self-defense, might not be part of any armed conflict at all. Armed conflict under international law is a term of art; it does not simply refer to any situation in which forces are shooting at each other. While all hostilities between armed forces of states are governed by the laws of war, hostilities in non-international armed conflict have to rise to a certain level of sustained intensity in order to qualify. And the speeches consistently reserve the right to use force should groups arise that the president concludes he needs to attack with force but which are not part of the current conflict or, indeed, any armed conflict. Under such circumstances, the first-term speeches imply, the inherent right of self-defense of a state— and the inherent powers of the president to protect the nation under the Constitution—would permit the use of lethal force anyway. This is one of several implications found in Brennan's claim in April 2012 that "the United States is in an armed conflict with Al Qaeda, the Taliban, and associated forces, in response to the 9/11 attacks . . ." Brennan concludes this same sentence by adding, "and we may *also* use force consistent with *our inherent right of national self-defense*" (emphasis added).

Brennan's "also" packs a lot of content into four letters. It acknowledges uses of force against non-state actors where the level of hostilities has not necessarily risen to the level of systematic, sustained fighting required to produce an armed conflict subject to the laws of war. And it acknowledges also that the current conflict does not exhaust the lawful uses of force in counterterrorism that the United States reserves the right to undertake.

It is not an anomaly in the speeches. Koh, too, carefully preserved this self-defense category. Addressing different targeting questions in his ASIL speech, he referred at different points to "a state that is engaged in an armed conflict *or in legitimate self-defense"* and to a state "acting in self-defense *or* during an armed conflict" (emphasis added). The use of "or," like Brennan's use of "also," appears intended to preserve this further category of belligerency *as distinct from belligerency in armed conflict.* The basic, implicit position here is that self-defense is a broader category than armed conflict but that this form of belligerency short of armed conflict is governed legally by the same fundamental principles as full-blown armed conflict.

Notably, the speeches appear to take the view that this category is—at least for now—a hypothetical one, since the speeches cast all of the uses of force actually undertaken by the United States in counterterrorism so far as part of the ongoing and preexisting armed conflict authorized by the AUMF. The self-defense theory, however, becomes critical as the administration begins imagining the end of the AUMF conflict—as the president did at the outset of his second term.

A Conflict across Personality, Space, and Time

The proposition that the United States is at war, for purposes of both domestic and international law, necessarily raises questions: With whom is it at war? Where does the war take place? At what point will it end? These are questions with easy answers when the enemy is a state; but the answers are far harder when the war is against a non-geographically specific, non-state actor. The first-term speeches thus spend a good deal of time on a constellation of issues one might call "the who, where, and when of counterterrorism."

The text of the AUMF authorizes the use of force against the "nations, organizations, or persons" determined by the president to have "planned, authorized, committed, or aided" the September 11, 2001, attacks and those who harbored them. At the time Congress passed the resolution, that meant Al Qaeda and, harboring it, the Afghan Taliban. Over time, the administration has come to think of it as authorizing force against those who are "part of" or "substantially supporting" those two groups. The speeches spell out a somewhat wider set of adversaries who, sometimes long after September 11, have joined themselves to Al Qaeda and its cause. The government's view is that the war is not limited to Al Qaeda itself but also includes its "affiliates," at least when those affiliates qualify—to use the term that prevails in legal briefs and sometimes in the speeches themselves—as "associated forces." This term does not appear in the text of the AUMF, but it pervades the administration's interpretations of it—and it does so now with Congress's explicit blessing, at least for purposes of detention.[2]

Obama alluded to this point in the sentence we quoted earlier from his 2009 National Archives speech: "Now let me be clear: we are indeed at war with Al Qaeda *and its affiliates.*" And administration officials fleshed out this point in the speeches that followed Obama's. Speaking October 18, 2011, at the Heritage Foundation in Washington, D.C. (see Appendix: Johnson—A), Pentagon General Counsel Jeh Johnson stated that Al Qaeda is "a far more decentralized organization than it was ten years ago, and relies on affiliates to carry out its terrorist aims. We know that Al Qaeda is likely to continue to metastasize and try to recruit affiliates to its cause." A few months later, at the Wilson Center, Brennan surveyed the

---

2. See Section 1021 of the National Defense Authorization Act for Fiscal Year 2012, Public Law 112-81.

major Al Qaeda affiliates, observing, "We've always been clear that the end of bin Laden would neither mark the end of Al Qaeda nor our resolve to destroy it," and that as "the Al Qaeda core falters, it continues to look to its affiliates and adherents to carry on its murderous cause." Brennan added that it was "worrying to witness Al Qaeda's merger with [the Somali group] al-Shabaab, whose ranks include foreign fighters, some with US passports." He described Al Qaeda in the Arabian Peninsula as "Al Qaeda's most active affiliate," one that "continues to seek the opportunity to strike our homeland." And he also took note of two other groups, Al Qaeda in the Islamic Maghreb and the Nigerian Boko Haram, which he described respectively as "another Al Qaeda affiliate" and "a group that appears to be aligning itself with Al Qaeda's violent agenda and is increasingly looking to attack Western interests in Nigeria in addition to Nigerian government targets."

The use of the word "affiliate"—or sometimes "associated forces"—in these speeches is surely not an accident. It is an intentional framing of the activity and identity of these groups so as to bring them within the scope of co-belligerency for purposes of international law. The concept of co-belligerency defines how, when a state is already fighting one party, it might add new belligerents to its list of enemies—as well as how it might announce that it regards these new groups as lawfully targetable under the conduct rules of armed conflict. The administration has taken internally a highly fact-dependent approach to determining when an affiliate is sufficiently integrated with Al Qaeda to warrant treatment as a co-belligerent force, and it has not, in fact, treated all affiliates as associated forces for purposes of the AUMF.

Johnson, in a February 22, 2012, speech at the Yale Law School (see Appendix: Johnson—B), fleshed out the administration's approach to the question of when an affiliate becomes close enough to come within the AUMF's scope:

> An "associated force," as we interpret the phrase, has two characteristics to it: (1) an organized, armed group that has entered the fight alongside Al Qaeda, and (2) is a co-belligerent with Al Qaeda in hostilities against the United States or its coalition partners. In other words, the group must not only be aligned with Al Qaeda; it must have also entered the fight against the United States or its coalition partners. Thus, an "associated force" is not any terrorist group in the world that merely embraces the Al Qaeda ideology. More is required before we draw the legal conclusion that the group fits within the statutory authorization for the use of military force passed by the Congress in 2001.

Yet, while "more is required," the administration consistently reserves the point that the war is not limited to core Al Qaeda forces and to the Taliban but extends to any affiliated or associated organization—or individual—that meaningfully joins the fight against the United States. That includes groups that did not exist on September 11, 2001. And as we noted earlier, the first-term speeches also always reserve the president's independent authority to use lethal force to protect the country against an imminent threat arising from any source, including brand-new threats unrelated to those of the past decade.

The speeches address the geography of the conflict at several junctures. The fundamental question is whether armed conflict has geographic boundaries, inside of which the law of war applies and outside of which the government must resort to ordinary domestic criminal law and international human rights law. Many commentators assert that the armed conflict is limited legally to particular theaters of conflict or hot battlefields. The administration, however, has consistently rejected this notion. Holder addressed this point in his Northwestern speech:

> Our legal authority is not limited to the battlefields in Afghanistan. Indeed, neither Congress nor our federal courts have limited the geographic scope of our ability to use force to the current conflict in Afghanistan. We are at war with a stateless enemy, prone to shifting operations from country to country. Over the last three years alone, Al Qaeda and its associates have directed several attacks—fortunately, unsuccessful—against us from countries other than Afghanistan. Our government has both a responsibility and a right to protect this nation and its people from such threats.

Brennan also addressed the geography question directly in his Harvard speech—albeit in a fashion that blended it with questions of the circumstances under which force is lawful:

> [A]s President Obama has stated on numerous occasions, we reserve the right to take unilateral action if or when other governments are unwilling or unable to take the necessary actions themselves. That does not mean we can use military force whenever we want, wherever we want. International legal principles, including respect for a state's sovereignty and the laws of war, impose important constraints on our ability to act unilaterally—and on the way in which we can use force—in foreign territories.

Indeed, the geographic question ultimately shades into a question of when force is appropriate. This often presents more of a policy question, given persons who are lawful targets, than one of law. Having the legal authority to attack does not, after all, necessarily mean that doing so is wise or prudent. "Associated forces" in, for example, Yemen or Somalia contain large numbers of fighters whose interests and activities do not involve the United States directly. And Brennan, in his Wilson Center speech, laid out a series of prudential factors the administration considers before authorizing strikes. "Even if it is lawful to pursue a specific member of Al Qaeda, we ask ourselves whether that individual's activities rise to a certain threshold for action and whether taking action will, in fact, enhance our security," he emphasized. Most importantly, he said, "when considering lethal force we ask ourselves whether the individual poses a significant threat to US interests. . . . We do not engage in lethal action in order to eliminate every single member of Al Qaeda in the world." Brennan had offered a bit more detail in his Harvard speech, describing a standard that approaches imminence:

> Others in the international community—including some of our closest allies and partners—take a different view of the geographic scope of the conflict, limiting it only to the "hot" battlefields. As such, they argue that, outside of these two active theatres, the United States can only act in self-defense against Al Qaeda when they are planning, engaging in, or threatening an armed attack against US interests if it amounts to an "imminent" threat.
>
> In practice, the US approach to targeting in the conflict with Al Qaeda is far more aligned with our allies' approach

than many assume. This administration's counterterrorism efforts outside of Afghanistan and Iraq are focused on those individuals who are a threat to the United States, whose removal would cause a significant—even if only temporary—disruption of the plans and capabilities of Al Qaeda and its associated forces. Practically speaking, then, the question turns principally on how you define "imminence."

We are finding increasing recognition in the international community that a more flexible understanding of "imminence" may be appropriate when dealing with terrorist groups, in part because threats posed by non-state actors do not present themselves in the ways that evidenced imminence in more traditional conflicts. After all, Al Qaeda does not follow a traditional command structure, wear uniforms, carry its arms openly, or mass its troops at the borders of the nations it attacks. Nonetheless, it possesses the demonstrated capability to strike with little notice and cause significant civilian or military casualties. Over time, an increasing number of our international counterterrorism partners have begun to recognize that the traditional conception of what constitutes an "imminent" attack should be broadened in light of the modern-day capabilities, techniques, and technological innovations of terrorist organizations.

And at the Wilson Center, he likewise described "significant threat" in a fashion that seemed to approach imminence:

And what do we mean when we say significant threat? I am not referring to some hypothetical threat, the mere possibility that a member of Al Qaeda might try to attack us at some point in the future. A significant threat might be posed by an individual who is an operational leader of Al Qaeda or one of its associated forces. Or perhaps the individual is himself an operative, in the midst of actually training for or planning to carry out attacks against US persons and interests. Or perhaps the individual possesses unique operational skills that are being leveraged in a planned attack. The purpose of a strike against a particular individual is to stop him before he can carry out his attack and kill innocents. The purpose is to disrupt his plans and his plots before they come to fruition.

As a matter of law, however, the "when" of counterterrorism largely comes down to a question of discretion. The existence of an ongoing armed conflict means that, legally speaking, the administration can strike—assuming the target is a lawful one—whenever it wants. It does not have to do a separate analysis of the lawfulness of a resort to force each time; a single conflict is, after all, already under way. The one exception to this rule is that Brennan acknowledged that operations undertaken not as part of an ongoing armed conflict but as an exercise in self-defense must satisfy the heightened standard of "imminent" threat—a standard the administration claimed to be approaching, though not quite reaching, as a matter of policy more broadly away from hot battlefields anyway.

In the closing months of its first term, however, the administration began to directly grapple with a different aspect of the "when" of counterterrorism: the question of when the conflict might end and what the end of the conflict might look like. Johnson addressed this question directly in a speech at Oxford University in November 2012 (see Appendix: Johnson—C). "How will this conflict end?" he asked, going on to note that it is an "unconventional conflict, against an unconventional enemy, and will not end in conventional terms." For that reason, he said, it is obvious that two things will *not* define the "end" of the conflict: "We cannot and should not expect Al Qaeda and its associated forces to all surrender, to all lay down their weapons in an open field, or to sign a peace treaty with us. They are terrorist organizations. Nor can we capture or kill every last terrorist who claims an affiliation with Al Qaeda."

Johnson declined to offer a prediction as to when the conflict would end, or even as to whether we are approaching the end. But he did say that on the "present course," there will come "a tipping point at which so many of the leaders and operatives of Al Qaeda and its affiliates have been killed or captured" that the organization will thus no longer be able to "attempt or launch a strategic attack against the United States, such that Al Qaeda as we know it, the organization that our Congress authorized the military to pursue in 2001, has been effectively destroyed." At that point, he argued, "our efforts should no longer be considered an 'armed conflict' against Al Qaeda and its associated forces. Rather, [we have] a counterterrorism effort against *individuals* who are the scattered remnants of Al Qaeda, or are parts of groups unaffiliated with Al Qaeda, for which the law enforcement and intelligence resources of our government are principally responsible, in cooperation with the international community—with our military assets available in reserve to address continuing and imminent terrorist threats."

This passage represents an important articulation of the conditions that make up the end of the formal armed conflict as a legal matter—and it foreshadows in a significant respect the first major speech Obama would give on these matters in his second term. But it bears noting that Johnson did not simply say that once these conditions are met, actions against terrorist threats will necessarily revert to the hands of law enforcement alone. Johnson, rather, carefully named both law enforcement and the intelligence resources of the US government, in cooperation with the international community; and, he added, the military assets remain in reserve for both continuing and imminent threats. The drones, in other words, will remain in the air for targeted killings of individuals and remnants of groups—not just Al Qaeda and its affiliates, but potentially other imminent threats. And the United States, Johnson said, will not permit Al Qaeda or other terrorist groups, affiliated with Al Qaeda or not, that pose a threat to the United States to establish territorial safe havens—or reestablish them.

Given that all tools of today's counterterrorism-on-offense will appear to remain on the table, it's reasonable to ask what the end of the conflict really means. The answer is that although the tools might remain available, they would revert to being exceptional measures, rather than simply how the current unconventional war is fought. The legal hurdle for resort to exceptional measures goes up, to take into account the feasibility of law enforcement and the cooperation of the international community. Johnson's Oxford speech offers a major statement of principle for both foreseeing the end of the current conflict and beginning to articulate the legal paradigm for counterterrorism past the current armed conflict.

To summarize the first-term speeches as simply as possible on this point, the United States regards itself as fighting an armed conflict determined geographically neither by some preexisting locational designation nor by such non-legal concepts as hot battlefields. Instead, the scope of the conflict hinges on the fact that the conduct of actual hostilities has breached the traditional threshold for application of the laws of war—that is, they have been sustained and intense. This having happened, the conduct of hostilities now lawfully includes hostilities initiated in any particular place by the United States against lawful targets. The conflict was triggered temporally by an initiation of hostilities against the United States—on 9/11 at the latest. And the ensuing armed conflict against these terrorists includes those who have taken up their cause and joined the fight, which has continued, despite the passage of years, without pause up through today.

Targeting and the Use of Force

The first-term speeches focus to a large extent on a handful of novel and controversial counterterrorism activities—specifically targeted killing and drone warfare, and notably targeted killing *through* drone missile strikes. Brennan noted the controversies in his Wilson Center speech, saying that "there continues to be considerable public and legal debate surrounding these technologies and how they are sometimes used in our fight against Al Qaeda." While the fundamental legal controversies of the Bush administration focused on detention and interrogation, the fundamental legal controversies of the Obama administration deal with targeting of individuals with lethal force. This is partly because of concern in the advocacy and international communities about the destabilizing effects of new technologies that enable discreet and less-attributable uses of force against individual targets. It is also partly because the ability to use highly discretionary, precision targeting at a distance upsets the view that armed conflict as a legal regime exists only in defined geographical spaces.

As a consequence, the speeches focus in considerable part on these practices. As Brennan himself put it: "What has clearly captured the attention of many . . . is [the] practice [of] identifying specific members of Al Qaeda and then targeting them with lethal force, often using aircraft remotely operated by pilots who can be hundreds if not thousands of miles away."

The speeches robustly defend the use of drones and other high-tech weapons on both legal and policy grounds. Koh addressed the legality of drone targeting as early as his 2010 ASIL speech, in a statement echoed in many later speeches:

> [S]ome have challenged *the very use of advanced weapons systems*, such as unmanned aerial vehicles, for lethal operations. But the rules that govern targeting do not turn on the type of weapons system used, and there is no prohibition under the laws of war on the use of technologically advanced weapons systems in armed conflict—such as pilotless aircraft or so-called smart bombs—so long as they are employed in conformity with applicable laws of war. Indeed, using such advanced technologies can ensure both that the best intelligence is available for planning operations and that civilian casualties are minimized in carrying out such operations.

Reflecting the centrality of this legal position to the administration's view of the conflict, it reappears nearly verbatim in other speeches. It was reiterated by Jeh Johnson in his Yale speech. Holder also echoed the theme at Northwestern.

Brennan also defended drone use on policy grounds in his Wilson Center speech as part of his broader defense of targeted strikes:

Remotely piloted aircraft in particular can be a wise choice because of geography, with their ability to fly hundreds of miles over the most treacherous terrain, strike their targets with astonishing precision, and then return to base. They can be a wise choice because of time, when windows of opportunity can close quickly and there may be just minutes to act.

They can be a wise choice because they dramatically reduce the danger to US personnel, even eliminating the danger altogether. Yet they are also a wise choice because they dramatically reduce the danger to innocent civilians, especially considered against massive ordnance that can cause injury and death far beyond its intended target.

In addition, compared against other options, a pilot operating this aircraft remotely—with the benefit of technology and with the safety of distance—might actually have a clearer picture of the target and its surroundings, including the presence of innocent civilians. It's this surgical precision—the ability, with laser-like focus, to eliminate the cancerous tumor called an Al Qaeda terrorist while limiting damage to the tissue around it—that makes this counterterrorism tool so essential.

In April 2012 Brennan officially confirmed the use of targeted strikes by means of drones. Prior to that official confirmation, officials delivering the earlier speeches faced a problem in addressing concerns over drone use: everything that they might want to say they had to express hypothetically. This made the speeches unwieldy, at times, but officials nonetheless sought to address the two broad concerns about targeted strikes using drones. First, what did the United States see as the legal principles governing sovereign strikes across borders from sometimes great distances? Second, what law governed the conduct of these strikes?

Regarding the first question—that of territorial sovereignty— the administration has held, broadly speaking, a consistent view of the applicable international law since at least the 1980s. The position is that, where possible, the United States seeks consent from the affected state before conducting operations on its soil. Where, however, a state is unwilling or unable to deal with the terrorist group, the United States reserves the right to act. Holder stated the doctrine simply:

> International legal principles, including respect for another nation's sovereignty, constrain our ability to act unilaterally. But the use of force in foreign territory would be consistent with these international legal principles if conducted, for example, with the consent of the nation involved—or after a determination that the nation is unable or unwilling to deal effectively with a threat to the United States.

The United States sees this as a principle of both permission and limitation regarding other states' territorial sovereignty. At least on the surface, the principle is a neutral one between states; the United States is not claiming for itself rights it would not grant to others. On the contrary, Brennan specifically noted in his Wilson Center speech that the technologies and techniques in question will not remain solely in the possession of the United States and that the principles that the United States declares enable and restrain it must also both enable and restrain other states:

The United States is the first nation to regularly conduct strikes using remotely piloted aircraft in an armed conflict. Other nations also possess this technology. Many more nations are seeking it, and more will succeed in acquiring it. President Obama and those of us on his national security team are very mindful that as our nation uses this technology, we are establishing precedents that other nations may follow, and not all of them will be nations that share our interests or the premium we put on protecting human life, including innocent civilians.

If we want other nations to use these technologies responsibly, we must use them responsibly. If we want other nations to adhere to high and rigorous standards for their use, then we must do so as well. We cannot expect of others what we will not do ourselves. President Obama has therefore demanded that we hold ourselves to the highest possible standards—that, at every step, we be as thorough and deliberate as possible.

At the same time, one has to see at least a little fiction in the neutrality of the "unable or unwilling" standard. One should not read these speeches as tolerant, say, of Syrian drone strikes on US territory to reach those members of the fighting opposition who found sanctuary here and whom the United States proved "unwilling" to give up.

As to the conduct of such strikes, as we noted above, the law of targeting in armed conflict establishes the standard. In the same speech formally acknowledging targeted strikes with drone aircraft, Brennan laid out the administration's position that their use conforms to the principles of necessity, distinction, proportionality, and humanity:

Here, I think it's useful to consider such strikes against the basic principles of the laws of war that govern the use of force.

Targeted strikes conform to the principle of necessity—the requirement that the target have definite military value. In this armed conflict, individuals who are part of Al Qaeda or its associated forces are legitimate military targets. We have the authority to target them with lethal force just as we targeted enemy leaders in past conflicts, such as German and Japanese commanders during World War II.

Targeted strikes conform to the principle of distinction—the idea that only military objectives may be intentionally targeted and that civilians are protected from being intentionally targeted. With the unprecedented ability of remotely piloted aircraft to precisely target a military objective while minimizing collateral damage, one could argue that never before has there been a weapon that allows us to distinguish more effectively between an Al Qaeda terrorist and innocent civilians.

Targeted strikes conform to the principle of proportionality—the notion that the anticipated collateral damage of an action cannot be excessive in relation to the anticipated military advantage. By targeting an individual terrorist or small numbers of terrorists with ordnance that can be adapted to avoid harming others in the immediate vicinity, it is hard to imagine a tool that can better minimize the risk to civilians than remotely piloted aircraft.

For the same reason, targeted strikes conform to the principle of humanity, which requires us to use weapons that will not inflict unnecessary suffering.

The first-term speeches also address an issue particular to targeted killings—that is, the lawfulness of strikes directed against pre-identified, known individuals, such as high-level terrorist leaders. Koh noted the objections some critics had raised and responded thus in his ASIL address:

> [S]ome have suggested that the *very act of targeting* a particular leader of an enemy force in an armed conflict must violate the laws of war. But individuals who are part of such an armed group are belligerents and, therefore, lawful targets under international law. During World War II, for example, American aviators tracked and shot down the airplane carrying the architect of the Japanese attack on Pearl Harbor, who was also the leader of enemy forces in the Battle of Midway. This was a lawful operation then, and would be if conducted today. Indeed, targeting particular individuals serves to narrow the focus when force is employed and to avoid broader harm to civilians and civilian objects.

Johnson reinforced this view in his speech at Yale:

> In an armed conflict, lethal force against known, individual members of the enemy is a long-standing and long-legal practice. What is new is that, with advances in technology, we are able to target military objectives with much more precision, to the point where we can identify, target, and strike a single military objective from great distances.
>
> Should the legal assessment of targeting a single identifiable military objective be any different in 2012 than it was in 1943, when the US Navy targeted and shot down over the Pacific the aircraft flying Admiral Yamamoto, the com-

mander of the Japanese navy during World War II, with the specific intent of killing him? Should we take a dimmer view of the legality of lethal force directed against individual members of the enemy because modern technology makes our weapons more precise?

The speeches also specifically address the domestic law side of this question concerning targeted strikes: do they breach Executive Order 12333, which prohibits "assassinations"?[3] Johnson said in his Yale speech that the term "assassinations" should "be rejected in this context. Under well-settled legal principles, lethal force against a valid *military* objective, in an armed conflict, is consistent with the law of war and does not, by definition, constitute an 'assassination'." Holder took a still broader view—one that dates back to the Reagan administration at least: assassinations must be killings that are unlawful on other grounds. An otherwise lawful killing cannot be an assassination within the meaning of the executive order:

> Some have called such operations "assassinations." They are not, and the use of that loaded term is misplaced. Assassinations are unlawful killings. Here, for the reasons I have given, the US government's use of lethal force in self-defense against a leader of Al Qaeda or an associated force who presents an imminent threat of violent attack would not be unlawful— and therefore would not violate the executive order banning assassination or criminal statutes.

---

3. See Section 2.11 of Executive Order 12333, "United States Intelligence Activities," December 4, 1981.

One of the deepest arguments over targeted killing is whether there exists some legal obligation to seek to capture a targeted person before attacking using lethal force. This is to ask whether there is "parsimony," a serial ordering in the use of force. In this conception of the laws of war, a drone missile strike could only be launched, if at all, following some determination that other measures would likely be unavailing or perhaps even following an actual attempt at capture.

The administration, unsurprisingly, did not take this view in the first-term speeches. They are clear that, the applicable legal regime being the law of targeting in armed conflict, there is no legal obligation to capture. Similarly, there is no obligation to give warning or offer surrender before launching an attack. At the same time, the administration has made it clear that, as a policy matter, it does prefer to capture whenever possible. As Brennan put it in his Wilson Center address:

> [O]ur unqualified preference is to only undertake lethal force when we believe that capturing the individual is not feasible. I have heard it suggested that the Obama administration somehow prefers killing Al Qaeda members rather than capturing them. Nothing could be further from the truth. It is our preference to capture suspected terrorists whenever feasible.
>
> For one reason, this allows us to gather valuable intelligence that we might not be able to obtain any other way. In fact, the members of Al Qaeda that we or other nations have captured have been one of our greatest sources of information about Al Qaeda, its plans, and its intentions. And once in US custody, we often can prosecute them in our federal courts or

reformed military commissions—both of which are used for gathering intelligence and preventing terrorist attacks.

There is really only one situation in which these speeches acknowledge an obligation to privilege the capture over the killing of an opponent who has not completed the legal act of surrender. That is when the individual target is a US citizen. We note that it is not clear in the speeches the extent to which the administration regards this obligation as strictly legal, as a mixture of law and interpretive policy, or as a matter of lines that situations up to this point have not required it to draw definitively. But the administration clearly linked in the first term some consideration of capture to the due process it owes its own citizens in the targeting context—a point that also becomes important in light of the president's second-term shift.

The US government's targeting of its own citizens abroad using drones became a reality with the 2011 missile attack that killed the radical Yemeni-American cleric Anwar al-Awlaki. The strike aroused—and continues to arouse—much heated debate within the United States, with critics charging that the president, on his sole say-so, had tried and executed an American citizen without due process (which is synonymous in the view of most critics with some form of judicial review). The criticism came from both the Left and the libertarian Right. It was noted that Harold Koh's March 2010 ASIL address, which preceded the al-Awlaki drone strike but which took place when al-Awlaki was already on a target list, was silent as to domestic law issues of citizenship but seemed in retrospect to say nothing that would imply that an American citizen could not be targeted like any other lawful target.

Later speeches addressed the specific question under domestic constitutional law of targeting US citizens, summarizing the position taken by the Office of Legal Counsel in a memo described in some depth to the *New York Times*.[4] The starting point in those speeches was that citizenship as such was no bar to targeting in American law stretching back at least to World War II. In his Northwestern speech, Holder said:

> Now, it is an unfortunate but undeniable fact that some of the threats we face come from a small number of US citizens who have decided to commit violent attacks against their own country from abroad. Based on generations-old legal principles and Supreme Court decisions handed down during World War II, as well as during this current conflict, it's clear that US citizenship alone does not make such individuals immune from being targeted.

While US citizenship confers no immunity against targeting, according to the administration, the question remains as to whether and in what fashion due process places constraints on the targeting of citizens. Holder acknowledged that it does, saying that the government

> . . . must take into account all relevant constitutional considerations with respect to US citizens—even those who are leading efforts to kill innocent Americans. Of these, the most relevant is the Fifth Amendment's due process clause,

---

4. Charlie Savage, "Secret US Memo Made Legal Case to Kill a Citizen," *New York Times*, October 8, 2011, http://www.nytimes.com/2011/10/09/world/middleeast/secret-us-memo-made-legal-case-to-kill-a-citizen.html?pagewanted=all.

which says that the government may not deprive a citizen of his or her life without due process of law.

The Supreme Court has made clear that the due process clause does not impose one-size-fits-all requirements but instead mandates procedural safeguards that depend on specific circumstances.

But importantly, Holder did not accept the main point urged by many critics with respect to targeting a US citizen: that constitutional due process requires *judicial* review, intervention, permission, or oversight in some fashion. He responded directly to this claim, rather, and robustly denied the underlying premise:

> Some have argued that the president is required to get permission from a federal court before taking action against a US citizen who is a senior operational leader of Al Qaeda or associated forces. This is simply not accurate. "Due process" and "judicial process" are not one and the same, particularly when it comes to national security. The Constitution guarantees due process, not judicial process.

In Holder's account, the executive branch can satisfy due process requirements by reviewing targeting decisions carefully in order to establish that several basic factual predicates as to the target have been satisfied. These predicates, in Holder's account, are threefold:

> An operation using lethal force in a foreign country, targeted against a US citizen who is a senior operational leader of Al Qaeda or associated forces, and who is actively engaged in planning to kill Americans, would be lawful at least in the

following circumstances: First, the US government has determined, after a thorough and careful review, that the individual poses an imminent threat of violent attack against the United States; second, capture is not feasible; and third, the operation would be conducted in a manner consistent with applicable law-of-war principles.

A few things are worth highlighting in this statement. First, what Holder described as three predicates is really four predicates—because the circumstances he defends as lawful are limited, in addition to the categories he enumerates, to circumstances of "a senior operational leader of Al Qaeda or associated forces." Second, Holder carefully *did not say* that a strike would be illegal if all of these conditions were not all met. Rather, he seemed to leave open the question of where the true due process minimum lies. His point, in other words, was not that a strike is illegal if these conditions are not met— but that it is certainly legal if they are.

Moreover, the term "imminent threat," in the administration's use of it, is a bit of a term of art; as the Brennan language quoted above suggests, it does not mean quite what the common-sense understanding of the phrase might convey. Holder emphasized—consistent with Brennan's comments and with the US view of imminence in other national security law circumstances—that it does not mean imminence in some immediate temporal sense. It does not mean that this is the last chance to act before disaster strikes. Rather, it incorporates a more flexible notion of a window being open to address a threat which, left unaddressed, has its own momentum toward an unacceptable outcome. The Constitution, Holder added,

. . . does not require the president to delay action until some theoretical end-stage of planning when the precise time, place, and manner of an attack become clear. Such a requirement would create an unacceptably high risk that our efforts would fail and that Americans would be killed.

Whether the capture of a US citizen terrorist is feasible is a fact-specific and, potentially, time-sensitive question. It may depend on, among other things, whether capture can be accomplished in the window of time available to prevent an attack and without undue risk to civilians or to US personnel. Given the nature of how terrorists act and where they tend to hide, it may not always be feasible to capture a US citizen terrorist who presents an imminent threat of violent attack. In that case, our government has the clear authority to defend the United States with lethal force.[5]

As chief legal officer of the United States, Holder is the executive branch official with the greatest authority to opine on the domestic and constitutional law issues involved in targeting US citizens. Unsurprisingly, therefore, his remarks have been echoed by other officials speaking on the topic. Brennan simply said at the Wilson Center that, in the case of American citizens, "We ask ourselves additional questions," and then referred to Holder's speech.

---

5. The themes of Holder's speech are spelled out in somewhat more detail in a "white paper" on the same subject leaked to *NBC News* as this chapter was nearing publication. See Department of Justice white paper "Lawfulness of a Lethal Operation Directed Against a U.S. Citizen Who Is a Senior Operational Leader of Al-Qa'ida or An Associated Force," undated, http://www.lawfareblog.com/wp-content/uploads/2013/02/020413_DOJ _White_Paper.pdf. We do not treat the white paper as it has not been released to the public as an official administration statement.

Other speeches likewise emphasize the view that targeting is inherently an executive branch function. Johnson, in his Yale speech, for example, referred to Judge John D. Bates's 2010 decision to dismiss the al-Awlaki lawsuit[6] when he said:

> Contrary to the view of some, targeting decisions are not appropriate for submission to a court. In my view, they are core functions of the executive branch and often require real-time decisions based on an evolving intelligence picture that only the executive branch may timely possess. I agree with Judge Bates of the federal district court in Washington, who ruled in 2010 that the judicial branch of government is simply not equipped to become involved in targeting decisions.

In short, the Obama administration in its first term staked out a fairly simple position with respect to the targeting of Americans abroad: due process applies, but it means in practice heightened standards of internal review—not the involvement of courts in reviewing targeting decisions.

The Legal Power to Detain the Enemy

From the time the new president took office, the Obama administration expressed consistent policy anxiety about the power to detain enemy forces in global counterterrorism operations. The president took office promising to close the Guantánamo Bay

---

6. Memorandum Opinion, *Al-Aulaqi v. Obama*, 10-cv-1496, DDC (December 7, 2010), http://www.lawfareblog.com/wp-content/uploads/2010/12/Al-Aulaqi-Decision-Granting-Motion-to-Dismiss-120710.pdf.

detention facility, and his administration in its first-term speeches consistently defended the propriety of using the criminal justice system to handle terrorist suspects. More generally, his administration strove to put at least rhetorical distance between itself and the Bush administration on detention matters. Even as Congress stymied the plan to shutter Guantánamo, the administration remained firm that it would not bring new detainees there and it opposed congressional efforts to impede transfers from the facility—both to the United States for trial and to other countries for release. In this respect, the administration clearly evinced an interest in shrinking this country's detention footprint. The speeches clearly and consistently reflect this.

At the same time, however, the speeches also consistently assert—in line with the administration's litigating positions in dozens of habeas corpus cases—a robust vision of the president's detention power under law-of-war authorities. These two themes are somewhat discordant with one another— amounting to an insistence that the Obama administration has as broad power as did its predecessor to behave in ways it generally prefers not to behave. Yet both themes are clearly present—often in adjacent paragraphs of the same speeches.

The administration at first broached the subject of the scope of its detention power tentatively, perhaps understanding that the assertion of broad detention powers would be toxic on the political Left and perhaps because President Obama himself had grave reservations about claiming long-term detention powers. When Obama spoke at the National Archives, for example, he spoke of long-term detention only in the conditional tense. He insisted that his administration would prosecute anyone who could be prosecuted and would transfer those whom it could safely transfer. And he hypothesized the possibility of a residual group—though by the time he did so, it was hardly a matter of conjecture that a residual group of Guantánamo detainees would certainly exist:

> Now, finally, there remains the question of detainees at Guantánamo who cannot be prosecuted yet who pose a clear danger to the American people. And I have to be honest here—this is the toughest single issue that we will face. We're going to exhaust every avenue that we have to prosecute those at Guantánamo who pose a danger to our country. But even when this process is complete, there may be a number of people who cannot be prosecuted for past crimes, in some cases because evidence may be tainted, but who nonetheless pose a threat to the security of the United States.

Obama then made it clear that should such people exist, he had no intention of releasing them: "Al Qaeda terrorists and their affiliates are at war with the United States, and those that we capture—like other prisoners of war—must be prevented from attacking us again."

At the same time, Obama also disclaimed any interest in an executive-centered detention policy:

> [W]e must recognize that these detention policies cannot be unbounded. They can't be based simply on what I or the executive branch decide[s] alone. . . . We must have clear, defensible, and lawful standards for those who fall into this category. We must have fair procedures so that we don't make mistakes. We must have a thorough process of periodic review, so that any prolonged detention is carefully evaluated and justified.

I know that creating such a system poses unique challenges. And other countries have grappled with this question; now, so must we. But I want to be very clear that our goal is to construct a legitimate legal framework for the remaining Guantánamo detainees that cannot be transferred. Our goal is not to avoid a legitimate legal framework. In our constitutional system, prolonged detention should not be the decision of any one man. If and when we determine that the United States must hold individuals to keep them from carrying out an act of war, we will do so within a system that involves judicial and congressional oversight. And so, going forward, my administration will work with Congress to develop an appropriate legal regime so that our efforts are consistent with our values and our Constitution.

In practice, the president's insistence on congressional sanction for detention has meant only the tiniest substantive change in the claimed scope of detention authority, but it has meant a consistently narrower claimed source of authority for detentions. Instead of relying on broad claims of executive authority for detention, as the Bush administration sometimes did, the Obama administration has relied exclusively on the 2001 AUMF. As Johnson explained in his Yale speech:

Ten years [after it was passed], the AUMF remains on the books, and it is still a viable authorization today. In the detention context, we in the Obama administration have interpreted this authority to include ". . . those persons who were part of, or substantially supported, Taliban or Al Qaeda forces or associated forces that are engaged in hostilities against the United States or its coalition partners."

This interpretation of our statutory authority has been adopted by the courts in the habeas cases brought by Guantánamo detainees, and in 2011 Congress joined the executive and judicial branches of government in embracing this interpretation when it codified it almost word-for-word in Section 1021 of this year's National Defense Authorization Act, ten years after enactment of the original AUMF.

The most substantial statement laying out both the domestic and international law justifications for the administration's claimed detention power in the first term came from Koh, who dealt with the subject at length in his ASIL speech:

Some have asked what legal basis we have for continuing to detain those held on Guantánamo and at Bagram [Airfield, Afghanistan]. But as a matter of both international and domestic law, the legal framework is well-established. As a matter of international law, our detention operations rest on three legal foundations. First, we continue to fight a war of self-defense against an enemy that attacked us on September 11, 2001, and before, and that continues to undertake armed attacks against the United States. Second, in Afghanistan we work as partners with a consenting host government. And third, the United Nations Security Council has, through a series of successive resolutions, authorized the use of "all necessary measures" by the NATO countries constituting the International Security Assistance Force (ISAF) to fulfill their mandate in Afghanistan. As a nation at war, we must comply with the laws of war, but detention of enemy belligerents to prevent them from returning to hostilities is a well-recognized feature of the conduct of armed conflict, as the drafters of Common Article 3 and Additional Protocol II [of the Geneva Conventions] recognized and as our own Supreme Court recognized in *Hamdi v. Rumsfeld.* The federal courts have confirmed our legal authority to detain in the Guantánamo habeas cases, but the administration is not asserting an unlimited detention authority. For example, with regard to individuals detained at Guantánamo, we explained in a March 13, 2009, habeas filing before the D.C. federal court—and repeatedly in habeas cases since—that we are resting our detention authority on a domestic statute—the 2001 Authorization for Use of Military Force (AUMF)—as informed by the principles of the laws of war. Our detention authority in Afghanistan comes from the same source.

In explaining this approach, let me note two important differences from the legal approach of the last administration. First, as a matter of domestic law, the Obama administration has not based its claim of authority to detain those at Gitmo [Guantánamo] and Bagram on the president's Article II authority as commander-in-chief. Instead, we have relied on legislative authority expressly granted to the president by Congress in the 2001 AUMF.

Second, unlike the last administration, as a matter of international law, this administration has expressly acknowledged that international law informs the scope of our detention authority. Both in our internal decisions about specific Guantánamo detainees, and before the courts in habeas cases, we have interpreted the scope of detention authority authorized by Congress in the AUMF as informed by the laws of war. Those laws of war were designed primarily for traditional armed conflicts among states, not conflicts against a diffuse, difficult-to-identify terrorist enemy. Therefore, construing what is "necessary and appropriate" under the AUMF requires some "translation," or analogizing principles from the laws of war governing traditional *international* conflicts.

Koh concluded,

[W]e have based our authority to detain not on conclusory labels, like "enemy combatant," but on whether the factual record in the particular case meets the legal standard. This includes, but is not limited to, whether an individual joined with or became part of Al Qaeda or Taliban forces or associated forces, which can be demonstrated by relevant evidence of formal or functional membership, which may include an oath of loyalty, training with Al Qaeda, or taking positions with enemy forces. Often these factors operate in combination. While we disagree with the International Committee of the Red Cross on some of the particulars, our general approach of looking at "functional" membership in an armed group has been endorsed not only by the federal courts, but also is consistent with the approach taken in the targeting context by the ICRC in its recent study on Direct Participation in Hostilities (DPH).

In short, while the first-term speeches consistently articulated the aspiration to close Guantánamo and expressed policy anxiety about broad uses of detention, they also reserved on a legal level relatively spacious authority to hold members or substantial supporters of enemy forces and they stoutly asserted the consonance of doing so with both domestic law and international legal obligations.

The only caveat here is that the administration disclaimed both the authority to detain American citizens in military custody and the authority to use military detention for suspects caught here at home. Brennan's language on this point is careful, however. He does not quite disclaim the legal power to use military detention domestically or against Americans. Rather, he says it is the "firm position" of the administration that it will not happen—"in keeping with long-standing tradition." This suggests more of a policy judgment than a legal conclusion that detention authorities cannot reach Americans or American shores under the Constitution or current law.

Finally, Jeh Johnson's Oxford University speech in November 2012 looked down the road to ask what happens to remaining detainees when the conditions under which today's armed conflict can be considered over have been satisfied, and the law of armed conflict is thus no longer the applicable paradigm. Johnson's answer was both careful and tentative, more of an effort to hazard legal possibilities than to state an approach to policy. "At that point," Johnson said,

> [W]e will also need to face the question of what to do with any members of Al Qaeda who still remain in US military detention without a criminal conviction and sentence. In general, the military's authority to detain ends with the "cessation of active hostilities." For this particular conflict, all I can say today is that we should look to conventional legal principles to supply the answer and that both our nations [the United States and Great Britain] faced similar challenging questions after the cessation of hostilities in

World War II and our governments delayed the release of some Nazi German prisoners of war.

In other words, while the first-term speeches articulate some vision of what the end of hostilities will look like, they articulate almost no vision at all of what that will mean for the authority to detain beyond the broadest acknowledgment that the authority to detain will ultimately atrophy.

Interrogating the Enemy

In sharp contrast to its detention powers—where the administration has, while regretfully, explored the boundaries of its authority—the Obama administration has made an assiduous point of not approaching, even in concept, the outer edges of its legal powers to interrogate the enemy. Obama in his first days in office shut down the CIA's high-value detainee interrogation program and bound all interrogations to the Army Field Manual, thus banning any kind of enhanced interrogation techniques.[7] The Army Field Manual quite deliberately authorizes only interrogation techniques well short of the legal lines. So the result of making it a government-wide standard has been to eliminate any need to consider—as the Bush administration famously did— what specific techniques are lawful and what techniques cross the line into torture or into cruel, inhuman, or degrading treatment. The first-term speeches, as a consequence, do not address this question. Rather, they lay out the policy steps the administration has taken with respect to interrogation and they

---

7. See Executive Order 13491, "Ensuring Lawful Interrogations," January 22, 2009, http://www.whitehouse.gov/the_press_office/EnsuringLawful Interrogations.

defend the proposition that more aggressive interrogation techniques are unnecessary and counterproductive.

Obama himself addressed the point in his National Archives address:

> I know some have argued that brutal methods like water-boarding were necessary to keep us safe. I could not disagree more. As commander-in-chief, I see the intelligence. I bear the responsibility for keeping this country safe. And I categorically reject the assertion that these are the most effective means of interrogation. What's more, they undermine the rule of law. They alienate us in the world. They serve as a recruitment tool for terrorists and increase the will of our enemies to fight us, while decreasing the will of others to work with America. They risk the lives of our troops by making it less likely that others will surrender to them in battle, and more likely that Americans will be mistreated if they are captured. In short, they did not advance our war and counterterrorism efforts—they undermined them, and that is why I ended them once and for all.

Notice here that, in contrast to the administration's discussions of its other authorities, this is not fundamentally a legal argument. It is a policy argument regarding the efficacy and costs of aggressive interrogations. Indeed, the speeches quite consistently avoid discussion of the legal limits on interrogation, focusing instead on the policy steps the administration has taken, both bureaucratically and substantively, to stop mistreatment of detainees and on the refutation of claims both that more aggressive tactics are warranted and that law enforcement interrogations are insufficient. At his Harvard Law School speech, Brennan addressed both points:

Now, there has been a great deal of debate about the best way to interrogate individuals in our custody. It's been suggested that getting terrorists to talk can be accomplished simply by withholding *Miranda* warnings or subjecting prisoners to so-called "enhanced interrogation techniques." It's also been suggested that prosecuting terrorists in our federal courts somehow impedes the collection of intelligence. A long record of experience, however, proves otherwise.

Consistent with our laws and our values, the president unequivocally banned torture and other abusive interrogation techniques, rejecting the claim that these are effective means of interrogation. Instead, we have focused on what works. The president approved the creation of a High-Value Detainee Interrogation Group, or HIG, to bring together resources from across the government—experienced interrogators, subject-matter experts, intelligence analysts, and linguists—to conduct or assist in the interrogation of those terrorists with the greatest intelligence value both at home and overseas. Through the HIG, we have brought together the capabilities that are essential to effective interrogation and ensured they can be mobilized quickly and in a coordinated fashion.

Claims that *Miranda* warnings undermine intelligence collection ignore decades of experience to the contrary. Yes, some terrorism suspects have refused to provide information in the criminal justice system, but so have many individuals held in military custody, from Afghanistan to Guantánamo, where *Miranda* warnings were not given. What is undeniable is that many individuals in the criminal justice system have provided a great deal of information and intelligence—even after being given their *Miranda* warnings. The real danger is *failing* to give a *Miranda* warning in those circumstances where it's appropriate, which could well determine whether a terrorist is convicted and spends the rest of his life behind bars, or is set free.

Moreover, the Supreme Court has recognized a limited exception to *Miranda*, allowing statements to be admitted if the unwarned interrogation was "reasonably prompted by a concern for public safety." Applying this public safety exception to the more complex and diverse threat of international terrorism can be complicated, so our law enforcement officers require clarity.

Therefore, at the end of 2010, the FBI clarified its guidance to agents on use of the public safety exception to *Miranda*, explaining how it should apply to terrorism cases. The FBI has acknowledged that this exception was utilized last year, including during the questioning of Faisal Shahzad, accused of attempting to detonate a car bomb in Times Square. Just this week in a major terrorism case, a federal judge ruled that statements obtained under the public safety exception *before* the defendant was read his *Miranda* rights are, in fact, admissible at trial.

Because of the Obama administration's policy choices with respect to interrogation, the law of interrogation is something of a hole in the first-term speeches—an area they self-consciously decline to address. While the administration famously withdrew all Bush administration guidance on the subject, it has not replaced it with its own—certainly not in public and likely not in private either.

The Use of Criminal Trial in Federal Courts

One consistent theme in the first-term speeches is the defense of the domestic criminal justice system as an instrument of counter-terrorism—even as an instrument of warfare against terrorists. This is really a defensive point. At the outset of the Obama administration, the administration talked proudly of its plans to try Guantánamo detainees in federal court. Indeed, such plans played prominently in the president's executive order to close Guantánamo.[8] But as the politics of Guantánamo changed and the public and congressional mood turned against federal court trials for terrorists, the point necessarily became more of a defense of federal court trials in principle and less of an ebullient promise to use them to resolve legacy cases from the Bush administration. One of the speeches, David Kris's Brookings talk, is wholly devoted to this subject. Several of the others include significant passages noting the effectiveness of the criminal justice apparatus in neutralizing large numbers of terrorists and inducing their cooperation over time while objecting strongly to congressional efforts to impede the use of the system both in legacy cases and in the future.

In important respects, however, the speeches lay out virtually no new doctrine vis-à-vis the criminal justice system, since the authority to indict and try terrorist suspects in domestic courts is—rhetoric aside—not the subject of serious dispute. Nor, really, are the general parameters of that authority. Con-

---

8. See Executive Order 13492, "Review and Disposition of Individuals Detained at the Guantánamo Bay Naval Base and Closure of Detention Facilities," January 22, 2009, http://www.gpo.gov/fdsys/pkg/FR-2009-01-27/pdf/E9-1893.pdf.

gress can, subject to constitutional limitation, criminalize whatever behavior it wants to proscribe, after all.

The first-term speeches thus lay out doctrine with respect to the claimed powers of the president only in the negative sense that they object to legislative proposals that would limit executive flexibility in the use of the system. Some of these proposals—restrictions on transfers of Guantánamo detainees to the United States for trial, for example—have been enshrined in law. Others, by contrast, were earlier-stage legislative proposals the administration sought to head off.

In the course of opposing these measures, the speeches make clear that this administration, at least, regards the criminal justice system as the exclusive means of handling terrorist suspects arrested domestically and US citizens captured anywhere. In his Harvard Law School speech, Brennan stated both points explicitly:

> [I]t is the firm position of the Obama administration that suspected terrorists arrested inside the United States will, in keeping with long-standing tradition, be processed through our Article III courts—as they should be. Our military does not patrol our streets or enforce our laws—nor should it. . . .

> Similarly, when it comes to US citizens involved in terrorist-related activity, whether they are captured overseas or at home, we will prosecute them in our criminal justice system. There is bipartisan agreement that US citizens should not be tried by military commissions. Since 2001, two US citizens were held in military custody and, after years of controversy and extensive litigation, one was released; the other was prosecuted in federal court. Even as the number

of US citizens arrested for terrorist-related activity has increased, our civilian courts have proven they are more than up to the job.

As noted earlier, however, this appears to be a statement of policy, not law. The administration has not taken the position, at least not in public, that the law bars it from processing an alien captured domestically through the military system or from holding another citizen in military detention. As to law, rather, the administration in the speeches is not really proposing anything new with respect to the criminal justice system. It is proposing something more modest: not to fix what it doesn't regard as broken.

The Use of Criminal Trial by Military Commission

By contrast, the first-term speeches do propose something new with respect to trial by military commission, and they reflect a sense on the administration's part that it has something of a burden of persuasion with respect to commissions. Obama as a senator and candidate had opposed the Military Commissions Act of 2006 and during the campaign had strongly implied—if never quite stating—that he would end the use of commissions altogether. Upon taking office, he seemed initially to head in this direction, freezing all commission proceedings and creating a presumption in his executive order on Guantánamo in favor of the use of federal courts.[9] But then the administration shifted gears. By the summer of 2009, it was working with Congress on a new Military Commissions Act that

9. Ibid. See Section 4(c)(3).

kept the essential structure of the old law in place while adopting marginally more restrictive rules of evidence and somewhat more generous due process rules.[10] The speeches thus have to do the delicate dance of defending military commissions—which have become particularly important since Congress blocked the planned federal court trial of the 9/11 conspirators—while at the same time hinging their legitimacy on a set of less-than-dramatic reforms without which Obama did not support the institution.

Obama himself began this pivot in his National Archives speech, in which he declared:

> Military commissions have a history in the United States dating back to George Washington and the Revolutionary War. They are an appropriate venue for trying detainees for violations of the laws of war. They allow for the protection of sensitive sources and methods of intelligence-gathering; they allow for the safety and security of participants; and [they allow] for the presentation of evidence gathered from the battlefield that cannot always be effectively presented in federal courts.
>
> Now, some have suggested that this represents a reversal on my part. They should look at the record. In 2006, I did strongly oppose legislation proposed by the Bush administration and passed by the Congress because it failed to establish a legitimate legal framework, with the kind of meaningful due process rights for the accused that could stand up on appeal.
>
> I said at that time, however, that I supported the use of military commissions to try detainees provided there were

---

10. See Title XVIII of the *National Defense Authorization Act for Fiscal Year 2010*, Public Law 111-84, enacted October 28, 2009.

several reforms and, in fact, there were some bipartisan efforts to achieve those reforms. Those are the reforms that we are now making. Instead of using the flawed commissions of the last seven years, my administration is bringing our commissions in line with the rule of law. We will no longer permit the use of statements that have been obtained using cruel, inhuman, or degrading interrogation methods. We will no longer place the burden to prove that hearsay is unreliable on the opponent of the hearsay. And we will give detainees greater latitude in selecting their own counsel and more protections if they refuse to testify. These reforms, among others, will make our military commissions a more credible and effective means of administering justice, and I will work with Congress and members of both parties, as well as legal authorities across the political spectrum, on legislation to ensure that these commissions are fair, legitimate, and effective.

This statement set the script for the subsequent speeches, which draw a sharp line between the supposedly illegitimate commissions of the prior administration and the kinder, gentler commissions of the 2009 MCA, which have a legitimate role to play in American counterterrorism. At the most superficial level, the speeches seldom refer to military commissions without the word "reformed" appended in front. What's more, they generally emphasize the nature of the reforms, as well as bureaucratic changes since the 2009 MCA designed to enhance their openness and transparency. In his Yale speech, for example, Johnson said,

We worked with the Congress to bring about a number of reforms to military commissions, reflected in the Military

Commissions Act of 2009 and the new *Manual for Military Commissions*. By law, use of statements obtained by cruel, inhuman, and degrading treatment—what was once the most controversial aspect of military commissions—is now prohibited.

. . .

We are working to make that system a more transparent one by reforming the rules for press access to military commissions' proceedings [and by] establishing closed-circuit TV and a new public website for the commissions system.

Similarly, at Harvard, Brennan emphasized,

[R]eformed military commissions also have their place in our counterterrorism arsenal. Because of bipartisan efforts to ensure that military commissions provide all of the core protections that are necessary to ensure a fair trial, we have restored the credibility of that system and brought it into line with our principles and our values. Where our counterterrorism professionals believe trying a suspected terrorist in our reformed military commissions would best protect the full range of US security interests and the safety of the American people, we will not hesitate to utilize them to try such individuals. In other words, rather than a rigid reliance on just one or the other, we will use both our federal courts and reformed military commissions as options for incapacitating terrorists.

As a result of recent reforms, there are indeed many similarities between the two systems and, at times, these reformed military commissions offer certain advantages.

The speeches also generally make a point of citing the areas of common ground between the two systems—the broad point being that both honor the basic norms of fair trial. As David Kris put it at Brookings:

> Before I focus on the differences between these systems, however, I want to acknowledge the similarities of the two prosecution systems. Whether you're in civilian court or a military commission, there is the presumption of innocence; a requirement of proof beyond a reasonable doubt; the right to an impartial decision-maker; similar processes for selecting members of the jury or commission; the right to counsel and choice of counsel; the right to qualified self-representation; the right to be present during proceedings; the right against self-incrimination; the right to present evidence, cross-examine the government's witnesses, and compel attendance of witnesses; the right to exclude prejudicial evidence; the right to exculpatory evidence; protections against double jeopardy; protections against ex post facto laws; and the right to an appeal. Both systems afford the basic rights most Americans associate with a fair trial.

Because the administration had to defend the propriety of both federal court and military commission trials, it inevitably had to spell out as well some of its thinking about when to use each system. The speeches consistently argue for a fact-specific, case-by-case judgment based on what Brennan called in his Harvard speech "a practical, flexible, results-driven approach that maximizes our intelligence collection and preserves our ability to prosecute dangerous individuals."

In his Brookings speech, Kris discussed at some length the advantages and disadvantages of the different systems. Holder condensed this discussion in his speech at Northwestern into a list of considerations that inform the case-by-case determination of which system to deploy—a list that tends to emphasize the advantages of the federal courts:

> Several practical considerations affect the choice of forum. First of all, the commissions only have jurisdiction to prosecute individuals who are a part of Al Qaeda, [who] have engaged in hostilities against the United States or its coalition partners, or who have purposefully and materially supported such hostilities. This means that there may be members of certain terrorist groups who fall outside the jurisdiction of military commissions because, for example, they lack ties to Al Qaeda and their conduct does not otherwise make them subject to prosecution in this forum. Additionally, by statute, military commissions cannot be used to try US citizens.
>
> Second, our civilian courts cover a much broader set of offenses than the military commissions, which can only prosecute specified offenses, including violations of the laws of war and other offenses traditionally triable by military commission. This means federal prosecutors have a wider range of tools that can be used to incapacitate suspected terrorists. Those charges, and the sentences they carry upon successful conviction, can provide important incentives to reach plea agreements and convince defendants to cooperate with federal authorities.
>
> Third, there is the issue of international cooperation. A number of countries have indicated that they will not cooperate with the United States in certain counterterrorism efforts—for instance, in providing evidence or extraditing suspects—if we intend to use that cooperation in pursuit of a

military commission prosecution. Although the use of military commissions in the United States can be traced back to the early days of our nation, in their present form they are less familiar to the international community than our time-tested criminal justice system and Article III courts. However, it is my hope that, with time and experience, the reformed commissions will attain similar respect in the eyes of the world.

In the end, the commissions system became the Obama administration's disfavored but essential step-child, whose embrace was necessary if somewhat distasteful. Congress had made commissions the exclusive means of handling the highest profile terrorism cases around, and the administration—having worked on and signed the 2009 MCA—has no principled objections to them, however much many officials might prefer the domestic courts. The result, in the speeches, is an awkward embrace—one carefully designed not to encourage the belief that the step-child was the equal of the natural-born son but also careful to reserve his legitimacy in the narrow instances in which the administration envisions showing him in public.

Cyber-Operations and the Law of Armed Conflict

The first-term speeches are notably reticent on a topic of major importance in general, though of less relevance to the conflict with Al Qaeda: cyber-operations. These can include offensive cyber-operations conducted by the United States, defensive or counter-cyber-operations by the United States responding to an attack from another party, or offensive or defensive operations by other parties. The complications are many, including whether the party is a state or a non-state actor, the problems of attributing a cyber-attack as a practical as well as legal matter, and many more. These questions have obviously taken on great salience since the appearance of newspaper and journalistic accounts both of US cyber-vulnerabilities and of US participation in offensive cyber-operations, including the Stuxnet worm and "Olympic Games" attacks against Iran's nuclear capabilities. Notwithstanding the undoubted importance of this array of questions, however, the speeches focus instead largely on targeting and detention questions. Until late in the first term, cyber-operations were entirely missing from the speeches; and throughout the first four years, the administration's position remained substantially underdeveloped as a public doctrinal matter. Only an address by Harold Koh on September 18, 2012, at Fort Meade, Maryland (see Appendix: Koh—B) began to take up questions of international law applicable to cyber-operations and, in particular, the question of the law of armed conflict.

Koh's speech proceeded in a question-and-answer format. The starting legal proposition is that, yes, "established principles" of international law apply in cyberspace. The field is difficult because cyberspace requires the transference of principles developed in other settings into new circumstances, but the process of adaptation and evolution is not uncommon in international law when dealing with new technologies. Presumably for this reason—and, one can say, consistent with the approach the speeches take in new technologies of drones and other weapons—the emphasis is on the adaptation of "established principles" to new situations and technologies in careful and plausible ways.

In line with that basic framing, Koh said that cyber-activities may "in certain circumstances constitute uses of force" within the meaning of the UN Charter and customary international law. That legal conclusion is most likely to be reached with respect to cyber-activities that "proximately result in death, injury, or significant destruction." These effects are viewed by analogy to the kinds of effects that kinetic weapons would produce which, Koh said, is a matter of "common sense." Having said this, it follows, Koh said, that a "state's national right of self-defense . . . may be triggered by computer network activities that amount to an armed attack or imminent threat thereof."

Having laid out the *jus ad bellum* proposition that cyber-activities can constitute an armed attack or imminent threat, the speech stated that such activities and responses to them must apply the rules of *jus in bello*—rules governing the conduct of hostilities. These include the basic principles of distinction and proportionality: limitation of attacks to legitimate military targets and related rules of the laws of war applicable to any weapons system and its use, cyber-systems included. Koh added that states should conduct legal reviews of weapons systems, including cyber-systems, to ensure that they conform to the laws of war as weapons systems. Furthermore, states are legally responsible for cyber-activities carried out by their proxies, such as non-state actors.

In keeping with the understanding that establishing a framework for international law applicable to cyber-activities depends upon adaptation of existing rules and norms, the speech noted a number of important areas in which the US government has not yet reached a legal position or settled on the correct approach. These include the question of "dual-use infrastructure" in cyberspace—the communications networks, for example, upon which both civilian and military functions depend. And, in addition, there is the problem of "attribution" of the attack: the difficulty of figuring out who is responsible for a given attack and the resulting practical ability of parties to have at least plausible deniability of participating in the cyber-attacks for which they are, in fact, responsible.

Finally, the speech emphasized that the laws of war are not the only international legal rules applicable in cyberspace and that, in any given situation, more than one legal regime might be invoked. Not everything in cyberspace is about uses of force, Koh said. Questions of human rights and free expression, as well as cyber-crime and cyber-security, all involve important bodies and principles of international and domestic law applicable to cyber-activities. These also must be brought into an integrated approach to these difficult cyber-related questions.

Secrecy and Transparency, Accountability and Oversight

In his 2009 National Archives speech, President Obama devoted a fair number of words not to the substance of counterterrorism authority but to the openness with which the government wields that authority. That is, he laid out an agenda for striking a balance between national security secrecy and transparency:

> National security requires a delicate balance. On the one hand, our democracy depends on transparency. On the other hand, some information must be protected from public disclosure for the sake of our security—for instance, the movement of our troops, our intelligence-gathering, or the information we have about a terrorist organization and its affiliates. In these and other cases, lives are at stake.
>
> . . .

I ran for president promising transparency, and I meant what I said. And that's why, whenever possible, my administration will make all information available to the American people so that they can make informed judgments and hold us accountable. But I have never argued—and I never will—that our most sensitive national security matters should simply be an open book. I will never abandon—and will vigorously defend—the necessity of classification to defend our troops at war, to protect sources and methods, and to safeguard confidential actions that keep the American people safe.

President Obama then made a commitment regarding secrecy and transparency, one that he described as different from the policies of prior administrations:

Here's the difference though: whenever we cannot release certain information to the public for valid national security reasons, I will insist that there is oversight of my actions by Congress or by the courts.

We're currently launching a review of current policies by all those agencies responsible for the classification of documents to determine where reforms are possible and to assure that the other branches of government will be in a position to review executive branch decisions on these matters. Because in our system of checks and balances, someone must always watch over the watchers—especially when it comes to sensitive administration information.

Whether this commitment offered in any meaningful sense more than Congress and the courts could already undertake is uncertain. Certainly, Obama's administration has not overseen dramatic reform of the classification process to address the over-classification of things that do not need classification, nor has it dramatically enhanced administrative cooperation with the congressional oversight process. The general lack of complaint from members of these committees likely indicates satisfaction with the level of disclosure. But the subsequent speeches make no reference to reform of the oversight process itself to make it more responsive to the emergence of new technologies and methods such as targeted drone strikes.

The president offered a second commitment in the National Archives speech, this one regarding the so-called "state secrets" doctrine:

> This is a doctrine that allows the government to challenge legal cases involving secret programs. It's been used by many past presidents—Republican and Democrat—for many decades. And while this principle is absolutely necessary in some circumstances to protect national security, I am concerned that it has been over-used. It is also currently the subject of a wide range of lawsuits. So let me lay out some principles here. We must not protect information merely because it reveals the violation of a law or embarrassment to the government. And that's why my administration is nearing completion of a thorough review of this practice.
>
> And we plan to embrace several principles for reform. We will apply a stricter legal test to material that can be protected under the state secrets privilege. We will not assert the privilege in court without first following our own formal process, including review by a Justice Department

committee and the personal approval of the attorney general. And each year we will voluntarily report to Congress when we have invoked the privilege and why because, as I said before, there must be proper oversight over our actions.

Again, the administration's use of the privilege looks less-than-dramatically different from that of its predecessors, though there probably are some differences. In general, in court cases, the administration has taken a hard line in favor of executive branch secrecy and the state secrecy doctrine. And it has certainly undertaken a hard line approach to the prosecution of leak cases—leading, not surprisingly, to the criticism that it was willing to prosecute leaks aggressively that were not tacitly approved, but has tolerated leaks as a substitute for providing official information on matters like drone strikes. Indeed, over the course of the past four years, the "covert" status of the program of targeted drone strikes in Pakistan reached absurd lows, even as the administration continued to defend against Freedom of Information Act requests surrounding this most open of secrets. Brennan addressed this problem in his Wilson Center speech, in which he publicly and officially acknowledged targeted strikes for the first time. He began by quoting Harvard Law School Professor Jack Goldsmith about the need to convey more information to the public about these programs, and then added, "Well, President Obama agrees." Brennan said that while he would never reveal sensitive operational information,

> [W]e reject the notion that any discussion of these matters is to step onto a slippery slope that inevitably endangers

our national security. Too often, that fear can become an excuse for saying nothing at all—which creates a void that is then filled with myths and falsehoods. That, in turn, can erode our credibility with the American people and with foreign partners, and it can undermine the public's understanding and support for our efforts. In contrast, President Obama believes that—done carefully, deliberately, and responsibly—we can be more transparent and still ensure our nation's security.

So let me say it as simply as I can. Yes, in full accordance with the law—and in order to prevent terrorist attacks on the United States and to save American lives— the US government conducts targeted strikes against specific Al Qaeda terrorists, sometimes using remotely piloted aircraft, often referred to publicly as drones. And I'm here today because President Obama has instructed us to be more open with the American people about these efforts.

To put the matter bluntly, the speeches over-promise on matters of transparency relative to what the administration, in a formal sense, managed to deliver in its first term. In many respects, the administration's most significant contribution to openness in national security legal policy has been the speeches themselves; and these, for obvious reasons, cannot be their own subject—except in the very limited recursive sense that Brennan made his own speech an issue in his speech.

This, in broad strokes, is the framework the administration laid out in its speeches during its first term, and it represents the basic lay of the legal landscape from the administration's point of view when the president took the podium at the

National Defense University in May 2013. Before turning to that speech, in chapter 2 we evaluate the first-term framework, which was stronger in some areas than it was in others—and which called out for development and refinement in certain areas.

CHAPTER 2

The Good, the Bad, and the Underdeveloped

Having laid out what senior Obama administration officials said about the legal authorities to confront Al Qaeda in the first term, let us turn to more normative questions. Are the authorities the administration has claimed the right ones? Where is the administration's baseline framework a strong one? Where is it weak? Where is it wrong? And where is it insufficiently developed—and thus in need of further public elaboration? In this chapter, we take on the task of analyzing and critiquing the administration's first-term framework.

In the main, we will argue, the administration got a great deal right in these speeches. It adopted—by discussing these matters through speeches—a creative (though far from perfect) method of describing its legal framework to the public, one that allows a relatively rich substantive conversation scrubbed carefully of operational details. Despite the criticism the administration received for refusing to release the internal legal memoranda that often lie beneath its speeches, the administration managed to put a lot of information before the public regarding the authorities it claims and the theories under which it operates. Moreover, the substance of many of its positions regarding drones and targeted killing had much to recommend it—as did its positions regarding the basic framework for detention law and the appropriate trial frameworks for terrorism cases. In other words, the administration managed to find a way to say a lot about certain matters—matters about which secrecy was the default when it came into office. And the substance of what it said generally provides a good basis for long-term institutional settlement of contested issues in areas of great consequence.

But the framework the administration laid out has significant weaknesses, too. Sometimes the framework is substantively suboptimal, as a matter of law or policy. The administration painted itself into needless corners regarding the framework for detention, for example. In many areas, the administration's framework suffered from its inability to work with Congress. And in some areas, the administration just neglected key aspects of a desirable legal framework. The administration, for example, has resolutely refused to define the legal limits on interrogation, thus leaving the long-term vitality of its framework in that area subject to doubt.

Moreover, significant aspects of the framework remained question marks—both because of limits on what the administration felt it could say and, in some areas, because, even in secret, the framework's parameters had not yet been fully agreed upon or developed internally. As became dramatically clear at the outset of the second term, much of the framework—which relies heavily on the Authorization for the Use of Military Force (AUMF) as its source of domestic legal authority—could prove fragile to the extent that the continued fraying of Al Qaeda's core and US disengagement in Afghanistan produced a conflict that the AUMF, focused as it is on September 11, 2001, describes badly and thus authorizes imperfectly. As the second-term administration looks beyond current adversaries that it regards as covered by the AUMF, it increasingly must ask whether its framework is sufficient, or sufficiently adaptable, for use against threats and what legal regimes will govern those threats. Institutional settlement must contemplate not only what the end of the current conflict would mean with regards to the formal end of AUMF authority; it must also contemplate what the end of the current conflict would mean for the continued targeting authority against the residual threats connected to the current conflict—not to mention what it would mean for those detained within the current conflict. And it must address how these institutional and legal structures for national security abroad would function with regard to a completely new future threat, unrelated to Al Qaeda and acknowledged not to be covered by the current AUMF.

Some substantive areas remained particularly thin in the first-term speeches. The speeches said very little about cyber-operations, for example, both because of classified information constraints and because the legal parameters of this nation's view of the matter remain very much disputed internally—though this is apparently in rapid evolution. And while the administration said quite a lot about the substantive law of targeting, it said much less about the procedural rules it uses to authorize potential strikes—other than that due process in targeting an American citizen does not require judicial review and that, in all cases, exacting review procedures are employed within the executive branch.

In short, as we will explain, the first-term framework represents a significant series of steps toward a legal posture that can represent the United States broadly—across party control over the executive branch—over the years to come and can address new national security situations abroad beyond the conflict legally bracketed by the AUMF. But it is still very much a work in progress, a fact that became obvious when the president pivoted on key points at the outset of his second term.

In Defense of Articulating Law Using Speeches

Before evaluating the substance of the framework laid out in the speeches, let's pause a moment to consider the administration's method of talking about law. The idea of laying out a legal framework using a series of speeches, rather than by releasing underlying legal memoranda or in legal briefs to courts, has engendered unsurprising controversy. Yet, controversial or not, it is a principal mode by which the administration has offered its legal and policy views. John Brennan, the administration's CIA director for its second term, promised in his confirmation hearing that there "need[s] to be continued speeches that are going to be given by the Executive Branch to explain our counterterrorism programs."[1] Attorney General Eric Holder, testifying before the Senate Judiciary Committee on the same day as the filibuster of the Brennan vote by Senator Rand Paul (R-KY),

---

1. See "Open Hearing on the Nomination of John O. Brennan to be Director of the Central Intelligence Agency," United States Senate, Select Committee on Intelligence, 114th Congress, 1st sess., February 7, 2013, http://intelligence.senate.gov/130207/transcript.pdf.

stated that the president would soon address the question of drone strikes—which he has now done.[2]

The speeches are often criticized on grounds that they are "merely" speeches, and so amount as a legal matter to nothing more than public relations, and a clumsy public relations effort at that. One journalist noted that Holder's speech on targeted killing has no footnotes, cites no cases, and falls "far short of the level of detail contained in the Office of Legal Counsel memo [that underlies it]—or in an account of its contents published in October by the *New York Times* based on descriptions by people who had read it."[3] In a recent district court decision dismissing a suit against the government, Judge Colleen McMahon described the speeches as "an extensive public relations campaign."[4] As we intimated in the introduction, however, this criticism of the speeches in our view lacks merit. Yes, the speeches are a public relations effort, but the specific public relations they embody entail explaining the legal views of the United States to the general public. The US government has a variety of methods by which to communicate its legal views, each addressed to varying audiences, for different legal and policy purposes. Each involves different forms of governmental

2. See Peter Finn, "Holder Says Obama Plans to Explain Drone Policy," *Washington Post,* March 6, 2013, http://www.washingtonpost.com/world/national-security/holder-says-obama-plans-to-explain-drone-policy/2013/03/06/0d9a64b8-867b-11e2-999e-5f8e0410cb9d_story.html.

3. Charlie Savage, "U.S. Law May Allow Killings, Holder Says," *New York Times,* March 5, 2012, http://www.nytimes.com/2012/03/06/us/politics/holder-explains-threat-that-would-call-for-killing-without-trial.html?_r=2&hp.

4. *New York Times v. U.S. Department of Justice,* 11-civ.-9336 (SDNY, January 2, 2013), http://www.lawfareblog.com/wp-content/uploads/2013/01/Drone-Ruling.pdf.

and diplomatic protocol with different degrees of technical legal precision. Each responds to different public purposes. The government has used many different modes of communication across history and in the present day. These modes have evolved as the nature of government, the subjects and objects of law in a democratic society, the relations among states, and communications technologies have all likewise evolved. In an era of foreign relations conducted bilaterally, the government often conveyed its legal views in diplomatic notes or in letters between diplomats; the correspondence between Secretary of State Daniel Webster and British Ambassador Lord Ashburton, which yielded the Caroline doctrine, is one famous example.[5] As the range of matters conducted in multilateral fora increased in diplomatic conferences and, eventually, in such venues as the League of Nations and the United Nations, speeches and accompanying written versions came to convey a state's legal views. Presidents have often conveyed the government's legal views by means of formal messages to Congress, including through the State of the Union Address or an Annual Message to Congress—that is, communications from one branch of government to another. President Theodore Roosevelt transmitted the "Roosevelt Corollary" to the Monroe Doctrine, for example, through the Annual Message to Congress.[6]

---

5. On the "Caroline Affair," including discussion of the exchange of diplomatic notes framing the respective legal views of the American and British governments through Secretary of State Webster and Lord Ashburton, leading finally to the Webster-Ashburton Treaty of 1842, see Samuel Flagg Bemis, *A Diplomatic History of the United States* (New York: Henry Holt & Co., 1938), pp. 259–263.

6. The Roosevelt Corollary to the Monroe Doctrine stated that European states should not intervene in the Americas to deal with, for example, default on debts, and said that the United States would, in effect, police these situa-

The US government has also used the flexible form of the internal "memorandum" to state its views. These are prepared ostensibly as internal documents from counsel or from a subordinate official to a senior official, but often with the idea of releasing them publicly later as statements of US government legal and diplomatic views. An example is the Clark Memorandum of 1928, drafted under signature of the under-secretary of state to the secretary of state, and addressing the Roosevelt Corollary to the Monroe Doctrine in both legal and diplomatic terms. Released publicly in 1930, it was formally drafted as an internal State Department memo but was intended to reach a broader diplomatic audience abroad. The Office of Legal Counsel's normal operations follow this pattern to this day.

"White papers" are certainly not unknown in US government practice, as the Justice Department's recent white paper on targeted killing attests. Yet as a form of organizational, governmental communication, the white paper is more typically a device of parliamentary democracies, a device by which officials convey findings, recommendations, and conclusions— generally *to* the government rather than *on behalf of* the government to the public.

For many observers, however, when it comes to the authoritative expression of the government's legal views, the most definitive form is the legal brief filed in a court case by the

tions. It was transmitted to Congress as part of President Theodore Roosevelt's "annual messages to Congress" of 1904 and 1905; these annual messages were a historically earlier form of the State of the Union Address. See "Theodore Roosevelt's Corollary to the Monroe Doctrine (1905)," in the US government online historical government document archive, http://www.ourdocuments .gov/doc.php?flash=true&doc=56.

government's lawyers. Being formal legal documents consisting of legal reasoning put to a coordinate branch—which is to make a ruling on the basis of law—briefs are often treated as the purest expression of the government's legal views. Yet there are important reasons to be cautious in seeing court briefs as the most authoritative statement of the government's views, especially in matters implicating foreign relations or national security. Briefs might be addressed to a judge and address legal arguments, but they are addressed to a particular case, and the accepted practice of litigation is to offer arguments strategically aimed at winning a particular case, rather than offering a considered general view applicable across policy as a whole. Briefs are allowed to argue in the alternative, and so might express many things that are not the government's core legal view. Particularly as a mechanism to declare the government's views on foreign relations and international law and diplomacy, legal briefs in US courts necessarily over-emphasize US court cases and precedents, rather than the international precedents, which may be actual court cases but may also be real-world events and practices.

The US government has reasons to use all these different rhetorical forms for expressing its views of the law. But we should not dismiss speeches in public venues as less useful than these other mechanisms. Particularly where, as in the cases of the speeches considered in this book, they are the products of the interagency process and have been vetted, discussed, and revised by multiple agencies of the executive, there are good reasons to see them as authoritative statements of the government's views. Speeches have been used this way often in the past, including in national security and foreign affairs, to express views of law and legal policy. To take an example that figures heavily in this book, many of the basic international law doctrines on the use of force that are correctly regarded as the legal views of the US government were first offered in a speech in 1989 by then-State Department legal adviser Abraham Sofaer. The speech was cleared through the interagency process; later—suitably footnoted—it appeared in the Military Law Review.[7] Few statements by a senior US government lawyer in recent years have contained so many consequential and authoritative declarations of the US government on international law and the use of force.

Speeches by senior officials and general counsels have some distinct advantages in articulating law. Because speeches are not tied to the facts of any particular court case or to its procedural peculiarities, a pattern of speeches can allow for the incremental public development of legal and policy positions while still permitting interagency review. Speeches can address the many issues in foreign relations, national security, and international law and politics that will never come close to a court case, and so will never be expressed in any brief to a court. And perhaps most importantly, they can do so in a fashion that protects sensitive diplomatic and intelligence information and thus facilitates the release of information the government would otherwise feel compelled to keep secret. It's all well and good to criticize the speeches for being less forthcoming or detailed than the government's internal legal memoranda. But in practical terms, the alternative to the speeches may not be *more* disclosure—it may well be far less.

---

7. Abraham Sofaer, "Terrorism, the Law, and the National Defense," Sixth Annual Waldemar A. Solf Lecture, US Army Judge Advocate General School, Charlottesville, Virginia (1989); reprinted in *Military Law Review*, Vol. 126, No. 1, pp. 89–123 (1989).

Even the supposedly terrible feature of these national security speeches—that they simply assert conclusions, rather than reason their way to them using dense argumentation and footnotes—is not entirely a matter of disability in these very specialized fields. After all, the US government has always seen international law as a matter of law and international politics and diplomacy conjoined. How states, and particularly great powers, see the law is an element of what the law is, in fact—so the project of defining the law, a project in which the United States has an outsized role, is indeed partly and necessarily a project consisting of this country's stating its conclusions. Important questions of international law have no clear answers. When the United States declares itself and offers a position on the law, it is useful to hear—from the standpoint of stable international relations— even if that position is conclusory.

The speeches, in other words, serve several important law-articulation purposes, from articulating *opinio juris* to facilitating domestic accountability to providing far greater openness than was likely in their absence.

What the Speeches Get Right

The administration's most important accomplishment in the first-term speeches lies in their treatment of the subject of drone strikes and targeted killing and, more broadly, the extraterritorial use of force against transnational terrorist groups. These speeches integrate these subjects into a larger framework of domestic and international law that governs the conflict. Targeted killing was a subject about which the executive branch had said literally nothing before the Obama administration came in. Drone strikes had been rare enough and obscure enough that they required no public defense. And they were diplomatically sensitive enough that they required silence— something that remains true in the situations in which, for example, the US government has worked to obtain sovereign consent to the strikes from countries that do not want their collaboration to be made public. The Obama administration, in ramping up the strikes, had to think through the legal, moral, and strategic factors justifying them and how to regulate them and, in addition, what it could and could not reveal publicly about programs conceived from the beginning as covert under domestic law. Notwithstanding a great deal of criticism, the first-term speeches got the big picture just about right.

The Nature of the Conflict at Home and Abroad

It is no small thing that the speeches—clearly and consistently— acknowledge that international law applies to America's conduct of the conflict. By the end of the Bush administration, the United States was no longer actively contesting this point and, indeed, had embraced it some years earlier. So the recognition represented an incremental change, not a watershed. But it was a significant incremental change nonetheless. It created, in certain areas, a greater common legal basis for discussion with allied governments and non-governmental organizations. Perhaps more importantly, it terminated the US government's implicit, and quite damaging, earlier insistence that strong, muscular counterterrorism actions must involve some degree of flouting of international law—rather than receiving its sanction under, at least, a plausible reading of it. And at a symbolic level, it is significant that the president himself gave speeches acknowledging that international law imposes constraints.

It is important not to overstate the significance of the administration's embrace of international law, however—at least if "embrace" means accepting wholesale the legal views of other actors in the international community that the United States has not traditionally accepted. As we explained in chapter 1, the administration's views of the substantive content of that law remain far from those of even close allies—not to mention human rights groups, academics, and UN officials, many of whom reject the opening legal premise that there can even be an "armed conflict" with a transnational non-state actor group. While in some areas certain international actors may be persuadable, more often they will not be. The law will remain sharply contested. The still-considerable value of the speeches lies in clearly articulating to this audience how the United States views international law in certain crucial areas. Even if there is no agreement about the law as such, US behavior regarding other states and allies should not appear merely capricious, nor its claims in law and diplomacy ad hoc. For many of this nation's closest allies, substantive legal agreement would be nice, but the most important thing is having an authoritative articulation of US views that permits, when necessary, an agreement to disagree and nonetheless work together.

The speeches, in short, allowed the Obama administration to finish the project begun in the last few years of the Bush administration: the United States is now arguing only about what international law permits or requires of American counterterrorism—not about whether it applies or makes demands. This represents a salutary narrowing of the field of dispute.

In a similar fashion, transported to the domestic legal level, the deliberate downplaying in the speeches of arguments based on inherent presidential power represents a significant move toward institutional settlement within the American political system about the nature of the conflict in question. While the first-term speeches always reserve the option of unilateral presidential actions to defend the nation, a fact that becomes important in the second term, they also accept congressional restrictions on executive latitude in certain important areas[8]— and in no area do they defend steps the administration has taken without primary reference to the powers that Congress has given it.

But having acknowledged the binding nature of both domestic and international legal restrictions, the first-term speeches also rightly insist on the permissive nature of the law they embrace—that is, they insist that Congress has given the executive branch wide power and latitude and, further, that international law does not preclude robust self-defense against terrorist enemies on the soil of countries that refuse to prevent their territories from being used to stage violent attacks on other nations. The administration sees international law in the use of force as being both permissive and limiting. Many of its critics, by contrast, see mostly limits.

Much as it has enraged the political Left, the international activist community, and some today on the American Right, the war and self-defense framework for overseas operations is a simple and lawful operational necessity in a world in which

---

8. See, for example, the acceptance in Department of Defense general counsel Jeh Johnson's October 18, 2011, speech to the Heritage Foundation that the restrictions Congress has placed on transfers from Guantánamo are simply something the administration has had to deal with: "After living with this provision now for almost a year, I will tell you that it is onerous and near impossible to satisfy. Not one Guantánamo detainee has been certified for transfer since this legal restriction has been imposed."

people in countries and locations impossible to reach by law enforcement means continue to threaten the United States and its people. This framework does not always mean recourse to hostilities, of course. Notwithstanding the fevered fears of administration critics, particularly in the wake of the Rand Paul filibuster, there will be no Reapers over Rome, no CIA blasting away people sitting in cafes on the sole secret say-so of the president, whether in Paris, France, or Paris, Texas. There are many places in the world where the United States can pursue terrorists through law enforcement, interdiction of terrorist financing, and other non-hostilities-based tools of counterterrorism; the speeches are rightly clear that the existence of an armed conflict in no sense precludes the use of these tools. But there are also places in the world that are weakly governed, ungoverned, or simply hostile to the United States, where terrorist groups responsible for September 11 have fled, or in which new, affiliated terrorist groups or cells have arisen. The armed conflict framework is essential to reaching these actors and denying them sanctuary.

Likewise, while the administration's understanding of its domestic law authorities, grounded in the AUMF, carries risks that we discuss below, it represents—at least for now—a more-than-plausible understanding of Congress's will that the United States should make war on those responsible for September 11 and those fighting alongside them. The speeches' claim that this authorization includes the use of force against groups and individuals who have affiliated themselves with Al Qaeda's side even many years after September 11 is also right. These groups, including groups or cells that did not exist on September 11, certainly see themselves as having entered an existing conflict, and affiliated with one combatant side of it; they have taken on the mantle of its cause, its operations, and its methods. Congress, for its part, has never renounced its expressed will in the AUMF—which, indeed, it has reiterated in different ways.[9] Neither has it ever suggested that the instrument authorized hostilities only against those it originally named. The courts have endorsed a broader view of the conflict as well.[10]

The much-criticized geographical and temporal open-endedness of the conflict that the speeches claim also ranks, in reality, among the virtues—not the vices—of the framework they lay out. The message of the United States to its allies and enemies alike cannot be that it will use force against terrorists only in certain "hot battlefields" and geographically defined theaters of conflict and that they can thus regain haven and impunity by moving to other failed states or permissive environments. "Hot battlefields" and "zones of conflict," while popular terms in public commentary, are not legal terms or concepts.

The speeches, it is important to note, are not simply adopting the early Bush administration's view of a "global war on terror." The position is more careful than that. The traditional international law threshold for application of the laws of war includes any geographical point of contact between the forces of states in an inter-state war, on the one hand, and a factual judgment of whether a certain level of hostilities exists in the

---

9. Congress in 2012 specifically reaffirmed—as least as regards detention authority—that the AUMF was still a vital document and reached members and supporters of enemy groups, including associated forces. See National Defense Authorization Act for Fiscal Year 2012 ("NDAA"), Pub. L. 112-81, § 1021, 125 Stat. 1297, 1562 (2012). It has also repeatedly funded operations conducted under the AUMF.

10. See, for example, *Khan v. Obama*, 655 F.3d 20, 21 (D.C. Cir. 2011), which affirmed the detention of a petitioner found to be "part of" Hezb-i Islami Gulbuddin, an associated force of Al Qaeda and the Taliban.

case of conflicts between states and non-state actors, on the other. The Bush administration, confronting the novel situation of a transnational non-state adversary, concluded that it could apply the law of war globally and to anyone it liked–whether it engaged in actual hostilities or not. This was something of a case of the tail of law wagging the dog of war because, in reality, the Bush administration had no intention of conducting actual hostilities in all the places where it claimed a state of armed conflict existed and where it therefore asserted theoretical application of the law of armed conflict. In effect, the Bush administration, at least during the early years after September 11, wanted recourse to the law of war where it wished to set aside ordinary civilian laws, in order to detain or interrogate suspected Al Qaeda members or sympathizers.

This was needlessly provocative in its excessive breadth—and it had consequences. The International Committee of the Red Cross and others in the international community expressed alarm at this departure from the traditional conduct-of-hostilities standard and began elaborating legal views that purported to put geographical limits on where the law of war applied. In other words, important parts of the international community came to see the law-of-war framework as limited to Afghanistan, and sometimes parts of Pakistan, irrespective of whether lawfully targetable fighters and terrorists, fleeing US forces, sought to relocate themselves in new havens.

The Obama administration, for its part, has disavowed the "global war on terror" rubric and re-embraced a more traditional "conduct-of-hostilities" standard. Under this view, the law of war applies in places in which hostilities take place; in other words, the Obama administration rejects both the "global war on terror" that supplants all other law everywhere and any artificial legal geographic limits. The question, in this formulation, is where the enemy strategically chooses to go and whether the United States thinks it strategically prudent to attack it there, thus initiating hostilities in that location and triggering the law of war as part of a larger armed conflict already under way. The speeches thus rightly return the United States to its—and international law's—traditional way of thinking about geography and armed conflict with a non-state actor. Notably, the courts have accepted a degree of geographical open-endedness in the context of the Guantánamo detention cases.[11]

If the legal geography of war is an issue for the administration's critics, so too is the question of when the war ends. Here too the administration has the better of the argument. Critics have argued that it is patently absurd that September 11 could still provide, so many years later, a basis on which to claim an armed conflict, especially against groups that did not even exist in 2001. But there is much to recommend the functional, practical view taken in the first-term speeches of when, in principle, the war ends. After all, the United States managed to attack and kill Osama bin Laden only in 2011, after years of debate among intelligence analysts, academics, and others over whether Al Qaeda's scattered senior leadership was actually in command of anything anymore. Materials captured in the bin Laden raid showed an organization degraded as a consequence of constant intelligence-driven strikes. Yet it also showed a leadership still actively directing the organization—

---

11. See, for example, *Salahi v. Obama*, 625 F.3d 745, 750 (D.C. Cir. 2010), which reversed a grant of habeas corpus notwithstanding the fact that the detainee was captured in Mauritania, nowhere near any hot battlefield, and transferred to US custody.

and directing affiliated groups whose relationship to the core many had begun to question.

In short, while the administration's current position is often derided as a world-wide war without end—a criticism we will confront in greater depth in chapter 5—this position is really just another way of saying the conflict is a real, actual armed conflict. It goes where the participants go and lasts until they are no longer meaningfully capable of fighting. To be sure, there are other international law principles at play—the rights of neutral states and sovereignty, for example, as well as the obligations of sovereign neutral states. But the conduct of hostilities, wherever they take place, is governed by the law of war for as long as the enemy continues to be able to fight. This is actually not a radical position. It is a sensible one, rooted in the ordinary law of war. When one initiates a war, after all, one does not announce that one will confront enemy forces in Location A but leave them alone when they are preparing for battle in Location B. And one generally does not put a time limit on the conflict either. To the contrary, a certain open-endedness in time and space is inherent in the project of warfare.

At the same time, however, the administration also deserves credit for defending in the speeches the exclusivity of law enforcement as the means of confronting the enemy domestically and of handling US nationals captured anywhere. As we explained in the previous chapter, the speeches territorially bifurcate the conflict and its legal framework. Within the territorial United States, law enforcement and domestic criminal law constitute the legal authority for the conduct of counterterrorism. This is a change from Bush administration policies, at least from the first term. The Bush administration made several efforts to use the law-of-armed-conflict rules to cover the detention of Americans and the handling of non-citizens captured domestically. They all failed, and by the end of the Bush administration the government had largely abandoned them. The speeches represent the formalization of that abandonment, an important recognition of the split personality of the conflict—that, while war abroad, the conflict invokes a very different set of authorities stateside.

All in all, with the caveat that the administration only began to describe in the first term an end of the conflict and what might follow it, the speeches of that period described the parameters of the conflict in a fashion that was reasonably clear, reasonably comprehensive, to our minds compelling, and a plausible and defensible—though certainly contested—reading of both domestic and international law.

Drones and Targeted Killing

In addition to laying out many of the structural basics regarding the conflict itself, the first-term speeches did a good—though by no means complete—job of laying out the legal parameters for targeted killing, particularly using drone technologies. By the beginning of the second Obama term, the criticism of drone warfare and targeted killing had greatly increased; the international activist community has vowed to make drones the Obama administration's Guantánamo. And the president felt compelled to say more. But Harold H. Koh, legal adviser to the Department of State, actually addressed the relevant issues in his March 25, 2010, address to the American Society of International Law ("The Obama Administration and International Law") in Washington, D.C. The combination of the years of silence preceding Koh's ASIL speech, the fact that drone strikes still notionally take place within a covert action program, and the administration's refusal to release the memos that underlie the speeches conspired to support the myth that American targeted killing remains shrouded in silence and secrecy. In fact, however, the administration in the first term put a considerable amount on the table, and most of what it has said constitutes the right positions for the United States to be taking.

These speeches, for starters, are entirely correct to treat targeted killing and drone warfare as targeting functions in armed conflict. For all the disparaging talk of these strikes as "assassinations," there is nothing so novel either about a drone or about the targeting of high-level individuals as to, from a legal point of view, require a profoundly different framework for operations. Drones are simply another air platform—governed by the same rules as any other air weapon system. They are another of the many "standoff" weapon systems used by the United States and others; other examples would be cruise missiles fired from ships and missiles fired from over-the-horizon aircraft. The shipboard personnel who, without any personal risk, fire a cruise missile from a computer console deep inside a vessel at sea are as remote from the "battlefield" as are drone operators. The originally voguish but now shopworn idea that drones are some psychologically distancing weapon, categorically different from other remote platform systems, is flat-out wrong. Drone pilots often suffer greater levels of stress than do others who conduct strikes; unlike nearly all other remote platform operators, they often engage in lengthy surveillance of an individual target, with video feeds that enable them to enter into that target's daily life. This is simply unimaginable for cruise missile operators or the pilots of the typical manned aircraft, both of which strike with far less situational awareness of what is actually taking place on the ground.

The novelty of the drone lies only in its additional ability to function as a particularly sophisticated intelligence-collection platform. The drone's lengthy "loiter" time enables dramatically more precise targeting. And this precision itself causes some drone strikes to look more like extra-judicial killings of individuals than like conventional law-of-war targeting aimed at undifferentiated combatant groups.[12] But that appearance is essentially an illusion; it cannot be that the ability to target precisely requires the adoption of some model of domestic criminal law or international human rights law. To the contrary, the administration in the speeches quite reasonably rejects the notion that the ability to target well conveys a legal obligation not to target at all.

Accepting that the basic paradigm for overseas counterterrorism action is armed conflict, the speeches are basically on firm ground as to the conduct of operations—that is, the rules under which the use of force and targeting must take place. Their basic point is that any use of force must conform to the fundamental principles of the laws of war: necessity, distinction and discrimination, proportionality, and humanity. One can argue with this point only to the extent to which one does

---

12. Drones are not always used for targeted killing of identified individuals; they are a flexible air platform and are also used in conventional targeting of groups of combatants. Although the government has not made public information that would explain this, this is likely the best understanding of so-called "signature strikes" taken against groups on the basis of their observed behaviors as a group—organized, for example, as a weapons-bearing group of Taliban fighters preparing to board a truck crossing from Pakistan to Afghanistan. See the discussion of "signature strikes" as conventional targeting in Robert Chesney, "Drones and the War on Terror: When Can the United States Target Alleged American Terrorists Overseas?" Written Statement Submitted to the US House of Representatives Committee on the Judiciary, February 27, 2013, Fn. 3.

not accept that warfare is at least a component of the operative framework.

The first-term speeches are also correct in their insistence that, at least under current domestic law, targeting is inherently an executive function and hence a responsibility of the commander in chief. In one sense, this is entirely uncontroversial—provided one accepts the armed conflict or self-defense paradigm. The controversy arises for those who reject this framing or who believe that it needs to be significantly qualified given that targeted killing does not always look like part of a traditional armed conflict taking place on an obvious battlefield.

Holder was explicit about the executive's exclusive responsibility for targeting in his March 5, 2012, speech to the Northwestern University School of Law in Chicago. And the absence of a prospective judicial role is unquestionably correct under the law as it stands, which simply does not provide for judicial involvement in targeting. Whether some as-yet-unwritten statutory framework might usefully provide for judicial involvement presents a more difficult question.[13] It also presents difficult issues of separation of powers, as well as prudential questions of judicial competence in these matters; it is not clear that even a statutory mandate for judicial review would be regarded as constitutional in every respect by the courts

13. Thoughtful proposals for new review processes have arisen. See, for example, Jennifer C. Daskal, "The Geography of the Battlefield: A Framework for Detention and Targeting Outside the 'Hot' Conflict Zone," 161 *University of Pennsylvania Law Review* 1165 (2013), http://scholarship.law.upenn.edu/penn_law_review/vol161/iss5/1. Others have proposed enhanced non-judicial oversight regimes. See Neal K. Katyal, "Who Will Mind the Drones?" *New York Times*, February 20, 2013, http://www.nytimes.com/2013/02/21/opinion/an-executive-branch-drone-court.html.

themselves. Whether some legislative framework might ultimately provide a limited judicial role is a matter for debate. But in any case, today that role does not exist. Suffice it for now to say that Holder's insistence that Yemeni-American cleric Anwar al-Awlaki—whom he did not name but whose case clearly gave rise to the speech in the first place—had no due process or Fourth Amendment right to prospective judicial review of his targeting clearly has merit.

The speeches further get right that while targeting should not involve judicial process, it must result from *some process*. The Department of Defense has elaborate processes in place for targeting in ordinary armed conflict, and these have provided the basis for targeting across this unconventional armed conflict under the AUMF. Those processes include targeting on conventional battlefields; because they are not really contested, they are not described in detail in the speeches—merely incorporated by reference to the care with which the military reviews targeting decisions. Moving, then, from ordinary battlefield targeting to covert, formally unacknowledged programs—whether conducted by the military or by the CIA—the speeches become quite vague. With the important exception of Brennan's comments at Harvard and at the Wilson Center, the administration said very little at all. The first-term speeches, in short, did a better job stating that processes exist than they did in describing the contours of those processes.

Finally, the administration articulated in these speeches a perfectly reasonable standard for the exceptionally rare situation that involves the targeting of the American citizen overseas. The leak of the administration's white paper on targeted killing and the furor that resulted threw up a great deal of smoke around this issue, fueled in some part by inelegant wording in the white paper itself. But the underlying theory in the white paper is sound.[14]

There exists no general immunity from targeting for US citizens who sign up to wage war against their own country. Americans have fought in foreign armies against their country in numerous armed conflicts in the past, and their citizenship has never relieved them of the risks of that belligerency—nor does it convey any need for judicial review of targeting decisions. US nationals fought for Axis countries during World War II, for example. And it would have been impossible to prosecute the Civil War had some principle required the Union Army to refrain from targeting US citizens—or required judicial review of targeting decisions directed against citizens. This principle is no different if a rebel leads Al Qaeda operations against the United States in Yemen than if he leads an army against US forces in Virginia.

Moreover, whatever the Constitution's guarantee of due process may require before targeting a US citizen aligned with the enemy overseas—and the administration assumes it does impose some demands—the administration is hardly out on a limb when it asserts that these requirements are more than satisfied by a high-level, rigorous internal judgment that this person is a senior operational leader of Al Qaeda or its affiliates

---

14. For a more focused defense of the administration's position on the killing of Americans overseas, see Benjamin Wittes, "Prepared Statement of Benjamin Wittes, Senior Fellow, The Brookings Institution, before the House Committee on the Judiciary: 'Drones and the War on Terror: When Can the U.S. Target Alleged American Terrorists Overseas?'" February 27, 2013, http://judiciary.house.gov/hearings/113th/02272013_2/Wittes%2002272013.pdf.

who poses an imminent threat, whose capture is not feasible, and whose targeting would be consistent with the laws of war.

To understand why this position must be correct, consider an example from an entirely different context: a domestic hostage situation. In such situations, even law enforcement will use targeted killings, and it will do so without judicial pre-approval when the threat to the lives of the hostages is adequately serious and when there are no available alternatives. What's more, police officers will not wait until the threat to the hostages is imminent in the sense that the hostage-taker is literally lifting his gun to kill innocents in real time. Rather, they will often act—including with lethal force—within the windows of opportunity that circumstances may offer them. Nobody takes the position that such actions constitute unlawful extra-judicial killings. Rather, we accept that the preservation of the lives of the hostages justifies the use of lethal force based on standards totally different from the standards of proof and evidence that would suffice before a judge or jury. Importantly, we generally do not consider the standards ordinarily applied to such uses of lethal force against US citizens as matters of due process—though this is the language many commentators use in discussing targeted killings—but instead in terms of the Fourth Amendment's balancing test of *Tennessee v. Garner*[15] and *Scott v. Harris*.[16] As the Supreme Court put it in *Garner*, "[w]here the officer has probable cause to believe that the suspect poses a threat of serious physical harm, either to the officer or to others, it

---

15. 471 US 1 (1985).
16. 550 US 372 (2007).

is not constitutionally unreasonable to prevent escape by using deadly force."[17]

The case that truly meets the administration's legal test—and only one such case, that of al-Awlaki, has presented itself to date—is not profoundly different from this hostage situation. Yes, the action was taken by military or covert operatives, not police and not pursuant to law enforcement authorities. And yes, the imminence of the harm al-Awlaki threatened was, in some temporal sense, less certain. Al-Awlaki was not, after all, literally holding hostages, and the precise window of time in which he posed a serious threat to American lives was not entirely clear. The nature of terrorist plots, which involve great secrecy and operational security, means that authorities may not know how imminent a threat really is; hostage-takers are less subtle. In another sense, however, the problem al-Awlaki posed was far less controllable and far more threatening than an ordinary hostage standoff. Remoteness gave him relative security. And, critically, the government *had no other obvious tool by which to neutralize the threat he posed*. Indicting him and seeking his extradition from a country that did not have custody of him, cannot generally keep track of its prisoners, and lacks full control over its territory was not a promising avenue. A capture operation would have involved much greater risk to US forces and a much greater affront to the sovereignty of a country that seems to allow unacknowledged American air strikes but is not especially eager to have American boots on the ground. To have declined to act in that situation would have been, perhaps, to decline the last and only opportunity to prevent an attack on American civilians—and the Constitution no

---

17. 471 US at 11.

more requires that than it requires that police forego the shot at the hostage-taker.

A great deal of confusion and anxiety about the targeting of American citizens has flowed from the inelegant discussion in the white paper of the word "imminent." Neither the white paper nor Holder's speech makes clear what precise legal question the concept of imminence is addressing in its analysis. It is a bit of a mystery, in fact, whether the administration is using it to address resort-to-force matters under international law, to tackle domestic separation-of-powers questions, to address issues of the constitutional rights of the targets, as a possible defense against criminal prohibitions on killing Americans, or perhaps as a prudential invocation of the standards of international human rights law. What is clear is that the administration, for whatever reason, limited itself in targeting Americans overseas to circumstances of an imminent threat. The criticism of its view of imminence rests, we submit, on a misreading of the white paper. Although it is true that the administration is using the term in a manner slightly relaxed from its common-sense meaning, as Brennan acknowledged, many commentators and media figures are dramatically overstating the degree of relaxation. To wit, the white paper should emphatically *not* be over-read as authorizing—as one journalist put it—the killing of top Al Qaeda leaders "even if there is no intelligence indicating they are engaged in an active plot to attack the US."[18]

In reality, the white paper says something much more modest: that a finding of imminence does not require "clear

---

18. Michael Isikoff, "Justice Department Memo Reveals Legal Case for Drone Strikes on Americans," *NBC News*, February 4, 2013, http://open channel.nbcnews.com/_news2013/02/04/16843014-justice -department-memo-reveals-legal-case-for-drone-strikes-on-americans?lite.

evidence" that "a specific attack" will take place in the "immediate future." It goes on to say that for those senior Al Qaeda
leaders who are "continually planning attacks," one has to consider the window of opportunity available in which to act
against them and the probability that another window may not
open before an attack comes to fruition. The result is that a
finding of imminence for such a senior-level Al Qaeda operational leader can be based on a determination that such a
figure is "personally and continually" planning attacks—not on
a determination that any one planned attack is necessarily
nearing ripeness.

The confusion arises largely out of a single, poorly worded
passage of the white paper:

> . . . a high-level official could conclude, for example, that
> an individual poses an "imminent threat" of violent attack
> against the United States where he is an operational leader
> of Al Qa'ida or an associated force and is personally continu-
> ally involved in planning terrorist attacks against the United
> States. Moreover, where the al-Qa'ida member in question
> has recently been involved in activities posing an imminent
> threat of violent attack against the United States, and there is
> no evidence suggesting that he has renounced or abandoned
> such activities, that member's involvement in al-Qa'ida's
> continuing terrorist campaign against the United States would
> support the conclusion that the member poses an imminent
> threat.[19]

---

19. Department of Justice white paper, "Lawfulness of a Lethal Operation Directed Against a U.S. Citizen Who is a Senior Operational Leader
of Al-Qa'ida or An Associated Force," http://msnbcmedia.msn.com/i/msnbc/
sections/news/020413_DOJ_White_Paper.pdf.

The temptation is to read this passage broadly, as stating that targeting may be predicated on nothing more than an un-renounced history of plotting attacks—and without regard for the target's present-day activities. Such a reading, however, places the white paper at odds both with other public admin-istration statements—including Holder's—and with the his-tory of US interpretation of "imminence" in the international law context. The better way to understand the passage is that the first sentence of the paragraph states the general rule: that an Al Qaeda operational leader may be considered an immi-nent threat if he is "personally continually" planning attacks against the United States. The second sentence states the view that when evaluating whether a potential target is personally and continually planning such attacks, his recent activity is important to that evaluation; a recent history of plotting major attacks will tend to support the inference that a person is cur-rently plotting as well—at least to the extent it is not contra-dicted by some sort of renunciation of violence.

Read this way, the passage seems both correct and unsur-prising. If one is trying to assess whether al-Awlaki was person-ally and continually planning major attacks against the United States, after all, surely it is not irrelevant that he had only recently coaxed Umar Farouk Abdulmutallab onto a plane with a bomb,[20] exchanged e-mails with would-be terrorists in Britain

20. See Government's Sentencing Memorandum, *United States of America v. Umar Farouk Abdulmutallab*, No. 2:10-cr-2000 (E.D. Mich., February 10, 2012), pp. 13–14. The document notes the defendant's following of and meet-ings with Anwar al-Awlaki to discuss jihad and martyrdom missions, the defen-dant's subsequent training at an Al Qaeda in the Arabian Peninsula camp, al-Awlaki's introduction of the defendant to an AQAP bomb-maker, al-Awlaki's instructions to the defendant about the need to attack a US airliner over US soil, and al-Awlaki's arranging for a martyrdom video by the defendant.

about how to carry out attacks on aviation there,[21] and corresponded with Nidal Hasan in the run-up to the latter's shooting at Fort Hood.[22] To the contrary, surely this pattern of behavior supports an inference—at least to *some* extent—that this is a person who is continually plotting attacks of this nature. And surely it is also relevant that the possible target has not merely failed to renounce participation in such attacks but is also continuing to release videos calling for them.

Whether a pattern of this sort would adequately and *on its own* support a finding that an individual is continually involved in plotting major attacks would likely depend on how recent the pattern was, and how extensive. But there is nothing especially remarkable about the government's position that for senior operational figures, recent past leadership conduct of an operational nature can serve as probative evidence of a figure's current role.

Regimes for Detention and Trial

The speeches reflect evident discomfort on the subject of detention. In many ways, however, that discomfort makes them all the more powerful on the subject. It is one thing, after all, for Bush administration officials to defend a broad authority to detain the enemy—quite another thing for the Obama administration to do it after so many of its officials, the

---

21. See Thomas Joscelyn, "Awlaki's Emails to Terror Plotter Show Operational Role," *Long War Journal,* March 2, 2011, http://www.longwarjournal.org/archives/2011/03/anwar_al_awlakis_ema.php.

22. See generally "Anwar Awlaki E-Mail Exchange with Fort Hood Shooter Nidal Hasan," *Intelwire,* July 19, 2012, http://news.intelwire.com/2012/07/the-following-e-mails-between-maj.html.

president included, criticized Bush administration detention policy.

The discomfort aside, these speeches lay out a series of quite reasonable positions regarding the law of detention. Though, as we describe below, they also reflect the administration's bungled thinking regarding key aspects of detention policy, on the key questions of law they are quite sound. Unlike the area of targeted killing, detention is an area in which the administration benefits from a considerable body of both judicial precedent and, more recently, legislation—a subject we turn to in chapter 4. So when officials insist upon their authority to detain people who are "part of" or "substantially supporting" enemy forces, they are not writing on a blank slate. Indeed, notwithstanding the ongoing questioning by human rights groups and editorial writers of the legality of non-criminal counterterrorism detention, they are really just stating the law. And while the law is hotly disputed in the political space, the authority to detain the enemy is no longer meaningfully in play among the branches of the US government.

The core elements of detention law as articulated in the speeches are all essentially sound given the basic premise of an armed conflict. Detaining the enemy is an inherent part of warfare, the humane alternative to killing the enemy. The parameters of detention authority, as the speeches insist, are properly bounded by international law and, domestically, by the AUMF. And, critically, the administration insists on the authority not merely to capture and hold people in military custody but also to transfer detainees *from* military custody— both abroad for release to foreign governments and to the domestic criminal justice system. This latter point is a matter of active contest between the administration and the legislature, which has restricted the authority to remove detainees from Guantánamo.

The speeches also get right the fundamental principles at work in bringing terrorists to trial. They robustly and consistently defend the use of the civilian criminal justice apparatus as a principal instrument of counterterrorism, and the exclusive one operative domestically and with respect to US citizens. But they also defend the propriety of a significant alternative tribunal and the legitimacy of military commissions as an alternative forum for certain criminal cases. The speeches here thus walk a peculiar tightrope. They defend commissions from the suspicions of the Left and reserve not merely the possibility of their use for legacy cases but their legitimacy as a prospective matter for crimes that have not yet taken place. But at the same time, they also respond to the Right's demand for the primacy of commissions and military authorities more generally by insisting on the primacy of civilian justice as the central tool of counterterrorism domestically.

At times, they walk this tightrope gracefully. Former Assistant Attorney General David Kris did so with particular cogency in his June 11, 2010, address to the Brookings Institution in Washington, D.C., "Law Enforcement as a Counterterrorism Tool." This speech was, notably, a distillation of a law review article he later published.[23] More often, because of the administration's unfortunate conflation of these issues with the marginally related project of closing Guantánamo, the high-wire

---

23. David S. Kris, "Law Enforcement as a Counterterrorism Tool," *Journal of National Security Law & Policy*, Vol. 5, No. 1, June 2011, http://jnslp.com/2011/06/26/law-enforcement-as-a-counterterrorism-tool.

balancing act has been clumsy. But the administration's core point is both correct and fundamentally important. Closing off, or encumbering the use of, the criminal justice system as a tool of counterterrorism makes no sense; the criminal courts of the United States have been one of the true workhorses of the war on terror. But, conversely, the development of an alternative tribunal with fair rules and procedures adapted to the project of trying the war crimes of those held in military custody is not a project that should be rejected on principle. Commissions might have advantages for certain cases, and they are essential in any case if only because Congress will not permit certain detainees to be brought to the United States for trial.

However uncomfortably and awkwardly (and notwithstanding whatever apologetics), in short, the first-term speeches thus preserve all of the essential government interests in a detention and trial regime. And they do it in the broader context of describing cogently the larger regime of warfare and civilian justice in which these powers exist and describing as well the powers, values, and restraints associated with those regimes.

What the Speeches Get Wrong

While the first-term speeches did an impressive job of laying out the law of the overarching nature of the conflict, of targeted killing, and of detention and trial, they were far from perfect or complete. In certain areas, the framework they laid out was flawed—both because on some issues the administration has adopted wrongheaded positions and because, in some areas, the speeches simply omitted discussion of points that are actually important to address.

The Refusal to Go to Congress or Force Congress to the Table

Perhaps the greatest flaw in the first-term speeches—and in the administration's policy, more generally—is the failure to involve, and thereby implicate, Congress pervasively in the framework they lay out. We are not romantic about the role that Congress has played in the national security arena during the Obama administration; far from shrouding itself in glory, it has shown itself, by turns, overly contentious and overly timid on issues of counterterrorism policy and has offered little constructive in the way of a larger, settled institutional architecture for terrorism and national security.[24] To see the short-sightedness of this approach, particularly for congressional Republicans, imagine for a moment that Mitt Romney had won the election and thereby taken responsibility for the conduct of America's armed conflict.

Romney and his team would have quite reasonably assumed on taking office that they had in their hands all of the same tools used in counterterrorism by the Obama administration—including targeted killings, drone warfare, bases in Africa, and so on. They would have assumed that if these tools are lawfully available to one president, they are also available to the next. But politically, that's a complicated proposition. Many Democrats, after all, believe that these tools of counterterrorism-on-offense could be entrusted—and only barely—to President

---

24. There are exceptions to this general characterization that warrant note. In 2011, for example, House Armed Services Committee Chairman Buck McKeon sought to update the AUMF to make it more clearly authorize current military operations. His efforts were spurned by the administration.

Obama and his administration. A Republican administration wielding the same tools brings out latent anxieties that partisan loyalties may have kept quiet. Over time, in our counterfactual world, these Democrats pivot to the mounting global suspicion of drone warfare and targeted killing as a violation of the laws of war or, indeed, some sort of war crime—as, indeed, some legislators of both parties are doing, even under Obama. Suddenly, what seems like a strong bipartisan consensus behind the basic tools becomes the next Guantánamo, a sharply contested use of presidential power facing an ongoing legitimacy crisis both at home and abroad.

The point of this little thought experiment is to say that congressional Republicans who have done little to support the Obama administration in a policy that they in fact see as successful, lawful, legitimate, and correct have missed an important opportunity to solidify permanent tools of any administration in the future. This is wrong on the part of the Congress, but it also represents a failure on the part of the administration.

The first-term speeches, after all, were notably devoid of any significant legislative proposals, though they do occasionally voice opposition to unfortunate congressional initiatives. Indeed, they generally failed to note or propose any ongoing role for Congress in the creation and management of the legal framework for the conflict. This absence reflects the Obama administration's larger unwillingness to expend political capital to move Congress to create statutory frameworks for the long run in national security. The Bush administration's foolish refusal to go to Congress to reach a common statutory ground left it with a massive legitimacy deficit on Guantánamo, detention, interrogation, and trial that could not be overcome by the executive branch alone. One might have thought that a fundamental lesson of the Bush years was that, in national security, the presidency is strengthened, not weakened, by going to Congress; yet the Obama administration has likewise largely failed to force Congress to grapple with these issues. And the speeches notably reflect that failure.

This broad failure—a failure of omission—connects in important ways to areas, discussed below, in which the speeches leave the framework underdeveloped.

A Detention Law without a Practical Detention Policy

While the first-term speeches describe the law of detention quite admirably, the administration has talked itself into something of a box about detention *policy*. These speeches reiterate almost mechanically President Obama's commitment to close Guantánamo—a promise the administration has long since shown itself as incapable of keeping. Doing so would, after all, require aggressively confronting Congress, which is tenaciously committed to *maintaining* Guantánamo. And the administration has repeatedly revealed that it is no more prepared to spend the political capital staring down the legislature on this matter than it is prepared to work with the legislature on developing the larger framework. Because Congress refuses to permit the building of any alternative detention site in the United States, the administration has little room to maneuver here. It cannot bring new non-Afghan detainees to any facility other than Guantánamo, as a result of Afghan restrictions on the use of the Bagram air base for detention and of the fact that it has no other site for long-term detentions. Yet the speeches emphasize that the administration will not, as a matter of policy, bring new detainees to Guantánamo. The result is that the speeches both wall off the use of, and shroud in disrepute and opprobrium, the one facility to which Congress and circumstances will both allow the administration access for an important counterterrorism authority. In large part because of policy ground that the administration, in the speeches and elsewhere, refuses to yield, it has been left without a detention site both for prospective detentions and for those currently at Bagram whom it does not wish to turn over to Afghan custody as the United States draws down troops from Afghanistan.

The absence of a detention site has caused consternation among senior military officers—some of which consternation has even spilled out in public. In congressional testimony in 2011, Admiral William McRaven—then commander of the Joint Special Operations Command (JSOC) and now commander of US Special Operations Command—had the following exchange with Senator Lindsey Graham (R-SC):

> SENATOR GRAHAM: . . . If you caught someone tomorrow in Yemen, Somalia, you name the theater, outside of Afghanistan, where would you detain that person?
>
> ADMIRAL MCRAVEN: Sir, right now, as you're well aware, that is always a difficult issue for us. When we conduct an operation outside the major theaters of war in Iraq or Afghanistan . . . we put forth a concept of operation. The concept of operation goes up through the chain of command . . . and is eventually vetted through the interagency, and the decision by the president is made for us to conduct a particular operation. Always as part of that CONOP are options for detention. No two cases seem to be alike. As you know,

there are certain individuals that are under the AUMF, the use of military force, and those are easier to deal with than folks that may not have been under the authority for AUMF. In many cases, we will put them on a naval vessel and we will hold them until we can either get a case to prosecute them in US court or…

…

SENATOR GRAHAM: What's the longest we can keep somebody on the ship?

ADMIRAL MCRAVEN: Sir, I think it depends on whether or not we think we can prosecute that individual in a US court or we can return him to a third party country.

SENATOR GRAHAM: What if you can't do either one of those?

ADMIRAL MCRAVEN: Sir, it — again, if we can't do either one of those, then we'll release that individual and that becomes the — the unenviable option, but it is an option.

Following up later on, Senator Kelly Ayotte (R-NH) pushed McRaven further:

SENATOR AYOTTE: And, Admiral, would it not be helpful ten years into the war on terror to have a long-term detention and interrogation facility that would be secure for individuals where we need to gather further intelligence?

ADMIRAL MCRAVEN: Ma'am, I believe it would be very helpful.

SENATOR AYOTTE: And as far as you understand it, is Guantánamo Bay still off the table in terms of being used for that type of facility?

ADMIRAL MCRAVEN: As far as I understand it, it is, yes, ma'am.[25]

Other senior military officials have, less publicly, voiced similar concerns, sometimes more pointedly.

The speeches reflect administration policy, rather than defining it; so in that sense, the problem is not the speeches themselves but the underlying policy standoff. The administration can neither work its will on Congress nor bring itself to back down and yield to Congress's will. On the other hand, each major speech represents an opportunity to back down, to reshape the dispute, or to proffer some sort of deal that changes the terms of the standoff. Yet, instead, each speech simply reiterates the premise: Guantánamo is disreputable and must be closed to avoid strengthening the enemy. Each speech— even while defending detention under the rule of law—thus also subtly casts American aspersions upon it. It is a hard dance

25. See Robert Chesney, "What Would We Do with Detainees Captured Outside Afghanistan? Must-Read Testimony from McRaven and Allen on Counterterrorism Policy," *Lawfare*, June 29, 2011, http://www.lawfareblog.com/2011/06/what-would-we-do-with-detainees-captured-outside-afghanistan-must-read-testimony-from-mcraven-and-allen-on-counterterrorism-policy.

to defend detention, while simultaneously apologizing for it and promising to close the one facility under one's full control at which it can take place. Obama, as we will see in Chapter 3, has made this problem significantly worse with his opening national security speech of his second term.

More damaging still, the speeches, as McRaven's testimony makes clear, offer no answer to the problem of what to do with future detainees, not just where to put them. Indeed, while defending the authority to detain, the first-term speeches largely ignore the problem of future detentions, preferring to treat detention as a legacy problem from the last administration. While none of them ever says this directly, they largely proceed under the assumption that new captures will either produce detentions in theater by local proxies or be handled through the criminal justice system. This latter assumption works only as long as the number of new captures remains small enough that they do not overwhelm the criminal justice system's capacity. As one of the present authors has put it:

> As long as the numbers stay small, proxy detention in the theater of operations presents a viable option for a high percentage of cases. As long as the numbers stay small, the domestic criminal justice system can plausibly absorb and handle most of the relatively rare cases in which rendition or proxy detention is not a reliable alternative. And as long as the number of new detainees entering the US detention system is a rounding error on the number of detainees leaving it—either through release or transfer to foreign custody—the newcomers can be hidden among the declining overall population. The American public and the world at large will continue to see a declining detainee population

and are likely not to care that the aggregate number of detainees masks some new entrants into the system.

The trouble is that it seems unlikely that the numbers will remain small forever. Eventually—and eventually may come soon—the United States will have to deploy forces to some location in the world where it lacks a local partner with the capacity to conduct our detentions for us. What happens then?[26]

What happens then is that the policy of having no location for detention—no Guantánamo and no replacement for it—comes back to bite the administration hard. The speeches have offered a lot of opportunities for the administration to strike a different chord on detention policy, either to promise the sort of confrontation with Congress that might actually trigger a congressional retreat or to signal a retreat of the administration's own. Either approach could provide an opportunity to answer the problem McRaven had to acknowledge before Congress. The obstinate refusal to confront the problem does not. And it was not until the beginning of the second term that the administration publicly tipped its hand regarding how it envisioned squaring this circle.

A Practical Interrogation Policy without Underlying Law

Whereas, with respect to detention, the administration's first-term speeches reflect sound law underlying an unsound policy,

26. Benjamin Wittes, *Detention and Denial: The Case for Candor After Guantanamo* (Washington, D.C.: Brookings Institution Press, 2011), p. 30.

the interrogation arena presents something of the opposite environment. On interrogation, the administration has a policy that binds all interrogations by US forces to either law enforcement standards or the Army Field Manual. It is a policy that, at least for now, is serving the country well. Notwithstanding the insistence of voices on the political Right, there is little evidence that—at this stage of America's fight against Al Qaeda—the lack of a CIA coercive interrogation program is causing a significant gap in America's intelligence efforts. Yet ironically, while the administration's policy is defensible, it peculiarly lacks a law of similar strength and conviction— relying instead only on an executive order that contains an important loophole.[27]

---

27. See Executive Order 13491, "Ensuring Lawful Interrogations," January 22, 2009, http://www.whitehouse.gov/the_press_office/Ensuring LawfulInterrogations. The executive order revokes all previous legal guidance given by the Department of Justice on the subject of interrogation to the extent it is not consistent with its requirements that "an individual in the custody or under the effective control of an officer, employee, or other agent of the United States Government, or detained within a facility owned, operated, or controlled by a department or agency of the United States, in any armed conflict, shall not be subjected to any interrogation technique or approach, or any treatment related to interrogation, that is not authorized by and listed in Army Field Manual 2 22.3 (Manual)." And it forbids officials "in conducting interrogations, [to] rely upon any interpretation of the law governing interrogation—including interpretations of Federal criminal laws, the Convention Against Torture, Common Article 3, Army Field Manual 2 22.3, and its predecessor document, Army Field Manual 34 52 issued by the Department of Justice between September 11, 2001, and January 20, 2009." But the document contains an important caveat: a clause that reads "unless the Attorney General with appropriate consultation provides further guidance." This means that even consistent with the current executive order, an administration that really wanted to could read the law differently, more permissively, than the current administration does right now.

This may not be the world's biggest problem. The legal ban on assassinations has rested on nothing more than an executive order since the administration of Gerald Ford, yet is nonetheless considered widely as an institutionally settled matter (though what counts as an assassination, as we have seen, remains a hotly disputed matter between the executive branch and critics of targeted killing).[28] On the other hand, the administration's triumphant cries that it has "banned torture" will ring a bit hollow if some later administration comes along and takes a different approach—a possibility the administration's path certainly leaves open. In declining either to seek congressional ratification of its ban on coercive interrogation or to articulate the legal (as opposed to policy) limits on interrogation, the administration risks leaving the issue unsettled in a particularly unhealthy manner. Republican candidates during the 2012 election competed among themselves as to who had the greatest enthusiasm for waterboarding—a competition facilitated by the legal uncertainty governing what the next president could or could not authorize. Just as the first-term speeches missed an opportunity to seek a stable detention policy, they also missed repeated opportunities to solidify the law of interrogation. Missing these opportunities may not seem like a big deal today, but it will seem far more consequential should the country ever find itself embroiled anew in bitter fights over detainee treatment.

What the Speeches Leave Out or Leave Underdeveloped

The preceding discussion has pointed to significant things the first-term speeches get right and to a much smaller, though still

28. See, e.g., Sofaer, "Terrorism, the Law, and the National Defense," and Koh, "The Obama Administration and International Law."

important, list of things that the speeches get wrong or that constitute important and negative omissions. But these speeches also include matters that they develop partially—yet inadequately—and that require fuller public articulation and explication. This might plausibly come through additional speeches, like the one the president gave in May 2013, though it might also come through some of the alternative means discussed above.

The End of the Conflict and Extra-AUMF Threats

Some of the most important areas of underdevelopment in these speeches relate to the fragility of the AUMF as a basis for overseas counterterrorism operations into a future that law does not well describe. The AUMF is, after all, by its terms tied to the September 11 attacks. While it has supported the use of force against any number of groups, it will not do so forever as the conflict continues to morph. At some point, and with respect to at least some groups, the AUMF simply looks too remote. The president, of course, retains the authority, in both international and domestic law, to use force to attack these groups as an exercise of self-defense to the extent they pose an imminent threat to the United States. But such operations would not be part of the existing armed conflict authorized by the AUMF.

Department of Defense general counsel Jeh Johnson's speech on the end of the conflict ("The Conflict Against Al Qaeda and Its Affiliates: How Will It End?"), delivered to the Oxford Union at Oxford University on November 30, 2012, clearly signaled that the Obama administration is exploring these longer-run issues about when the conflict ends and what comes after that end—a fact dramatically reinforced by President Obama's own speech six months later. This reflects a laudable instinct to get beyond a reflexive invocation of the AUMF for every modern counterterrorism need. But at the end of the day, as Johnson's speech recognizes, there is both a legal question of when the conflict is deemed to end and a strategic reality. The legal question involves imagining what the end of the conflict will look like, as a set of hypothetical conditions given without reference to when those conditions might be met. The strategic reality, on the other hand, is that for the practical future, the United States will be engaged in a variety of activities, including the use of force, against transnational non-state terrorist groups and non-state armed forces that are in some legally relevant sense affiliated with Al Qaeda and its ideology, goals, and methods. These uses of force will not be drone strikes alone, but will also include different forms of discrete, limited special operations with human teams under varying levels of covertness. They will include offering military and intelligence advisers to governments that are battling insurgencies. And, in some cases, the United States may conduct strikes in support of those governments in their civil wars.

In other cases, local intelligence networks might well transition to become proxy forces run and financed by the United States, perhaps by the CIA. Johnson's speech was only the first tentative exploration of what the end of the conflict might look like and how it might come about. It was firm about the return to the condition of "peace." Perhaps it was too firm, though, as we explain in chapter 3, it was far less so than the president's own words the following May. For it is possible that what should replace the AUMF is not a lapsing of the AUMF but some superseding piece of legislation authorizing uses of force against a vision of the enemy that is less focused on the September 11 attacks. Even on its own terms, Johnson's speech was tentative as to what those conditions of peace mean in the face of continuing threats even from degraded terrorist adversaries. It was utterly cautious in not purporting to suggest when peace might come about.

Johnson's caution left important areas for further doctrinal development. And it was largely these themes Johnson teased with which Obama would run in his second term's first major address. He would do so with far less caution than Johnson displayed. First, to judge from the reactions to Johnson's speech—in which many commentators noticed chiefly the passage declaring that the United States could not have a permanent war—it left a need for the administration to be clear and forthright that peace would likely not mean an end to targeted killing, drone strikes, covert actions, military and intelligence assistance in several places, and proxy forces in others. Some people might find that to be a distinction between peace and war that carries little difference. However, in our judgment the difference would be at least somewhat significant in terms of the legal authorities and justifications that would undergird the legitimacy of the actions—thus making them rarer and more limited. In any event, Johnson's speech addressed movingly and directly the nature of war, security, emergency, and peace. But he left unclear what powers would really ebb or how completely.

Second, Johnson's speech touched on—but ultimately failed to settle—certain transitional issues with respect to the expiration of the conflict. Johnson most directly addressed the consequences of the war's end for detention, noting that one consequence of the end of a conflict would be that the legal authority of the laws of war to detain would—at least eventually—come to an end. Johnson went on to note World War II-era precedents for continuing to hold German POWs well past the day of "surrender." And he declined to address the matter further. There are, of course, other possibilities for an administration to consider for handling those detainees whose release it regards as unthinkable. Perhaps, for example, the administration should consider domestic law-based detention based on assessments of individual dangerousness and membership in terrorist organizations. Such ideas raise many legal issues, and we raise them here as examples of legal authorities that the government might have to consider over time—and develop in detail to the American public in the future, though they seem off the political table for now.

Third, and most fundamentally, any discussion of the lapsing of the AUMF necessarily raises the question—unaddressed in Johnson's speech but current in discussions within the executive branch and the legislature—of what sort of statutory authorization might replace it. In other words, it is far from certain that Congress and the administration will be content to have *no* authorization for the use of force against overseas enemy non-state actors. It may be, rather, that to maintain counterterrorism-on-offense, Congress will choose to supplant the current AUMF with a new one. Indeed, press reports have indicated that the administration has considered seeking just that for threats in Africa.[29] The first-term speeches left unclear

---

29. Julian E. Barnes and Evan Perez, "Terror Fight Shifts to Africa: U.S. Considers Seeking Congressional Backing for Operations Against Extremists," *Wall Street Journal,* December 6, 2012, http://online.wsj.com/article/SB10001424127887323316804578163724113421726.html.

whether the post-AUMF environment would really be one of peace or whether it would be one of some other AUMF.[30]

This final point suggests the larger weakness in the framework the speeches lay out: the framework's reliance on the AUMF is so pervasive that its vitality depends hugely on that law's continuing relevance. The growth of extra-AUMF threats—that is, actors that are in some sense related to Al Qaeda but lie outside of the AUMF's coverage—threatens to upset the AUMF's vitality. These threats include, for example, groups related only by ideological inspiration to Al Qaeda. As the relationship between new groups and Al Qaeda becomes more remote, it will ultimately become necessary to acknowledge that the United States is targeting a threat or group *not* covered by the AUMF. This will require either abstention or separate justification in international law, presumably under America's "active self-defense" views; it might well trigger domestic law issues and clashes between Congress and the executive. This problem requires further public discussion.

There are, after all, new threats that lie entirely beyond the AUMF—that is, national security threats that have no relationship *at all* to the matrix of threats linked to Al Qaeda, September 11, our current adversaries, or their causes. The day will thus come when the United States has to deal with some major

30. For a discussion of the necessity of a post-AUMF authorization and some options for its contours, see Robert Chesney, Jack Goldsmith, Matthew C. Waxman, and Benjamin Wittes, "A Statutory Framework for Next-Generation Terrorist Threats," published by the Hoover Institution's Jean Perkins Task Force on National Security and Law, http://www.scribd.com/doc/127191153/A-Statutory-Framework-for-Next-Generation-Terrorist-Threats.

terrorist threat that is not even plausibly within the AUMF's scope. Perhaps it will be from some terrorist group in Latin America, maybe from Hezbollah. But there will certainly be threats from non-state groups outside of the AUMF conflict that some president will someday feel compelled to address with force. It has been easy, over the last dozen years of armed conflict under the AUMF, to assume that all uses of force authorized by the president for reasons of national security are part of the same existing armed conflict—or that, to the extent they are not, they are part of a different armed conflict as soon as they are undertaken, because they involve some new state-to-state conflict. Yet the modern evolution of warfare toward more micro-targeted projections of force—toward very small wars—suggests that presidents may well in the future seek to *avoid* the sustained violence that would legally establish an armed conflict.

The speeches take the view, as matters of both domestic and international law, that the president can preempt threats outside of the AUMF under the rubric of self-defense. The speeches do so obliquely in most cases, by referring to armed conflict *or* self-defense. But the point is significantly underdeveloped relative to its growing theoretical importance in American counterterrorism. The United States considers the Somali group Al Shabaab to be only partially covered by the AUMF, for example. And it considers Al Qaeda in the Islamic Maghreb (AQIM) and the Nigerian Boko Haram to be even further removed from the AUMF's coverage. As such groups loom larger in the American threat matrix, will the United States be content merely to see the AUMF fade into irrelevance? The first-term speeches left open the question of whether such groups would be handled as self-defense matters, as law enforcement matters, as both, or with some new legislative authorization.

Answering this question is a project that is not severable from the project of imagining the end of the conflict. It involves both spelling out in greater detail the US self-defense doctrine and imagining what statutory law, if any, will replace the AUMF as it gradually recedes over time. Obama would address these questions directly in 2013, and we return to them in chapter 3.

The Procedural Dimensions of Targeting

The first-term speeches nowhere mention "kill lists," "nominations," or the other terms associated with the targeted killing programs. What we know of these terms comes from newspaper reporting, accurate or not—uniformly based on anonymous sources. That descriptions of the bureaucracy of target selection can appear in the press yet have no description in official speeches is reason enough to believe that the bureaucratic processes for targeted killing decisions have to be better outlined and defended. Indeed, while the speeches did an admirable job describing the law of targeted killing and rightly insisted that there must be rigorous executive processes to minimize mistakes in target selection, they did little—almost nothing—to describe those internal processes.

Administration officials balk at describing the processes as giving a road map to decision-making in a fashion that could tip off the enemy. But there is no reason this needs to be so, and there is no reason such a discussion of process needs to divulge the intelligence that underlies any strike.

Targeted killing aims to be individuated and is driven by multiple sources of intelligence that might include human intelligence, signals intelligence, and surveillance by drones. A targeted killing decision has to take into account fundamental law-of-war principles. The speeches raised these fundamental principles over and over. What they did not do is to put them concretely into clear and accurate, if necessarily general and abstract, descriptions of how we know the principles have been satisfied. When it comes to actually deciding to engage the targeted person, how do we know we have the correct person in the drone sensors, as a matter of distinction and discrimination? How do we know what levels of civilian collateral damage can be reasonably anticipated as a question of proportionality? How do we know whether this is excessive in relation to the value of the target? And how do we know whether there are ways, using the strategic "persistence" of drones, to select a better moment or place so as to reduce or eliminate the civilian harm? The administration needs to find a way to develop a better public understanding of how it addresses the analysis of intelligence sources and makes different kinds of factual determinations and of how it puts the legal requirements it has announced into practice.

The president's aides paint a fawning picture of Obama as St. Thomas Aquinas cogitating over strikes in a way that no other president could ever do in order to apply just-war theory to them.[31] In fact, the process likely resembles more closely the military's air targeting rules, combined with certain high-level

---

31. See for example, Jo Becker and Scott Shane, "Secret 'Kill List' Proves a Test of Obama's Principles and Will," *New York Times,* May 29, 2012: "Aides say Mr. Obama has several reasons for becoming so immersed in lethal counterterrorism operations. A student of writings on war by Augustine and Thomas Aquinas, he believes that he should take moral responsibility for such actions."

reviews. But it is important not merely to optimize the procedures associated with targeting but to explain them. This is a subject on which a single additional speech could go a long way.

The Blurring of Title 10 and Title 50 Activities and CIA Covert Uses of Force

Another area that could use further public development is the evident, if gradual, merger that is taking place between the legal and regulatory authorities of the military under Title 10 and those of the intelligence community under Title 50.[32]

At this point, outsiders cannot know what exactly is underway here. But something clearly is. It is public knowledge, of course, that the Osama bin Laden raid was carried out by JSOC forces—specifically, Navy SEALS—but under the authority of the CIA; what that means, however, is less clear. The essential design elements of national security need to be public, as part of the long-run architecture of the use of force in counterterrorism, and there seems to be little reason why the administration cannot make the general policies public.

How and to what extent this merger takes place matters a lot. One could imagine its offering a win-win situation, if properly constructed—at once raising the standards of discrete, precise, intelligence-driven uses of force and offering better

---

32. See, e.g., Robert Chesney, "Military-Intelligence Convergence and the Law of the Title 10/Title 50 Debate," *Journal of National Security Law and Policy*, Vol. 5, 2012 , p. 539, SSRN at http://papers.ssrn.com/sol3/papers.cfm?abstract_id=1945392; Andru E. Wall, "Demystifying the Title 10-Title 50 Debate: Distinguishing Military Operations, Intelligence Activities & Covert Action," *Harvard National Security Journal*, Vol. 3 (2011), pp. 85–102.

oversight opportunities for those uses of force. Military personnel are legally bound by the laws of war no matter what, irrespective of which agency they are seconded to—the CIA or
anything else. JSOC will thus have its operational lawyers
involved in the planning of operations, and they will insist on
adherence to military interpretations of the laws of war for
operational conduct. At the same time, ironically, Title 10 is
far less demanding than Title 50 as a domestic law matter in
terms of reporting or oversight requirements to Congress; CIA
lawyers are reputedly far more expert at, and attuned to, the
requirements of covert action oversight and reporting than is
the military. A partial merger that has each service contributing
but still subject to its own internal standards has at least the
possibility of invoking the best of both worlds—high operational standards with high oversight standards.

On the other hand, a badly designed or implemented
arrangement could have exactly the opposite effect, resulting
in a gradual slippage among military special operators away
from scrupulous adherence to law-of-war standards as their
uniformed status becomes less salient. What's more, the gradual removal of actual CIA personnel from direct participation
in uses of force might reduce the pressures on the agency to
report fully to the oversight committees; after all, only military
special operators were actually present when the operation
went down. The administration should find a way to discuss
publicly the general structure of forces both practically and
legally in future speeches or other public communications.

Similarly, the administration should address publicly a
broader question: why is it ever operationally useful to have the
CIA involved, as civilians and not military personnel, in the use
of force? Why not simply turn all of the strike activities over to

military special operations, with intelligence gathering and analysis by the CIA? The bin Laden raid would provide the obvious template here; what's the operational need for anyone other than military personnel to use force—including flying an armed drone? Relatedly, what is the justification in domestic law—and, much more importantly, in international law—for civilian officers of the agency to participate in use-of-force operations? Why exactly are they not unlawful belligerents?

The CIA is in the rifle sights of anti-drone campaigners. These groups have made no secret of their desire to brand CIA participation in drone strikes as illegal, even a war crime. The agency's participation in drone warfare is a far easier public target than the military's, since the military's core mission is fighting wars and using weapons to do so—and its members wear uniforms and have a commitment to follow the laws of war.

Some explanation of the CIA's ongoing paramilitary role, particularly if the administration means to maintain it, seems essential. This may be a very difficult area to discuss publicly without confirming—or seeming to confirm—agency activity in countries whose cooperation is predicated on American silence. But somehow the administration needs to state directly its operational and legal views on the intelligence community's role in actions that have long looked like traditional military strikes.

The first-term speeches left a number of other areas ripe for further development. Most prominent is cyber-operations, which they treated on the explicit basis that administration thinking on the subject is still evolving and not quite ready for prime time. And the administration also spent more time in the speeches congratulating itself for openness than it did developing anything like new doctrines of openness. Indeed, the administration and Congress have both largely failed to address the law of secrecy, classification, leaks, accountability, transparency, congressional oversight, and the ever-present reality of Freedom of Information Act cases in a fashion that has kept pace with the role of covert activity in America's foreign policy arsenal. This failure has resulted in an endless tension between the purpose of the speeches and their effect—which is invariably to precipitate more calls for greater openness and disclosure.

These are the major virtues, vices, and gaps in the framework the administration has laid out for deployment of American military and covert powers against non-state terrorist enemies. In chapter 3, we look at the impact on this framework of a single speech near the beginning of Obama's second term: the president's May 2013 National Defense University address.

CHAPTER 3

The President's NDU Speech and the Pivot from the First Term to the Second

On May 23, 2013, President Obama delivered a major address on counterterrorism policy at the National Defense University in Washington, D.C.—the first major national security speech of his second term. Billed as a comprehensive statement of policy, it represented a crucial pivot in the Obama administration's understanding of long-term counterterrorism policy. The first-term speeches, as we have seen, mostly involved efforts to explain—and thereby shore up—the public legitimacy of existing counterterrorism policies. The stance of the speeches was chiefly explanatory and thus inevitably somewhat defensive. The first-term speeches put on the record a great deal more than critics have been willing to grant. But the appetite grows with the eating, and the clamor for the administration to say more about what it was doing—and under what legal authorities—had only expanded.

This speech was different. With it, the administration pivoted sharply away from simply seeking to declare and justify existing policy and moved to describing the future direction of counterterrorism—and the law and policy that, in the president's view, should govern it in the long term. The speech was ambitious in scope and, in some areas at least, marked a significant departure from the framework laid out during the first term.

We turn, therefore, to a close analysis of the president's NDU speech, examining it for both continuity and change from the first term with respect to the categories we have set out in chapters 1 and 2. We look here both at the speech itself and at its accompanying documents, and try to address the good, the bad, and the unanswered in the president's words.

In broad strokes, the NDU speech was a work of both significant virtues and significant vices—and significant contradictions. It defended robust actions under the Authorization for the Use of Military Force (AUMF) even as the president emphatically insisted that they must end. It defended drone strikes—and promised new limits on them. It promised, once again, the closure of Guantánamo and the end of non-criminal detention—without giving any sense of what would happen to those held at Guantánamo who could not plausibly face trial but for whom release remains unthinkable.

On the positive side of the ledger, the speech elaborated on then-Department of Defense General Counsel Jeh Johnson's November 30, 2012, Oxford Union address on the end of the conflict ("The Conflict against Al Qaeda and Its Affiliates: How Will It End?"). It tried to imagine a post-AUMF world—one in which some degree of return to normalcy coexists with a maintenance of counterterrorism-on-offense and the capacity to deny terrorists safe havens in ungoverned spaces in which to regroup and rebuild. This vision represents a potentially important basis for long-term operational flexibility in a post-AUMF world and seeks to propose stages by which to get there. But it also signifies a post-AUMF, post-armed-conflict world that uses the tools of belligerency and conduct of hostilities, and the laws that govern their use, rather more than some of the present war's critics understand in the term "peace."

On the more negative side, however, the president's presentation promised in key areas more end to the conflict than Obama is likely to be able to deliver. In important respects, he both sided with his critics in delegitimizing his own policies and cut off policy options that ought to be on the table for long-term institutional settlement of contested counterterrorism authorities. Whether one sees mostly virtue or mostly vice in the speech largely hinges on how one interprets passages that are legitimately—and probably intentionally—amenable to different readings. It probably also depends on what specific passages of the speech one focuses on. As we look here at the speech in its entirety, our account is necessarily mixed.

Indeed, the positive and the negative aspects of the speech are more than simply the sum of good policy points and bad. The speech ran the risk—not just in its policies, but in its modes of framing and justifying them—of wanting to have everything all ways. It is not obvious at all that the Guantánamo policies can be squared, for example, with the legal implications of the end-of-the-conflict policies. In sliding over glaring contradictions, the speech seemed to want to have its cake and eat it, too. Some of the contradictions might be bridged by time. As we explain below, the speech can be read as proposing one targeting policy for the duration of the AUMF conflict, another for the post-AUMF peace, and a third during some period of transition between them. But for some areas—particularly those where the president appeared to embrace, even wrap himself in, the arguments of his critics, while nonetheless reaching policies that appear quite inimical under those criticisms—the speech gave a sense of believing that a clever form of words can make the harsh antinomies of the real world disappear. Perhaps clever words can do that—but only for a time. There is much that is praiseworthy in this speech, but we cannot dismiss our fear that it hides the day of reckoning when the profound contradictions of policy must finally end in tears.

As the speech was clearly intended to make varying points to a variety of constituencies, its political background is crucial to understanding the various ways it can be reasonably read.

The Political Background to the NDU Speech

The NDU speech responded to a near-perfect storm of political conditions that came together for the administration in the spring of 2013. That hurricane had several constituent storms, each of which created significant pressure on the president to move the ball forward from what his administration had said during his first term.

The first of these was the need to explain significant developments and policy shifts within the administration with respect to drones and targeted killing. The 2012 election had created new stresses on the permanency of the nation's counterterrorism structures, precipitating a long set of bureaucratic processes toward formalization of certain rules that had been previously more ad hoc. The administration's senior officials, according to news accounts, had become increasingly nervous about the prospect of Mitt Romney winning the 2012 election and inheriting tools of counterterrorism, such as drone strikes, whose use was essentially discretionary within the very broad legal limits of the AUMF.[1] The Obama administration trusted itself with these authorities, but the prospect of someone else wielding them—particularly someone who might revive some of the executive power enthusiasms of the Bush administration—kept officials up at night.

The result was a confluence of two distinct motivations for seeking a more permanent and legitimate basis for offensive counterterrorism actions into the future: on the one hand, a genuine institutional belief in long-run codification of policy for future presidents, and, on the other hand, a particularly political belief in limiting the discretionary use by Republicans of such things as drones. Mixed motivations notwithstanding, the impulse toward codification of principles of both permission and limitation was a sound one. And by the beginning of its second term, the administration was far along in the creation of a formal set of policies—known as the playbook—which was designed to institutionalize the rules for drone strikes and to enshrine certain policy limitations that go beyond the legal limits on targeting authority. By May 2013, these policies were ready for the president's signature—and the administration wanted to announce them.

Other independent political developments were also coming to a head. One was a mass hunger strike at Guantánamo, which threatened the legitimacy—especially abroad—of the

1. See, for example, Scott Shane, "Election Spurred a Move to Codify U.S. Drone Policy," *New York Times,* November 24, 2012, http://www.nytimes.com/2012/11/25/world/white-house-presses-for-drone-rule-book.html?pagewanted=all&_r=0.

already uneasy truce between the president and Congress over detention policy at Guantánamo. Obama had never really accepted this truce, anyway—a truce under which Guantánamo remained open, detainees could not be transferred from it, but the government brought no new detainees there either and the administration maintained a public posture of seeking the facility's closure. The hunger strike, and then the forced feeding of detainees, put the question of indefinite detention without charges or trial squarely back on the political table. Though, legally speaking, nothing had changed, activists were talking about a "crisis" at Guantánamo, and the administration was feeling considerable heat.

This problem dovetailed with increasing talk of the end of the conflict—the subject about which Jeh Johnson had spoken the previous December. Johnson's speech had given hope to the nongovernmental organization community, which saw in the end of the conflict, at once, an end to the lawful right to detain terrorists as a legal incident of warfare, a mechanism to bring about the closure of Guantánamo, and an end—or at least a radical constriction—of kinetic military operations overseas. This vision on the part of the activists gelled nicely with aspects of the president's own self-image; Obama, after all, has long seen himself as the man who has sought to bring to a close the American military actions in Iraq and Afghanistan that he inherited from his predecessor. The idea of bringing about an end to the AUMF conflict, and thereby bringing about a true restoration of peace, clearly has internal resonance for him as well.

Also pushing the administration to speak were the effects of the concerted NGO and journalistic efforts to challenge the administration's claims of minimal, occasionally even near-zero, civilian casualties in drone strikes. In one infamous episode, John Brennan (at the time Obama's top counterterrorism adviser) had made the mistake of advancing the frankly absurd proposition that there had been no—that is to say, zero—civilian collateral deaths from drone strikes in 2011.[2] Activists had responded to the evident absurdity of that claim with questionable estimates of civilian harm of their own, ones that surely overstated civilian deaths.[3] After a period of several years of debate over civilian casualties, the issue had become a potent source of attack on the administration's policies.

Finally, there was the emergence of a new group of critics on the political right: the libertarian wing of the Republican Party, led by Senator Rand Paul (R-KY). In a peculiar merger of the civil libertarian language of the Left and the Right's own opposition to regulatory excess and governmental power, this group brandished the ideological claim that Obama had created an imperial presidency that ruled by decree, administrative rule-making, and executive order both in the domestic sphere and in foreign affairs and national security. It also adopted ACLU-like anxieties about the drone strike against Anwar al-Awlaki, the American citizen, executed—on this view—by the president on his sole say-so following his denomination as a terrorist solely by the executive and blown up with a missile without a judicial hearing. Leave aside the actual facts of the al-Awlaki case, the man's operational role in some of the

2. Scott Shane, "C.I.A. is Disputed on Civilian Toll in Drone Strikes," *New York Times,* August 11, 2011, http://www.nytimes.com/2011/08/12/world/asia/12drones.html.

3. For an excellent overview of civilian deaths in drone strikes and the controversy over it, see Ritika Singh, "A Meta-Study of Drone Strike Casualties," *Lawfare,* July 22, 2013, http://www.lawfareblog.com/2013/07/a-meta-study-of-drone-strike-casualties/.

worst terrorist near-misses of the previous several years, and the implausibility of his capture. Al-Awlaki was offered purely as an abstraction. From this, the claim broadened to encompass the possibility of drone strikes, as Senator Ted Cruz (R-TX) put it, against "a US citizen on US soil who is not flying a plane into a building, who is not robbing a bank, who is not pointing a bazooka at the Pentagon, but who is simply sitting quietly at a cafe, peaceably enjoying breakfast."[4] What law, in other words, stops the imperial president from secretly naming some citizen a terrorist and blowing him up with a drone strike on US soil?

This strain of thought exploded onto the public's radar screen in Senator Paul's famous thirteen-hour filibuster on the Senate floor on March 6, 2013. Paul's impassioned rhetoric and demands for simple answers to questions about when and where American citizens could be targeted reached directly to anxieties felt by Americans on the right, as well as many on the left. The anxiety about legitimacy and the absence of judicial process was genuine and real, even if inchoate and not necessarily focused on anything that, in light of the facts, even made much rational sense. Paul's filibuster came in the context of the confirmation of Brennan to head the CIA in March 2013. Brennan was confirmed, but not without facing a raft of hostile questions and not before he had promised more speeches from the administration on counterterrorism.

---

4. Senator Cruz's statement took place at the outset of the Rand Paul filibuster, a full transcript of which is available at Raffaela Wakeman, "Senator Paul's Filibuster: Get Yer Transcript and Video Here!" *Lawfare*, March 7, 2013, http://www.lawfareblog.com/2013/03/senator-pauls-filibuster-get-yer-transcript-and-video-here/.

All of this formed the political backdrop as the president took the podium at NDU. This backdrop collectively amounted to a multifaceted and intensifying argument over the legitimacy of counterterrorism-on-offense, continuing detention, and the fundamental building blocks of the president's light-footprint strategy. The president's speech was accompanied by two written documents, each issued within a day of the speech itself: a Fact Sheet released by the White House under the heading, "U.S. Policy Standards and Procedures for the Use of Force in Counterterrorism Operations Outside the United States and Areas of Active Hostilities"; and a letter from Attorney General Eric Holder to Senator Patrick Leahy, chairman of the Senate Judiciary Committee. The letter principally addressed, in greater detail than had prior statements, the circumstances and intelligence at issue in the al-Awlaki case and declassified information both about the strike itself and about three other Americans (including al-Awlaki's sixteen-year-old son) who had been killed in drone strikes aimed at others.

Taking the three together, the NDU speech constituted the most comprehensive single statement to date of the US government's present and future policies for counterterrorism. And it laid out a vision that in some ways built upon the vision the speeches described during the first term but that in some ways was dissonant with that vision.

The Fundamental Nature of the Conflict and its End

With respect to the immediate present, the president affirmed in all significant respects the fundamental view of the conflict that has lain at the heart of the legal framework for the Bush administration and the Obama administration alike: from September 11, 2001, down to today, the United States has been at war. Under both "domestic law, and international law," the president reiterated, "the United States is at war with Al Qaeda, the Taliban, and their associated forces." In saying this, he reaffirmed the fundamental view of his administration, laid out in the first-term speeches, that the administration is entitled to lethally target the enemy and, when it captures enemy forces, detain enemy fighters and operatives for the duration of hostilities.

The president's speech also reaffirmed the fundamental US legal view that armed conflict does not have a predetermined "legal geography." The United States is legally entitled to pursue and target the enemy wherever it goes, though limited by the legal rights of neutral sovereign states, who also have legal obligations as conditions of their neutrality. The president emphasized that America "cannot take [drone] strikes wherever we choose; our actions are bound by consultations with partners and respect for state sovereignty." But Obama also reaffirmed the US view that "where foreign governments cannot or will not effectively stop terrorism in their territory," then the United States reserves the right to act on their soil.

So far, there is no daylight between this speech and the ones that came before it.

But new in the NDU speech was a clear statement that, notwithstanding these legal authorities, as a matter of policy— not law as such, and thus revisable according to circumstances— the United States will now limit its conduct of hostilities in places beyond the existing zones of active conventional combat. Brennan had hinted at this position in his April 30, 2012, Wilson

Center speech ("The Ethics and Efficacy of the President's Counterterrorism Strategy") with his suggestion that the United States does not target all of those whom it could hit lawfully. But the president's NDU speech and, particularly, the Fact Sheet, whose very title suggests different policy choices "Outside [of] Areas of Active Hostilities," went further. They made it clear that an entirely different set of targeting rules governs US forces outside of theaters in which force protection remains a matter of high salience.

In principle, such policy choices are no different from when the US military limits its combat activities in any place of active hostilities—adopting more restrictive rules of engagement, for example, as part of a campaign to win hearts and minds in a counterinsurgency setting. In the course of a far-flung counterterrorism campaign, policy and strategic considerations may include many factors that might reasonably cause the United States to adopt more restrictive rules than the law would demand. As the president noted, we "cannot use force everywhere."

But talking about such policy choices in the context of a speech focused on winding down the war gives them a different sheen. Indeed, where the NDU speech really broke new ground was in articulating the architecture of counterterrorism beyond the current AUMF armed conflict—or, at least, in beginning to do so. Apart from Johnson's Oxford Union speech in November 2012, the NDU speech was the first serious public consideration of when this war will finally be over and how the United States will pursue counterterrorism as a matter of law and policy beyond the AUMF conflict. What's more, unlike Johnson's speech, the president's NDU speech offered a window into the time frame for the conflict's end.

The window was more a matter of hints and tea leaves than clear signaling. But the president seemed to attach significance to the withdrawal from Afghanistan in 2014, and he talked about the conflict's end as a matter of urgency both in general terms and with respect to detention. The most direct signaling occurred near the speech's end, when he said that he looked "forward to engaging Congress and the American people in efforts to refine, and ultimately repeal, the AUMF's mandate." He added that he would "not sign laws designed to expand this mandate further." If this is so, it appears likely that, under the framework of the NDU speech and the Fact Sheet, the AUMF would be retired in stages.

The president made four fundamental assertions regarding the end of the conflict: first, that America cannot live with permanent war; second, that threats today look increasingly similar to those from before September 11, 2001; third, that it is time to recognize criteria for the end of the AUMF conflict, narrow the AUMF, and put it on a path toward repeal; and, fourth, that we should make a transition to legal policies for drone warfare and other self-defense actions suited to a post-conflict regime. Each of these propositions is controversial and contested, and we examine each in turn.

Obama began with the almost philosophical idea—at once abstract and emotionally suggestive—that the American republic cannot live with "permanent" war. He quoted James Madison's warning: "No nation could preserve its freedom in the midst of continual warfare."[5] After a dozen years of war, he said, America is "at a crossroads" and we must "define the nature and scope of this struggle, or else it will define us."

---

5. James Madison, "Political Observations," April 20, 1795.

In framing the issue thus, the president solidly allied him-self with the Left's critics of his administration's policies. Hav-ing waged the war for four years, the president was now warning about the dangers of continuing to do so. It is hard to quarrel with Obama's aspiration here; nobody wants a perpetual armed conflict. The trouble is that the United States is not the only party to the conflict with a vote on its nature. America can define the struggle however it likes, but the realism of that definition also depends on how its terrorist adversaries frame it and how able they are to make a reality of their understand-ing. Mere forms of words do not vanquish hard threats, and winning is more than a matter of verbal definition. Put a differ-ent way, it is possible that while America may no longer be interested in war, war remains interested in America. And the aspiration does not answer the question of how war powers—whose use may remain necessary—figure into a post-conflict legal framework.

Obama's second point was an effort to respond preemp-tively to this realist critique. Granted, the president said, our "nation is still threatened by terrorists . . . but we have to rec-ognize that the threat has shifted and evolved from the one that came to our shores on 9/11." After ten years of experience in dealing with heightened security efforts at home and war abroad, this is the "moment to ask ourselves hard questions—about the nature of today's threats and how we should confront them." As a definition of victory in this war, no president can "promise the total defeat of terror," he said. Our enemies are groups and networks of groups, and the meaning of victory and defeat must correspond to what they are. Today, the president continued, the "core of Al Qaeda in Afghanistan and Pakistan is on the path to defeat. Their remaining operatives spend more time thinking about their own safety than plotting against us." They did not direct the attacks in either "Benghazi or Boston. They've not carried out a successful attack on our homeland since 9/11." While preserving the caution that the core of Al Qaeda is on the path to defeat, the president emphasized that the threat today is more diffuse in terms of groups, terrorist networks, and affiliates, and in terms of geography.

The NDU speech didn't soft-pedal the dangers of these diffuse groups. The president singled out Al Qaeda in the Arabian Peninsula—the Al Qaeda affiliate which counted Anwar al-Awlaki as an operational leader—as the most active in plotting against the US homeland. At the same time, he noted, extremists have gained a "foothold in countries like Libya and Syria," but the ability of these groups to focus and reach beyond those countries and regions where they are based is limited. The result is likely to be more localized threats to Western interests, including to business interests and to allied governments seeking to battle these groups in their own territories. Further, Obama said, there is a "real threat from radicalized individuals here in the United States." The current, direct threats to the United States and its people, then, according to the president, are "lethal yet less capable Al Qaeda affiliates; threats to diplomatic facilities and businesses abroad; homegrown extremists. This is the future of terrorism."

And this, the president said, is all but enough to declare victory in the armed conflict. Indeed, the president, in arguing for moving toward the conflict's formal legal end, declared that the "scale of this threat closely resembles the types of attacks we faced before 9/11."

Again, it's hard to fault the aspiration. But the president's vision of victory—predicated as it is on the threat picture's resemblance to the pre-9/11 era—does not obviously support his conclusion. It would be of scant comfort to those who would use the tools of warfare to deal with overseas terrorists to learn that the president would be satisfied with having merely wound back the threats to those of the pre-9/11 era and thus concluded that we can now safely return to the thinking, planning, and responses of the years preceding that day. After all, it was precisely because we did not adequately contemplate, by September 10, the emergence of groups that could carry out a 9/11-like attack that the attack was successful. We failed to anticipate such events and, as a result, we failed to take the kinds of forcible actions in the 1990s that might have rendered much less safe and usable the safe havens where the terrorist groups were able to plan and execute a highly complex, years-long enterprise.

Obama's third proposition was something of a response to this concern. For Obama clearly didn't mean to embrace such an abandonment of military options in confronting emergent, incipient, and ongoing terrorist threats. He appeared to imagine something more intermediate: maintaining key aspects of counterterrorism-on-offense, while yet calling it peace.

This would be a peace of unusual military muscularity, one that may well not satisfy the Left's critics who share the president's vision of the conflict's end, but for whom this military (and CIA paramilitary) muscularity would represent a contradiction, even hypocrisy. One way to imagine this peace is as analogous to the peace of the Cold War, in which a struggle was indeed underway, but only a hot conflict in dribs and drabs over the course of sixty years. More often, it took the form of proxy wars fought on the fringes of the great powers, with military or paramilitary intelligence forces used in small-scale belligerent actions short of full-on war. Another way to understand it as peace is simply to look to the past 150 years of American history; the number of years in which, even during times generally regarded as "peacetime" by most people, the United States was not engaged in forms of belligerency and the use of hostilities short of full-scale war by its forces abroad is very small.[6] Small-scale military or paramilitary actions using tools of hostilities have been a feature of American peacetime for most of its history, and the same is true of many other great powers. The idea of an absolute binary in international or domestic law, between "armed conflicts" conceived as full-on war and all other extraterritorial situations being necessarily governed by human rights law and law enforcement tools, is by far the historical novelty, not the norm. This figures as part of the deep architecture of the president's speech, because its conception of a return to normalcy contemplates a return to *this* historical norm; the president clearly did not regard the speech's repeated references to using drones and other forms of hostilities even in time of peace as inventing anything new but, instead, as part of the ordinary, realistic conditions of peace. He was not wrong about that.

This deep architecture about what normal uses of force are needed even in peacetime informs how Obama framed the

---

6. Mary L. Dudziak, in *War Time: An Idea, Its History, Its Consequences* (New York: Oxford University Press, 2012), provides a useful timeline (in its appendix) of US uses of military force over its history, as shown by its award of campaign medals, along with a discussion of how much a continuous part of American history military operations are even in times understood as "peace." See the book reviews by Samuel Moyn, May 24, 2012, on *Lawfare,* http://www.lawfareblog.com/2012/05/war-time-an-idea-its-history-its-consequences/, and Kenneth Anderson, "Time Out of Joint," 91 *Texas Law Review* 859 (May 2013).

conditions for what it means for the conflict to be over —which he framed in terms of a reduction in the general threat level against the homeland and the American people to levels more closely associated with pre-9/11 conditions. But since those responses were lacking in crucial respects, the conditions for the end of the conflict also implicitly include some permanent infrastructure for addressing threats in the form of plots, individuals, groups, and networks of groups—an architecture that is manifestly not just a robust form of law enforcement or the criminal law. We have learned from bitter experience, the president said, that "left unchecked, these threats can grow." And we have learned that if "dealt with smartly and proportionally, these threats need not rise to the level that we saw on the eve of 9/11." The president was not talking about just the FBI here.

In other words, even as Obama insisted that "this war, like all wars, must end," he also declared in the same sentence that "our systematic effort to dismantle terrorist organizations must continue." Even as he quoted Madison on the dangers of perpetual warfare, he also declared that American policy should aim to "dismantle networks that pose a direct danger and make it less likely for new groups to gain a foothold, all while maintaining the freedoms and ideals that we defend." Even as he promised to bring combat operations in Afghanistan to an end, he also promised "a series of persistent, targeted efforts to dismantle specific networks of violent extremists that threaten America."

To put it simply, the conditions of the "end of the conflict," in Obama's formulation, seem to mean the reduction of threat to levels that can be managed without large-scale warfare and, crucially, without need for the legal appellation of "armed conflict." They do not appear to involve the abandonment of instrumentalities of military action. Rather, the president appeared to be describing ongoing belligerent actions—using military or paramilitary forces—conducted under the laws of armed conflict, in national self-defense, whether as a continuing response to a continuing terrorist threat or as a response to newly arising threats.

But this formulation, and the long-run paradigm for the peacetime use of belligerent or covert intelligence forces that it proposes, raises issues of its own. The critic will instantly object, and with no small justice, that giving up the legal framework of armed conflict has genuine legal consequences. For example, it is quite unclear, as we discuss below, how the United States can continue to detain people under the laws of war whom it cannot easily set free in practice to the extent it considers itself at peace. More fundamentally, giving up the legal claim to armed conflict also makes much less clear the basis on which the United States can conduct even limited hostilities, such as drone strikes or Joint Special Operations Command raids, against the various groups that the president insists on dismantling or against new groups that arise and count themselves the children or grandchildren of Al Qaeda. Against some of these groups, at least, it seems neither legally required nor factually supported to believe that the conditions of victory have been met in the ordinary sense of destroying and dismantling the enemy and its ability to conduct hostile terrorist acts against the United States. Why give up legal authorities, in both international law and domestic law, that continue to be legally and factually warranted?

The NDU speech didn't straightforwardly address this question. It rested, rather, on the factual characterization of a threat reduced to manageable levels combined with the normative claim that a republic's moral nature is threatened by permanent warfare. Together, these yield the conclusion that, where the reduced threat permits, a state of war should end even if that means giving up certain legal privileges associated with war. Conservative critics will tend to question the factual and normative premise. But the criticism from the president's left may end up being just as sharp. What's the difference between war and peace, anyway, if peacetime entails something that looks remarkably like the conduct of hostilities? In one sense, critics on both the left and the right will be asking the same question of the Obama administration: what is the cash-out in real terms for giving up the legal framework of an armed conflict under the AUMF? The Right fears it gives up too much; the Left fears it gives up too little.

The president had an answer to this critique, but he laid it out only very elliptically in his speech. The answer is that the sort of ongoing but occasional use of force he described can be justified legally as a matter of self-defense—and that this authority is actually robust enough to keep enemy groups at bay and incapable of projecting force against the United States. Military or paramilitary means can be small scale, discrete, and limited and can be conducted according to the terms of the laws of armed conflict. The United States has done so since the beginning of the age of international terrorism. It has a long-developed international law jurisprudence that provides the framework for doing this sort of thing, even outside of the AUMF armed conflict. There might be many issues to be worked out as to the proper standards for invoking rights of national self-defense, not to mention issues related to when it is appropriate to look to Congress or to the president's own authorities in domestic law for such operations. But the basic proposition of forcible belligerent responses to international terrorism in particular, outside of and beyond those of the human rights and law enforcement paradigms, has not been an issue legally for the United States at least since the 1980s. Hostilities with an intensity short of armed conflict in the legal sense might still be very intense—intense enough, Obama seemed to be saying, to stay on offense against the groups he wants the latitude to dismantle.

At the same time, however, the NDU speech recognized that there exists a meaningful difference between wartime under the AUMF and peacetime. The return to peace thus imposes greater restrictions on when, where, and against whom the tools of war—drone strikes, most obviously—may be deployed. These specific policies, mostly related to targeted killing and drone strikes, constituted the fourth point made by the president in describing the end of the conflict: specific new rules and policies for the use of force as the AUMF conflict winds down.

We turn then to consider the new policies that the NDU speech and the accompanying White House Fact Sheet announced.

Targeted Killings and Drone Strikes: A Strong Defense—and New Restrictions

Although the NDU speech was billed as comprehensive, its central core addressed targeted killing and drone warfare—particularly in light of the accompanying White House Fact Sheet and Attorney General Holder's letter to Senator Leahy on the targeting of US citizens abroad.

The speech is noteworthy on this score first for the president's strong defense of drone strikes as ethical, effective, and legal. To some degree, this aspect of the speech simply rehashed ground that Brennan had covered earlier in his Wilson Center speech. But it was notable this time for coming from the president's own lips. After describing sometimes alternative, sometimes complementary, means of achieving counterterrorism aims, Obama acknowledged candidly that despite a "strong preference for the detention and prosecution of terrorists, sometimes this approach is foreclosed." The terrorists flee to "some of the most distant and unforgiving places on earth. . . . In some of these places—such as parts of Somalia and Yemen—the state lacks the capacity or will to take action." Moreover, he said, it is also "not possible for America to simply deploy a team of Special Forces to capture every terrorist. . . . [T]here are places where it would pose profound risks to our troops and local civilians—where a terrorist compound cannot be breached without triggering a firefight with surrounding tribal communities." In these cases, the local communities pose no threat to the United States; in other cases, putting "US boots on the ground may trigger a major international crisis," the president said, and he offered the Osama bin Laden raid in Pakistan as an example. The "fact that we did not find ourselves confronted with civilian casualties, or embroiled in an extended firefight, was a testament to the meticulous planning and professionalism of our Special Forces, but it also depended on some luck," he noted.

It is in this context, Obama said, that the United States has adopted the methods of drone warfare. And while he acknowledged that this form of warfare raises profound questions, he didn't apologize for it. As to effectiveness, the president pointed to terrorist communications found in the bin Laden compound lamenting the effectiveness of the drones. As a matter of legality, he invoked armed conflict under the AUMF and later referred to self-defense.

The president then offered a defense of the ethics of drone strikes, describing them as the tool of war least harmful to civilians in many circumstances. There is a "wide gap," he said, between "US assessments of such casualties and nongovernmental reports." He acknowledged as a "hard fact that US strikes have resulted in civilian casualties, a risk that exists in every war. And for the families of those civilians, no words or legal construct"—like lawful collateral damage, for example—"can justify their loss." But he then asked what the ethical point of comparison should be; heartbreaking tragedies must be weighed "against the alternatives. To do nothing in the face of terrorist networks would invite far more civilian casualties," not just among Americans, but in the "very places like Sana'a and Kabul and Mogadishu where terrorists seek a foothold. . . . [T]he terrorists we are after target civilians, and the death toll from their acts of terrorism against Muslims dwarfs any estimate of civilian casualties from drone strikes. So doing nothing is not an option."

This is an important moral assertion by the president. The unstated premise of many critics of drone strikes is that the proper moral comparison for drone strikes is against the policy of no use of military force at all. The speech insisted that this is a red herring. The real alternative is the use of other weapons systems or forms of kinetic military activity. Conventional airpower or missiles, Obama said, "are far less precise than drones, and are likely to cause more civilian casualties and more local outrage. And invasions of those territories lead us to be viewed as occupying armies." In other words, the value of drones requires not merely understanding their tactical value in a particular attack, but an assessment of their strategic value compared to other means that might have worse geopolitical consequences.

Obama acknowledged the limits of what drones can do and the problems of the global resentment and blowback they can induce. But he nonetheless declared that they frequently provide the most ethical and effective tool of war. Neither "conventional military action nor waiting for attacks to occur offers moral safe harbor," he concluded. And "neither does a sole reliance on law enforcement in territories that have no functioning police or security services—and indeed have no functioning law."[7] It was the strongest defense of the administration's

---

7. In this part of the speech, President Obama—probably coincidentally—channeled themes that the present two authors developed the previous month in a debate at the Oxford Union. Compare the president's comments, quoted above, to the arguments on the subject delivered by both of the present authors at the April 25, 2013, Oxford Union debate over the following resolution: "This House Believes Drone Warfare is Ethical and Effective." Wittes concluded:

> Now from the other side you're going to hear a lot of talk about civilian casualties, and I want to be candid about this up front. Any weapons system that you use—weapons are dangerous things. And when you target people, people make mistakes, and that produces civilian deaths. And drones are not different from other weapons in that regard—except in one sense, which is that they give you more opportunity to do less of that. That's not to say there are not civilian casualties. There are.
>
> Now one thing you will *not* hear the other side talk about, I suspect, with respect to the civilian casualties is the question of the null hypothesis—that is to say, what the alternatives are. What if you didn't use a drone in this situation? What would you do instead? Now often, drone opponents

posture on drones given yet—and all the more important coming from the president himself.

But having defended drone strikes energetically, the president also announced that he was reining them in. Obama did not immediately alter the hard legal framework and authorities under which drone strikes take place. But he did, in promising an end to the AUMF conflict, suggest that a change in legal framework was inevitably coming down the pike. And he also adopted new policies for strikes—at least outside of active combat theaters—that anticipate these changes. These policies for targeted drone strikes, applied in the *current* AUMF conflict, represent a significant policy determination not to have recourse to the more capacious existing legal authority to hit lawful targets beyond zones of active hostilities.

The United States recognizes the legitimate concerns that many people have regarding a perceived ability to strike with drones across borders at discrete targets with potentially little attribution, transparency, or risk. It recognizes this both in the legal context of the existing AUMF armed conflict, on the one

---

operate with a sort of assumption—I think it's a lazy assumption—that the null hypothesis is some lesser use of violence or maybe no use of violence at all. Maybe it would be law enforcement. Maybe if you didn't use a drone in a particular situation, we'd have peace. We'd have nothing. I think this is very, very rarely the case. And I want to be very candid with you about what I think the null hypothesis is, which is often greater uses of violence. The alternative to drone use in many instances is air strikes, on-the-ground human interventions, and Tomahawk cruise missiles—all of which have less capacity for discrimination, for proportionality, and more capacity for civilian deaths than do drones.

Video of the debate is available at Benjamin Wittes, "Oxford Union Debate on Drone Warfare," *Lawfare,* May 3, 2013, available at http://www.lawfareblog.com/2013/05/oxford-union-debate-on-drone-warfare/.

hand, and in the post-AUMF conflict setting, on the other. It has therefore announced policies to govern its targeting with drones, both those attacks undertaken beyond areas of active hostilities in the current AUMF armed conflict and attacks in the future, post-AUMF conflict—thus merging to some degree the AUMF conflict with whatever will succeed it.

These policies were described in the NDU speech, but were laid out with greater specificity and organization in the Fact Sheet. The Fact Sheet stated that these are "counterterrorism policy standards and procedures that are either already in place or will be transitioned into place over time."

These policies are something less than law; the law remains, at least for now, the targeting rules of the law of armed conflict. The policies are subject to change; the Fact Sheet added that officials are "continually working to refine, clarify, and strengthen our standards and processes for using force." They are also subject to waiver; the Fact Sheet noted that they do "not limit the president's authority to take action in extraordinary circumstances when doing so is both lawful and necessary to protect the United States or its allies." That said, they are clearly more than just a discretionary policy declaration. They are intended to establish a basic framework grounded in law and policy together, one that can and will evolve over time, within a basic legal paradigm of both international and domestic law. They are a framework meant to create a bridge between targeting under the AUMF and targeting under the self-defense framework of the regime to which Obama aspires to move.

One important implication of designing policy in this fashion is that the passage from "wartime" to "peacetime" is a transitional and gradual one, legally and in fact. The policies for drone strikes are now largely the same for the AUMF armed conflict—outside of Afghanistan and Pakistan—as they will be for addressing the "transitional" threats that remain and the same as they will be for self-defense actions even once the "conflict" as such is deemed over. This is, we suspect, how the administration squares the circle between the assertion that "this war, like all wars, must end" and the promise that our "systematic efforts to dismantle terrorist organizations must continue"— including with drone strikes. Analytically, the NDU speech and the Fact Sheet preserved a transitional period under the AUMF conflict in which recourse to the legal authorities of the current armed conflict are still available, though in gradually diminishing ways, as existing, ongoing enemy terrorist groups presumably lose their capacities to confront America as a result of the continuing degradation caused by drone strikes and other American measures.

Eventually, this will give way to actions taken entirely under what the US government understands to be its inherent sovereign right of self-defense in international law. Those rights of inherent self-defense include, in the US view, the lawfulness in some circumstances of using military and paramilitary force against non-state adversaries.

The NDU speech and Fact Sheet thus appeared to address three conceptually distinct legal periods: the current AUMF conflict prior to the end of combat operations in Afghanistan; the post-AUMF conflict of peacetime (but which will continue to have ongoing and new threats); and a transitional period between withdrawal from Afghanistan and the full lapsing or repeal of the AUMF—in which the government might use force, depending on the facts of the situation, based on the AUMF, self-defense, or both.

Targeting in Transition:
"Continuing, Imminent" Threats

At least as far as drone targeting outside of areas of active hostilities is concerned, the NDU speech announced a simple device for harmonizing the rules of targeting as a matter of policy through this transition from war to self-defense in peacetime. That is to say, the rules will be the *same* for all three periods, whether the legal authority is the current armed conflict, any transitional period, or post-conflict self-defense. Since the rules for the post-conflict period of formal peace are, legally speaking, the most restrictive, the device works by applying those rules as a policy matter to restrict conduct in the earlier periods.

As a matter of both international and domestic constitutional law, inherent national self-defense entitles the president to target people with lethal force, including with drones, in situations of imminent attack. So the speech limited targeting outside of active combat theaters to situations of "continuing, imminent threats"; the speech and the Fact Sheet also used the phrases "continuing, imminent," as well as "continuing and imminent." This appears to tighten up the criteria for using force in any given situation as long as the armed conflict continues. Remember, the administration's earlier statements—in the first-term speeches—had reserved the right to act in the face of continuing and *significant* threats. But while Brennan had mentioned in his September 16, 2011, Harvard speech ("Strengthening Our Security by Adhering to Our Values and Laws") that there was a convergence between the US view and an increasingly flexible allied notion of imminence, he had acknowledged that a gap remained. And the United States had not previously restricted itself to drone strikes only in situations of *imminent* attack—except, notably, with regard to US citizens. Now, however, imminence has become part of the formula—albeit as a matter of policy, not yet law. As Obama put it, "not every collection of thugs that labels themselves Al Qaeda will pose a credible threat to the United States." The Fact Sheet adds that it is "simply not the case that all terrorists pose a continuing, imminent threat to US persons; if a terrorist does not pose such a threat, the United States will not use lethal force."

How big a change this is depends on how one reads the phrases "continuing, imminent" threat and "continuing and imminent" threat—particularly in relation to the earlier standard of "continuing and significant" threat. The correct reading of this language remains a matter of considerable opacity both in the speech and in the Fact Sheet. Do these phrases mean that a threat must be *both* continuing *and* imminent—with imminence further restricted by a requirement that the imminent threat be continuing, not evanescent? Or do these two words denote distinct categories, with lethal force lawful against both continuing threats and imminent threats? Or, in a third alternative, is this a way of saying that an "imminent" threat can also be a "continuing" one, in which the concept of "continuing" broadens the notion of imminence such that a threat is imminent in a continuous fashion? Or, finally, is "continuing and imminent" some kind of collective term of art?

In our view, the position most plausibly intended by the administration here is that targeting is lawful *against a threat that is continuing on the part of some actor, and could result in an attack at any particular point in time—and therefore is continuously imminent with respect to that actor, whether that actor is a group, network, individual, or, for that matter, a state.* We believe this in part because the NDU speech and the Fact Sheet referred not just to plots or even to individuals, but instead to groups and networks. The president said that the United States would target, with persistence, networks over time; in that case, the imminent threat is posed over time by the group, given evidence of its nature, aims, and past behaviors. Moreover, as we discussed in the prior two chapters, earlier statements by the administration with respect to drone strikes in general and to al-Awlaki in particular describe a flexible, non-temporal sense of the word "imminent." In particular, they describe a sense of imminence that permits the United States to go on offense and pick its own moments to strike— certainly not being confined, as many of the speeches have said, to a reactive posture of having to wait for threats to ripen before striking. As the president further declared in the NDU speech, merely waiting for attacks to occur, or holding off a response until the perceived last moment in order to demonstrate a threat's imminence before responding to it with force, offers "no moral safe harbor."

In other words, the current language likely reflects an incremental narrowing of the previous "continuing and significant" threat language used by Brennan at Harvard, something that brings the United States still closer to allied countries' increasingly flexible conceptions of imminence. The exact contours of the shift, however, remain unclear. And this analytic gloss on the administration's view may not be correct. This is an area that cries out for greater clarification from the administration in the wake of the NDU speech.

The speech and its accompanying documents laid out other limits on drone strikes as well. The Fact Sheet said, as an initial matter, that it is the "policy of the United States" not to use "lethal force when it is feasible to capture a terrorist suspect." This seems to go further than previous statements that it is the unqualified preference of the United States to capture, rather than kill. Rather, the language sounds increasingly like the feasibility language that Holder used in his March 5, 2012, speech at Northwestern University and that the Department of Justice's 2011 white paper used with respect to the targeting of US citizens: that force would only be authorized when capture was not feasible. Indeed, Obama made it clear at NDU that under the new playbook, "the high threshold that we have set for taking lethal action applies to all potential terrorist targets, regardless of whether or not they are American citizens."

Yet the president also made it clear that "feasible" is not a standard easily or frequently met, and that the feasibility analysis includes both the risk to US forces and the risk to civilians of attempting to capture the target. It also includes broader strategic concerns such as those raised by the president about putting US forces on the ground in countries like Pakistan and thereby risking a "major international crisis." In other words, feasible does not mean feasible in the technical sense of accomplishable. It means, rather, accomplishable without undue harm to other interests—tactical, strategic, and political.

The Fact Sheet outlined a set of other preconditions for undertaking a drone strike:

- Near certainty that the terrorist target is present
- Near certainty that non-combatants will not be injured or killed

- An assessment that the relevant governmental authorities in the country where action is contemplated cannot or will not effectively address the threat to US persons
- An assessment that no other reasonable alternatives exist to effectively address the threat to US persons

These conditions are striking in that they appear to contemplate the evolution from the full availability of armed conflict targeting rules to something much more restricted. That said, it is hard to believe that the second "near certainty"—that noncombatants will not be injured or killed—can be a workable formula, even in the context of peacetime self-defense operations. Kinetic military operations always carry risks to civilians. And setting the bar for actions unrealistically high runs the risk of raising expectations of perfection in targeting that simply cannot be achieved. This risks, in turn, undermining the credibility of an otherwise ethically and legally defensible structure when the reality inevitably falls short of the stated policy.

Finally, the president made a brief, passing reference to what are called in the press "signature strikes"—the practice of targeting groups of people based not on individual identification but on broader patterns of behavior indicative of belligerency. He referred to the gradual transition out of the Afghanistan war and the need to protect US and coalition forces in that transition from attacks in their counterinsurgency war. In the "Afghan war theater," he said, we "must . . . and will continue to support our troops." (It is likely that the phrase "Afghan war theater" in this phraseology is intended to include border areas of Pakistan and targets engaged in counterinsurgency operations operating over the Pakistani border.) This means, continued the president, that US forces "will continue to take strikes against high value Al Qaeda targets, *but also against forces that are massing to support attacks on coalition forces.*" These strikes are, he added, intended to wind down as the counterinsurgency war winds down.

This passage did not address, however, the use of signature strikes in places such as Yemen, that is, outside of what the Obama administration has acknowledged as active combat theaters. So it is not clear whether the same criteria that apply to individuated strikes outside of hot battlefields also apply to signature strikes, although that seems to us unlikely. This question is important because, while the United States has not admitted as much, it appears to have been all but acting as a cobelligerent of the Yemen government in its civil war against a common enemy—using mostly airpower and, in a conventional way, targeting groups of hostile enemy forces. The president came closer to stating this directly than has any other official on the record, saying in this speech that in "Yemen, we are supporting security forces that have reclaimed territory from AQAP"—reclaimed, that is, an area the size of Maryland with 1.2 million people held and governed by the insurgent forces for nearly a year. The president went on to note this same role in assisting a coalition of African nations pushing the group al-Shabaab out of its strongholds and, even more notably, using drones and other assets to assist France in driving Al Qaeda groups out of their strongholds in Mali.

It is not clear from the speech and its accompanying materials how the president means to continue using drone strikes in such settings. It is plausible to believe, however, that in circumstances where the purpose of the strike is part of—in military support of—an allied government's counterinsurgency campaign against terrorist and insurgent forces, the administration will regard it as outside the framework the president articulated altogether and simply view it as conventional warfare. On the other hand, it's plausible also to believe that the new criteria are centrally about Yemen and Africa. This is also an area that is critical for the administration to flesh out further in the future.

Targeting of US Nationals: Defending the al-Awlaki Killing

As we noted above, the claim that Obama played judge, jury, and executioner in killing the radical cleric Anwar al-Awlaki in a drone strike has been a potent driver of anger and angst on both the political right and the political left. Targeted killing has been at the center of a well-organized and increasingly vocal advocacy campaign against drone warfare. The strength and persistence of this campaign—and an awareness of its potential to reshape public perception over time—led Obama to address the al-Awlaki strike directly in his NDU speech and led Holder to do so in his letter to Leahy the day before.

The president actually said nothing that went beyond what Holder had earlier said in his Northwestern University speech as far as legal standards were concerned. What the president did at NDU, however, was to announce that he was declassifying the fact of the drone strike against al-Awlaki, as well as the fact of the deaths of three other Americans in drone strikes, in order to "facilitate transparency and debate." And the president and Holder robustly set out the practical, and quite damning, facts of al-Awlaki's "actively plotting to kill US citizens," including with respect to the 2009 Detroit plot and the 2010 plot to bring down US-bound cargo planes—

thus moving the discussion off the purely abstract question of due process for an American citizen. Holder's letter contained more details about al-Awlaki's role and reiterated the legal standard the attorney general laid out in his Northwestern speech. The letter also noted—adding to the president's speech—that of the four US citizens known to have been killed during the Obama administration by drone strikes in targeted killing operations outside of "areas of active hostilities," only al-Awlaki was specifically targeted. Holder said the other three, including al-Awlaki's son, were not "specifically targeted by the United States."

Yet even as Obama strongly defended the al-Awlaki killing, he simultaneously and quite paradoxically sought to ally himself with his critics. So while he defended his actions, he also acknowledged different ways in which oversight might be made more robust, including more detailed congressional briefings, an independent review board for drone strikes, or even judicial review. On the latter two, the president was gently skeptical, raising both constitutional and practical concerns:

> Going forward, I've asked my administration to review proposals to extend oversight of lethal actions outside of warzones that go beyond our reporting to Congress. Each option has virtues in theory, but poses difficulties in practice. For example, the establishment of a special court to evaluate and authorize lethal action has the benefit of bringing a third branch of government into the process, but raises serious constitutional issues about presidential and judicial authority. Another idea that's been suggested—the establishment of an independent oversight board in the executive branch—

avoids those problems, but may introduce a layer of bureau-cracy into national security decision-making without inspiring additional public confidence in the process. But despite these challenges, I look forward to actively engaging Congress to explore these and other options for increased oversight.

The president here—as with his discussion of the end of the conflict—was trying at once to represent his own policies and to align himself with his critics. The trouble is that Obama has not at all changed his substantive views—that al-Awlaki was a lawful target and that it required no court order to kill him—and he is not, in fact, friendly to proposals to judicialize or bureaucratize targeting decisions. He is willing to "engage" such ideas and "review" them, but probably not to embrace them or, were Congress to pass them, sign them into law. So at the end of the day, he is signaling openness—sort of—to something to which he is not, in fact, open so as to emphasize a values affinity with a political base alienated from him on targeting questions. But the dance is unpersuasive. And by and large, the Left is unpersuaded.

Also in the fear-alleviating vein, the president addressed, almost in passing, another point of increasing angst on both the left and the right: the targeting of US citizens on US soil. This was the subject of the Paul filibuster, after all. And the president attempted to dispense with it once and for all. "For the record," he said, and to "dismiss some of the more outlandish claims that have been made" concerning drone strikes on US territory, "I do not believe it would be constitutional for the government to target and kill any US citizen—with a drone, or with a shotgun—without due process, nor should any president deploy armed drones over US soil."

The central aim of this statement is clear, although—as we noted in chapter 2—in many situations of ordinary law enforcement, US citizens are targeted and killed without *judicial* due process. Moreover, the president's "should" was less than an ironclad commitment *never* to deploy armed drones over US soil on behalf of himself and future presidents. Just as no president would ever forswear the possibility of using tanks on American soil, Obama was rightly careful not to preclude the possibility, senators Paul and Cruz notwithstanding.[8]

Denial of Territory to Terrorist Groups

Occupying a considerable space in the NDU speech was a discussion by the president of strategies for working with allied governments in Africa and elsewhere to ensure that radical Islamist insurgents do not take control of entire political spaces. Almost entirely ignored by the commentary on the speech, this "territorial denial" aspect of counterterrorism is emerging as among the new centerpieces of US counterterrorism-on-offense. Drone warfare must be understood as part of a series

---

8. For an explanation of why no president can entirely exclude the possibility of drone use on US soil, see Jack Goldsmith, "Of Course President Obama Has Authority, Under Some Circumstances, to Order Lethal Force Against a U.S. Citizen on U.S. Soil (and a Free Draft Response to Senator Paul for John Brennan)," *Lawfare,* February 23, 2013, http://www.lawfareblog .com/2013/02/of-course-president-obama-has-authority-under-some -circumstances-to-order-lethal-force-against-a-u-s-citizen-on-u-s-soil-and-a -free-draft-response-to-senator-paul-for-john-brennan/.

of activities aimed at denying radical Islamist terrorist groups territory from which to operate. The president's speech contained many statements pointing to the need to deny these groups safe haven. The president spent considerable time describing the strategies by which the United States and other Western allies are working with governments in Africa and elsewhere, embracing them as allies in a common fight against these terrorist groups.

Some emerging threats arise, said the president, from groups that are "collections of local militias interested in seizing territory." Some of them might be content with that—though the destabilizing effects of radical Islamist groups seizing territory within already fragile and lightly governed spaces cannot be written off as a geopolitical matter independent of anything else. While "we are vigilant for signs that these groups may pose a transnational threat, most are focused on operating in the countries and regions where they are based." In that case, the US response will be partly one of assessing the conventional geopolitical risks of instability. The United States might subsequently provide aid ranging from security assistance to economic and development help to prevent these groups from growing stronger.

Obama also talked about addressing "underlying grievances and conflicts that feed extremism—from North Africa to South Asia." Many critics will see this as a reflexive invocation of the "root causes" thesis about terrorist groups—presumably a debate that ended on 9/11—that served as something between a justification for terrorist violence and a reason not to undertake robust counterterrorism. The criticism is not unreasonable. But in context, the best way to understand the president's comments probably relates closely to this idea of territorial denial. Obama referred to the fact that the revolts in Arab countries have created openings for both political and social reform, but also openings for radical Islamist groups. These changes in the Arab world touch on every aspect of US interests, from geopolitics to counterterrorism, and policymakers will have to take all of those into account. Some places will "undergo chaotic change before things get better." In all these places, however, the geopolitical interests of the United States are intertwined with the counterterrorism strategies, and they intertwine with "all the elements of national power to win a battle of wills, a battle of ideas," including economic and development aid and efforts to assist countries and societies in transition.

Obama in the NDU speech used the word "territory" in two subtly distinct ways. First, the president referred to "remote" parts of Yemen, Somalia, and Afghanistan after the end of the US combat mission there, among other places, and said that America has an interest in ensuring that "Al Qaeda can never again establish a safe haven to launch attacks" in these nearly unreachable places—remote places where terrorists are able to train, regroup, and plot. Territory in this sense means small bits of land, often inaccessible to the United States and even to the notional sovereign states, where transnational terrorists hide. Often, as the president explained, drones are the only feasible tool for reaching them. Terrorist groups must be denied haven in this sense—whether by using drones or, preferably, by using drones and simultaneously strengthening the sovereign state and its ability and will to control its own territory.

But a second strategic meaning of "territory" has emerged in counterterrorism and has taken center stage in recent years.

This is the case in which a sovereign government faces an insurgency by an extremist group that has aspirations not just to control a tiny bit of territory for terrorist camps, but instead to take political control of whole territories, perhaps even an entire country. These groups form internal insurgencies with regional or larger sympathies. They might have terrorist wings of their own, or might be hospitable to foreign terrorist groups joining them with transnational aims. The president said that the United States acts, and will continue to act, in "partnerships with other countries" on this front—pushing back against Islamist insurgencies seeking to control territory and play host to terrorists. The president specifically framed this as territory—as "reclaimed territory from AQAP" in Yemen, for example. The United States is helping a coalition of African nations "push al-Shabaab out of its strongholds," he said; US military aid, including drones, helped "French-led intervention to push back Al Qaeda in the Maghreb, and help[ed] the people of Mali reclaim their future."

The strategic aim here is clear, and it is the most important area of growth in US counterterrorism-on-offense: locating drones as part of a unified geopolitical strategy that puts emphasis on ensuring that terrorist groups and Islamist insurgencies do not seize whole political territories, put entire populations under their brutal rule, and create country-size safe havens for transnational terrorist groups.

Detention Policy and the Future of Guantánamo

Obama's discussions of drones and targeting, and the future of the conflict and its end, all had much to recommend them—

though they had weaknesses too and raised plenty of questions, as we have seen. But there were parts of the speech that were just plain bad—political, naïve, and counterproductive.

Obama indulged most flamboyantly his broader tendency in the speech to align himself with critics of his own administration's policies when he spoke about detentions at Guantánamo Bay—a subject on which the NDU speech simply lacked candor and seriousness. This subject represented the speech's low point. Obama's justified frustration with congressional interference in his efforts to close the detention facility has led him in this direction before. Only a few weeks before the NDU speech, he had vented at a press conference that:

> . . . the notion that we're going to continue to keep over one hundred individuals in a no-man's land in perpetuity, even at a time when we've wound down the war in Iraq, we're winding down the war in Afghanistan, and we're having success defeating Al Qaeda's core, we've kept the pressure up on all these transnational terrorist networks. When we transfer detention authority in Afghanistan, the idea that we would still maintain forever a group of individuals who have not been tried, that is contrary to who we are. It is contrary to our interests and it needs to stop.
>
> . . .
>
> I think all of us should reflect on why exactly are we doing this. Why are we doing this? I mean, we've got a whole bunch of individuals who have been tried who are currently in maximum security prisons around the country. Nothing's happened to them. Justice has been served. It's been done in a way that's consistent with our Constitution; consistent

with due process; consistent with rule of law; consistent with our traditions.[9]

The president's comments here were bewildering, because his own policies had given rise to the vast majority of the concerns about which he so earnestly spoke. Remember that Obama himself had imposed the moratorium on repatriating people to Yemen. And Obama himself had insisted that nearly fifty detainees at Guantánamo could neither be tried nor transferred. To be sure, Obama would hold such people in a domestic facility, rather than at Guantánamo Bay. But that does not seem like a difference that makes detention at Guantánamo inconsistent with our Constitution, due process, the rule of law, or our traditions.

In the NDU speech, Obama once again draped himself in the rhetoric of his left-wing critics while neither facing his own role in perpetuating non-criminal detention nor proposing a viable means of ending it. After offering legal, diplomatic, and budgetary arguments against the facility, he declared that "I have tried to close GTMO. I transferred sixty-seven detainees to other countries before Congress imposed restrictions to effectively prevent us from either transferring detainees to other countries, or imprisoning them in the United States." He complained—rightly—about the transfer restrictions and he then thumped his bin Laden-killing chest a bit: "Given my administration's relentless pursuit of Al Qaeda's leadership, there is no

9. Barack Obama, "News Conference by the President," April 30, 2013, http://www.whitehouse.gov/the-press-office/2013/04/30/news -conference-president.

justification beyond politics for Congress to prevent us from closing a facility that should never have been opened." He then announced that he was lifting the moratorium on transfers to Yemen and that he was reappointing envoys to facilitate detainee transfers.

Had he stopped there, Obama would merely have reiterated his long-standing case for doing detention somewhere other than Guantánamo—a position with which reasonable people might disagree but which surely represents a matter of long-standing administration (and campaign) commitment. But Obama then went further to make an in-principle case against the sort of detention his administration has never, in fact, promised to end:

> . . . history will cast a harsh judgment on this aspect of our fight against terrorism and those of us who fail to end it. Imagine a future—ten years from now or twenty years from now—when the United States of America is still holding people who have been charged with no crime on a piece of land that is not part of our country. Look at the current situation, where we are force-feeding detainees who are being held on a hunger strike. . . . Is this who we are? Is that something our Founders foresaw? Is that the America we want to leave our children?
>
> Our sense of justice is stronger than that.

Obama here was not-so-subtly linking the closure of Guantánamo to the speech's broader theme, the end of the conflict:

> During the past decade, the vast majority of those detained by our military were captured on the battlefield. In Iraq, we

turned over thousands of prisoners as we ended the war. In Afghanistan, we have transitioned detention facilities to the Afghans, as part of the process of restoring Afghan sovereignty. So we bring law-of-war detention to an end, and we are committed to prosecuting terrorists wherever we can.

The "glaring exception to this time-tested approach," he said, is Guantánamo. In other words, even as his administration has defended the legality of virtually every detention ongoing at the facility, even as it contends that all of these detentions are authorized by the AUMF, Obama wags his finger at the public regarding the judgment of history and the sort of America we are going to leave our children. Yet he does so with no coherent plan to end the detentions that are taking place at the facility. The finger-wagging, after all, took place the very same day that Obama lifted his own self-imposed moratorium on Yemeni repatriations. So the finger-wagging might properly have been self-directed.

What's more, as Obama himself recognized, "even after we take [all the] steps [he proposed] one issue will remain—just how to deal with those GTMO detainees who we know have participated in dangerous plots or attacks but who cannot be prosecuted, for example, because the evidence against them has been compromised or is inadmissible in a court of law."

Yet for this group, Obama proposed nothing, saying only that "once we commit to a process of closing GTMO, I am confident that this legacy problem can be resolved, consistent with our commitment to the rule of law." Obama, in other words, offered no window into the basis for this confidence. And it's not as though these cases have never been reviewed before. The president's own task force, set up at the outset of the administration, identified forty-eight detainees (two of whom have since died) who meet "three core criteria":

> First, the totality of available information—including credible information that might not be admissible in a criminal prosecution—indicated that the detainee poses a high level of threat that cannot be mitigated sufficiently except through continued detention; second, prosecution of the detainee in a federal criminal court or a military commission did not appear feasible; and third, notwithstanding the infeasibility of criminal prosecution, there is a lawful basis for the detainee's detention under the AUMF.[10]

That number has surely risen in the years since, as the willingness to repatriate Yemenis has waned and legal rulings have reduced the number of detainees who might plausibly face criminal trials. Whatever the real number is today, there is only one way to resolve the problem other than maintaining this group of people in custody. And that is *not* maintaining this group of people in custody. Is Obama really going to free Abu Zubaydah—against whom a criminal case has not yet materialized? What about Mohammed Qatani, the would-be September 11 hijacker who was turned away from this country's borders in Orlando, Florida, with Mohammed Atta waiting for him on the other side of customs? Until the president is willing to say that he means to set these people free, pieties about what sort of country we are, however earnestly felt, ring hollow and are beneath the rest of the speech. Because whether

---

10. Guantánamo Review Task Force, *Final Report,* January 22, 2010, http://www.justice.gov/ag/guantanamo-review-final-report.pdf.

Obama faces it squarely or not, we are, in fact, the sort of country that detains people under the law of war, rather than letting them commit acts of terrorism against us.

And more to the point, he is the kind of president who does so.

Detention is another reason it might be very difficult to declare the end of the conflict to which the speech aspires. For once again, the detainees get a vote as to whether they are still at war with the United States. And some of them manifestly still are. Obama's unwillingness, even as he insists on a return to the normalcy of peacetime, to begin articulating the steps that true peace would compel—not just the closure of the facility but the freeing of its detainees—suggests once again that at least part of him imagines something less than real peace is at hand.

Conclusion

Obama had words on other subjects, too. On the cluster of closely linked issues that include secrecy and transparency, surveillance and privacy, reporting and journalism, classified information, leaks and leak prosecutions, he once again tried to straddle a line between defending an administration that has, in fact, been aggressive and sharing values with a base that objects to that aggressiveness. The dance, once again, left a lot of people cold—and rightly so. For Obama consistently put himself on both sides of the issues. We must, he said,

> . . . keep information secret that protects our operations and our people in the field. To do so, we must enforce conse- quences for those who break the law and breach their com-

mitment to protect classified information. But a free press is also essential for our democracy. . . . I'm troubled by the possibility that leak investigations may chill the investigative journalism that holds government accountable.

Inhibiting investigative journalism that holds government accountable—or, at least, the sources on which that journalism relies—is precisely the point of prosecuting leakers of classified information. And troubled though the president might be, the briefs filed by his administration express no sense of doubt or qualification when it comes either to the prosecution of leakers or to the demands that reporters provide information to investigators. Yet the president also called for a "media shield law" and for the attorney general to review guidelines for "investigations that involve reporters." It was largely a continuation of a pattern in the speeches of self-congratulation for openness from an administration that is not, in fact, especially open.

In this case, it also reflected a broad pattern within this one speech of trying to straddle lines. Defending secrecy while allying himself with the reporters who erode it is of a piece with defending detention while decrying it and insisting that we're not the sort of country that does it. It is also of a piece with promising to end a war even as he also promises to continue its prosecution. At its best, the speech promised a plausible bridge across these apparent antinomies—as when the president seemed to describe a transitional period between war and peace with targeting standards that would be lawful across that transition. At its worst, however, the speech sought to ally the president with his critics at the risk of delegitimizing his own policies and the men and women who have to implement them. Whether it will be remembered principally for the virtues or principally for the vices will largely depend on whether the transition he described materializes in fact and how the government manages it, if and when it does.

CHAPTER 4

The Speeches in Interaction with Other Branches of Government

The Obama administration intended the president's May 23, 2013, speech on US counterterrorism strategy at the National Defense University as a comprehensive statement of its approach to the conflict, one that would fundamentally reshape the conversation nationally—both bolstering support for aggressive counterterrorism measures and preparing the public for a wind-down of the legal war. But within a few weeks of the president's speech, events intervened and sent the conversation veering away from drones, the end of the conflict, and hunger-striking detainees and toward a subject the speeches had previously ignored almost completely.

A young man named Edward Snowden, a contractor at the National Security Agency (NSA), absconded abroad with tens of thousands, hundreds of thousands, or even millions of NSA documents, a large number of which he then proceeded to

dispense among a group of media outlets and individual journalists. These documents revealed major NSA surveillance
activities both in the form of the collection in bulk of telephony
metadata—data that identifies which telephone numbers are
calling which other telephone numbers and when but does not
include the contents of the communications—and the cooperation of US Internet and communications companies in the
collection of communications contents directed at non-US
persons overseas. They also revealed any number of collaborative relationships with foreign intelligence services for collection overseas, various technical aspects of US collection
practices, NSA targeting of foreign leaders, and many other
details.

The firestorm that erupted from the Snowden revelations
went on for months, with Congress demanding answers and
contemplating changes in the law, international allies furious
at US spying on them and their citizens, and the public ener-
gized in a fashion that neither drones nor detention had yet
accomplished in terms of mobilizing people en masse. Part of
the administration's response involved, once again, speeches.

And so it was that Robert S. Litt, general counsel to the
Office of the Director of National Intelligence, took the podium
at the Brookings Institution on July 19, 2013, to emphasize
that all of the activity Snowden had compromised had been
authorized by Congress and approved by the courts. In his
speech, "Privacy, Technology, and National Security: An Overview of Intelligence Collection," he said:

> These programs are not illegal. They are authorized by
> Congress and are carefully overseen by the congressional
> intelligence and judiciary committees. They are conducted

with the approval of the Foreign Intelligence Surveillance Court and under its supervision. And they are subject to extensive, court-ordered oversight by the executive branch. In short, all three branches of government knew about these programs, approved them, and helped to ensure that they complied with the law.

In Litt's account, " . . . the conclusion that the bulk metadata collection is authorized under section 215 is not that of the intelligence community alone." Rather, he emphasized, "Applications to obtain this data have been repeatedly approved by numerous judges of the FISA [Foreign Intelligence Surveillance Act] Court, each of whom has determined that the application complies with all legal requirements. And Congress reauthorized section 215 in 2011, after the intelligence and judiciary committees of both houses had been briefed on the program and after information describing the program had been made available to all members. In short, all three branches of government have determined that this collection is lawful and reasonable—in large part because of the substantial protections we provide for the privacy of every person whose telephone number is collected."

Similarly, Litt also argued that the larger targeting of foreign call contents under the FISA Amendments Act was not the work of the executive branch alone.

A few months later, on January 17, 2014, speaking at the Justice Department, President Obama ("Remarks by the President on Review of Signals Intelligence") also addressed these programs and specifically promised reforms of the section 215 program—reforms under which the government would get out of the business of holding large metadata databases.

He promised enhanced judicial review and he promised as well to "consult with the relevant committees in Congress to seek their views, and then seek congressional authorization for the new program as needed." More broadly, he stated that "I am open to working with Congress to ensure that we build a broad consensus for how to move forward" on surveillance authorities.

The point that Litt made explicitly and Obama made implicitly—that all three branches of government are deeply implicated in these programs—clearly has merit with respect to the NSA programs the two were discussing. But the point actually has more general application to many of the controversies that have arisen repeatedly over the administration's assertions of muscular counterterrorism authorities. Critics of these authorities often frame them as expressions of unaccountable executive power. There was a time when this criticism had some merit. The early George W. Bush administration claimed broad, inherent executive authority for detention, interrogation, surveillance, and other controversial actions, after all.

But the criticism has persisted long past its truth. Indeed, the legal framework outlined in the speeches did not spring full-grown from Zeus's head. It has not, as many critics believe, resulted from an executive-only lawmaking process lacking in significant involvement from Congress or signoff from the judiciary. It did not, as many of those same critics assume or argue, develop without reference to—or uninfluenced by—international law. Rather, the framework developed over time in a complex and iterative set of interactions with the other branches of government and with a deep awareness of the United States' international obligations. Many key aspects of the framework, though certainly not all, are written in statute, and the courts have both reviewed some aspects and actively declined to review others. The courts have also themselves crafted important features of the framework.

In this chapter, we review the involvement of the other branches of government in the development of the framework described in the speeches. We explore the degree to which each branch is implicated in major aspects of the administration's position. We also look, to the extent the administration claims compliance with international law, at the degree to which the international system and its actors—other countries and international nongovernmental organizations (NGOs)—have had their voices heard, even as outsiders to government, in the development of the framework and have exerted leverage to influence it.

The bottom line, as we shall explain, is that for all the talk of the framework being a "trust-me" executive-based system without external review or input, the other branches of government have actually been deeply involved in its creation and continuing evolution. What's more, in many cases the limits on their involvement in overseeing its implementation have as much to do with their own institutional reticence as with executive ambitions.

Nor is the framework uninfluenced by activist groups which are not part of the constitutional structure of the United States and have no official juridical place in the elaboration of the legal framework that binds the US government. As with any cause about which people or groups feel strongly, the democratic and judicial processes offer mechanisms of input and influence. The American Civil Liberties Union, Human Rights First, Human Rights Watch, and the Center for Constitutional Rights—just to take a few organizations that broadly find the legal framework problematic—have not lacked for voice to address any of the three branches of government. The framework, for all that these groups remain dissenters from it, bears indelible marks of their influence as well.

Similarly, actors of the international community—whether international organizations and their officials or other states through their foreign ministries—have also made their views known. This involves mainly a set of political and diplomatic pressures. Broadly speaking, other countries have their greatest impact through bilateral diplomacy. But these pressures have undoubtedly had an impact on the framework. The international community's many voices have ranged from guardedly ambiguous to hostile dissent with respect to the rules that the US government has put in place. And you can see the input of other countries on the framework in, for example, negotiations over the terms of drone strikes in Pakistan or Yemen. You can see it in discussions with different countries over detention, particularly with respect to those countries' own detained nationals. You can also see it in the angry denunciations of US electronic collection practices from the governments of Germany and Brazil. In his speech at the Justice Department, President Obama announced changes to the rules for intelligence collection against foreign allied leaders and announced as well that the United States would consider the privacy interests of foreigners abroad in conducting espionage in the future. More generally, in the wake of the Snowden revelations, the blow-back the United States has received in numerous bilateral relationships has produced a significant rethinking at the highest levels of government about how aggressively this nation should really be collecting in a number of different contexts.

But the framework has also seen influence from UN officials and NGOs, who have had their greatest impact through political stances taken in the media and public forums. NGOs have also had a significant voice through judicial processes, not just in the United States but elsewhere as well. As a political matter, this dissent has registered over the years and will continue to do so in the future on matters ranging from drone targeting to habeas hearings.

In this chapter, we consider the role of actors external to the executive branch on the legal framework described in the speeches across the major positions on which the administration has staked out ground and across the major authorities it has claimed.

The Nature of the Conflict

At this stage, both other branches of government have substantially signed on to the most basic element of the speeches' framework: that there is, in fact, a state of armed conflict between the United States and Al Qaeda and its associated forces and that this armed conflict extends beyond the hot battlefields of Afghanistan. The fundamental propositions— that an armed conflict exists; that it is not limited to Afghanistan but extends at least to those places from which the enemy strikes, plans and plots, and creates safe havens for operations; that the law of war applies to operations in the context of this armed conflict; and that the armed conflict includes Al Qaeda's co-belligerent forces—are all contested by advocacy groups, international organizations, and prominent figures in the legal academy. Importantly, however, they are contested neither by the Congress nor by the courts.

Consider Congress's role first. Congress passed the Authorization for the Use of Military Force (AUMF), which contained a broad authorization for the administration to use military force against those responsible for the September 11, 2001, attacks and those who harbored them—and, implicitly, those who joined the fight on their side.[1] It never specified either temporal or geographic limits on the fight. And as the fight has expanded both geographically and in terms of the list of groups incorporated within the executive's understanding of the authorization, Congress has never amended it. To the contrary, Congress has consistently funded operations under the AUMF. And in 2012, the legislature specifically reaffirmed—at least as regards detention authority—that it remained a vital document, one that reached both members and supporters of enemy groups, including associated forces. It did so, once again, without reference to geography and without imposing time limitations:

> Congress affirms that the authority of the president to use all necessary and appropriate force pursuant to the Authorization for Use of Military Force (Public Law 107-40; 50 US C. 1541 note) includes the authority for the Armed Forces of the United States to detain covered persons (as defined in subsection (b)) pending disposition under the law of war.[2]

---

1. See the Authorization for the Use of Military Force (AUMF), Pub L. 107-40, 115 Stat. 224 (2001).

2. The National Defense Authorization Act for Fiscal Year 2012 (NDAA) reaffirmed detention authority under the AUMF. See Pub. L. 112-81, § 1021, 125 Stat. 1297, 1562 (2012). The NDAA does not speak to the question of targeting authority.

Indeed, Congress has sometimes pushed the administration toward a *greater,* not lesser, sense of the AUMF's geographic and temporal sweep. For example, in the 2012 National Defense Authorization Act (NDAA), Congress sought to require military detention for terrorist suspects captured *domestically* or anywhere else in the world.[3] The administration fought this provision, managed to get it watered down in a conference committee, and then interpreted it nearly out of existence.[4] The speeches, likewise, repeatedly push back against congressional efforts to further militarize the conflict. David Kris's June 11, 2010, speech at the Brookings Institution ("Law Enforcement as a Counterterrorism Tool"), as we described in chapter 1, is entirely devoted to defending the use of the civilian criminal justice system—that is, to the non-exclusivity of law-of-war tools. And both Jeh Johnson in his October 18, 2011, speech to the Heritage Foundation and John Brennan at Harvard Law School ("Strengthening Our Security by Adhering to Our Values and Laws," September 16, 2011), likewise devoted significant energy to resisting the congressional urge to treat counterterrorism as a purely military endeavor.

In other words, far from pushing the boundaries of what Congress has willed, the administration—in the speeches and in practice—has *resisted* the full sweep of the pure conflict model as the legislature has sought to authorize it. The speeches describe a hybrid conflict, one which draws upon multiple—including non-military—sources of national power. Congress

---

3. Ibid., § 1022.

4. See Benjamin Wittes, "Initial Comments on the Implementing Procedures for NDAA Section 1022," *Lawfare,* February 28, 2012, http://www.lawfareblog.com/2012/02/initial-comments-on-the-implementing-procedures-for-ndaa-section-1022/.

as an institution—notwithstanding members who oppose drone strikes, insist on closing Guantánamo, and express discomfort with the signals intelligence activity of the United States—sees it far less in complicated, hybrid terms. It sees the country as much less ambiguously and much more plainly at war.

The courts too are, at this point, deeply implicated in the framework. The Supreme Court accepted in *Hamdi* that a state of armed conflict existed between Al Qaeda and the Taliban, on the one hand, and the United States on the other. Writing for a plurality of the court, Justice Sandra Day O'Connor stated, "The AUMF authorizes the president to use 'all necessary and appropriate force' against 'nations, organizations, or persons' associated with the September 11, 2001, terrorist attacks." She consistently discussed the issue of Yaser Hamdi's detention in terms of the laws of war. She accepted further that this armed conflict was temporally open-ended: " . . . we understand Congress' grant of authority for the use of 'necessary and appropriate force' to include the authority to detain for the duration of the relevant conflict, and our understanding is based on longstanding law-of-war principles."[5]

In subsequent Guantánamo detention cases, the lower courts have recognized both that this armed conflict extends beyond the hot battlefield of Afghanistan and that the executive branch's authority to use force extends beyond core Al Qaeda and Taliban forces and includes "associated forces."[6] For example, in one case, the US Court of Appeals for the District of Columbia Circuit reversed and vacated a district court grant of habeas corpus despite the fact that the detainee

5. *Hamdi v. Rumsfeld*, 542 US 507 (2004).
6. *Khan v. Obama*, 655 F.3d 20, 21 (D.C. Cir. 2011).

in question had been captured in Mauritania, nowhere near any hot battlefield, and transferred to US custody.[7] In another case, the D.C. Circuit affirmed the detention of a petitioner found to be "part of" Hezb-i Islami Gulbuddin, which it found to be an associated force of Al Qaeda and the Taliban. In still other cases, the D.C. Circuit found that Abu Zubaydah's force was an associated force of Al Qaeda and that detainees captured in Abu Zubaydah's safe houses in urban Pakistan were subject to detention.[8] The Supreme Court has not granted certiorari in any Guantánamo cases.

Moreover, the courts have largely accepted the executive's view of its international law obligations. While as a domestic law matter the courts have extended a limited form of habeas to Guantánamo detainees, neither they nor Congress has done anything to disturb the executive branch's long-declared legal view that the human rights regime contained in, notably, the International Covenant on Civil and Political Rights does not bind the US government extraterritorially. So when the United States engages in hostilities against terrorist targets in one place or another, it is the law of war that applies and not the corpus of international human rights law that would apply domestically in times of peace. Moreover, in addition to rejecting the claim (so well accepted among human rights groups) that no state of armed conflict exists under international law, the courts have also rejected the claim that hostilities are over for purposes of either international or domestic law.[9] Christof Heyns, the UN special rapporteur on extrajudicial, summary, or arbitrary

7. *Salahi v. Obama*, 625 F.3d 745, 750 (D.C. Cir. 2010).

8. *Abdul Razak Ali v. Obama*, No. 11-5102 (December 3, 2013).

9. *G. Al Bihani v. Obama*, 590 F.3d 866, 874 (D.C. Cir. Jan. 5, 2010).

executions, can shrug off the US legal view that targeted drone strikes on Al Qaeda or allied groups are an ongoing, legitimate response against those who carried out the 9/11 attacks or later associated themselves to those groups, declaring in a 2012 speech that it's "difficult to see how any killings carried out in 2012 can be justified as in response to [events] in 2001."[10] However, all three branches of the US government think otherwise. And all three branches have considered legal views and reasoning for why the United States government has a perfectly plausible basis on which, even today, to continue hostilities.

To put the matter bluntly, as to the nature of the conflict, the speeches do not simply reflect the aspirational views of the executive branch with respect to either domestic law or international law. They reflect core points on which the three branches of government have reached a strong consensus and which broadly draw upon long-standing legal views of the US government on national security in both domestic and international law: the United States is in a state of armed conflict with Al Qaeda and its co-belligerents that reaches beyond the borders of Afghanistan, now and into the indeterminate future—even though President Obama aspires to wind down the conflict.

Matters are very different with respect to this nation's interlocutors in international law, where many countries and international organizations simply disagree with the whole international law approach taken by the United States from September 11 until the present. Many are deeply concerned

---

10. Owen Bowcott, "Drone strikes threaten 50 years of international law, says UN rapporteur," *The Guardian*, June 21, 2012, http://www.theguardian.com/world/2012/jun/21/drone-strikes-international-law-un.

that the approach the United States has taken will become permanently embedded—as we, in fact, urge that it should become—in the national security legal architecture of the United States. The depth of unease, even antipathy, toward US policy has to be understood for what it is: irreconcilable viewpoints that often create a ships-passing-in-the-night conversation that goes nowhere at the glacial pace of "transatlantic dialogue." With many of these critics, the starting points between them and the US government are simply so far apart that the US government, with all the best will in the world, cannot bridge the gap. And it shouldn't try. Seeking to find workable compromises simply shows weakness in these conversations and suggests a lack of confidence in the moral and legal legitimacy of the fundamental framework. It thus serves as an invitation to move the goal posts and demand more. With those who reject the propriety of the entire construction of the conflict as warfare, there really is little to discuss.

Yet this does not mean that the international community has no impact on the framework. The gulf between the United States and many international actors is nowhere near as dire as one might think from listening to discussions in the European Parliament or at academic conferences. For many of the United States' allies in NATO and elsewhere, for example, it is possible to agree to disagree on basic aspects of the framework and to work together despite having disparate views of what law, if any, authorizes given steps. Agreement to disagree takes place at the grand level as to the nature of the conflict as a whole, but it also takes place on narrower legal questions. In some cases, the disagreement is of sufficient gravity that the other state—even a close ally like the United Kingdom—will not participate in certain activities with the United States. In other cases, the disagreement might not rise to this level but might simply mean that the different countries have different legal theories as to why their joint activity is proper. In these situations, which tend to predominate in bilateral relations with states with which the United States has common counterterrorism interests, the US government has a strong incentive to seek to work out at least policy compromises. And this need to work with allies creates an ongoing incentive on the part of the United States to narrow the field of disagreement where possible.

The attempt to create as wide a zone of overlap as possible with other countries produces all sorts of specific accommodations to allies and trade-offs with other countries. The Bush administration released all the British detainees from Guantánamo early on because it was important to Tony Blair's government in the period surrounding the Iraq War, to cite only one example. For present purposes, the more important point is that the need to find practical common ground often affects the legal framework itself, sometimes profoundly, even on such macro matters as the nature of the conflict itself. The speeches themselves sometimes reflect this impact. For example, in Brennan's speech at Harvard Law School, as we noted in chapter 2, Brennan described how European views of "imminence" in targeting were becoming more flexible, moving toward the US position, and also how US views of what sort of threat was required before lethal force was appropriate were evolving toward the European view that it must be an imminent threat. In the president's May 23, 2013, speech on US counterterrorism strategy at National Defense University, as we described in chapter 3, that convergence went further, with the United

States adopting "imminence" of threat as a condition for strikes. More generally, the highly restrictive criteria Obama adopted in the NDU speech for drone strikes represent an attempt to alleviate international pressure on the United States by embracing criteria that, as we have described, would be lawful in peacetime too, not just during an armed conflict. The pressures that led to these new criteria were predominantly international pressures—friction with Pakistan and with European allies, mainly—not domestic ones.

The US view of the nature of the conflict, in short, has had a considerable number of legal influences. Far from a project of executive freelancing, it has seen the impact of, and buy-in from, all three branches of government and significant influence from allies overseas and interest groups domestically.

Surveillance Authorities

As a general matter, the Snowden revelations and the surveillance controversy they unleashed lie beyond the scope of this volume. For one thing, the story broke as we were nearing the book's completion. For another thing, even as of this writing in mid-2014, the administration has not responded to them using speeches in quite the same systematic way as it did with respect to the controversies over drones and targeted killing earlier in the administration. Other than Litt's speech at Brookings, Obama's at the Justice Department, and a number of testimonies by the NSA and intelligence community leaderships, formal speeches have been relatively sparse. Lisa Monaco, Brennan's successor as counterterrorism adviser, gave one at New York University in November 2013, but largely did not address the question of legal authorities.[11] Similarly, then-NSA director General Keith Alexander has given a number of speeches, but these have largely been policy defenses of NSA's conduct, not elaborations of legal theories to justify them.[12] The administration, rather, has justified its policy to a considerable degree by doing precisely what it has refused to do with respect to drones: declassifying large numbers of underlying legal documents and court opinions and making them available for the public to evaluate on its own.

At the same time, these document releases have highlighted the point Litt made in the speech we quoted at the beginning of this chapter: the surveillance architecture, like the nature of the conflict, is by no means an executive-only affair. The two programs that have garnered the lion's share of the controversy—bulk metadata collection under section 215 of the Patriot Act and acquisition of foreign communications content under section 702 of the FISA Amendments Act—both proceed under statutory authority. While the statutory authority for the metadata program is controversial, the authority for collection under section 702 is fairly straightforward. Both programs proceed under the supervision of the FISA Court. Both have produced significant compliance issues, which have led to energetic FISA Court interventions. And both programs, as Litt noted, have been repeatedly briefed to

---

11. Lisa Monaco, address at NYU Law School Center on Law and Security, November 19, 2013, http://www.whitehouse.gov/the-press-office/2013 /11/19/remarks-prepared-delivery-assistant-president-homeland -security-and-coun.

12. See, for example, General Alexander's speech at the Black Hat USA 2013 convention, available on YouTube at http://www.youtube.com/watch?v =4Sg4AtcW0LU.

the intelligence committees of the Congress, and Congress has reauthorized the authorities knowing in some detail how the government was using them.

More generally, it is simply impossible to argue that the American surveillance architecture is an under-regulated bastion of executive authority. Indeed, Congress has given the subject bipartisan and almost neurotic attention over a long period of time, beginning with the passage of the wiretapping statute in 1968, continuing through the FISA in 1978, the Electronic Communications Privacy Act in 1986, major FISA amendments in 1994, 2001, 2007, and 2008, and numerous other enactments along the way. While one can fault Congress in any number of ways for the manner of its regulation of intelligence collection, one cannot reasonably question that it has— repeatedly, consistently, and over many years—monitored and adjusted the legal framework at work here and tried to help it keep pace with technological developments. Notably, the impact of outside NGOs during many of these legislative efforts is plainly visible, too. While outside groups like the ACLU often opposed changes and reforms to the surveillance architecture, they have sometimes supported changes as well. The ACLU, for example, was integral to the passage of the FISA. And its opposition to other aspects of major collection authorities led to substantial changes in them. For example, during the debates over the FISA Amendments Act of 2008, which gave rise to the section 702 authority, opposition from civil liberties groups to the proposed core authorities prompted the inclusion of numerous limitations and reporting requirements that would not have been in law otherwise.

Congress has, to be sure, left certain areas unregulated in statute—particularly with respect to intelligence collection against non-US citizens and permanent residents that is conducted overseas. But these were deliberate legislative forbearances, not oversights or executive power grabs. That is, Congress specifically chose *not* to regulate overseas collection against non-US persons but to leave these areas to governance by executive order.[13] Notably, Congress in recent years has narrowed the zone of legal policy it is content for the president to govern in that fashion. Until 2008, espionage directed at US persons overseas also fell outside of the FISA. Now, by contrast, Congress and the FISA Court are involved there, too.[14]

Generally speaking, the legal architecture of American surveillance has seen little impact from formal international law mechanisms, but that's because there really is no international law of espionage. Unlike the laws of war, which developed in the international arena, spying is just one of those things that international law assumes countries will do and leaves to domestic law and the bilateral relationships between international actors to regulate. The impact of bilateral relationships on the contours of US intelligence policy is very visible indeed. For example, the so-called Five Eyes agreement among the United States, the United Kingdom, Canada, Australia, and New Zealand—an agreement which involves a close intelligence-sharing partnership and a joint agreement not to spy on one another's governments—creates a qualitatively different understanding between the United States and these countries than exists with other countries, even close allies like Germany and Israel. And the reaction of countries like Brazil and Germany to NSA sur-

---

13. This area is regulated by Executive Order 12333.
14. See section 704 of the FISA Amendments Act of 2008, Pub. L. 110-261.

veillance led directly to President Obama's embrace in his speech in January of new restraints on NSA's targeting of foreign allied leaders—and, more broadly, of the consideration of privacy concerns in overseas surveillance.

To put the matter simply, the contours of American surveillance law and policy have been set and reset over a long iterative dialogue among the executive branch, the Congress, the courts, interest groups, and foreign actors. Responsibility for its contours do not lie exclusively in the intelligence community or, more generally, in the presidency.

Detaining and Trying the Enemy

At this point, we can say much the same thing about US detention policy and trial by military commissions, which have both seen deep involvement from the courts and from Congress. Detention certainly *used* to be an exclusively executive affair. The Bush administration resisted involvement from the courts and claimed both inherent executive power and power under the AUMF to detain the enemy. More recently, Congress itself resisted getting involved and putting its name behind US detention operations, leaving them almost entirely to the administration and the courts.[15] There was a time, and it wasn't even that long ago, when one could fairly treat detention as an area of "trust us" executive lawmaking.

But this is no longer the case. While Congress kept itself out of the fray for a long time, it is now very much in it—erring

---

15. For a critique of this congressional posture, see Benjamin Wittes, *Detention and Denial: The Case for Candor after Guantánamo* (Washington: Brookings, 2011).

these days not on the side of keeping its hands off but on the side of excessive micromanagement of detainee handling. The 2012 NDAA, as we have seen, authorized detention in general terms. And Congress has slapped a series of restrictions on executive handling of detention. It has banned moving detainees to the United States for trial, for example, and it has restricted transfers overseas to narrow circumstances that made such transfers all but impossible. More recently, it has relaxed those overseas transfer restrictions, while retaining those on transfers to the United States. Notably, the executive branch—while complaining about the transfer restrictions repeatedly in the speeches and in various signing statements associated with the legislation in which they appeared—has respected them. Indeed, the transfer restrictions have greatly frustrated the administration's planned closure of Guantánamo Bay. Yet the administration has chosen to live with them, effectively acknowledging Congress's authority over the matter. Congress has even become involved in regulating military detention *outside* of Guantánamo, passing one provision that requires reporting before releases or transfers from the Bagram Airfield in Afghanistan.[16] At this point, the US detention architecture bears indelible marks of Congress's involvement and approval.

The involvement of the courts has been even deeper. Since the *Boumediene* decision,[17] the D.C. Circuit, which reviews the habeas decisions rendered under the authority *Boumediene* created, has become the primary articulator of the substantive

---

16. See Robert Chesney, "The NDAA and Detention in Afghanistan: Congress Takes a Step Toward Greater Involvement," *Lawfare*, December 20, 2012, http://www.lawfareblog.com/2012/12/the-ndaa-and-detention-in -afghanistan-congress-takes-a-step-toward-greater-involvement/.

17. *Boumediene v. Bush*, 553 US 723 (2008).

and procedural law of detention under the AUMF. In a wide range of opinions handed down since 2010, the court has defined the substantive scope of the government's detention authority, the rules for the use of hearsay, and the rules for the construal of evidentiary material admitted.[18] In other words, much as in the surveillance space, the framework discussed in the speeches is not one cooked up in the executive branch alone. It has the assent of Congress and the active involvement of the judiciary in its substantive formation and creation.

In this area, moreover, the impact of international law and NGO actors is very clear as well. The United States claims to be acting within its rights under the Geneva Conventions. Guantánamo detainees receive visits from the International Committee of the Red Cross, the official arbiter of the conventions, and the ICRC has not challenged the legality of the detentions there. And while the administration does not accept the insistence of many human rights groups that detentions at Guantánamo are unlawful, it does—as we have seen—accept the normative argument they have advanced that the facility must close. Current US detention authority, in other words, reflects a diverse set of inputs from sources well beyond the three branches of government.

The development of military commission trials has followed a similar trajectory. These were also once promulgated on executive authority alone. But in the *Hamdan* decision,[19] the Supreme Court insisted on a role for Congress in establishing

---

18. See Benjamin Wittes, Robert Chesney, Larkin Reynolds, et al., "The Emerging Law of Detention 2.0: The Guantánamo Habeas Cases as Lawmaking," Brookings, May 12, 2011, http://www.brookings.edu/research/reports/2011/05/guantanamo-wittes.

19. *Hamdan v. Rumsfeld*, 548 US 557 (2006).

any commissions the executive might use. Modern military commissions have thus resulted from a complex interaction of all three branches of government. Since the *Hamdan* decision, Congress—under two successive administrations and under legislative control of both parties—has authorized the commissions in two separate major pieces of legislation. It has also repeatedly tinkered with the authorizing legislation. The courts, meanwhile, have reviewed military commission convictions and, in the process, limited the availability of key charges before the commissions. Specifically, D.C. Circuit cases have called into question whether material support for terrorism and conspiracy are available as charges in military commissions on grounds that they are not traditional offenses under the international laws of war. This point, in turn, highlights the impact of international law norms on the development of the architecture the speeches defend. In the military commission system, a statutorily authorized court's convictions are being reviewed by an Article III court that is limiting Congress's ability to proscribe conduct, and the federal court is doing so based on the authority of international law. That is hardly an example of the executive branch running amok.

Targeting, Drone Strikes, and Secrecy

There really are only two areas in which the executive branch has insisted on a near-exclusive role. The first is targeting. Indeed, if the speeches' framework as a general matter reflects interactions among the three branches that is more robust than is generally recognized, targeting represents something of an exception to the rule.

In his NDU speech, President Obama seemed to give a bit of ground on the subject of judicial review of targeting, suggesting he had "asked my administration to review proposals to extend oversight of lethal actions outside of war zones" and discussing the pros and cons of such proposals. This was a considerable departure from the first-term speeches, which had been entirely uncompromising on this point. Targeting, said then-Attorney General Eric Holder, Secretary of Homeland Security Jeh C. Johnson, and several others, is an inherently executive function. (Holder addressed the issue at Northwestern University School of Law on March 5, 2012, as did Johnson, who at the time was general counsel for the Department of Defense, in his February 22, 2012, address at Yale Law School, "National Security Law, Lawyers, and Lawyering in the Obama Administration.")

The administration then took the view that there is no role for the courts in targeting decisions outside the territorial United States, whether in advance or after the fact—even in cases involving a US citizen. The role of Congress is limited to oversight through secret reports to the intelligence committees or to the armed services committees. Beyond that, the Obama administration said, on any of the legal framings of this conflict, targeting with lethal force is inherently and exclusively an executive function. Notably, the administration has not followed up on the NDU speech by endorsing any proposal to "judicialize" any aspects of targeting. So on this matter, the Obama administration does sound—with the exception of Obama's own 2013 speech—remarkably like the early Bush administration. Targeting with lethal force abroad runs not just to the executive generally, but to the constitutional functions most associated with it: the commander-in-chief power, the power to protect national security and defense, and the power to conduct foreign relations.

Moreover, the administration contends that only the executive has the specialized, dedicated agencies and agents able to perform this inherently discretionary and probabilistic task well; the nature of defending the country through force requires executive focus and the expertise of military and national security personnel acting in a highly coordinated way that no other branch of government can do. What's more, the act of the courts playing Monday morning quarterback will inevitably damage the ability of the executive to make the best decisions in an uncertain environment in real time. Congress always has political avenues by which to rein in a president whose adventures exceed the legislature's appetite; the courts, for their part, have developed a long history of deference and refusal to get involved, particularly with decisions for how force is to be used, when, how, and against whom.

If all of this sounds like just so much unilateral executive policymaking, there are two important considerations to take into account. The first is that to the extent one conceives of the conflict as a true armed conflict pitting the United States against a belligerent force and governed by the law of armed conflict, the Obama administration's view of the matter has a solid foundation in law. Targeting in this conflict is not, in principle, any different from targeting in any other conflict in which the United States has engaged in the past. It is *always* an executive affair. The military, of course, must respect the international law of war, even when engaged in hostilities with an unlawful and criminal belligerent, and it must follow particularly the law of targeting in armed conflict. But as we have explained, those laws—particularly as the Obama administration understands them—give capacious ground in which to operate. Notably, they do not call for judicial review of, or statutory foundation for, targeting decisions. It is noteworthy that in one of the earliest speeches setting out the administration's legal framework, Harold Koh made reference to the targeting of Admiral Yamamoto during World War II in his March 25, 2010, address to the American Society of International Law ("The Obama Administration and International Law"). The Obama administration, in other words, is not shy about seeing its targeting decisions in this conflict as similar to targeting decisions in any other war, nor is that an eccentric view

Second, to the extent the judiciary has played no role in targeting, that is at least in significant degree because it has affirmatively declined to get involved in the matter. The ACLU offered the courts the opportunity to get involved in the Anwar al-Awlaki targeting before the drone strike that killed him, but US District Judge John Bates declined, arguing both that al-Awlaki's father—whom the organization represented—had no standing to bring the action and that targeting was a political question from which the courts had to abstain in any event.[20] After the strike, the ACLU reformulated the case as a wrongful death action[21] under *Bivens;*[22] Judge Rosemary Collyer dismissed that.[23] At this stage, in other words, there is no evident

---

20. See *Al-Aulaqi v. Obama*, No. 10-1469 (DDC Dec. 7, 2010).

21. See complaint in *Al-Aulaqi v. Panetta*, No. 12-01192, filed July 18, 2012.

22. *Bivens v. Six Unknown Named Agents of Federal Bureau of Narcotics*, 403 US 388 (1971).

23. See opinion in *Al-Aulaqi v. Panetta*, No. 12-01192, filed April 4, 2014. For an account of the oral argument before Judge Collyer, see Raffaela Wakeman and Jane Chong, "A Recap of Friday's Oral Arguments in *Al-Aulaqi v. Panetta*," *Lawfare*, July 19, 2013, http://www.lawfareblog.com/2013/07/a-recap-of-fridays-oral-arguments-in-al-aulaqi-v-panetta/.

interest on the part of the federal courts in reviewing targeting judgments.

The fact that the courts have not involved themselves in targeting activities so far reflects the fact that the situations involved have been plausibly presented as part of an armed conflict abroad—the least likely case for a court to insert itself, either at the front end or the back. This creates a genuine oddity with respect to detention, where even foreigners held at Guantánamo are entitled to at least some form of habeas and judicial review. If one targets such combatants with lethal force instead of merely capturing them, however, the judicial posture is utterly different. It is entirely understandable that the ACLU and human rights groups would take the view that it is important to have at least the same level of judicial scrutiny on targeting people as would exist were the target captured instead of killed. Yet it seems unlikely that the judiciary will in the long run insert itself into targeting decisions made abroad, unless brought into the process by statute, though it may take a certain amount of lower-court tumult to establish this point firmly.

Similarly, Congress is playing in this area more or less the role it wants to play. The intelligence committees of both houses of Congress have been kept informed in detail on drone strikes. The Senate Intelligence Committee chair, Dianne Feinstein, has expressed her confidence in the drones program and has described the information she has received about it.[24]

---

24. See Dianne Feinstein's website, "Feinstein Statement on Intelligence Committee Oversight of Targeted Killings," news release, February 13, 2013, http://www.feinstein.senate.gov/public/index.cfm/press-releases ?ID=5b8dbe0c-07b6-4714-b663-b01c7c9b99b8. Feinstein said, "The committee has devoted significant time and attention to targeted killings by drones. The committee receives notifications with key details of each strike

Indeed, only relatively recently has the question of drone strikes really been live within Congress and even then less because of any actual drone strikes than because of the hypothetical possibility of a domestic strike against a US citizen. The killing of al-Awlaki raised few eyebrows in the legislature. While the congressional left wing and the Rand Paul wing of the Republican right in 2013 did raise the issue with new strength, it did not arise with the kind of strength necessary actually to legislate limits on the authority to use drones to kill foreign terrorists.

There is certainly room for more robust congressional oversight of this process. In an ideal world, we would see legislation reforming the intelligence oversight statutes to reflect a range of activities that are currently pushed into a "covert" or "not covert" binary. These activities probably ought to have a broader spectrum of different reporting and oversight requirements. The connections and interrelationships with the US military—Joint Special Operations Command (JSOC) particularly—and the reporting and oversight processes to the armed services committees ought to be reformed as well. As of this writing, some positive steps have been taken on this final matter. Rep. Mac Thornberry has introduced reasonably good legislation addressing the reporting of JSOC activities to the armed services

---

shortly after it occurs, and the committee holds regular briefings and hearings on these operations—reviewing the strikes, examining their effectiveness as a counterterrorism tool, verifying the care taken to avoid deaths to non-combatants and understanding the intelligence collection and analysis that underpins these operations. In addition, the committee staff has held thirty-five monthly, in-depth oversight meetings with government officials to review strike records (including video footage) and question every aspect of the program." Feinstein also complained about the lack of access to Office of Legal Counsel memoranda.

committees.[25] Congress has also become involved to try to force
the administration to release the Office of Legal Counsel (OLC)
memos that underlie drone strikes. This came up particularly
during the Brennan confirmation as director of the CIA and
during a judicial nomination fight in 2014.

But all of this operates at the level of oversight, reporting,
and articulating in domestic law the increasingly important
relationships between the military and JSOC, on the one hand,
and the CIA, on the other. What Congress has not tried to
do—and in our judgment should not try to do—is to codify in
statute the law of targeting. Congress cannot possibly intervene
usefully to define matters of targeting that rest upon interpretations of the international law of war. The law of war has to
remain as a specialized body of law, a source of professional
formation and identity for the professional military, defined
through its lawyers, the members of the Judge Advocate General's Corps, and their interactions with foreign counterparts
both in practice and in negotiations.

In short, the posture of both other branches of government
in this area is one of informed and self-conscious abstention.
If the courts and Congress have been marginalized in the law
of targeting, they have both been very willing partners in their
own marginalization.

There is one other area in which the executive branch has
insisted assiduously on its own primacy, and that is secrecy. The
Obama administration talks a good game about secrecy, but it
generally has been mostly talk in that realm. At least until the

25. See H.R. 1904, introduced May, 9, 2013, sponsored by Rep. Mac
Thornberry (R-Texas), referred to House Armed Services Committee. See
http://thornberry.house.gov/legislation/sponsoredlegislation.htm for text,
cosponsors, and progress

Snowden affair, it did very little actually to open up and certainly kept major disclosures as matters of its sole discretion.

The Snowden episode changed that somewhat in two ways. For one thing, it forced significant disclosures and declassifications by an administration that suddenly had to respond to an onslaught of allegations. More fundamentally, however, it also caused the administration to contemplate in a serious way submitting to legislation that would require a great deal more public disclosure of data and documents concerning FISA-related matters. Indeed, all major reform proposals, including those the administration backs, would require significant new disclosures. As of this writing, no such legislation has passed, but the mere fact of its contemplation with administration blessing marks something of a change.

It's also a notable exception to the more general rule, which is that the Obama administration—like virtually all administrations—wants to decide for itself, in the exercise of its own discretion, what material to make public. And it has shown no particular appetite for the courts or the Congress or the international community imposing new obligations of disclosure upon it.

Conclusion

The broad point here is that the framework the speeches elucidate is not narrowly the Obama administration's doctrine of the conflict—though the speeches often present themselves that way and certainly have been received that way by a great many commentators. In important respects, rather, they reflect a broader articulation of the state of American law vis-à-vis the conflict, an articulation that actually speaks for the other two branches of government as well and incorporates in important respects the viewpoints of allies and even critics of the framework. It thus, we believe, is likely to have strong legs—the legs of a great deal of policymaking, legislation, court decisions, and international negotiation. The framework will, of course, continue to evolve. But we suspect it will prove much more durable than those who blithely call for an "end of the conflict" may expect.

CHAPTER 5

The Framework and Its Discontents

Not everyone, needless to say, admires the framework laid out in the Obama administration's national security speeches. Indeed, the speeches themselves arose in the first place because not everyone admired the actions which they justified. The impetus to deliver them arose out of a perception that the administration's critics had successfully seized the moral high ground and that the administration was at risk of losing a war over public legitimacy for its core national security policies. Thus the speeches, as we have previously observed, at many points speak directly to the Obama administration's critics, as though in dialogue with them. This is true, in particularly striking fashion, of the president's own addresses, which often implicitly concede the voice of moral authenticity to the administration's human rights-oriented critics and plead with them for the regrettable necessity of the administration's actions.

Yet the administration's critics, for their part, have generally not granted absolution. To the contrary, they have—from a variety of different perspectives—critiqued the speeches' framework or else brushed it off with disdain, creating a kind of ongoing public relations war over the perception of lawfulness and legitimacy across a range of government counterterrorism activities.

In our view, however, the speeches and their framework actually hold up remarkably well against the administration's critics. The framework of law and legitimacy that the administration has laid out is not without its problems, some of which we have detailed. Taken as a whole, however, the legal, ethical, and policy framework is far more robust, as a matter of law, morality, and legitimacy, than the critics acknowledge. Moreover, in our view at least, it compares favorably with all of the alternatives the various strains of critics have proposed in its stead.

In the process of analyzing the speeches, we have at many points engaged the critics and summarized their objections. In this chapter, however, we give them their fuller due in the sense of summarizing their positive visions of what the framework ought to look like in place of the vision the US government presents. That is, what is the framework of national security law and policy the critics would have, instead of the speeches' framework, to address transnational terrorism and counterterrorism? A full treatment of this subject would require a book of its own, so we are necessarily dealing in summary here—a summary of several distinct, if overlapping, leading critical positions. We quite deliberately aim to present the forest, rather than the trees, for each of these viewpoints. And we readily grant that our brisk summaries of the complex legal and ethical positions outlined by administration critics risk some caricature, as well as some lumping together of views that may diverge in significant respects. Our goal is to present in broad outlines the affirmative frameworks that critics pose by way of considering what the alternatives to the speeches' framework look like alongside each other and alongside the administration's approach. It allows us to ask how they measure up.

Four principal strands of criticism have emerged during Barack Obama's two terms:

1. Domestic American Left-progressives—left, that is, of Obama—who believe the president has embraced too much of the war framework of his predecessor.
2. Members of the international community—international organizations and officials, sovereign states including US friends and allies, international nongovernmental organizations (NGOs) of many kinds, and international law academics—who dispute US interpretations of its international obligations and construe those obligations as precluding much of the war framework.
3. National security hawks—mostly conservatives in the Republican Party—who believe the administration is insufficiently committed to the war powers model of counterterrorism.
4. Libertarians—mostly on the political right and typified by Republican Senator Rand Paul—who are skeptical of surveillance, drone strikes, and detention authorities, at least when directed at US citizens.

We consider each in turn.

American Progressives to Obama's Left

A great many of the critiques of US government policy to which the speeches address themselves have been advanced by domestic American progressives: ordinary citizens, media commentators, politicians, law professors, and advocacy organizations. These voices represent the wing of the Democratic Party to the left of the president on national security issues. Their criticisms are legion and have been increasing in number and intensity as American Left-progressives gradually realize that what they believed President Obama would do in office has been very different from what he has, in fact, done. What's more, these groups occupy a particular psychological space for the Obama administration. They represent not just his political base but a voice of moral authenticity for Obama. Their criticisms clearly bother him more than do those from elsewhere on the political spectrum.[1] And the speeches consequently spend a great deal of time responding to suggestions from the Left of impropriety and illegality on the administration's part.

The gap between hopes and disappointed experience on the left has many complicated expressions and involves a certain cognitive dissonance. It runs the gamut from a belief that the president broke his promise to close the Guantánamo Bay detention facility to a widespread belief that, given congressional Republican intransigence on the subject, the failure is not truly Obama's fault—or, at least, is more a matter of insuf-

---

1. See, for example, Daniel Klaidman, *Kill or Capture: The War on Terror and the Soul of the Obama Presidency* (New York: Houghton Mifflin Harcourt, 2012), pp. 128–136, recounting a meeting between Obama and civil liberties advocates before the president's National Archives speech in Washington, D.C., on May 21, 2009.

ficient will and verve on Obama's part than willful wrong choices. It also involves the somewhat more active failure on the part of the American progressives themselves to have taken candidate Obama at his word as to how he would prosecute the war against Al Qaeda and associated forces, wherever—as he said several times during the 2008 campaign—they might go and with the technologies at America's disposal. It also has a lot to do with a genuine whiplash many progressives feel— and rightly so—at the contrast between the tone at times of Obama the candidate and the reality of the Obama administration's attitudes in office toward war powers. While the Obama campaign promised a more focused effort against Al Qaeda, it also talked a lot about law enforcement and it talked a great deal about ending wars. While Obama was actually always careful not to promise an end to noncriminal detention or an end to the conflict, the tone he set promised more than his specific words. And this created a genuine surprise when his approach to Al Qaeda and America's transnational non-state enemies turned out to involve a sword—and an ever-sharper and longer one at that—against the authors of 9/11 and those who would continue their work and affiliate themselves to those groups. Finally, Obama's critics on the Left have also been horrified by the surveillance revelations of 2013, which raise the specter for them of the bad old days of the intelligence scandals of the 1970s.

What with anger at the administration's not-minor— though also not-unusual—hypocrisies, an intense focus on the promises the president broke, and a refusal to listen coolly and dispassionately to the promises he kept, the Left has generated an emotional intensity that goes beyond simple disagreement, disappointment, or dismay. There is a palpable sense of betrayal.

And the resentment is exacerbated by having to choose between allowing that Obama's policies must still be counted as preferable to any plausible Republican alternative and the less-resigned belief that Obama's adoption of the positions of his predecessors has permanently and institutionally shifted the mean of legitimate actions by presidents—that Obama, to put it differently, has given up any meaningful moral or legal distinction between the parties on national security matters. These critics, most prominently Glenn Greenwald, decry the unwillingness of other liberals to call Obama on his positions almost as loudly as they decry the positions themselves.[2]

Though there are many strains of the Left's dissent from Obama's framework, there are some common threads to the alternative framework of law and policy on these issues for American progressives. We can identify the basic propositions of that alternative, the institutional pillars of the positive Left framework, straightforwardly enough, as they have all come up before. To be sure, not every commentator subscribes to every one of these propositions; indeed, probably relatively few do. But some combination of them forms the intellectual core of nearly all strains of the Left's critique of the speeches' framework:

1. The legal paradigms for the use of force beyond US borders involve a binary choice between armed conflict governed by the laws of war (interpreted so as to incorporate a large, though vague, dollop of human

2. See, for example, Glenn Greenwald, "Repulsive Progressive Hypocrisy," *Salon*, February 8, 2012, http://www.salon.com/2012/02/08/repulsive_progressive_hypocrisy.

rights law obligations) and operations governed directly under human rights law through domestic law enforcement authorities.

2. It is not legally possible for a state to be in an armed conflict with a transnational non-state actor; and, in any case, there cannot be a *global* armed conflict against a non-state actor. Even assuming for purposes of argument that there could be an armed conflict against Al Qaeda, there are still grave problems with the law, legitimacy, and policy of that putative war. Consequently, the Authorization for Use of Military Force (AUMF) does not authorize the conflict as the administration is prosecuting it. Nor, under international law, could it: that conflict is not lawful.

3. An armed conflict must have a delimited geography. Cross-border counterterrorism activities outside of recognized conventional conflict zones, moreover, have to take place under international human rights law. Human rights law, meanwhile, does not allow for status-based targeting, and it likewise does not allow first resort to lethal force. It thus legally requires a preference for capturing, rather than killing, the target and permits the use of deadly force only to address a truly "imminent" threat. Imminence is defined far more temporally than in the administration's conception of it. And human rights law does not have a legal category, either, for armed conflict's "lawfully anticipated collateral damage."

4. Even if the law-of-armed-conflict standards were to apply, their proper understanding would disallow targeting on the basis of "membership" in an enemy

organization alone and would instead require that the person pose an imminent threat to Americans or American territory. Moreover, it would follow the interpretive guidance of the International Committee of the Red Cross (ICRC) on the meaning of direct participation in hostilities, including its requirement of a "continuous combat function" for targeting a civilian who takes part in hostilities when he or she is not actually taking part.

5. The scope of national self-defense, outside of an existing armed conflict, against a transnational non-state terrorist group requires an imminent threat, where imminence is measured by the literal words of the *Caroline* doctrine.[3] Moreover, it is temporally limited to the threat posed by the particular plot by particular individuals at that time; it does not extend to the group at large or to the members behind the plot. That is to say that there is no notion of an "ongoing" or "active" imminent threat persisting over time by virtue of a terrorist group, membership, or network against which

---

3. The *Caroline* doctrine is the classic nineteenth-century formulation of the imminent threat that permits an immediate forcible response by one state on the territory of another. In the words of then-US Secretary of State Daniel Webster to the British ambassador to the United States, such an incursion was permissible in self-defense only where the threat was "instant, overwhelming, leaving no choice of means, and no moment of deliberation." See Daniel Webster, Letter to Henry Stephen Fox, in K.E. Shewmaker, ed., *The Papers of Daniel Webster: Diplomatic Papers, vol. 1, 1841-1843* (Hanover, NH: Dartmouth College Press, 1983), p. 62. Although oft-quoted as the customary international rule, in practice the United States and other states do not take those words literally as the legal standard defining an imminent threat.

the United States could act at a time of its choosing.

6. Drone strikes on the territories of other countries violate the sovereignty of those countries and public statements by those countries denying consent to US operations must be taken at face value. In accordance with the United Nations Charter, the proper forum in which to deal with states in which non-state terrorist groups have taken safe haven is the Security Council. Alternatively, the aggrieved state can act through bilateral mechanisms to strengthen the safe-haven state's ability to deal with the problem. The rule claimed by the US government—consent when possible but the "unable or unwilling" test when not—is not found in the UN Charter, whose literal words permit resort to force by a state only in case of an armed attack upon its territory. In any case, however, international human rights standards must apply to any action taken, even with the consent of the affected state, because state consent cannot waive the human rights of individuals harmed by any attack.

7. It follows from the absence of an armed conflict outside of Afghanistan that law-of-war detention pending the end of hostilities is not a lawful option. Consequently, the applicable standard for any detainee is to charge him in a civilian court or to let him go.

8. Outside of a conventional armed conflict, an American citizen cannot be targeted by the executive without robust prospective judicial review. US citizens enjoy their core constitutional rights against US government action abroad and judicial review must be available to vindicate those rights even when the executive branch

has determined that the individual is a senior operational leader who poses an ongoing threat and whose capture is not feasible.

9. A targeted killing program outside of a conventional armed conflict in a defined geographic area is unlawful *per se*, and more so in the absence of judicial review and other safeguards of due process for US citizens and even for non-US persons. Reliance upon internal executive branch procedures instead—yielding "kill lists," using intelligence-driven targeting recommendations—is legally insufficient and immoral.

10. Assuming that the armed conflict model against Al Qaeda and associated forces is accepted as the legal paradigm, or simply recognizing that the administration lawlessly invokes it as the model, it is time to repeal or sharply curtail the AUMF underlying the armed conflict or to declare the end of hostilities—thereby ending whatever authority the AUMF may grant. In its stead, the administration should adopt means of cross-border counterterrorism that fit with the human rights and law enforcement model backed up with a highly limited vision of self-defense to respond to truly imminent threats as in ordinary peacetime.

11. The National Security Agency (NSA) big data surveillance programs are illegal under US law, violating the Fourth Amendment properly understood and exceeding the authority Congress granted the administration under the Foreign Intelligence Surveillance Act. Privacy, moreover, is not merely a right protected in domestic law but an international legal obligation that has extraterritorial effect and thus limits the authority

of the United States to spy against even foreigners overseas. NSA programs must therefore be radically restructured both to tighten the data the NSA can collect, whether on Americans or anyone else, and to limit use of this data. The administration and Congress also need to radically enhance mechanisms of oversight and disclosure to permit far more public knowledge and to replace secret intelligence community processes with court hearings.

12. More generally, transparency, accountability, and oversight in intelligence work all require deep reform—as does government secrecy. This reform should push pervasively in the direction of government revealing publicly the rationales, policies, and criteria that lie behind operations and revealing operational details to a far greater extent than any rules or laws now require.

13. Given the current weaknesses of oversight and the lack of such accountability mechanisms, the theft of US government secrets by self-appointed whistleblowers and the revelation of those secrets through the media—including foreign media—merit praise, not prosecution or punishment.

14. Both the American public and administration officials wildly overestimate the risks of terrorism and its harms. The fixation on 9/11 has spawned government structures that have strong institutional incentives to drive risk estimates upward and to perpetuate themselves and their funding streams. Simple cost-benefit analysis suggests that Americans are in, if not precisely a moral panic any longer, the long inertial tail of a moral panic. The result is a wasteful commitment of

resources and energy that starves other social priorities of resources. Moreover, on account of blowback and global resentments created by the US government's secret war model, the approach to counterterrorism and American security is not just hugely wasteful, but also counterproductive to US interests and actively threatening to US and foreign liberties. In its strongest form, this thesis sees terrorism as a lesser threat than the aggregated US responses to terrorism.

15. At the most fundamental level of political morality, the United States cannot be in a permanent state of war and retain its open, democratic character.

Let us start by acknowledging that this critique is not simply knee-jerk opposition or a litany of complaints, however much it is framed that way in the public debate. It is, rather, a robust alternative vision of what US national security policy and counterterrorism could look like. Moreover, there are many points of overlap between it and the Obama administration speeches. These overlaps concern not just issues like Guantánamo, where the administration says many things that sound like the Left's agenda, albeit with complex countervailing currents and without the demonstrated political will to effectuate what therefore amount to hortatory statements.

The Left's framework shares with Obama's, in particular, a view about the necessity of an endgame—a way in which to draw the conflict to a close, or at least a way that can be understood to have drawn it to a close. Although many would see the remarks by then-Pentagon General Counsel Jeh Johnson on the end of the conflict (Oxford University, November 30,

2012) and President Obama's National Defense University (NDU) speech on May 23, 2013 as merely soothing, meaningless words for an important constituency, we think they express a deep desire on the part of the government and the American people for a way to reach a resolution. War *should* be a state of exception, the administration and its critics on the left agree: permanent war undermines open societies, the American experience of war is that they do end, and this war ought to be no different—even accepting it as a war. But Obama and his critics on the left also agree that this war *is* somehow different. For that reason, we have an obligation to think through what the end looks like and the legal regimes governing uses of force and many other things into the future. After the war, what will (or ought to) have changed in both practical and legal terms as to how the US government uses force, keeps detainees, and acts in relation to nearly every issue taken up in this book?[4]

The American liberal framework could conceivably work to keep the United States safe using a much heavier reliance on traditional law enforcement and a much lesser reliance on military force, intelligence operations, and espionage. It is a particularly plausible vision if one adopts a sufficiently relaxed idea of what sort and how many successful attacks the United States might be willing to absorb in exchange for restraint in

---

4. See Mary L. Dudziak, *War Time: An Idea, Its History, Its Consequences* (New York: Oxford University Press, 2012). For three distinct critical appraisals of *War Time* and the question of the end of the war that began in 2001, see Kenneth Anderson, "Time Out of Joint," *Texas Law Review* 91, no. 859 (2013), http://papers.ssrn.com/sol3/papers.cfm?abstract_id=2242245; Samuel Moyn, "Book Review," *Lawfare* (blog), May 24, 2012, http://www.lawfareblog.com/2012/05/war-time-an-idea-its-history-its-consequences/; and Eric Posner, "The Longest Battle," *New Republic*, February 6, 2012, http://www.newrepublic.com/book/review/mary-dudziak-war-time.

the exercise of muscular governmental powers. But it surely bears consideration that the Obama administration has never been able to embrace the framework of its liberal critics, except in certain vague terms that amount to statements of aspiration and values affinity. Guantánamo must close, the administration agrees—yet it remains open. This war, like all wars, must end, it agrees—even as it prosecutes the war further. Surveillance authorities threaten privacy, the president acknowledges—yet he does not broadly renounce them.

There is a reason (several interrelated reasons, really) why the administration has not taken—and feels it cannot take—the plunge. The first is the problem of ungoverned spaces. Law enforcement authorities are at their most potent where sovereign power is at its zenith. Where the FBI can show up at people's doors and wield their very considerable coercive powers, where the power to arrest exists unmediated by foreign law enforcement, where the courts are sitting and competent, and where prisons don't have revolving doors, there is no need for the tools of warfare. But renouncing those tools when large swaths of territory lack any sort of governance and when those territories form safe havens for groups that are actively plotting against the United States leaves gaps that policymakers with actual responsibility for security have tended to find unacceptable. And nobody has really figured out how to reach terrorists camped out in the Pakistani tribal areas, in Somalia, and in Yemen without the tools of warfare.

Moreover, as we have already seen, the presence or absence of a war is not simply a definitional matter which one side determines by diktat. The other side gets at least something of a vote. And events sometimes have a way of not cooperating with one side's desires to reach an end. The administration, for its part, has discovered over the past few years that bringing this conflict to an end is much harder, messier, shifting, and uncertain than things might seem to liberal critics. This is particularly true while troops are on the ground in Afghanistan. But the problem never quite goes away. It is never quite the right moment to give up the authority of the AUMF—and that reality might persist for some time to come. When exactly is the right time to lock yourself as a matter of law into the highly restrictive targeting rules of peacetime? And when exactly is the right time to obligate yourself to free Abu Zubaydah and Hambali (Riduan Isamuddin) and the other high-value detainees against whom criminal charges have not materialized?

The unrealism of the Left's critique persists for policymakers when considering the rules within armed conflict: the factual determinations of whether parties are covered by the AUMF or not, the determinations of who is an associated force and who is not, and the genuine feasibility of the standards. These are questions the administration's critics can afford to regard with great doctrinal strictness. For those responsible for actual operators, those who have to consider matters of force protection and military effectiveness, however, a set of rules that amounts to a list of "noes" has limited appeal. In the antiseptic environments of law schools, media organizations, and advocacy groups, these considerations can get short shrift. But they are not considerations that any administration can or will ignore over the long term.

Finally, intelligence creates a paradox for the administration's capacity to embrace its critics on the left. The essence of the Left's critique is that the administration should be more sparing in its use of force and be disciplined by tighter rules. To do this—the capture operation instead of the kill operation, for example, or the exceptionally close law enforcement partnerships that make overseas counterterrorism in the absence of military force at all possible in the first place—requires exquisitely good intelligence. Yet the Left's critics are as hostile to intelligence authorities as they are to kinetic military authorities or detention powers. The result is that the Left's critique—taken seriously across all of its numerous axes—leaves the administration no real area of permission beyond the most traditional of law enforcement approaches. The Obama administration swears by law enforcement. But at the end of the day the executive branch has been emphatic over more than twelve years now that it needs, and has lawfully available to it, tools beyond conventional law enforcement to address, as the president said, not just individuals and particular terror plots, but the groups and networks of groups that plan and launch these attacks. The Left's critique resists all of the major additional toolboxes with which our forces reach those groups hidden in places where the writ of US law does not run, yet the threat from such groups remains.

In this regard the Left plants its head firmly in the sand as to the conditions of effective control over territory that the rule of law requires in order to permit domestic law enforcement in a criminal law framework. The paradigm of law enforcement requires, in the first place, effective dominion over a sovereign territory. Where that does not exist (and it does not exist, as the president pointed out in his NDU speech, in remote mountains of Yemen and other hiding places for those who would do America grave harm), then the law enforcement paradigm has insufficient purchase for America's needs.

The International Community

The international community in this context refers to international organizations and their officials; sovereign states, including American friends and allies; human rights advocacy organizations; global media organizations and their leading journalists; and individuals in academic international law or similar fields who wield influence through their expertise. It's a loose, undemanding definition, not a strict academic one. And as a general matter, the community's activities in this space function as an additional fillip for the Left's critique. The practical realities of international politics are, after all, that the international community for these purposes is essentially a progressive-Left agglomeration. While there are many international community actors who do not fit any precise description of the "progressive Left," they don't matter much for present purposes. The preponderant, even overwhelming, effect of the international community's activities in this space is to act as a force multiplier for the Left's critique of the framework the speeches lay out.

This is because in most—nearly all—ways, much of the international community embraces the propositions offered above in the American progressive framework. Speaking loosely, international elites—or at least those of them that carry moral weight with Americans, rather than America's enemies—tend to embrace politically progressive values in roughly the American sense. And the American Left-progressive community, for its part, embraces not just progressive values in a domestic sense but liberal internationalism, as well—which is defined by Stanford University scholar Francis Fukuyama as the belief that international organizations and universal law can finally overcome the anarchy and injustice of an international order of equal, jostling, competing, warring sovereign states.[5] This convergence has been under way for a long time, so it is no surprise that the international community would join in nearly all of the above features of the America liberal framework.

There's another reason for the convergence: a big part of the American progressive critique is predicated on supposed US noncompliance with international law as defined by international organizations, both public ones such as UN human rights offices and private ones such as prominent international NGOs. Just as the international community broadly finds American liberal internationalism more congenial than American exceptionalism and hegemony, the American Left tends to take at face value pronouncements by, say, the ICRC, Human Rights Watch, and Amnesty International about what constitutes lawful targeting or when an armed conflict exists. The Left also tends to be the only movement in American politics that regards with any sort of seriousness the moral authority of United Nations bodies and special rapporteurs.

The differences, therefore, between the domestic progressive critique and the international community's critique are largely matters of nuance and emphasis. But they do matter. Among the most important are the following:

1. The international community is deeply concerned with the violations of sovereignty that it perceives as arising under the "unable or unwilling" doctrine. As a matter

---

5. Francis Fukuyama, *After the Neocons: America at the Crossroads* (New Haven, CT: Yale University Press, 2006), p. 7. Liberal internationalists, Fukuyama writes, "hope to transcend power politics altogether and move to an international order based on law and institutions."

of state practice, even in the UN Charter era, states have long embraced something like this test when it comes to international terrorism or insurgent movements that threaten them; the reason is simply that states believe they cannot tolerate insurgent or terrorist actors having safe havens. This history, however, does not stop the community, especially its international organizations and officialdom, from roundly condemning the United States in this regard.

2. The international community is also deeply concerned that drone warfare and targeted killing abet violations of sovereignty using technologies difficult or impossible to attribute. Small-scale attacks using drones are seen by many commentators as rendering the triggers and boundaries between war and peace more difficult to maintain. The international community—and particularly international organizations and their officials, academics, media, and NGOs—believes strongly that America's reliance on technology such as drones makes it too easy for the United States to use force because its forces are protected from risk. This concern (which one hears somewhat less, interestingly, from leading sovereign states) goes hand in hand with the belief that protection of American forces means greater risk to civilians. That this belief is very likely incorrect as a factual matter does not diminish its currency. It motivates a great deal of animus against the United States and is attached, for many, to a still further belief— rooted in some residue of the chivalric traditions of warfare—that there is something unsporting and dishonorable about not facing adversaries directly and

exposing oneself to risk in the course of attack. This alleged moral deficit of reliance upon armed drones, among other concerns, has led to debates in European national parliaments and in the European Parliament itself over resolutions condemning armed drones, among many other features of US counterterrorism policy.[6]

3. The American progressive community mostly distinguishes between constitutional protections for American citizens, even abroad, and international human rights obligations for everyone—and by and large is not disturbed by a higher constitutional standard protecting US citizens above the human rights baseline. For understandable reasons, however, many in the international community are not all that concerned with American domestic law, even its constitutional law. And many in the international community work off the presumption that states owe some measure of protection to everyone. This attitude has emerged with special fervor in the current debate over surveillance and a supposed international human right to privacy derived chiefly from language in the International Convention on Civil and Political Rights (ICCPR).

---

6. See, for example, David Keating, "MEPs concerned about EU drone programme," *European Voice*, February 27, 2014, http://www.european voice.com/article/2014/february/meps-concerned-about-eu-drone -programme/79878.aspx. On Germany's ongoing parliamentary debates over armed drones, see, for example, Judy Dempsey, "Germans Play for Time In the Debate on Drones," *New York Times*, July 22, 2013, http://www.nytimes .com/2013/07/23/world/europe/23iht-letter23.html?_r=0.

American advocacy organizations mostly want to ensure that Americans are not spied on. The international community wants privacy protections from American surveillance not just for Americans but for everyone. A similar dispute arose in the targeting context, where the heightened scrutiny the United States used in the Anwar al-Awlaki case rubbed many in the international community the wrong way. Why the additional process just for someone who happened to hold US citizenship, people wondered.

4. The international community is concerned to a higher degree, in our estimation, than is the American progressive community about the CIA's participation in the use of force. American progressives do not like it, but they do not talk about it all that much either. By contrast, it comes up frequently in, for example, reports by UN special rapporteurs. The then-UN special rapporteur for extrajudicial, summary, or arbitrary executions, Philip Alston, criticized CIA conduct of drone strikes on carefully hedged grounds in his final 2010 report on drone warfare to the United Nations, limiting his criticism to a presumed lack of transparency and accountability when strikes are conducted by the CIA rather than the US military.[7] Others have criticized CIA participation on far harsher grounds,

---

7. See Philip Alston, Report of the Special Rapporteur on extrajudicial, summary, or arbitrary executions, United Nations Human Rights Council, May 28, 2010, Addendum Study on Targeted Killings, A/HRC/14/24/Add.6, paras. 70-73, http://www2.ohchr.org/english/bodies/hrcouncil/docs/14session/A.HRC.14.24.Add6.pdf.

including that, as civilians, CIA personnel are unlawful combatants and their lethal drone strikes are war crimes.[8] The current UN special rapporteur for counterterrorism and human rights, Ben Emmerson, made an unusual intervention in 2013 into US domestic politics by effectively endorsing John Brennan for the CIA director post. Among other reasons, Emmerson indicated that while Brennan had been largely responsible for the shape of the drones program in the first Obama term, Emmerson believed Brennan at the CIA would bring the CIA under greater control.[9] Human Rights Watch and other human rights organizations

8. See, for example, Mary Ellen O'Connell, "Unlawful Killing with Combat Drones: A Case Study of Pakistan, 2004-2009," Notre Dame Legal Studies Paper, No. 09-43, 2009, https://webspace.utexas.edu/rmc2289/LT/Mary%20Ellen%20OConnell%20on%20Drones.pdf. "Members of the CIA are not lawful combatants and their participation in killing persons—even in an armed conflict—is a crime," O'Connell writes in the paper's abstract. On page 26 she adds: "The CIA operatives involved are not lawful combatants with the combatant's privilege to kill during an armed conflict." See also Benjamin Wittes, "Debate with Mary Ellen O'Connell on Targeted Killings and Drones," *Lawfare*, October 25, 2010, video of live event at International Law Weekend 2010 in which he and O'Connell debate the subject, http://www.lawfareblog.com/2010/10/wittes-v-oconnell-on-targeted-killing-and-drones/.

9. Spencer Ackerman, "UN's Top Drone Investigator Backs Brennan for Top CIA Job," *Wired*, February 7, 2013, http://www.wired.com/2013/02/un-drone-brennan/all/. "By putting Brennan in direct control of the CIA's policy [of targeted killings], the president has placed this mediating legal presence in direct control of the positions that the CIA will adopt and advance, so as to bring the CIA much more closely under direct presidential and democratic control," Emmerson said. "It's right to view this as a recognition of the repository of trust that Obama places in Brennan to put him in control of the organization that poses the greatest threat to international legal consensus and recognition of the lawfulness of the drone program."

have made many similar demands that the agency get out of the drone strikes business.[10]

5. The international community puts a particular emphasis on the notion that the mechanisms by which the international community defines law ought to bind, or nearly bind, the United States. The self-interest involved in this shoe-horning of the international community into American domestic political decision-making is obvious enough and nothing new. But it has taken on special importance today with the campaign arguing for the extraterritorial application of the main human rights treaty, the ICCPR. Acceptance by the United States of the extraterritorial application of the ICCPR has long been a goal of many in the international community. The extraterritoriality issue took on particular currency in 2014 both because of the ICCPR's references to privacy—which could function as a lever to limit US surveillance overseas—and because of the leaks of Harold Koh's 2010 memo, while he was still legal adviser at the State Department, arguing for a change in the US position.[11] The issue is important because acceptance of extraterritorial application of the ICCPR would go a long way toward cementing the

---

10. See, for example, Human Rights Watch, "US: Move Drone Strike Program to Military," March 21, 2013, http://www.hrw.org/news/2013/03/21/us-move-drone-strike-program-military.

11. The text of the memo was made public by the *New York Times* on March 6, 2014, http://www.nytimes.com/interactive/2014/03/07/world/state-department-iccpr.html. The memo is entitled "Memorandum Opinion on the Geographic Scope of the International Covenant on Civil and Political Rights" and is dated October 19, 2010.

binary choice of either armed conflict or human rights law. It is possible, with it as reigning law, that the US government's lawyers could still reach the same conclusions as they reach today with respect to the bottom line on questions like targeting certain terrorists with lethal force, detention authority, surveillance, and privacy. But the lift would be a great deal heavier—and that's precisely the point.

6. America's close friends and allies—NATO allies, of course, but also important (and increasingly unsettled) friends in the Pacific—raise a particular concern within the international community: that the US framework impedes cooperation among allies. The gap between the rules of war as interpreted by the United States and the legal frameworks embraced by other countries requires bridging. In the theaters of more conventional conflict, such as Afghanistan, allied forces over the years have worked out with the United States a number of protocols for how to deal with differences in legal rules. Some of America's allies, for example, were prohibited from some activity by weapons conventions to which they are party but the United States is not. Others might operate under different targeting rules with regards to civilian direct participation in hostilities and with regard to who is or is not a lawful target. In Afghanistan, as in Iraq, allied forces worked out ways of dealing with each other on these issues. But in the case of the broader conflict with Al Qaeda, which the United States sees as armed conflict but its allies generally do not, serious questions arise as to the ability of allies to assist the United States with intel-

ligence collection that leads to targeting decisions. Americans fly the drones and fire the missiles but, in many important situations, the intelligence comes partly from allied sources. Similar issues arise regarding detention, trials, and many other issues. So far, most of the important problems of differing rules have been worked out. But there have been cases in which different allied government officials have struggled over whether and to what extent they can find a basis for acting in coordination with the Americans. The greater the gap between US views of law and policy and those of its allies, the worse this problem will be.

So what are we to make of this as a framework? To a great extent, it suffers from the same disabilities and unrealisms as does the American progressive framework. But it also has problems of its own.

First, there is a ships-passing-in-the-night quality to how the international community conceives of international law and how the United States government does. The international community regards international law as though it were some neutral, universal, and objective set of rules—the authoritative enunciation, interpretation, and declaration of which lie in the hands of this international community. But it also sees international law as a malleable dough, in its own hands anyway, for reaching seemingly whatever conclusions it likes, particularly in areas of human rights and with respect to how the United States conducts hostilities under the laws of armed conflict.

Consider, for example, the sudden enunciation of a human right to privacy—that is, a right not to be the target of cross-border surveillance by intelligence agencies or at least to have one's interests factored into surveillance targeting decisions. A human right? Until a handful of NGOs and sympathetic states and academics discovered this new human right in the ICCPR and other instruments in the wake of the Edward Snowden revelations, no one who is regarded as serious appears to have thought of privacy in the language of international law—as distinct from the particular conceptions of particular political communities in their own constitutional arrangements and laws.

The presumption of the international community's framework of international law is that the US government does not care about international law. And it is certainly true that the United States does not embrace a vision of formally binding law that is rapidly changeable by the international community itself. In reality, however, the US government cares deeply about international law. But it understands it, and has always understood it, to be a fused enterprise of formal law, diplomacy, politics, and, above all, activity in the hands of sovereign states—a body of law found centrally in the actual practices of states and in the practices to which they have assented as law.

If that's the case, then the international community's framework is one that has trouble really engaging with the US government—even with the Obama administration, which is arguably more sympathetic to liberal internationalism than any US administration since the founding of the United Nations. When it comes to issues of fundamental national security, to war and armed conflict, and to interpretations of international law regulating those activities, not even the Obama administration is willing to abandon the traditional US government view of international law as law rooted in practice and understood pragmatically and prudentially.

The international community's invocation of international law is fundamentally political, a use of the rhetorical tools of law to constrain American resort to force, both in self-defense and in armed conflict. As such, it is perfectly understandable that American administrations of all stripes would not ultimately embrace the framework; their fundamental concern, after all, is to avoid limiting American flexibility in responding to the ongoing and emergent threats that they are responsible for repelling. These essential approaches cannot be reconciled, because the most basic aims of the United States and its international interlocutors clash.

Yet it also bears noting that America's allies are not political monoliths—just as the United States government is less a unitary executive than it is a jumble of voices. The views expressed in parliaments and international organizations are often very different from the cooperation that exists at the levels of military and intelligence agencies and interior ministries. The debates over armed drones inside some of America's NATO allies is a case in point; the debates in parliament are one conversation, but the discussions among the ministries of defense quite another. Particularly as the Ukraine crisis deepened in 2014, issues of national and European security seemed much more pressing to many American allies than did NSA surveillance matters that convulsed Europe only months earlier. Moreover, countries that actually fight wars on the ground (particularly when they express their views in non-public forums) often have far more textured understandings of the problems the United States faces than do those that free-ride most aggressively under the American security umbrella. So the apparently unified view of the international community against the speeches' framework is at least a little less unified than it sometimes appears.

Finally, the fundamental narrative running beneath the surface of the international community's framework has a deep moral problem. That narrative essentially starts with the idea of the United States as having every advantage—most importantly, the ability to use technology to dominate its adversaries and the ability to do so from a remote distance in which its forces are not at substantial risk. The United States, in this view, has leveraged its technological advantages to the extent that it is no longer constrained by the political costs of casualties among its own forces in using force. And international law therefore somehow needs to restore equilibrium, either by constraining the use of precision technologies, for example, or by imposing ever-greater legal burdens on any civilian death or injury. The community is thus far more concerned with minor US errors than with the grossest abuses of terrorist adversaries. This focus ignores the biggest drivers in the American shift toward capabilities for conducting operations from a remote distance and precision: that those adversaries see civilians as materiel for human shields. And, indeed, there is little impulse among the international community to make the adversary groups pay any price for these serious violations of law. On the contrary, at many turns, the positions of the international community, as it seeks to evolve the laws of war, make it easier for these forces to hide themselves among civilians or to get treated themselves as non-targetable civilians. The international community, indeed, tells the United States that its legal obligation is to find better and better ways to take precautions in attacks to spare the civilians.

The United States pushes itself using technology, training, law, and rules, and it achieves historic advances in the protection of civilians. And for this humanitarian service it is told by the international community that this apparently good thing is actually a bad thing—because its technologies make it too easy to use force to strike its adversaries.

The international community cannot forever have a framework that wants it both ways. And the Obama administration, in its speeches, is far from wrong in refusing to cede the legal or moral high ground to a framework based around a view of international law, what it is and how it is practiced, that neither it nor the administrations that have preceded it since the Second World War have ever embraced.

Libertarians on the Republican Right

The libertarian strain of criticism of the framework the administration has laid out is a relatively recent development. The people who articulate it are led by Senator Rand Paul (R-KY); the libertarian critique has emerged as one strand of a larger Tea Party opposition to government power. They come from a very different political space from the American progressive movement, but they reach similar conclusions, at least about a limited list of matters. That list consists of actions that the critics believe on constitutional grounds cannot be taken against American citizens anywhere in the world. Although there are signs that parts of the libertarian movement are gradually extending their notion of libertarian protection beyond American citizens to others as well, the libertarian movement in the Republican Party today is rooted in a view of the Constitution, not a view about universal human rights and international law—about which many on the libertarian Right have

244 SPEAKING THE LAW

traditionally been skeptical. Traditionally, libertarians have not been eager to acknowledge the power of a bunch of international bureaucrats to order Americans around.

So while right-wing civil libertarians might support the particular human right at issue, they tend not to find it in any framework rooted in international institutions or law. They find it, instead, in a purportedly originalist understanding of the Constitution—a reading that often ignores a great deal of case law. The consequence of this Constitution-based view of political values and their protection is that, with some exceptions, the libertarian concern with the speeches' framework deals almost exclusively with American citizens. To the extent the concern goes beyond that, it is usually because of a concurrent strain of non-interventionism and isolationism in the libertarian Right—not because of serious legal concerns about the rules of targeting, detention, or surveillance under international law.

In that light, Paul's filibuster in 2013 and his speechifying about drone strikes dealt narrowly with blowing up American citizens with drones—as did the remarks by Senator Ted Cruz (R-TX) about an American getting blown up in a café in the United States by a drone. Similarly, the conservative anxiety about NSA surveillance has been almost entirely a concern about collection of data on US persons, not—as with the comparable liberal anxiety—a concern about global privacy rights. When it comes to terrorists, in the view of the libertarian Right, if they are Americans, they are entitled to due process by means of judicial review—even if the facts are as damning as they were in al-Awlaki 's case and even if the practical ability of US forces to capture them is zero. In this view, intelligence collection against US citizens should proceed only under judicial warrants, notwithstanding long-standing Supreme

Court doctrine concerning the non-applicability of the Fourth Amendment to situations in which individuals voluntarily give data to third parties and the government collects that data from the third parties.[12]

This is a framework that's remarkably long on simple principles and remarkably short on context, statute, case law, or facts. After all, nobody conducts drone strikes on US soil, the entire predicate for the Paul filibuster. The libertarians offer a framework for national security counterterrorism that, more than any other framework considered here, carries no burden of actual governance and no obligation to actually confront the problems of protecting the people of the United States from those individuals, including the occasional American citizen, who come within a hair's breadth of blowing up airliners filled with other American citizens.

Notably, the libertarians do not tend to talk much about detention or military commissions. Since those held at Guantánamo are not American citizens, they tend not to excite the libertarian passion the way they do the Left's. So while some of the libertarians have offered criticism of US detention policy on a view that the Constitution requires that any person held by the US government be charged with a crime or freed, this basket of issues has never moved to the top of the libertarian constitutional list.

The emergence of leaks and stolen government documents on surveillance and the NSA, however, came exactly as libertarian conservatism was finding its stride politically. Unlike drone strikes—which inconveniently did not take place domestically and had affected few enough citizens to count on the

---

12. See, for example, *Smith v. Maryland*, 442 U.S. 735 (1979).

fingers of one hand—the Snowden documents at least theoretically affected all Americans who use telephones and computers. Privacy and Big Brother, spying on Americans—the libertarian movement has found a potent issue with these. And as with the Left, in Snowden it seems to have found a hero—at least to judge by the recent spate of teleconferences in which Snowden is a star performer and his unambiguous crimes treated as righteous acts of necessary civil disobedience to an illegitimate and unjust order.

So it is that right-wing libertarianism in the Republican Party manages to find common ground with the Democratic Party's libertarians in the technology world and Silicon Valley. The result is a ringing call that manages to sound in both political parties for privacy and for anti-surveillance protections rooted in a vision of the Constitution. It's a Constitution whose only value is maximizing individual liberty, which is to say a suicide pact. But it has become an undeniably potent political force.

To give it its due, the American trait of stubborn anti-government fervor (and the ferment that this strain of politics represents) is a good and salutary thing, at least over the long arc of history. There are good reasons to start from a presumption of liberty, rather than security or something else, so that strong government actions require some genuinely compelling necessity. That said, this is not a framework for governance—or anything close to it—and it barely even pretends to be one. It is a political mood, a statement of credo and commitment to small government and skepticism about national power. It's a powerful thing, but it actually does not present much in the way of an alternative—except in political and rhetorical terms—to the administration's framework.

Conservative National Security Hawks

The last critical framework we consider here is that of the conservative national security hawks. These are people deeply concerned about national security issues and deeply committed to ensuring that measures they would regard as necessary to the national defense and national security are not shunted aside by an administration too concerned to please well-intentioned, but ultimately foolish, civil libertarians. They are deeply committed both to the severity of the security threat and to the primacy of military and wartime tools in addressing this threat. They are deeply suspicious of the administration's rhetorical retreat from the war paradigm and its insistence on the value of law enforcement tools. Some of the most prominent of these conservative national security hawks are former Bush administration officials—former Office of Legal Counsel lawyer John Yoo, for example, and former Attorney General Michael Mukasey—and their platform has been, most notably, the Op-Ed page of the *Wall Street Journal*. This camp also includes a coalition of senators led by John McCain (R-AZ) and Lindsey Graham (R-SC). And it has often included former Vice President Dick Cheney, who has publicly lambasted the Obama administration for its retreats from Bush administration policies.

The positive framework proposed by the conservative national security hawks is simple: that the proper conception of the conflict with Al Qaeda and its associated forces is that of war, plain old armed conflict. They insist that US government policy must embrace the full implications of that condition or risk serious negative consequences. To these critics, the hybrid nature of the speeches' framework is a weak-kneed heresy from the true armed conflict model.

This premise actually leads in some peculiar directions. One might imagine that national security hawks would take comfort from the Obama administration's ramping up of drone warfare and its refinement as technology has evolved and intelligence-gathering has improved in key places. But many of them have not, both because they see deep hypocrisy in the drone war and because they believe that it is, as much as anything, a means of avoiding the hard tasks of war. So to take a leading example, Yoo has written in the *Wall Street Journal* and elsewhere that the Obama administration has embraced drone warfare because it refused to consider detaining the people it instead targets. "Ironies abound," Yoo wrote in 2012. Candidate Obama,

> campaigned on narrowing presidential wartime power, closing Guantánamo Bay, trying terrorists in civilian courts, ending enhanced interrogation, and moving away from a wartime approach to terrorism toward a criminal-justice approach. Mr. Obama has avoided these vexing detention issues simply by depriving terrorists of all of their rights—by killing them.[13]

In part, this is an accusation of hypocrisy: a claim that the self-righteous Obama administration has seized the moral high ground by incessantly harping on the wickedness of the Bush administration while taking Bush administration policies a step further and killing people, rather than merely detaining them. All this, moreover, merely to avoid the adverse publicity associ-

---

13. John Yoo, "Obama, Drones, and Thomas Aquinas," *Wall Street Journal*, June 7, 2012, http://online.wsj.com/news/articles/SB10001424052702303665904577452271794312802.

ated with wartime detention and to avoid having to answer for its foolish vows to close Guantánamo.

But the critique goes a step further, and urges—and this is what makes it a positive framework of policy, rather than simply criticism—that we are losing valuable intelligence by refusing to detain and interrogate. In some iterations, though not in McCain's or Graham's, it also complains of the unwillingness to use any tough interrogation methods on detainees, even techniques well short of waterboarding, and that this constitutes real harm to the US war effort. If it's a war, the conservative critique goes, treat it as a war. Be willing to capture and hold and interrogate people, rather than blowing them up individually in order to avoid confronting the evident absurdity of your political speeches. Yoo also criticized the legal theory under which the Obama administration defended the al-Awlaki strike on the basis that it gave serious consideration to his due process rights and to Fourth Amendment constraints; these don't apply to enemy combatants in warfare, he argued. And since, in addition, al-Awlaki and his fellow jihadis are also terrorists and unprivileged belligerents with no legal right to resort to force, much less to target civilians, it is justified morally and legally to use rough interrogation techniques on them, short of actual torture, that would not be legal against a lawful combatant or ordinary civilian.

Then-Attorney General Eric Holder's methodology for determining whether an American citizen could be targeted with a drone strike abroad assumed that an American citizen was owed due process, though not necessarily judicial process. Step one in Holder's approach was the determination that the American had in fact joined the enemy and was an otherwise targetable part of the enemy's forces, under ordinary laws-of-war criteria.

This was followed by a second step: consideration of whether capture was feasible. The first step was fine, according to the conservative critics, but the inquiry should end there. Because if this is really a war, once this American citizen was determined to be a member of the enemy forces, there need be no determination of whether due process is satisfied by targeting procedures or whether it would be feasible to seize or detain the American and present him for trial. Citizenship is not relevant to the targeting of hostile forces in war, and the American citizen is not entitled to any special consideration for capture. Mixing and mingling paradigms will do nothing good for either.

Indeed, the national security hawks believe as a general proposition that it is a mistake to mingle the war paradigm with US domestic law enforcement practices. The problem with the Obama administration, Yoo wrote in another opinion piece in the *Wall Street Journal* in 2013, is that it "is trying to dilute the normal practice of war with law-enforcement methods."[14] Similarly, the last Bush administration's attorney general, Mukasey, was scathing in 2009 in his denunciations of the then-new Obama administration's plans to try at least some Guantánamo detainees in federal courts on US territory. The war on terror is a war, Mukasey said, and the role of federal courts "in a war on terror—to use an unfashionably harsh phrase—should be, as the term 'war' would suggest, a supporting and not a principal role."[15] It is not a surprise that the conservative national

14. John Yoo, "The Real Problem With Obama's Drone Memo," *Wall Street Journal*, February 7, 2013, http://online.wsj.com/news/articles/SB10 001424127887323951904578288380180346300.

15. Michael Mukasey, "Civilian Courts Are No Place to Try Terrorists," *Wall Street Journal*, October 19, 2009, http://online.wsj.com/news/articles/ SB10001424052748704107204574475300052267212.

security hawks have been closely aligned with those in Congress who have pushed for prohibitions on terrorism trials in federal courts and have sought to create heavy presumptions in favor of military custody of suspects. They believe in the legitimacy, and the primacy, of the tools of war and that mingling these tools with civilian law enforcement turns war into a lukewarm hybrid that is inappropriate to the requirements of actual conflict.

One of the particular, often unstated, concerns of the national security hawks is defending the symbolic legitimacy of warfare as the appropriate paradigm. Given a choice between a military commission trial that may prove a long and difficult slog and a smooth, quick federal trial, the national security hawks will sometimes opt for the former precisely to avoid lessening our societal insistence on the legitimacy of the tools of warfare. Warfare is a form of toughness. Reversion to other authorities represents to them the refusal to face Al Qaeda for what it really is and at the same time a refusal, in the face of domestic and international disapproval, to take the hard steps the situation requires and hold to them over the length of the conflict, however long.

As a framework, the "it's all war" approach has the virtues of consistency and clarity. It is concrete, rather than abstract, and, unlike the Pauline position, which is almost entirely devoid of actual utility in governance, it has the virtue of suggesting approaches to real circumstances that arise in counterterrorism.

The essential problem is that it ignores both important constraints on American action and crucial ways in which, like it or not, the best approach for the United States is one that actually *does* mingle disparate elements of national power. The

Bush administration was never actually allergic to the use of law enforcement power or single-mindedly committed to military authorities, after all. So the purity of the warfare model is greater when its proponents are out of government than it was when they actually had to make decisions. Guantánamo was shrinking under the Bush administration, too. And the use of drone aircraft for targeted killing in some remote place in Yemen where no ground forces will ever set foot, in the context of a strategic and operational paradigm almost entirely driven by secret intelligence, is just different from conventional warfare. Whichever party is in power—and no matter how committed it is in theoretical terms to a warfare model of the conflict—it has to ask, when it captures a new detainee, what will happen after it's done questioning him. Sometimes, the best answer to that question will involve a federal court. These realities matter, and so does the fact of a war in which the conditions of winning are murky at best. The response of the tough, realist, national security conservative that it's over when the enemy stops fighting or is all killed does not make a great deal of sense to the American people anymore—and it does not facilitate allied cooperation either.

Like the administration's liberal critics, in other words, the national security hawks describe a mode of pursuing the conflict that lacks realism. The liberal critics pretend it isn't really an armed conflict. The conservative hawks pretend it's a caricature of the conflict we were fighting a decade ago. They deny the degree to which the world has changed, a world that was never that pure anyway. The virtue of the Obama administration's general approach has been to look for ways to pursue the war so as to stomp out and tamp down the threats that started it, maintaining a position that is flexible with regards to the use of force yet also nimble with respect to the use of other tools. The national security hawks' position that this is just a war like any other is not able to take account of the evident differences between this war and others—differences that are growing more, not less, pronounced as time goes on. The result is that it is not finally persuasive as an encompassing framework for the many distinct and distinguishable ways in which the United States will decide when it ought to employ hostilities, even on a tiny scale, now and into the future.

Conclusion

Each of these broad strains of thought offers something that could, at least in part, serve as an alternative framework for law, policy, and legitimacy with which to structure our national security and counterterrorism operations abroad. Of them, the American progressive framework (with which the international community framework is joined at the hip) is the most complete. The conservative libertarian framework is the least complete and the least satisfactory; its abstraction precludes it from being a framework for governance, at least not governance of an American people which expects the practical protection of both its liberties and its security. The conservative national security hawk framework offers a clear basis for governance and a toughness from which a great deal can be learned. But it is far too simple and clear-cut, and it is growing more and more outdated with every passing year. The situation is more complicated than this model allows.

In any case, the task is not to find ways to reduce, cut, fit, and stuff counterterrorism and national security into the traditional framework of conventional war and the law of war. The true problem is to shape out of something new, something old, something borrowed, and something owed a framework for the use of force and other tools that reflects the precision of our weapons, the discretion of attack, the intelligence-driven process of target identification and selection, the importance of law enforcement and international cooperation, and operations in both conventional warfare and outside of armed conflict. None of the alternatives to the framework the Obama administration has cobbled together over the past several years really poses a plausible means of taking on this project.

Even the American progressive framework—which is the most worked out, the most thoroughly elaborated in every way—fails in this regard. Its framers have had a lot of time to think about it. Yet the apparent similiarities between it and the often-very-similar language of the Obama administration's framework are deceptive. The American progressive framework is a framework of restraints only. The Obama administration's framework is one of both restraints and permissions. The Obama administration has been explicit in insisting on the ability to take on groups and networks, and not just plots as they arise—about the ability to counter threats to the United States based on patterns of behavior by a group over time either inside or outside of armed conflict. The American progressive framework would deny all of this. It seems hard to believe that any president, now or in the future, will give up this view and the interpretation of imminence that supports it. Such examples could be repeated across the elements of the framework of the speeches. This is why the Obama administration's national security policies have, at the end of the day, ended in frustration for American progressives who thought they had a champion in the man who had garnered so much progressive excitement.

And it's also why, despite Obama's evident desire to convince the Left that he really is one of them on these issues, he cannot embrace the progressive framework.

To put the matter simply, the administration's basic framework holds up pretty well in the face of all of the major strains of criticism emanating from these four basic stances, and also alongside the alternative positive frameworks for national security policy that each of these might offer. Much of the commentary on the speeches has sought in so many words to make the administration feel ugly and unloved for its supposedly intellectually impoverished and threadbare policy and legal framework. By and large, this is balderdash. The speeches have their problems, their blind spots, and their weak points. But to a remarkable extent, they put forward a coherent intellectual, legal, and moral set of positions that is vastly more robust than its critics are willing to credit—and more robust as well than those its critics would put forth in its place.

Conclusion

"Events, dear boy, events," former British Prime Minister Harold Macmillan is reputed to have said when asked what was most likely to blow things off course for his government. We draw this work to a close in mid-2014 as several distinct but related events have begun ramping up the pressure on the framework of law, policy, and strategy laid out in the Obama administration's national security law speeches. These will almost certainly drive important changes to the framework and they will almost certainly also retard the change to the framework the administration envisions: an overall end of the Al Qaeda conflict.

The landscape is changing quickly. Most importantly, the eruption onto the scene of the Islamic State of Iraq and Syria (ISIS, or the Islamic State) and the swift ground advance of its several thousand Sunni militants to seize wide swaths of Iraq and Syria have brought into focus—and collision—nearly every aspect of the administration's national security policies. ISIS's sudden emergence reveals vividly a broader trend toward the growth of Al Qaeda's offshoots across whole regions, with fighters recruited from widely dispersed places, including Europe and the United States. It is a strategic evolution of jihadist warfare to embrace regionally based and nationally based insurgency and conventional warfare, in addition to transnational terrorism. Whatever conditions allowed ISIS to emerge in Syria and Iraq—and something like the same model to appear as a threat in widely dispersed places such as Nigeria—the threat posed by ISIS and its model of jihad has largely unraveled the administration's hope that its second-term foreign policy legacy would be the winding down and end of the counterterrorism armed conflict against Al Qaeda.

ISIS's public debut took place even as other core pillars of the framework have come under pressure. With regards to targeted killing, drone warfare, and covert uses of force generally, the Justice Department, following years of pressure and litigation, finally released a redacted version of the 2010 Office of Legal Counsel (OLC) memorandum endorsing the president's legal authority to target Anwar al-Awlaki with a drone missile strike in 2011. The memo's release followed quickly on the heels of a controversy over the exchange of five Taliban detainees at Guantánamo for Bowe Bergdahl, the US soldier held by the Taliban in Afghanistan from 2009 to 2014.

Amidst all this, US forces captured Libyan militant Ahmed Abu Khattala, accused of being a mastermind in the 2012 attack in Benghazi that killed the US ambassador and three other Americans. Following Abu Khattala's capture, authorities brought him to the United States and arraigned him in federal court rather than sending him to Guantánamo, as some congressional Republicans demanded. Among other factors influencing the decision, the administration appears not to have believed that Abu Khatalla was covered by the Authorization for the Use of Military Force (AUMF). All this took place amidst a congressional debate over reform of surveillance authorities; debates over humanitarian intervention and the responsibility to protect against the threatened genocide of Yazidi and Christian communities in Iraqi towns taken by ISIS; and, finally, debates over the best strategic division of resources between the war against the jihadists and Al Qaeda, on the one hand, and the emerging geopolitical, state-on-state crises in Ukraine and the increased tensions in the South and East China Seas on the other.

We reach the end of this discussion in a world filled with wars and rumors of wars facing an administration that—and, we grant, hindsight is easy—appears to have anticipated a quite different endgame. These events, particularly in combination, raise important questions about the vitality of the Obama administration's framework and especially the administration's attempt to see the framework not as a permanent or long-run elaboration of national security policy to be bequeathed to future administrations but instead as an essentially *temporary* legal-political-strategic framework that would, so to speak, almost automatically zero itself out, wind itself down, and terminate, leaving the nation in a state of peace. Events, in some cases dire events, are today putting pressure on some of the framework's fundamental premises; they raise new strategic concerns; and they potentially draw to the surface unresolved contradictions. These events pose the broad question of how the framework will need to adapt and how the administration will need to reconceive its vision of what it will bequeath to future presidencies.

In these pages, we have sought to address the core categories of policy formulation and articulation of legal authority the Obama administration has put forth in its national security speeches. As a way of drawing a general conclusion, we consider what the administration would like to do in the way of drawing the conflict to a close against the pressures militating toward its perpetuation, even its expansion. And we consider the big questions the administration will have to face in the months and years—and in the speeches—to come.

The eruption in Iraq clearly took many people, the Obama administration included, by surprise. The conventional military strength of ISIS, its level of organization, equipment, and wealth, the speed of its ground advance as it seized enormous swaths of territory, the criminal brutality with which it executed captured Iraqi army soldiers (committing war crimes and crimes against humanity, and only too credibly threatening genocide along the way), and the barbarity with which it has governed captured territories and their populations were as shocking to American policymakers as they are unacceptable.

While the rise of ISIS might have taken the US national security community by surprise as a matter of the geopolitics of the Middle East, from the standpoint of counterterrorism strategy, what is taking place in Iraq is not all that surprising. It is the Iraq-Syria version of a more general morphing of transnational terrorist non-state actor groups into a broader category of radical Islamist insurgencies. The militants who make up these groups have an internal aspect and an external one. Internally, the trend over the last decade has been toward insurgency within particular countries or regions. The insurgents, who might include a sizable number of foreign jihadist fighters, seek to take over entire political territories, perhaps even states as a whole, to govern them and their local populations under extremist Islamist law. The external aspect is that the militants either have or actively support a transnational terrorist wing, one externally focused on attacking Western or US targets.

The pattern is not new with ISIS. It is, rather, the pattern the United States has had to confront over the last six years. It is clearly a large and growing part of the strategic task. The legal and policy problem is that the task of territorial denial to these Islamist insurgent groups is not quite the task Congress authorized with the AUMF and it looks less and less like the conflict the AUMF contemplated the more time goes on. The more the conflict looks like a broad effort to prop up a set of governments against these insurgencies—co-belligerency with governments from Yemen to Iraq against jihadist, terrorist insurgencies, rather than striking shadowy terrorists in relatively small numbers with missile strikes or special forces—the less apt the AUMF looks as a mechanism for authorizing it.

US counterterrorism doctrine has long understood that transnational terrorist groups, such as Al Qaeda, must have safe havens somewhere to function, places where they can establish safe houses, compounds, and camps for training, meeting, and planning. Drone strikes have proved remarkably effective in giving the United States a tool to engage in armed raids directly, but that presupposes that the insurgent group is, in fact, covered by the AUMF. As time has gone on, as we have seen, the groups have grown less and less associated with the AUMF-covered forces. ISIS—which was actually expelled by Al Qaeda—puts that problem in sharp relief. The more that transnational terrorist groups focused externally have attached themselves to—or risen again as—internal militant insurgencies in countries in Africa and elsewhere, the less plausible grows the framing of the conflict as the one Congress imagined in the AUMF and the more the AUMF seems to require reform.

The speeches themselves have laid out the essentials of both the strategic threat and the US response to that threat as a matter of strategy, policy, and law. As we explained in detail in chapter 3, the president's May 23, 2013, speech at the National Defense University (NDU) takes on explicitly the strategic shift in the nature of transnational terrorist groups. A 2014 speech at West Point essentially restates these points in terms of the new strategic terms posed by ISIS, Boko Haram in Nigeria, Yemen's Al Qaeda in the Arabian Peninsula (AQAP), jihadist groups still present in Mali, and other groups in other places.[1] The US national security community has long been committed to preventing a new recurrence of conditions of externally oriented terrorist groups sheltering not just in tiny locales serving as safe havens, but hosted by those governing a whole territory or even an entire state and its population. The strategic description is not wrong—to the contrary, it's only too correct. Yet, as a legal, political, and legitimacy question, it is hard to see how one extracts the broad, long-run authority to address these threats from the AUMF, particularly if one is committed for other reasons to winding down the AUMF conflict.

---

1. See "Remarks by the President at the United States Military Academy Commencement Ceremony," U.S. Military Academy–West Point, West Point, NY, May 28, 2014, http://www.whitehouse.gov/the-press-office/2014/05/28/remarks-president-united-states-military-academy-commencement-ceremony.

Ironically, the speeches—again, the key one here is Obama's NDU speech—also express a commitment to bringing the conflict to a close and explicitly reject any widening of the AUMF authority. The administration has also said that it prefers that Congress repeal the Iraq War AUMF. The Iraq War is over, after all—even with ISIS's hurtling advance, and the long years of preparation for it. Any additional uses of force could be undertaken through the president's Article II powers under the Constitution.

But this language, as we warned in chapter 3, has had a short shelf life. As we go to press, the administration is relying on the 2001 AUMF, quite implausibly, for an expanded set of operations against ISIS—the same AUMF it insists it wishes to see wound down. And it is relying as well on the 2002 Iraq AUMF it wishes to see repealed. Its view of both is strained to the point that the present authors, who have embraced a broad understanding of associated forces, cannot endorse it. Congressional action will be necessary to authorize force against ISIS if the administration means to take the action that Obama is now describing.

ISIS thus highlights long-lurking questions of domestic legal authority, executive power, and the role of Congress in defining the contours of the conflict, which will only become more difficult in the years to come. There are important ways in which ISIS is the next phase of the Iraq War. But there are other important ways in which it is genuinely something different: its connections to the civil war in Syria, more regionalized Shiite-Sunni struggles, and the core AUMF conflict against Al Qaeda and the Taliban. However one parses the conflicts, it is harder and harder to see a connection to the conditions contemplated by the 2001 AUMF or even the Iraq War AUMF, or arguably sufficient powers under Article II for the president to undertake what might have to be a very large conventional effort, even if conducted primarily from the air. As pinprick drone strikes against individual terrorists or terrorist groups become part of a general strategy of military and intelligence help to multiple countries facing multiple civil wars, the question of how much of this activity can be supported legally either under the existing AUMF or under the president's own authority, without some new authority from Congress, takes on much greater weight.

Another data point in the increasing obsolescence of the AUMF came with the capture of Abu Khatalla, who—the administration appears to have concluded—was not covered by the document at all. Hence, while he was kept on a military ship for a period of time, he was formally in FBI custody, not subject to detention under the laws of war.[2]

The speeches do not treat in any depth the question of what sort of instrument might replace the AUMF—as they assume, rather, that the war is ending. But as policymakers consider what sort of long-term intervention ISIS will require of the United States and contemplate operations against people outside of its coverage, the stance that we are heading toward the end of the conflict looks increasingly like a pose. Put simply, it's probably not possible to take on ISIS and the other scary groups that will crop up from time to time and simultaneously to bring the conflict to an end. We're going to

---

2. See Jack Goldsmith, "Civilian Trial is the Only Option for Abu Khattala," *Lawfare* (blog), June 18, 2014, http://www.lawfareblog.com/2014/06/civilian -trial-is-the-only-option-for-abu-khattala/.

have to decide which we want to do, and the framework should change to reflect our choice.

At some point, this administration or a future one will have to consider seriously what the future of congressional authorization for the conflict will and should look like. Are we really going to let the AUMF fade into irrelevance and declare ourselves at peace? Are we going to do so even while interpreting it far more aggressively than we ever have in the past to authorize a new conflict against ISIS? Are we really going to repeal the authorization? Or are we going to undertake imagining its legislative successors? This is perhaps the biggest question concerning the legal architecture of the next few years of American counterterrorism. As we finish this work, Congress is just beginning to stir on the subject.

A related question, festering for years now, is how to deal with the legacy detainees at Guantánamo. The administration has insisted for years that it is closing Guantánamo. It's likely not. As the furor over the release of Taliban detainees of apparently real value in exchange for an American soldier reflects, the marginal political capital it requires to remove each additional Guantánamo detainee is growing, not declining. While there are still some detainees who can be resettled, substantial political constraints now impede many repatriations and resettlements.

This problem interacts with the problem of the AUMF, because the AUMF presents the continuing legal authority for these detentions. So to the extent one repeals it or declares hostilities at an end before achieving appropriate dispositions for each detainee, one risks abnegating one's legal authority to detain in the process. There are a variety of possible answers here—ranging from gritting one's teeth and freeing people who have done horrible things or pose some measure of prospective threat to passing ancillary legislation. What is not viable, however, is to keep pretending that Guantánamo is closing and the war is ending when, in fact, there exists no plan for the disposition of several dozen Guantánamo cases irrespective of what happens to the larger conflict. One way or another, the administration owes more candor and clarity on this point than it has given so far.

Whether or not the war ends or somehow morphs, CIA lethal force actions will likely continue and may even increase under some circumstances. This will be partly because even in a peacetime environment—a genuine peacetime as traditionally understood in modern America—presidents will conclude that certain threats and groups are best addressed by covert lethal force. It will also be partly because covert US involvement is, with some countries, the price of US involvement that can then be denounced or denied by the country that gave its secret consent. In any case, the need for a clear defense of the legality and legitimacy of CIA participation in lethal force operations is rising, not declining. We have urged that this legal account must include formally recognizing the role CIA operations, like those of other states' intelligence agencies, have long had outside the contours of armed conflict in its technical meaning, as well as formal (and not merely de facto and inconsistent) treatment of the CIA as "incorporated" into the fighting forces of the United States in an armed conflict under the laws of war.

In this respect, the most interesting event of recent months in US national security politics was the release in June 2014 of a redacted version of the 2010 opinion on the targeted killing of Anwar al-Awlaki, the American citizen killed by a drone strike in Yemen.[3] In one respect, the document had something of an anticlimactic air to it. Much of the memo's contents had already been leaked to the press over the years. The memo, under the signature of David Barron, then-acting head of the OLC at the Department of Justice, also formed the basis both for Eric Holder's March 5, 2012, speech at Northwestern University and for the Justice Department's white paper, both of which were public documents already.

That said, the legal opinion is important in that it sheds light—albeit elliptically—on the legal rationale under which the Justice Department found that the killing of a Yemeni-American radical Islamist was a lawful use of lethal force not only by the military under the AUMF but also by the CIA under its own authorities. Much of this discussion is redacted, but it's possible to reconstruct a fair bit of it. The exercise poses important forward-looking questions that, in Syria and Iraq today, are becoming unavoidable as policy and legal questions. First, how robust do we want the agency's authority to be to use lethal force abroad in the coming years, particularly in an environment in which we purport to be curtailing military operations but in which threats posed by non-state groups continue and, if anything, multiply?

The legal reasoning in the redacted OLC opinion will be debated by scholars and lawyers for a long time to come. Its essence—at least the essence of the visible part of it—is that

---

3. See "Memorandum For The Attorney General Re: Applicability of Federal Criminal Laws and the Constitution to Contemplated Lethal Operations Against Shaykh Anwar al-Aulaqi," from Acting Assistant Attorney General David J. Barron, July 16, 2010, http://www.lawfareblog.com/wp-content/uploads/2014/06/6-23-14_Drone_Memo-Alone.pdf.

targeting an enemy belligerent in an armed conflict, including the non-international armed conflict that the US government sees itself as engaged in under the AUMF, is lawful under both the international law of armed conflict and US statutory and constitutional law. For present purposes, however, the memo is interesting because it at least partly resolves the puzzle we identified in chapter 2, where we noted that it was unclear precisely what legal question the idea of "imminence" of threat was addressing in the administration's thinking about targeted killing. That is, why is targeted killing limited to situations of imminent threat? The speeches, as we noted, do not answer this question. And it's a bit of a head-scratcher. Whether a threat is "imminent," after all, is no longer relevant once an armed conflict is underway; as we have said, once it's "game-on," imminence drops out of consideration.

The Barron memo does not directly explain why or in what way imminence matters in its analysis. Yet imminence nonetheless makes an appearance. The memo's imminence discussion is minimal—either because the memo is focused on other things or because the relevant discussion is redacted. The discussion that is there takes the form more of a recitation of the CIA's and Pentagon's factual conclusions about al-Awlaki than of an analysis of what work imminence is doing legally or what would constitute it factually. Yet reading between the lines, it's possible to exclude some of the conceivable roles for imminence—and, by doing so, to home in on the actual role the concept is playing and its probable, and very surprising, legal source.

First, as the preceding observations on the legal role of imminence once armed conflict is underway imply, "imminence" in its international law meaning is not at issue here. People think of imminence in the context of international law because it is part of analyzing the legality of a resort to force in self-defense. Yet the memo contains no resort-to-force analysis at all, because it finds (unsurprisingly) that the targeting of al-Awlaki was undertaken as part of an existing armed conflict.

Second, and by the same token, even in domestic legal terms imminence is *not* playing a role in the memo's separation-of-powers analysis. Imminence arises in that context too—for much the same reasons that it comes up in international law. The president has inherent Article II authority to defend the nation, after all, and defense includes preemption of "imminent" threats. Imminence in this domestic law sense is not identical to international law imminence, of course; it's merely homologous. But again, as in the international law sense, the domestic constitutional law issue of imminence only arises if one is initiating a conflict or use of force in the first instance. If a conflict is already underway, as the memo finds to be the case, or if Congress has authorized it, as the memo also finds, there is no reliance on Article II at all and this issue just does not come up.

Third, imminence in the memo also plays virtually no role in the discussion of legal defenses to claims that the government's lethal targeting violates domestic statutory criminal prohibitions against killing Americans. These discussions in the memo focus on the "public authority" justification—that is, the idea that the killing in question would not be unlawful because, under the facts as described, it has been authorized by Congress and is part of the activities contemplated by the laws of war that are, indeed, intentional killings but are not murder and are lawful in warfare. The notion of imminence shows up here, but purely as a description of al-Awlaki's threat. In no sense does the statutory analysis seem to hinge on it.

Finally, imminence in the OLC opinion does not seem to come from the domestic constitutional rights of suspects either. Imminence is not irrelevant to the Fourth Amendment line of cases here, but it's not the dispositive consideration either. The Fourth Amendment cases, which run from *Tennessee v. Garner*[4] through *Scott v. Harris*[5] and down more recently to *Plumhoff v. Rickard*,[6] involve a close factual examination of the individual case details; they inquire into reasonableness (or its absence) in the totality of the circumstances. The Fifth Amendment cases, for their part, involve a *Mathews v. Eldridge*[7] balancing test. Neither of these hinges necessarily on imminence.

So then where is imminence coming from? For our part, we suspect that the source of law for imminence in Holder's speech, in the white paper, and in this memo is the presidential covert action finding that authorized action against Al Qaeda in the first place. That is, the president, in issuing whatever finding gave rise to the killing of al-Awlaki, limited the authorization to situations involving imminent threats. This invocation was prudential, not legally required by any other source of law. But it nonetheless operates as law for the executive branch. If that is so, the opinion's imminence analysis is not very important under either international or domestic law, but quite important with respect to the internal operations of the executive.

There are a few pieces of evidence—not conclusive, but suggestive—supporting this view. The most important is that

---

4. *Tennessee v. Garner,* 471 U.S. 1 (1985).
5. *Scott v. Harris,* 550 U.S. 372 (2007).
6. *Plumhoff v. Rickard,* 134 S. Ct. 1156 (2014).
7. *Mathews v. Eldridge,* 424 U.S. 319 (1976).

the memo, by omission, excludes the other major possibilities. If the imminence requirement is not there because of constitutional separation of powers, international law, or the constitutional rights of the targets, it's got to be coming from *somewhere*. Internal executive branch law is one of the few remaining possibilities. Moreover, it's the only obvious possibility we can think of that would leave so little footprint in the memo. Indeed, if the imminence discussion is present but redacted, that suggests that the very source of law is classified. That is consistent with its appearance in a "finding." Alternatively, if the reason the discussion seems to be missing is that it isn't there at all, that is *also* consistent with its originating in a finding. After all, if we assume that imminence is only a requirement because the president (or *a* president, in an earlier administration) said it's a requirement, it follows that the concept means—at least in this context—whatever the president wants it to mean, assuming the president goes through any necessary executive branch steps so to qualify it. Thus, it may require very little legal analysis at all because, though binding for the executive branch, its interpretation lies in the hands of the president.

There is at least one piece of extrinsic evidence that the Obama administration has layered imminence requirements as a prudential matter on top of the targeted killing program. In his NDU speech, President Obama did exactly that with respect to non-US citizens: "America does not take strikes to punish individuals; we act against terrorists who pose a continuing and imminent threat to the American people, and when there are no other governments capable of effectively addressing the threat. . . . [T]he high threshold that we've set for taking lethal action applies to all potential terrorist targets, regardless of whether or not they are American citizens." Those standards are policy, not requirements of law, as we noted earlier, and revisable by the executive.

There's another dog that does not bark in the Barron memo—and doesn't bark in a manner that seems to suggest that policy is all imminence ever is in the administration's targeted killing rationales: the assassination ban in Executive Order 12333. The assassination ban does not seem to be discussed at all in the unredacted parts of the memo. It may offer a key—perhaps *the* key—to explaining why the finding limits targeted killings to situations of continuing and imminent threat, even when they are part of an armed conflict and thus lawful in both international and domestic law.

The CIA's authority to go after Al Qaeda is not originally rooted in the AUMF, though the AUMF arguably adds considerable support to it. It's rooted, rather, in findings under the covert action statute that predate the AUMF's signing by a day. When the lawyers were writing these findings, they could not rest the legal power of the CIA on the congressional authorization for force, which was not yet law. In the absence of an AUMF, they faced the problem when contemplating the use of lethal force of the ban on assassinations, which reads, "No person employed by or acting on behalf of the United States Government shall engage in, or conspire to engage in, assassination." The government has always understood the ban to cover only *unlawful* killings. In that regard, the assassination ban prohibits nothing that was not already unlawful. So the question of the ban's coverage boiled down to a question of whether a killing is lawful or not. If it is lawful, then it's not an assassination. If it's not lawful, it might well be.

This problem was not, as it turned out, new. The Clinton administration had confronted it in 1998 (as the 9/11 Commission later recounted) when considering lethal force actions against Osama bin Laden. "The administration's position," said the commission, was that "under the law of armed conflict, killing a person who posed an imminent threat to the United States would be an act of self-defense, not an assassination."[8] Notably, this view was taken by OLC chief Randy Moss—and, as the *Washington Post* described in October 2001, this interpretation of EO 12333's language won out over proposals to simply amend the executive order itself:

> Since the late Clinton administration, executive branch lawyers have held that the president's inherent authority to use lethal force—under Article 2, Section 2 of the Constitution—permits an order to kill an individual enemy of the United States in self-defense.
>
> In 1998, an interagency group led by then-Assistant Attorney General Randy Moss produced a highly classified memo of law on assassination. The group concluded that recent presidents—from Reagan in Libya to Bush in Iraq—had been needlessly cautious in ordering broad attacks against enemy headquarters if their real objective was to kill an individual leader. Because executive orders are entirely at the discretion of the president, they wrote, a president may issue contrary directives at will and need not make public that he has done so.

---

8. National Commission on Terrorist Attacks Upon the United States, *The 9/11 Commission Report* (Washington, DC: Government Printing Office, 2004), 132, http://www.9-11commission.gov/report/911Report.pdf.

Under customary international law and Article 51 of the U.N. Charter, according to those familiar with the memo, taking the life of a terrorist to preempt an imminent or continuing threat of attack is analogous to self-defense against conventional attack.

That interpretation won out over a proposal by Walter Dellinger, Moss's predecessor, who wanted to amend Executive Order 12333. Dellinger proposed to forbid assassination "without the prior written express authorization of the president." Presidential "findings" on lethal force, he said, "were too often drafted overbroadly simply 'to avoid calling what we're doing 'assassination'.'"[9]

In other words, when the CIA and the Bush administration in the immediate wake of September 11 confronted the problem of how to construct a finding that would not run afoul of the assassination ban, the answer was already sitting there in their laps: if they simply wrote the finding so as to limit the lethal force authorization to situations of imminent threat, then by definition they would not be authorizing assassinations.

This is, we suspect, what they did: the findings authorized lethal force only in situations of continuing and imminent threat so as to avoid conflict with the assassination ban. In other words, imminence arises out of domestic law, and it does not arise out of domestic *constitutional* law, either the constitutional rights of the targets or the constitutional separa-

---

9. Barton Gellman, "CIA Weighs 'Targeted Killing' Missions," *Washington Post,* October 28, 2001.

tion of powers. Rather, it arises out of presidentially self-imposed rules.

Restricting the finding to situations of imminent threat no doubt has a bunch of other salutary consequences legally. Because of the role imminence plays both in resort-to-force issues in domestic constitutional law and in international law, and because of the role it plays in restricting lethal force in human rights law, the restriction tends to harmonize (albeit imperfectly) US views of its authority to kill with those of other countries. It also tends to diminish the perception of illegitimate presidential unilateralism at the domestic level, since nobody doubts the president's authority to use force to counter an imminent threat. But it's important to realize that—in all probability—this is not the legal work the concept is actually doing. The legal work, rather, is in getting around the assassination ban and ensuring that CIA personnel who engage in targeted killings are not liable under criminal statutes that prohibit murder.

From the standpoint of the framework and the speeches, the OLC memo is thus arguably most important not for what it addresses in its unredacted portions—the targeting of a citizen by the military in the context of armed conflict. It is important, rather—indeed, crucial, if this admittedly speculative reading is correct—for what it likely actually addresses in its redacted portions: the targeting of anyone, citizen or noncitizen, *outside* the legal contours of an openly stated and acknowledged armed conflict by civilian CIA personnel. Or, more broadly, the conduct of hostilities and the use of force by CIA paramilitaries under covert action authorities in domestic law and not necessarily as part of an armed conflict as defined in international law. After all, this is what the future almost certainly holds, long after—and entirely unrelated to—today's armed conflict against Al Qaeda and associated forces.

For just as that authority predated the AUMF by a day, it will—unless amended or rescinded by the president—postdate it, too. That means that just as we have to think about the authority the military will have in a post-AUMF world, we also have to think about the authority the CIA will retain under these findings even after the AUMF's repeal, replacement, or reinvigoration. It would be a hollow kind of victory, after all, to find ourselves at peace yet still using force as though at war. And it would be a hollow kind of victory of a different sort to unilaterally declare ourselves at peace, formally decommissioning legal authorities for making war, overt and covert, only to discover that our enemies are persisting with lethal plans of their own.

The Obama administration, across two terms, has seen it as peculiarly its project to wind down and bring to a close America's wars: the two ground wars, Iraq and Afghanistan, and the transnational armed conflict against Al Qaeda and associated forces under the AUMF. It likes to think and talk about the end of the conflict or, more precisely, the end of *conflicts,* around which the president clearly desires to shape his foreign policy legacy. The president's aim is to bring to an end the era of American history set in motion by September 11: the United States of America, once again at peace.

That is not dishonorable as such—of course not. It is an important and valuable exercise to consider concretely what the conditions of war and peace really are, and what separates them in the current circumstances. Yet doing so requires thinking through systematically how the framework will change, building in suitable flexibility for future administrations to respond to future contingent events—events like the rise of ISIS. If it is to be more than just a public relations exercise, it requires enormous thought about what comes next across a number of different axes. In a meaningful sense, the future is now. One cannot be the president who ends wars, who returns us to peace and lectures us about the necessity of doing so, while also being the president who stretches old outdated legal documents to describe new situations.

In these pages, we have viewed the speeches—the care and effort of the interagency process in elaborating them, and their contents—as far more than a public relations exercise. We have argued that the speeches create a robust framework, necessarily incomplete on some matters as a consequence of absent political will, and contradictory on other matters. Yet for all that, it's a sturdy framework for future administrations to build upon, one that is dramatically better than the administration's critics acknowledge.

Our plea—and the conclusion to this work—is for the Obama administration as it approaches the end of its second term in 2016 to understand that its true legacy, the one that matters and will endure, is the framework it will leave to future administrations. Though peace in our time is always a tempting ideal and sometimes even achievable, with regard to the complex counterterrorism war on which this country embarked—tragically late—on September 11, determining the end of the war is less the project than is defining the parameters of the conflict's next phase. Institutional settlement around a sturdy framework, not peace in our time, is the legacy genuinely available to the Obama administration—and the one necessary to the nation into the future.

APPENDIXES

Addresses and Remarks by President Obama and Administration Officials on National Security Law

Appendix: Koh–B

Harold H. Koh, legal adviser to the Department of State, address to the USCYBERCOM Inter-Agency Legal Conference, "International Law in Cyberspace," Fort Meade, Maryland, September 18, 2012. [See pages 370–383.]

Appendix: Kris–A

David Kris, assistant attorney general for national security, "Law Enforcement as a CounterterrorismTool," address at the Brookings Institution, June 11, 2010. [See pages 384–397.]

Appendix: Johnson–A

Jeh C. Johnson, general counsel, Department of Defense, "Jeh C. Johnson Speech to the Heritage Foundation," Washington, D.C., October 18, 2011. [See pages 398–407.]

Appendix: Johnson–B

Jeh C. Johnson, general counsel, Department of Defense, "National Security Law, Lawyers, and Lawyering in the Obama Administration," address at Yale Law School, February 22, 2012. [See pages 408–416.]

Appendix: Johnson–C

Jeh C. Johnson, general counsel, Department of Defense, "The Conflict against Al Qaeda and Its Affiliates: How Will It End?" Oxford Union, Oxford University, November 30, 2012. [See pages 417–423.]

Appendix: Holder–A

Eric Holder, Attorney General, Department of Justice, Address at Northwestern University School of Law, March 5, 2012. [See pages 424–438.]

Appendix: Preston–A

Stephen W. Preston, general counsel, Central Intelligence Agency, "CIA and the Rule of Law," address at Harvard Law School, April 10, 2012. [See pages 439–449.]

Appendix: Brennan–A

John O. Brennan, assistant to the president for homeland security and counterterrorism, "Strengthening Our Security by Adhering to Our Values and Laws," address at Harvard Law School, September 16, 2011. [See pages 450–465.]

Appendix: Brennan–B

John O. Brennan, assistant to the president for homeland security and counterterrorism, "The Ethics and Efficacy of the President's Counterterrorism Strategy," Woodrow Wilson International Center for Scholars, Washington, D.C., April 30, 2012. [See pages 466–484.]

Appendix: Brennan–C

John O. Brennan, assistant to the president for homeland security and counterterrorism, "US Policy toward Yemen," Council on Foreign Relations, New York City, August 8, 2012. [See pages 485–493.]

Appendix: Litt–A

Robert S. Litt, general counsel with the Office of the Director of National Intelligence, "Privacy, Technology, and National Security: An Overview of Intelligence Collection," address at the Brookings Institution, Washington, D.C., July 19, 2013. [See pages 494–517.]

Appendix: Obama–A

President Barack Obama,
"Remarks by the President on National Security,"
the National Archives, Washington, D.C., May 21, 2009

. . .

These are extraordinary times for our country. We're confronting a historic economic crisis. We're fighting two wars. We face a range of challenges that will define the way that Americans will live in the twenty-first century. So there's no shortage of work to be done or responsibilities to bear.

. . .

In the midst of all these challenges, however, my single most important responsibility as president is to keep the American people safe. It's the first thing that I think about when I wake up in the morning. It's the last thing that I think about when I go to sleep at night.

And this responsibility is only magnified in an era when an extremist ideology threatens our people and technology gives a handful of terrorists the potential to do us great harm. We are less than eight years removed from the deadliest attack on American soil in our history. We know that Al Qaeda is actively planning to attack us again. We know that this threat will be with us for a long time and that we must use all elements of our power to defeat it.

Already, we've taken several steps to achieve that goal. For the first time since 2002, we're providing the necessary resources and strategic direction to take the fight to the extremists who attacked us on 9/11 in Afghanistan and Pakistan. We're investing in the twenty-first-century military and intelligence capabilities that will allow us to stay one step ahead of a nimble enemy. We have re-energized a global non-proliferation regime to deny the world's most dangerous people access to the world's deadliest weapons. And we've launched an effort to secure all loose nuclear materials within four years. We're better protecting our border and increasing our preparedness for any future attack or natural disaster. We're building new partnerships around the world to disrupt, dismantle, and defeat Al Qaeda and its affiliates. And we have renewed American diplomacy so that we once again have the strength and standing to truly lead the world.

These steps are all critical to keeping America secure. But I believe with every fiber of my being that in the long run we also cannot keep this country safe unless we enlist the power of our most fundamental values. The documents that we hold in this very hall—the Declaration of Independence, the Constitution, the Bill of Rights—these are not simply words written into aging parchment. They are the foundation of liberty and justice in this country, and a light that shines for all who seek freedom, fairness, equality, and dignity around the world.

I stand here today as someone whose own life was made possible by these documents. My father came to these shores in search of the promise that they offered. My mother made me rise before dawn to learn their truths when I lived as a child in a foreign land. My own American journey was paved by generations of citizens who gave meaning to those simple words—"to form a more perfect union." I've studied the Constitution as a student, I've taught it as a teacher, I've been bound by it as a lawyer and a legislator. I took an oath to preserve, protect, and defend the Constitution as commander-in-chief; and, as a citizen, I know that we must never, ever, turn our back on its enduring principles for expediency's sake.

I make this claim not simply as a matter of idealism. We uphold our most cherished values not only because doing so is right, but because it strengthens our country and it keeps us safe. Time and again, our values have been our best national security asset—in war and peace, in times of ease, and in eras of upheaval.

Fidelity to our values is the reason why the United States of America grew from a small string of colonies under the writ of an empire to the strongest nation in the world.

It's the reason why enemy soldiers have surrendered to us in battle, knowing they'd receive better treatment from America's armed forces than from their own government.

It's the reason why America has benefited from strong alliances that amplified our power and have drawn a sharp, moral contrast with our adversaries.

It's the reason why we've been able to overpower the iron fist of fascism and outlast the iron curtain of communism, and enlist free nations and free peoples everywhere in the common cause and common effort of liberty.

From Europe to the Pacific, we've been the nation that has shut down torture chambers and replaced tyranny with the rule of law. That is who we are. And where terrorists offer only the injustice of disorder and destruction, America must demonstrate that our values and our institutions are more resilient than a hateful ideology.

After 9/11, we knew that we had entered a new era—that enemies who did not abide by any law of war would present new challenges to our application of the law, that our government would need new tools to protect the American people, and that these tools would have to allow us to prevent attacks instead of simply prosecuting those who try to carry them out.

Unfortunately, faced with an uncertain threat, our government made a series of hasty decisions. I believe that many of these decisions were motivated by a sincere desire to protect the American people. But I also believe that all too often our government made decisions based on fear rather than foresight—that all too often our government trimmed facts and evidence to fit ideological predispositions. Instead of strategically applying our power and our principles, too often we set those principles aside as luxuries that we could no longer afford. And during this season of fear, too many of us—Democrats and Republicans, politicians, journalists, and citizens—fell silent.

In other words, we went off course. And this is not my assessment alone. It was an assessment that was shared by the American people who nominated candidates for president from both major parties who, despite our many differences, called for a new approach—one that rejected torture and one that recognized the imperative of closing the prison at Guantánamo Bay.

Now let me be clear: we are indeed at war with Al Qaeda and its affiliates. We do need to update our institutions to deal with this threat. But we must do so with an abiding confidence in the rule of law and due process—in checks and balances and accountability. For reasons that I will explain, the decisions that were made over the last eight years established an ad hoc legal approach for fighting terrorism that was neither effective nor sustainable—a framework that failed to rely on our legal traditions and time-tested institutions and that failed to use our values as a compass. And that's why I took several steps upon taking office to better protect the American people.

First, I banned the use of so-called enhanced interrogation techniques by the United States of America.

I know some have argued that brutal methods like waterboarding were necessary to keep us safe. I could not disagree more. As commander-in-chief, I see the intelligence. I bear the responsibility for keeping this country safe. And I categorically reject the assertion that these are the most effective means of interrogation. What's more, they undermine the rule of law. They alienate us in the world. They serve as a recruitment tool for terrorists and increase the will of our enemies to fight us, while decreasing the will of others to work with America. They risk the lives of our troops by making it less likely that others will surrender to them in battle, and more likely that Americans will be mistreated if they are captured. In short, they did not advance our war and counterterrorism efforts—they undermined them, and that is why I ended them once and for all.

Now, I should add, the arguments against these techniques did not originate from my administration. As Senator McCain once said, torture "serves as a great propaganda tool for those who recruit people to fight against us." And even under President Bush, there was recognition among members of his own administration—including a secretary of state, other senior officials, and many in the military and intelligence community—that those who argued for these tactics were on the wrong side of the debate and the wrong side of history. That's why we must leave these methods where they belong—in the past. They are not who we are, and they are not America.

The second decision that I made was to order the closing of the prison camp at Guantánamo Bay.

For over seven years, we have detained hundreds of people at Guantánamo. During that time, the system of military commissions that were in place at Guantánamo succeeded in convicting a grand total of three suspected terrorists. Let me repeat that: three convictions in over seven years. Instead of bringing terrorists to justice, efforts at prosecution met setback after setback, cases lingered on, and in 2006 the Supreme Court invalidated the entire system. Meanwhile, over 525 detainees were released from Guantánamo under not my administration, under the previous administration. Let me repeat that: two-thirds of the detainees were released before I took office and ordered the closure of Guantánamo.

There is also no question that Guantánamo set back the moral authority that is America's strongest currency in the world. Instead of building a durable framework for the struggle against Al Qaeda that drew upon our deeply held values and traditions, our government was defending positions that undermined the rule of law. In fact, part of the rationale for establishing Guantánamo in the first place was the misplaced notion that a prison there would be beyond the law—a proposition that the Supreme Court soundly rejected.

Meanwhile, instead of serving as a tool to counter terrorism, Guantánamo became a symbol that helped Al Qaeda recruit terrorists to its cause. Indeed, the existence of Guantánamo likely created more terrorists around the world than it ever detained.

So the record is clear: rather than keeping us safer, the prison at Guantánamo has weakened American national security. It is a rallying cry for our enemies. It sets back the willingness of our allies to work with us in fighting an enemy that operates in scores of countries. By any measure, the costs of keeping it open far exceed the complications involved in closing it. That's why I argued that it should be closed throughout my campaign, and that is why I ordered it closed within one year.

The third decision that I made was to order a review of all pending cases at Guantánamo. I knew when I ordered Guantánamo closed that it would be difficult and complex. There are 240 people there who have now spent years in legal limbo. In dealing with this situation, we don't have the luxury of starting from scratch. We're cleaning up something that is, quite simply, a mess—a misguided experiment that has left in its wake a flood of legal challenges that my administration is forced to deal with on a constant, almost daily, basis, and it consumes the time of government officials whose time should be spent on better protecting our country.

Indeed, the legal challenges that have sparked so much debate in recent weeks here in Washington would be taking place whether or not I decided to close Guantánamo. For example, the court order to release seventeen Uighur detainees took place last fall when George Bush was president. The Supreme Court that invalidated the system of prosecution at Guantánamo in 2006 was overwhelmingly appointed by Republican presidents—not wild-eyed liberals. In other words, the problem of what to do with Guantánamo detainees was not caused by my decision to close the facility; the problem exists because of the decision to open Guantánamo in the first place.

Now let me be blunt. There are no neat or easy answers here. I wish there were. But I can tell you that the wrong answer is to pretend like this problem will go away if we maintain an unsustainable status quo. As president, I refuse to allow this problem to fester. I refuse to pass it on to somebody else. It is my responsibility to solve the problem. Our security interests will not permit us to delay. Our courts won't allow it. And neither should our conscience.

Now, over the last several weeks we've seen a return of the politicization of these issues that have characterized the last several years. I'm an elected official; I understand these problems arouse passions and concerns. They should. We're confronting some of the most complicated questions that a democracy can face. But I have no interest in spending all of our time re-litigating the policies of the last eight years. I'll leave that to others. I want to solve these problems, and I want to solve them together as Americans.

And we will be ill-served by some of the fear-mongering that emerges whenever we discuss this issue. Listening to the recent debate, I've heard words that, frankly, are calculated to scare people rather than educate them—words that have more to do with politics than protecting our country. So I want to take this opportunity to lay out what we are doing and how we intend to resolve these outstanding issues. I will explain how each action that we are taking will help build a framework that protects both the American people and the values that we hold most dear. And I'll focus on two broad areas: first, issues relating to Guantánamo and our detention policy; but, second, I also want to discuss issues relating to security and transparency.

Now, let me begin by disposing of one argument as plainly as I can: we are not going to release anyone if it would endanger our national security, nor will we release detainees within the United States who endanger the American people. Where demanded by justice and national security, we will seek to transfer some detainees to the same type of facilities in which we hold all manner of dangerous and violent criminals within our borders—namely, highly secure prisons that ensure the public safety.

As we make these decisions, bear in mind the following fact: nobody has ever escaped from one of our federal, super-max prisons, which hold hundreds of convicted terrorists. As Republican Lindsey Graham said, the idea that we cannot find a place to securely house 250-plus detainees within the United States is not rational.

We are currently in the process of reviewing each of the detainee cases at Guantánamo to determine the appropriate policy for dealing with them. And as we do so, we are acutely aware that under the last administration, detainees were released and, in some cases, returned to the battlefield. That's why we are doing away with the poorly planned, haphazard approach that let those detainees go in the past. Instead we are treating these cases with the care and attention that the law requires and that our security demands.

Now, going forward, these cases will fall into five distinct categories.

First, whenever feasible, we will try those who have violated American criminal laws in federal courts—courts provided for by the United States Constitution. Some have derided our federal courts as incapable of handling the trials of terrorists. They are wrong. Our courts and our juries, our citizens, are tough enough to convict terrorists. The record makes that clear. Ramzi Yousef tried to blow up the World Trade Center. He was convicted in our courts and is serving a life sentence in US prisons. Zacarias Moussaoui has been identified as the twentieth 9/11 hijacker. He was convicted in our courts, and he too is serving a life sentence in prison. If we can try those terrorists in our courts and hold them in our prisons, then we can do the same with detainees from Guantánamo.

Recently, we prosecuted and received a guilty plea from a detainee, [Ali] al-Marri, in federal court after years of legal confusion. We're preparing to transfer another detainee to the Southern District Court of New York, where he will face trial on charges related to the

1998 bombings of our embassies in Kenya and Tanzania—bombings that killed over 200 people. Preventing this detainee from coming to our shores would prevent his trial and conviction. And after over a decade, it is time to finally see that justice is served, and that is what we intend to do.

The second category of cases involves detainees who violate the laws of war and are therefore best tried through military commissions. Military commissions have a history in the United States dating back to George Washington and the Revolutionary War. They are an appropriate venue for trying detainees for violations of the laws of war. They allow for the protection of sensitive sources and methods of intelligence-gathering; they allow for the safety and security of participants; and [they allow] for the presentation of evidence gathered from the battlefield that cannot always be effectively presented in federal courts.

Now, some have suggested that this represents a reversal on my part. They should look at the record. In 2006, I did strongly oppose legislation proposed by the Bush administration and passed by the Congress because it failed to establish a legitimate legal framework, with the kind of meaningful due process rights for the accused that could stand up on appeal.

I said at that time, however, that I supported the use of military commissions to try detainees, provided there were several reforms, and in fact there were some bipartisan efforts to achieve those reforms. Those are the reforms that we are now making. Instead of using the flawed commissions of the last seven years, my administration is bringing our commissions in line with the rule of law. We will no longer permit the use of statements that have been obtained using cruel, inhuman, or degrading interrogation methods. We will no longer place the burden to prove that hearsay is unreliable on the opponent of the hearsay. And we will give detainees greater latitude in selecting their own counsel and more protections if they refuse to testify. These reforms, among others, will make our military commissions a more credible and effective means of administering justice, and I will work with Congress and members of both parties, as well as legal authorities across the political spectrum, on legislation to ensure that these commissions are fair, legitimate, and effective.

The third category of detainees includes those who have been ordered released by the courts. Now, let me repeat what I said earlier: This has nothing to do with my decision to close Guantánamo. It has to do with the rule of law. The courts have spoken. They have found that there's no legitimate reason to hold twenty-one of the people currently held at Guantánamo. Nineteen of these findings took place before I was sworn into office. I cannot ignore these rulings because, as president, I too am bound by the law. The United States is a nation of laws and so we must abide by these rulings.

The fourth category of cases involves detainees who we have determined can be transferred safely to another country. So far, our review team has approved fifty detainees for transfer. And my administration is in ongoing discussions with a number of other countries about the transfer of detainees to their soil for detention and rehabilitation.

Now, finally, there remains the question of detainees at Guantánamo who cannot be prosecuted yet who pose a clear danger to the American people. And I have to be honest here—this is the toughest single issue that we will face. We're going to exhaust every avenue that we have to prosecute those at Guantánamo who pose a danger to our country. But even when this process is complete, there may be a number of people who cannot be prosecuted for past crimes, in some cases because evidence may be tainted, but who nonetheless pose a threat to the security of the United States. Examples of that threat include people who've received extensive explosives training at Al Qaeda training camps, or commanded Taliban troops in battle, or expressed their allegiance to Osama bin Laden, or otherwise made it clear that they want to kill Americans. These are people who, in effect, remain at war with the United States.

Let me repeat: I am not going to release individuals who endanger the American people. Al Qaeda terrorists and their affiliates are at war with the United States, and those that we capture—like other prisoners of war—must be prevented from attacking us again. Having said that, we must recognize that these detention policies cannot be unbounded. They can't be based simply on what I or the executive branch decide[s] alone. That's why my administration has begun to reshape the standards that apply to ensure that they are in line with the rule of law. We must have clear, defensible, and lawful standards for those who fall into this category. We must have fair procedures so that we don't make mistakes. We must have a thorough process of periodic review so that any prolonged detention is carefully evaluated and justified.

I know that creating such a system poses unique challenges. And other countries have grappled with this question; now, so must we. But I want to be very clear that our goal is to construct a legitimate legal framework for the remaining Guantánamo detainees that cannot be transferred. Our goal is not to avoid a legitimate legal framework. In our constitutional system, prolonged detention should not be the decision of any one man. If and when we determine that the United States must hold individuals to keep them from carrying out an act of war, we will do so within a system that involves judicial and congressional oversight. And so, going forward, my administration will work with Congress to develop an appropriate legal regime so that our efforts are consistent with our values and our Constitution.

Now, as our efforts to close Guantánamo move forward, I know that the politics in Congress will be difficult. These are issues that are fodder for thirty-second commercials. You can almost picture the direct mail pieces that emerge from any vote on this issue, designed to frighten the population. I get it. But if we continue to make decisions within a climate of fear, we will make more mistakes. And if we refuse to deal with these issues today, then I guarantee you that they will be an albatross around our efforts to combat terrorism in the future.

I have confidence that the American people are more interested in doing what is right to protect this country than in political posturing. I am not the only person in this city who swore an oath to uphold the Constitution—so did each and every member of Congress. And together we have a responsibility to enlist our values in the effort to secure our people and to leave behind the legacy that makes it easier for future presidents to keep this country safe.

Now, let me touch on a second set of issues that relate to security and transparency.

National security requires a delicate balance. On the one hand, our democracy depends on transparency. On the other hand, some information must be protected from public disclosure for the sake of our security—for instance, the movement of our troops, our intelligence-gathering, or the information we have about a terrorist organization and its affiliates. In these and other cases, lives are at stake.

Now, several weeks ago, as part of an ongoing court case, I released memos issued by the previous administration's Office of Legal Counsel. I did not do this because I disagreed with the enhanced interrogation techniques that those memos authorized, and I didn't release the documents because I rejected their legal rationales—although I do on both counts. I released the memos because the existence of that approach to interrogation was already widely known, the Bush administration had acknowledged its existence, and I had already banned those methods. The argument that somehow by releasing those memos we are providing terrorists with information about how they will be interrogated makes no sense. We will not be interrogating terrorists using that approach. That approach is now prohibited.

In short, I released these memos because there was no overriding reason to protect them. And the ensuing debate has helped the American people better understand how these interrogation methods came to be authorized and used.

On the other hand, I recently opposed the release of certain photographs that were taken of detainees by US personnel between 2002 and 2004. Individuals who violated standards of behavior in these photos have been investigated and they have been held accountable. There was and is no debate as to whether what is reflected in those photos is wrong. Nothing has been concealed to absolve perpetrators of crimes. However, it was my judgment—informed by my national security team—that releasing these photos would inflame anti-American opinion and allow our enemies to paint US troops with a broad, damning, and inaccurate brush, thereby endangering them in theaters of war.

In short, there is a clear and compelling reason to not release these particular photos. There are nearly 200,000 Americans who are serving in harm's way, and I have a solemn responsibility for their safety as commander-in-chief. Nothing would be gained by the release of these photos that matters more than the lives of our young men and women serving in harm's way.

Now, in the press's mind and in some of the public's mind, these two cases are contradictory. They are not to me. In each of these cases, I had to strike the right balance between transparency and national security. And this balance brings with it a precious responsibility. There's no doubt that the American people have seen this balance tested over the last several years. In the images from Abu Ghraib and the brutal interrogation techniques made public long before I was president, the American people learned of actions taken in their name that bear no resemblance to the ideals that generations of Americans have fought for. And whether it was the run-up to the Iraq war or the revelation of secret programs, Americans often felt like part of the story had been unnecessarily withheld from them. And that caused suspicion to build up. And that leads to a thirst for accountability.

I understand that. I ran for president promising transparency, and I meant what I said. And that's why, whenever possible, my administration will make all information available to the American people so that they can make informed judgments and hold us accountable. But I have never argued—and I never will—that our most sensitive national security matters should simply be an open book. I will never abandon—and will vigorously defend—the necessity of classification to defend our troops at war, to protect sources and methods, and to safeguard confidential actions that keep the American people safe. Here's the difference though: whenever we cannot release certain information to the public for valid national security reasons, I will insist that there is oversight of my actions by Congress or by the courts.

We're currently launching a review of current policies by all those agencies responsible for the classification of documents to determine where reforms are possible and to assure that the other branches of government will be in a position to review executive branch decisions on these matters. Because in our system of checks and balances, someone must always watch over the watchers—especially when it comes to sensitive information.

Now, along these same lines, my administration is also confronting challenges to what is known as the state secrets privilege. This is a doctrine that allows the government to challenge legal cases involving secret programs. It's been used by many past presidents—Republican and Democrat—for many decades. And while this principle is absolutely necessary in some circumstances to protect national security, I am concerned that it has been over-used. It is also currently the subject of a wide range of lawsuits. So let me lay out some principles here. We must not protect information merely because it reveals the violation of a law or embarrassment to the government. And that's why my administration is nearing completion of a thorough review of this practice.

And we plan to embrace several principles for reform. We will apply a stricter legal test to material that can be protected under the state secrets privilege. We will not assert the privilege in court without first following our own formal process, including review by a Justice

Department committee and the personal approval of the attorney general. And each year we will voluntarily report to Congress when we have invoked the privilege and why because, as I said before, there must be proper oversight over our actions.

On all these matters related to the disclosure of sensitive information, I wish I could say that there was some simple formula out there to be had. There is not. These often involve tough calls, involve competing concerns, and they require a surgical approach. But the common thread that runs through all of my decisions is simple: we will safeguard what we must to protect the American people, but we will also ensure the accountability and oversight that is the hallmark of our constitutional system. I will never hide the truth because it's uncomfortable. I will deal with Congress and the courts as co-equal branches of government. I will tell the American people what I know and don't know, and when I release something publicly or keep something secret, I will tell you why.

Now, in all the areas that I've discussed today, the policies that I've proposed represent a new direction from the last eight years. To protect the American people and our values, we've banned enhanced interrogation techniques. We are closing the prison at Guantánamo. We are reforming military commissions and we will pursue a new legal regime to detain terrorists. We are declassifying more information and embracing more oversight of our actions; and we're narrowing our use of the state secrets privilege. These are dramatic changes that will put our approach to national security on a surer, safer, and more sustainable footing. Their implementation will take time, but they will get done.

There's a core principle that we will apply to all of our actions. Even as we clean up the mess at Guantánamo, we will constantly reevaluate our approach [and] subject our decisions to review from other branches of government as well as the public. We seek the strongest and most sustainable legal framework for addressing these issues in the long term—not to serve immediate politics, but to do what's right over the long term. By doing that we can leave behind a legacy that outlasts my administration—my presidency—that endures for the next president and the president after that: a legacy that protects the American people and enjoys a broad legitimacy at home and abroad.

Now, this is what I mean when I say that we need to focus on the future. I recognize that many still have a strong desire to focus on the past. When it comes to actions of the last eight years, passions are high. Some Americans are angry; others want to re-fight debates that have been settled, in some cases debates that they have lost. I know that these debates lead directly, in some cases, to a call for a fuller accounting, perhaps through an independent commission.

I've opposed the creation of such a commission because I believe that our existing democratic institutions are strong enough to deliver accountability. The Congress can review abuses of our values, and there are ongoing inquiries by the Congress into matters like enhanced interrogation techniques. The Department of Justice and our courts can work through and punish any violations of our laws or miscarriages of justice.

It's no secret there is a tendency in Washington to spend our time pointing fingers at one another. And it's no secret that our media culture feeds the impulse that leads to a good fight and good copy. But nothing will contribute more than that to an extended re-litigation of the last eight years. Already, we've seen how that kind of effort only leads those in Washington on different sides to laying blame. It can distract us from focusing our time, our efforts, and our politics on the challenges of the future.

We see how the recent debate has obscured the truth and sends people into opposite and absolutist ends. On the one side of the spectrum, there are those who make little allowance for the unique challenges posed by terrorism, and would almost never put national security over transparency. And on the other end of the spectrum, there are those who embrace a view that can be summarized in two words: "Anything goes." Their arguments suggest that the ends of fighting terrorism can be used to justify any means, and that the president should have blanket authority to do whatever he wants—provided it is a president with whom they agree.

Both sides may be sincere in their views, but neither side is right. The American people are not absolutist, and they don't elect us to impose a rigid ideology on our problems. They know that we need not sacrifice our security for our values, nor sacrifice our values for our security, so long as we approach difficult questions with honesty and care and a dose of common sense. That, after all, is the unique genius of America. That's the challenge laid down by our Constitution. That has been the source of our strength through the ages. That's what makes the United States of America different as a nation.

I can stand here today, as president of the United States, and say without exception or equivocation that we do not torture and that we will vigorously protect our people while forging a strong and durable framework that allows us to fight terrorism while abiding by the rule of law. Make no mistake: if we fail to turn the page on the approach that was taken over the past several years, then I will not be able to say that as president. And if we cannot stand for our core values, then we are not keeping faith with the documents that are enshrined in this hall.

The Framers who drafted the Constitution could not have foreseen the challenges that have unfolded over the last 222 years. But our Constitution has endured through secession and civil rights, through world war and cold war, because it provides a foundation of principles that can be applied pragmatically; it provides a compass that can help us find our way. It hasn't always been easy. We are an imperfect people. Every now and then, there are those who think that America's safety and success require us to walk away from the sacred principles enshrined in this building. And we hear such voices today. But over the long haul the American people have resisted that temptation. And though we've made our share of mistakes, required some course corrections, ultimately we have held fast to the principles that have been the source of our strength and a beacon to the world.

Now this generation faces a great test in the specter of terrorism. And unlike the Civil War or World War II, we can't count on a surrender ceremony to bring this journey to an end. Right now, in distant training camps and in crowded cities, there are people plotting to take American lives. That will be the case a year from now, five years from now, and—in all probability—ten years from now. Neither I nor anyone can stand here today and say that there will not be another terrorist attack that takes American lives. But I can say with certainty that my administration—along with our extraordinary troops and the patriotic men and women who defend our national security—will do everything in our power to keep the American people safe. And I do know with certainty that we can defeat Al Qaeda. Because the terrorists can only succeed if they swell their ranks and alienate America from our allies, and they will never be able to do that if we stay true to who we are, if we forge tough and durable approaches to fighting terrorism that are anchored in our timeless ideals. This must be our common purpose.

I ran for president because I believe that we cannot solve the challenges of our time unless we solve them together. We will not be safe if we see national security as a wedge that divides America—it can and must be a cause that unites us as one people and as one nation. We've done so before in times that were more perilous than ours. We will do so once again.

. . .

Appendix: Obama–B

President Barack Obama,
"A Just and Lasting Peace,"
the 2009 Nobel Peace Prize Lecture,
Oslo, Norway, December 10, 2009

. . .

We must begin by acknowledging the hard truth: we will not eradicate violent conflict in our lifetimes. There will be times when nations—acting individually or in concert—will find the use of force not only necessary but morally justified.

I make this statement mindful of what Martin Luther King Jr. said in this same ceremony years ago: "Violence never brings permanent peace. It solves no social problem: it merely creates new and more complicated ones." As someone who stands here as a direct consequence of Dr. King's life work, I am living testimony to the moral force of non-violence. I know there's nothing weak—nothing passive—nothing naïve—in the creed and lives of [Mahatma] Gandhi and King.

But as a head of state sworn to protect and defend my nation, I cannot be guided by their examples alone. I face the world as it is, and cannot stand idle in the face of threats to the American people. For make no mistake: evil does exist in the world. A non-violent movement could not have halted Hitler's armies. Negotiations cannot convince Al Qaeda's leaders to lay down their arms. To say that force may sometimes be necessary is not a call to cynicism—it is a recognition of history, the imperfections of man, and the limits of reason.

. . .

I begin with this point because in many countries there is a deep ambivalence about military action today, no matter what the cause. And at times, this is joined by a reflexive suspicion of America, the world's sole military superpower.

But the world must remember that it was not simply international institutions—not just treaties and declarations—that brought stability to a post-World War II world. Whatever mistakes we have made, the plain fact is this: the United States of America has helped underwrite global security for more than six decades with the blood of our citizens and the strength of our arms. The service and sacrifice of our men and women in uniform has promoted peace and prosperity from Germany to Korea and enabled democracy to take hold in places like the Balkans. We have borne this burden not because we seek to impose our will. We have done so out of enlightened self-interest—because we seek a better future for our children and grandchildren, and we believe that their lives will be better if others' children and grandchildren can live in freedom and prosperity.

So yes, the instruments of war do have a role to play in preserving the peace. And yet this truth must coexist with another—that no matter how justified, war promises human tragedy. The soldier's courage and sacrifice is full of glory, expressing devotion to country, to cause, to comrades in arms. But war itself is never glorious, and we must never trumpet it as such.

So part of our challenge is reconciling these two seemingly irreconcilable truths—that war is sometimes necessary, and war at some level is an expression of human folly. Concretely, we must direct our effort to the task that President Kennedy called for long ago. "Let us focus," he said, "on a more practical, more attainable peace, based not on a sudden revolution in human nature but on a gradual evolution in human institutions."

"A gradual evolution of human institutions." What might this evolution look like? What might these practical steps be?

To begin with, I believe that all nations—strong and weak alike—must adhere to standards that govern the use of force. I—like any head of state—reserve the right to act unilaterally if necessary to defend my nation. Nevertheless, I am convinced that adhering to standards, international standards, strengthens those who do, and isolates and weakens those who don't.

The world rallied around America after the 9/11 attacks and continues to support our efforts in Afghanistan because of the horror of those senseless attacks and the recognized principle of self-defense. Likewise, the world recognized the need to confront Saddam Hussein when he invaded Kuwait—a consensus that sent a clear message to all about the cost of aggression.

Furthermore, America [cannot insist]—in fact, no nation can insist—that others follow the rules of the road if we refuse to follow them ourselves. For when we don't, our actions appear arbitrary and undercut the legitimacy of future interventions, no matter how justified.

And this becomes particularly important when the purpose of military action extends beyond self-defense or the defense of one nation against an aggressor. More and more, we all confront difficult questions about how to prevent the slaughter of civilians by their own government or to stop a civil war whose violence and suffering can engulf an entire region.

I believe that force can be justified on humanitarian grounds, as it was in the Balkans, or in other places that have been scarred by war. Inaction tears at our conscience and can lead to more costly intervention later. That's why all responsible nations must embrace the role that militaries with a clear mandate can play to keep the peace.

America's commitment to global security will never waver. But in a world in which threats are more diffuse, and missions more complex, America cannot act alone. America alone cannot secure the peace. This is true in Afghanistan. This is true in failed states like

Somalia, where terrorism and piracy are joined by famine and human suffering. And, sadly, it will continue to be true in unstable regions for years to come.

The leaders and soldiers of NATO countries, and other friends and allies, demonstrate this truth through the capacity and courage they've shown in Afghanistan. But in many countries, there is a disconnect between the efforts of those who serve and the ambivalence of the broader public. I understand why war is not popular, but I also know this: the belief that peace is desirable is rarely enough to achieve it. Peace requires responsibility. Peace entails sacrifice. That's why NATO continues to be indispensable. That's why we must strengthen UN and regional peacekeeping, and not leave the task to a few countries. That's why we honor those who return home from peacekeeping and training abroad to Oslo and Rome; to Ottawa and Sydney; to Dhaka and Kigali. We honor them not as makers of war, but as wagers of peace.

Let me make one final point about the use of force. Even as we make difficult decisions about going to war, we must also think clearly about how we fight it. The Nobel Committee recognized this truth in awarding its first prize for peace to Henry Dunant, the founder of the Red Cross and a driving force behind the Geneva Conventions.

Where force is necessary, we have a moral and strategic interest in binding ourselves to certain rules of conduct. And even as we confront a vicious adversary that abides by no rules, I believe the United States of America must remain a standard-bearer in the conduct of war. That is what makes us different from those whom we fight. That is a source of our strength. That is why I prohibited torture. That is why I ordered the prison at Guantánamo Bay closed. And that is why I have reaffirmed America's commitment to abide by the Geneva Conventions. We lose ourselves when we compromise the very ideals that we fight to defend. And we honor those ideals by upholding them not when it's easy, but when it is hard.

. . .

Appendix: Obama–C

Remarks by the president at the
National Defense University
(on US counterterrorism strategy)
Fort McNair, Washington, DC
May 23, 2013

For over two centuries, the United States has been bound together by founding documents that defined who we are as Americans and served as our compass through every type of change. Matters of war and peace are no different. Americans are deeply ambivalent about war, but having fought for our independence, we know a price must

---

[*Editors' Note:* President Barack Obama delivered this speech on May 23, 2013, at the National Defense University (NDU), Fort McNair, Washington, DC. A short section of introductory material has been edited out in this version. In addition, the president was interrupted by a heckler, Medea Benjamin of the anti-war and anti-drone organization Code Pink; the president chose to engage her with his own remarks, and the exchange is preserved in the official White House text of the address. We have therefore kept that exchange in the text as well. Finally, the NDU speech was accompanied by two additional documents that are important commentaries and emendations to the president's remarks and intended to be read with them. The first is a White House press statement, *Fact Sheet: US Policy Standards and Procedures for the Use of Force in Counterterrorism Operations Outside the United States and Areas of Active Hostilities* (May 23, 2013). The second is a *letter dated May 22, 2013, from Eric H. Holder, Jr., Attorney General, to Sen. Patrick J. Leahy, Chair of the Senate Judiciary Committee,* addressing drone operations in connection with US citizens. These two documents are included here as appendices to President Obama's NDU speech.]

be paid for freedom. From the Civil War to our struggle against fascism, on through the long twilight struggle of the Cold War, battlefields have changed and technology has evolved. But our commitment to constitutional principles has weathered every war, and every war has come to an end.

With the collapse of the Berlin Wall, a new dawn of democracy took hold abroad and a decade of peace and prosperity arrived here at home. And for a moment, it seemed the 21st century would be a tranquil time. And then, on September 11, 2001, we were shaken out of complacency. Thousands were taken from us, as clouds of fire and metal and ash descended upon a sun-filled morning. This was a different kind of war. No armies came to our shores, and our military was not the principal target. Instead, a group of terrorists came to kill as many civilians as they could.

And so our nation went to war. We have now been at war for well over a decade. I won't review the full history. What is clear is that we quickly drove Al Qaeda out of Afghanistan, but then shifted our focus and began a new war in Iraq. And this carried significant consequences for our fight against Al Qaeda, our standing in the world, and—to this day—our interests in a vital region.

Meanwhile, we strengthened our defenses—hardening targets, tightening transportation security, giving law enforcement new tools to prevent terror. Most of these changes were sound. Some caused inconvenience. But some, like expanded surveillance, raised difficult questions about the balance that we strike between our interests in security and our values of privacy. And in some cases, I believe we compromised our basic values—by using torture to interrogate our enemies and detaining individuals in a way that ran counter to the rule of law.

So after I took office, we stepped up the war against Al Qaeda but we also sought to change its course. We relentlessly targeted Al Qaeda's leadership. We ended the war in Iraq and brought nearly 150,000 troops home. We pursued a new strategy in Afghanistan and increased our training of Afghan forces. We unequivocally banned torture, affirmed our commitment to civilian courts, worked to align our policies with the rule of law, and expanded our consultations with Congress.

Today, Osama bin Laden is dead, and so are most of his top lieutenants. There have been no large-scale attacks on the United States, and our homeland is more secure. Fewer of our troops are in harm's way, and over the next nineteen months they will continue to come home. Our alliances are strong, and so is our standing in the world. In sum, we are safer because of our efforts.

Now, make no mistake, our nation is still threatened by terrorists. From Benghazi to Boston, we have been tragically reminded of that truth. But we have to recognize that the threat has shifted and evolved from the one that came to our shores on 9/11. With a decade of experience now to draw from, this is the moment to ask ourselves hard questions—about the nature of today's threats and how we should confront them.

And these questions matter to every American.

For over the last decade, our nation has spent well over a trillion dollars on war, helping to explode our deficits and constraining our ability to nation-build here at home. Our service members and their families have sacrificed far more on our behalf. Nearly 7,000 Americans have made the ultimate sacrifice. Many more have left a part of themselves on the battlefield, or brought the shadows of battle back home. From our use of drones to the detention of terrorist suspects, the decisions that we are making now will define the type of nation— and world—that we leave to our children.

So America is at a crossroads. We must define the nature and scope of this struggle, or else it will define us. We have to be mindful of James Madison's warning that "No nation could preserve its freedom in the midst of continual warfare." Neither I, nor any president, can promise the total defeat of terror. We will never erase the evil that lies in the hearts of some human beings, nor stamp out every danger to our open society. But what we can do—what we must do—is dismantle networks that pose a direct danger to us and make it less likely for new groups to gain a foothold, all the while maintaining the freedoms and ideals that we defend. And to define that strategy, we have to make decisions based not on fear, but on hard-earned wisdom. That begins with understanding the current threat that we face.

Today, the core of Al Qaeda in Afghanistan and Pakistan is on the path to defeat. Their remaining operatives spend more time thinking about their own safety than plotting against us. They did not direct the attacks in Benghazi or Boston. They've not carried out a successful attack on our homeland since 9/11.

Instead, what we've seen is the emergence of various Al Qaeda affiliates. From Yemen to Iraq, from Somalia to North Africa, the threat today is more diffuse, with Al Qaeda's affiliates in the Arabian Peninsula—AQAP—the most active in plotting against our homeland. And while none of AQAP's efforts approach the scale of 9/11, they have continued to plot acts of terror, like the attempt to blow up an airplane on Christmas Day in 2009.

Unrest in the Arab world has also allowed extremists to gain a foothold in countries like Libya and Syria. But here, too, there are differences from 9/11. In some cases, we continue to confront state-sponsored networks like Hezbollah that engage in acts of terror to achieve political goals. Others of these groups are simply collections of local militias or extremists interested in seizing territory. And while we are vigilant for signs that these groups may pose a transnational threat, most are focused on operating in the countries and regions where they are based. And that means we'll face more localized threats like what we saw in Benghazi, or the BP oil facility in Algeria, in which local operatives—perhaps in loose affiliation with regional networks—launch periodic attacks against Western diplomats, companies, and other soft targets, or resort to kidnapping and other criminal enterprises to fund their operations.

And, finally, we face a real threat from radicalized individuals here in the United States. Whether it's a shooter at a Sikh temple in Wisconsin, a plane flying into a building in Texas, or the extremists who killed 168 people at the Federal Building in Oklahoma City, America has confronted many forms of violent extremism in our history. Deranged or alienated individuals—often US citizens or legal residents—can do enormous damage, particularly when inspired by larger notions of violent jihad. And that pull toward extremism appears to have led to the shooting at Fort Hood and the bombing of the Boston Marathon.

So that's the current threat—lethal yet less capable Al Qaeda affiliates; threats to diplomatic facilities and businesses abroad; home-grown extremists. This is the future of terrorism. We have to take these threats seriously, and do all that we can to confront them. But as we shape our response, we have to recognize that the scale of this threat closely resembles the types of attacks we faced before 9/11.

In the 1980s, we lost Americans to terrorism at our embassy in Beirut; at our Marine barracks in Lebanon; on a cruise ship at sea; at a disco in Berlin; and on a Pan Am flight—Flight 103—over Lockerbie. In the 1990s, we lost Americans to terrorism at the World Trade Center; at our military facilities in Saudi Arabia; and at our embassy in Kenya. These attacks were all brutal; they were all deadly; and we learned that, left unchecked, these threats can grow. But if dealt with smartly and proportionally, these threats need not rise to the level that we saw on the eve of 9/11.

Moreover, we have to recognize that these threats don't arise in a vacuum. Most, though not all, of the terrorism we face is fueled by a common ideology—a belief by some extremists that Islam is in conflict with the United States and the West, and that violence against Western targets, including civilians, is justified in pursuit of a larger cause. Of course, this ideology is based on a lie, for the United States is not at war with Islam. And this ideology is rejected by the vast majority of Muslims, who are the most frequent victims of terrorist attacks.

Nevertheless, this ideology persists, and in an age when ideas and images can travel the globe in an instant, our response to terrorism can't depend on military or law enforcement alone. We need all elements of national power to win a battle of wills, a battle of ideas. So what I want to discuss here today is the components of such a comprehensive counterterrorism strategy.

First, we must finish the work of defeating Al Qaeda and its associated forces.

In Afghanistan, we will complete our transition to Afghan responsibility for that country's security. Our troops will come home. Our combat mission will come to an end. And we will work with the Afghan government to train security forces, and sustain a counterterrorism force, which ensures that Al Qaeda can never again establish a safe haven to launch attacks against us or our allies.

Beyond Afghanistan, we must define our effort not as a boundless "global war on terror" but rather as a series of persistent, targeted efforts to dismantle specific networks of violent extremists that threaten America. In many cases, this will involve partnerships with other countries. Already, thousands of Pakistani soldiers have lost their lives fighting extremists. In Yemen, we are supporting security forces that have reclaimed territory from AQAP. In Somalia, we helped a coalition of African nations push Al Shabaab out of its strongholds. In Mali, we're providing military aid to French-led intervention to push back Al Qaeda in the Maghreb and help the people of Mali reclaim their future.

Much of our best counterterrorism cooperation results in the gathering and sharing of intelligence, the arrest and prosecution of terrorists. And that's how a Somali terrorist apprehended off the coast of Yemen is now in a prison in New York. That's how we worked with European allies to disrupt plots from Denmark to Germany to the United Kingdom. That's how intelligence collected with Saudi Arabia helped us stop a cargo plane from being blown up over the Atlantic. These partnerships work.

But despite our strong preference for the detention and prosecution of terrorists, sometimes this approach is foreclosed. Al Qaeda and its affiliates try to gain footholds in some of the most distant and unforgiving places on Earth. They take refuge in remote tribal regions. They hide in caves and walled compounds. They train in empty deserts and rugged mountains.

In some of these places—such as parts of Somalia and Yemen—the state only has the most tenuous reach into the territory. In other cases, the state lacks the capacity or will to take action. And it's also not possible for America to simply deploy a team of special forces to capture every terrorist. Even when such an approach may be possible, there are places where it would pose profound risks to our troops and local civilians—where a terrorist compound cannot be breached without triggering a firefight with surrounding tribal communities, for example, that pose no threat to us; times when putting US boots on the ground may trigger a major international crisis.

To put it another way, our operation in Pakistan against Osama bin Laden cannot be the norm. The risks in that case were immense. The likelihood of capture, although that was our preference, was remote given the certainty that our folks would confront resistance. The fact that we did not find ourselves confronted with civilian casualties, or embroiled in an extended firefight, was a testament to the meticulous planning and professionalism of our special forces, but it also depended on some luck. And it was supported by massive infrastructure in Afghanistan.

And even then, the cost to our relationship with Pakistan—and the backlash among the Pakistani public over encroachment on their territory—was so severe that we are just now beginning to rebuild this important partnership.

So it is in this context that the United States has taken lethal, targeted action against Al Qaeda and its associated forces, including with remotely piloted aircraft commonly referred to as drones.

As was true in previous armed conflicts, this new technology raises profound questions—about who is targeted, and why; about civilian casualties and the risk of creating new enemies; about the legality of such strikes under US and international law; about accountability and morality. So let me address these questions.

To begin with, our actions are effective. Don't take my word for it. In the intelligence gathered at bin Laden's compound, we found that he wrote, "We could lose the reserves to enemy's air strikes. We cannot fight air strikes with explosives." Other communications from Al Qaeda operatives confirm this as well. Dozens of highly skilled Al Qaeda commanders, trainers, bomb-makers, and operatives have been taken off the battlefield. Plots have been disrupted that would have targeted international aviation, US transit systems, European cities, and our troops in Afghanistan. Simply put, these strikes have saved lives.

Moreover, America's actions are legal. We were attacked on 9/11. Within a week, Congress overwhelmingly authorized the use of force. Under domestic law, and international law, the United States is at war with Al Qaeda, the Taliban, and their associated forces. We are at war with an organization that right now would kill as many Americans as it could if we did not stop it first. So this is a just war—a war waged proportionally, in last resort, and in self-defense.

And yet, as our fight enters a new phase, America's legitimate claim of self-defense cannot be the end of the discussion. To say a military tactic is legal, or even effective, is not to say it is wise or moral in every instance. For the same human progress that gives us the technology to strike half a world away also demands the discipline to constrain that power—or risk abusing it. And that's why, over the last four years, my administration has worked vigorously to establish a framework that governs our use of force against terrorists—insisting upon clear guidelines, oversight, and accountability that are now codified in the "Presidential Policy Guidance" that I signed yesterday.

In the Afghan war theater, we must—and will—continue to support our troops until the transition is complete at the end of 2014. And that means we will continue to take strikes against high-value Al Qaeda targets, but also against forces that are massing to support attacks on coalition forces. But by the end of 2014, we will no longer have the same need for force protection, and the progress we've made against core Al Qaeda will reduce the need for unmanned strikes.

Beyond the Afghan theater, we only target Al Qaeda and its associated forces. And even then, the use of drones is heavily constrained. America does not take strikes when we have the ability to capture individual terrorists; our preference is always to detain, interrogate, and prosecute. America cannot take strikes wherever we choose; our actions are bound by consultations with partners and respect for state sovereignty.

America does not take strikes to punish individuals; we act against terrorists who pose a continuing and imminent threat to the American people and when there are no other governments capable of effectively addressing the threat. And before any strike is taken, there must be near certainty that no civilians will be killed or injured—the highest standard we can set.

Now, this last point is critical, because much of the criticism about drone strikes—both here at home and abroad—understandably centers on reports of civilian casualties. There's a wide gap between US assessments of such casualties and nongovernmental reports. Nevertheless, it is a hard fact that US strikes have resulted in civilian casualties, a risk that exists in every war. And for the families of those civilians, no words or legal construct can justify their loss. For me, and those in my chain of command, those deaths will haunt us as long as we live, just as we are haunted by the civilian casualties that have occurred throughout conventional fighting in Afghanistan and Iraq.

But as commander in chief, I must weigh these heartbreaking tragedies against the alternatives. To do nothing in the face of terrorist networks would invite far more civilian casualties—not just in our cities at home and our facilities abroad, but also in the very places like Sana'a and Kabul and Mogadishu where terrorists seek a foothold. Remember that the terrorists we are after target civilians, and the death toll from their acts of terrorism against Muslims dwarfs any estimate of civilian casualties from drone strikes. So doing nothing is not an option.

Where foreign governments cannot or will not effectively stop terrorism in their territory, the primary alternative to targeted lethal action would be the use of conventional military options. As I've already said, even small special operations carry enormous risks. Conventional airpower or missiles are far less precise than drones, and are likely to cause more civilian casualties and more local outrage. And invasions of these territories lead us to be viewed as occupying armies, unleash a torrent of unintended consequences, are difficult to contain, result in large numbers of civilian casualties, and ultimately empower those who thrive on violent conflict.

So it is false to assert that putting boots on the ground is less likely to result in civilian deaths or less likely to create enemies in the Muslim world. The results would be more US deaths, more Black Hawks down, more confrontations with local populations, and an inevitable mission creep in support of such raids that could easily escalate into new wars.

Yes, the conflict with Al Qaeda, like all armed conflicts, invites tragedy. But by narrowly targeting our action against those who want to kill us and not the people they hide among, we are choosing the course of action least likely to result in the loss of innocent life.

Our efforts must be measured against the history of putting American troops in distant lands among hostile populations. In Vietnam, hundreds of thousands of civilians died in a war where the boundaries of battle were blurred. In Iraq and Afghanistan, despite the extraordinary courage and discipline of our troops, thousands of civilians have been killed. So neither conventional military action nor waiting for attacks to occur offers moral safe harbor, and neither does a sole reliance on law enforcement in territories that have no functioning police or security services—and, indeed, have no functioning law.

Now, this is not to say that the risks are not real. Any US military action in foreign lands risks creating more enemies and impacts public opinion overseas. Moreover, our laws constrain the power of the president even during wartime, and I have taken an oath to defend the Constitution of the United States. The very precision of drone strikes and the necessary secrecy often involved in such actions can end up shielding our government from the public scrutiny that a troop deployment invites. It can also lead a president and his team to view drone strikes as a cure-all for terrorism.

And for this reason, I've insisted on strong oversight of all lethal action. After I took office, my administration began briefing all strikes outside of Iraq and Afghanistan to the appropriate committees of Congress. Let me repeat that: not only did Congress authorize the use of force, it is briefed on every strike that America takes. Every strike. That includes the one instance when we targeted an American citizen—Anwar al-Awlaki, the chief of external operations for AQAP.

This week, I authorized the declassification of this action, and the deaths of three other Americans in drone strikes, to facilitate transparency and debate on this issue and to dismiss some of the more outlandish claims that have been made. For the record, I do not believe it would be constitutional for the government to target and kill any US citizen—with a drone, or with a shotgun—without due process, nor should any president deploy armed drones over US soil.

But when a US citizen goes abroad to wage war against America and is actively plotting to kill US citizens, and when neither the United States nor our partners are in a position to capture him before he carries out a plot, his citizenship should no more serve as a shield than a sniper shooting down on an innocent crowd should be protected from a SWAT team.

That's who Anwar al-Awlaki was—he was continuously trying to kill people. He helped oversee the 2010 plot to detonate explosive devices on two US-bound cargo planes. He was involved in planning to blow up an airliner in 2009. When Farouk Abdulmutallab—the Christmas Day bomber—went to Yemen in 2009, al-Awlaki hosted him, approved his suicide operation, helped him tape a martyrdom video to be shown after the attack, and his last instructions were to blow up the airplane when it was over American soil. I would have detained and prosecuted al-Awlaki if we captured him before he carried out a plot, but we couldn't. And as president, I would have been derelict in my duty had I not authorized the strike that took him out.

Of course, the targeting of any American raises constitutional issues that are not present in other strikes—which is why my administration submitted information about al-Awlaki to the Department of Justice months before al-Awlaki was killed, and briefed the Congress before this strike as well. But the high threshold that we've set for taking lethal action applies to all potential terrorist targets, regardless of whether or not they are American citizens. This threshold respects the inherent dignity of every human life. Alongside the decision to put our men and women in uniform in harm's way, the decision to use force against individuals or groups—even against a sworn enemy of the United States—is the hardest thing I do as president. But these decisions must be made, given my responsibility to protect the American people.

Going forward, I've asked my administration to review proposals to extend oversight of lethal actions outside of warzones that go beyond our reporting to Congress. Each option has virtues in theory, but poses difficulties in practice. For example, the establishment of a special court to evaluate and authorize lethal action has the benefit of bringing a third branch of government into the process, but raises serious constitutional issues about presidential and judicial authority. Another idea that's been suggested—the establishment of an independent oversight board in the executive branch—avoids those problems, but may introduce a layer of bureaucracy into national security decision-making without inspiring additional public confidence in the process. But despite these challenges, I look forward to actively engaging Congress to explore these and other options for increased oversight.

I believe, however, that the use of force must be seen as part of a larger discussion we need to have about a comprehensive counterterrorism strategy—because for all the focus on the use of force, force alone cannot make us safe. We cannot use force everywhere that a radical ideology takes root; and in the absence of a strategy that reduces the wellspring of extremism, a perpetual war—through drones or special forces or troop deployments—will prove self-defeating and alter our country in troubling ways.

So the next element of our strategy involves addressing the underlying grievances and conflicts that feed extremism—from North Africa to South Asia. As we've learned this past decade, this is a vast and complex undertaking. We must be humble in our expectation that we can quickly resolve deep-rooted problems like poverty and sectarian hatred. Moreover, no two countries are alike, and some will undergo chaotic change before things get better. But our security and our values demand that we make the effort.

This means patiently supporting transitions to democracy in places like Egypt and Tunisia and Libya—because the peaceful realization of individual aspirations will serve as a rebuke to violent extremists. We must strengthen the opposition in Syria, while isolating extremist elements—because the end of a tyrant must not give way to the tyranny of terrorism. We are actively working to promote peace between Israelis and Palestinians—because it is right and because such a peace could help reshape attitudes in the region. And we must help countries modernize economies, upgrade education, and encourage entrepreneurship—because American leadership has always been elevated by our ability to connect with people's hopes, and not simply their fears.

And success on all these fronts requires sustained engagement, but it will also require resources. I know that foreign aid is one of the least popular expenditures that there is. That's true for Democrats and Republicans—I've seen the polling—even though it amounts to less than 1 percent of the federal budget. In fact, a lot of folks think it's 25 percent, if you ask people on the streets. Less than 1 percent—still wildly unpopular. But foreign assistance cannot be viewed as charity. It is fundamental to our national security. And it's fundamental to any sensible long-term strategy to battle extremism.

Moreover, foreign assistance is a tiny fraction of what we spend fighting wars that our assistance might ultimately prevent. For what we spent in a month in Iraq at the height of the war, we could be training security forces in Libya, maintaining peace agreements between Israel and its neighbors, feeding the hungry in Yemen, building schools in Pakistan, and creating reservoirs of goodwill that marginalize extremists. That has to be part of our strategy.

Moreover, America cannot carry out this work if we don't have diplomats serving in some very dangerous places. Over the past decade, we have strengthened security at our embassies, and I am implementing every recommendation of the Accountability Review Board, which found unacceptable failures in Benghazi. I've called on Congress to fully fund these efforts to bolster security and harden facilities, improve intelligence, and facilitate a quicker response time from our military if a crisis emerges.

But even after we take these steps, some irreducible risks to our diplomats will remain. This is the price of being the world's most powerful nation, particularly as a wave of change washes over the Arab world. And in balancing the trade-offs between security and active diplomacy, I firmly believe that any retreat from challenging regions will only increase the dangers that we face in the long run.

And that's why we should be grateful to those diplomats who are willing to serve.

Targeted action against terrorists, effective partnerships, diplomatic engagement and assistance—through such a comprehensive strategy we can significantly reduce the chances of large-scale attacks on the homeland and mitigate threats to Americans overseas. But as we guard against dangers from abroad, we cannot neglect the daunting challenge of terrorism from within our borders.

As I said earlier, this threat is not new. But technology and the Internet increase its frequency and in some cases its lethality. Today, a person can consume hateful propaganda, commit to a violent agenda, and learn how to kill without leaving home. To address this threat, two years ago my administration did a comprehensive review and engaged with law enforcement.

And the best way to prevent violent extremism inspired by violent jihadists is to work with the Muslim American community—which has consistently rejected terrorism—to identify signs of radicalization and partner with law enforcement when an individual is drifting toward violence. And these partnerships can only work when we recognize that Muslims are a fundamental part of the American family. In fact, the success of American Muslims and our determination to guard against any encroachments on their civil liberties is the ultimate rebuke to those who say that we're at war with Islam.

Thwarting homegrown plots presents particular challenges in part because of our proud commitment to civil liberties for all who call America home. That's why, in the years to come, we will have to keep working hard to strike the appropriate balance between our need for security and preserving those freedoms that make us who we are. That means reviewing the authorities of law enforcement, so we can intercept new types of communication, but also build in privacy protections to prevent abuse.

That means that—even after Boston—we do not deport someone or throw somebody in prison in the absence of evidence. That means putting careful constraints on the tools the government uses to protect sensitive information, such as the state secrets doctrine. And that means finally having a strong Privacy and Civil Liberties [Oversight] Board to review those issues where our counterterrorism efforts and our values may come into tension.

The Justice Department's investigation of national security leaks offers a recent example of the challenges involved in striking the right balance between our security and our open society. As commander in chief, I believe we must keep information secret that protects our operations and our people in the field. To do so, we must enforce consequences for those who break the law and breach their commitment to protect classified information. But a free press is also essential for our democracy. That's who we are. And I'm troubled by the possibility that leak investigations may chill the investigative journalism that holds government accountable.

Journalists should not be at legal risk for doing their jobs. Our focus must be on those who break the law. And that's why I've called on Congress to pass a media shield law to guard against government overreach. And I've raised these issues with the attorney general, who shares my concerns. So he has agreed to review existing Department of Justice guidelines governing investigations that involve reporters, and he'll convene a group of media organizations to hear their concerns as part of that review. And I've directed the attorney general to report back to me by July 12.

Now, all these issues remind us that the choices we make about war can impact—in sometimes unintended ways—the openness and freedom on which our way of life depends. And that is why I intend to engage Congress about the existing Authorization to Use Military Force, or AUMF, to determine how we can continue to fight terrorism without keeping America on a perpetual wartime footing.

The AUMF is now nearly twelve years old. The Afghan war is coming to an end. Core Al Qaeda is a shell of its former self. Groups like AQAP must be dealt with, but in the years to come, not every collection of thugs that label themselves Al Qaeda will pose a credible threat to the United States. Unless we discipline our thinking, our definitions, our actions, we may be drawn into more wars we don't need to fight, or continue to grant presidents unbound powers more suited for traditional armed conflicts between nation-states.

So I look forward to engaging Congress and the American people in efforts to refine, and ultimately repeal, the AUMF's mandate. And I will not sign laws designed to expand this mandate further. Our systematic effort to dismantle terrorist organizations must continue. But this war, like all wars, must end. That's what history advises. That's what our democracy demands.

And that brings me to my final topic: the detention of terrorist suspects. I'm going to repeat one more time: as a matter of policy, the preference of the United States is to capture terrorist suspects. When we do detain a suspect, we interrogate him. And if the suspect can be prosecuted, we decide whether to try him in a civilian court or a military commission.

During the past decade, the vast majority of those detained by our military were captured on the battlefield. In Iraq, we turned over thousands of prisoners as we ended the war. In Afghanistan, we have transitioned detention facilities to the Afghans, as part of the process of restoring Afghan sovereignty. So we bring law-of-war detention to an end, and we are committed to prosecuting terrorists wherever we can.

The glaring exception to this time-tested approach is the detention center at Guantánamo Bay. The original premise for opening GTMO—that detainees would not be able to challenge their detention—was found unconstitutional five years ago. In the meantime, GTMO has become a symbol around the world for an America that flouts the rule of law. Our allies won't cooperate with us if they think a terrorist will end up at GTMO.

During a time of budget cuts, we spend $150 million each year to imprison 166 people—almost $1 million per prisoner. And the

Department of Defense estimates that we must spend another $200 million to keep GTMO open at a time when we're cutting investments in education and research here at home and when the Pentagon is struggling with sequester and budget cuts.

As president, I have tried to close GTMO. I transferred sixty-seven detainees to other countries before Congress imposed restrictions to effectively prevent us from either transferring detainees to other countries or imprisoning them here in the United States.

These restrictions make no sense. After all, under President Bush, some 530 detainees were transferred from GTMO with Congress's support. When I ran for president the first time, John McCain supported closing GTMO—this was a bipartisan issue. No person has ever escaped one of our super-max or military prisons here in the United States—ever. Our courts have convicted hundreds of people for terrorism or terrorism-related offenses, including some folks who are more dangerous than most GTMO detainees. They're in our prisons.

And given my administration's relentless pursuit of Al Qaeda's leadership, there is no justification beyond politics for Congress to prevent us from closing a facility that should have never been opened. (Applause.)

AUDIENCE MEMBER: Excuse me, President Obama—

MR. OBAMA: So—let me finish, ma'am. So today, once again—

AUDIENCE MEMBER: There are 102 people on a hunger strike. These are desperate people.

MR. OBAMA: I'm about to address it, ma'am, but you've got to let me speak. I'm about to address it.

AUDIENCE MEMBER: You're our commander in chief—

MR. OBAMA: Let me address it.

AUDIENCE MEMBER: —you can close Guantánamo Bay.

MR. OBAMA: Why don't you let me address it, ma'am.

AUDIENCE MEMBER: There's still prisoners—

MR. OBAMA: Why don't you sit down and I will tell you exactly what I'm going to do.

AUDIENCE MEMBER: That includes fifty-seven Yemenis.

MR. OBAMA: Thank you, ma'am. Thank you. (Applause.) Ma'am, thank you. You should let me finish my sentence.

Today, I once again call on Congress to lift the restrictions on detainee transfers from GTMO. (Applause.) I have asked the Department of Defense to designate a site in the United States where we can hold military commissions. I'm appointing a new senior envoy at the State Department and Defense Department whose sole responsibility will be to achieve the transfer of detainees to third countries.

I am lifting the moratorium on detainee transfers to Yemen so we can review them on a case-by-case basis. To the greatest extent possible, we will transfer detainees who have been cleared to go to other countries.

AUDIENCE MEMBER: —prisoners already. Release them today.

MR. OBAMA: Where appropriate, we will bring terrorists to justice in our courts and our military justice system. And we will insist that judicial review be available for every detainee.

AUDIENCE MEMBER: It needs to be—

THE PRESIDENT: Now, ma'am, let me finish. Let me finish, ma'am. Part of free speech is you being able to speak, but also, you listening and me being able to speak. (Applause.)

Now, even after we take these steps one issue will remain—just how to deal with those GTMO detainees who we know have participated in dangerous plots or attacks but who cannot be prosecuted, for example, because the evidence against them has been compromised or is inadmissible in a court of law. But once we commit to a process of closing GTMO, I am confident that this legacy problem can be resolved, consistent with our commitment to the rule of law.

I know the politics are hard. But history will cast a harsh judgment on this aspect of our fight against terrorism and those of us who fail to end it. Imagine a future—ten years from now or twenty years from now—when the United States of America is still holding people who have been charged with no crime on a piece of land that is not part of our country. Look at the current situation, where we are force-feeding detainees who are being held on a hunger strike. I'm willing to cut the young lady who interrupted me some slack because it's worth being passionate about. Is this who we are? Is that something our Founders foresaw? Is that the America we want to leave our children? Our sense of justice is stronger than that.

We have prosecuted scores of terrorists in our courts. That includes Umar Farouk Abdulmutallab, who tried to blow up an airplane over Detroit; and Faisal Shahzad, who put a car bomb in Times Square. It's in a court of law that we will try Dzhokhar Tsarnaev, who is accused of bombing the Boston Marathon. Richard Reid, the shoe bomber, is, as we speak, serving a life sentence in a maximum security prison here in the United States. In sentencing Reid, Judge William Young told him, "The way we treat you . . . is the measure of our own liberties."

AUDIENCE MEMBER: How about Abdulmutallab—locking up a 16-year-old—is that the way we treat a 16-year-old? (Inaudible) —can you take the drones out of the hands of the CIA? Can you stop the signature strikes killing people on the basis of suspicious activities?

MR. OBAMA: We're addressing that, ma'am.

AUDIENCE MEMBER: —thousands of Muslims that got killed— will you compensate the innocent families—that will make us safer here at home. I love my country. I love (inaudible)—

MR. OBAMA: I think that—and I'm going off script, as you might expect here. (Laughter and applause.) The voice of that woman is worth paying attention to. (Applause.) Obviously, I do not agree with much of what she said, and obviously she wasn't listening to me in much of what I said. But these are tough issues, and the suggestion that we can gloss over them is wrong.

When that judge sentenced Mr. Reid, the shoe bomber, he went on to point to the American flag that flew in the courtroom. "That flag," he said, "will fly there long after this is all forgotten. That flag still stands for freedom."

So, America, we've faced down dangers far greater than Al Qaeda. By staying true to the values of our founding, and by using our constitutional compass, we have overcome slavery and civil war and fascism and communism. In just these last few years as president, I've watched the American people bounce back from painful recession, mass shootings, natural disasters like the recent tornadoes that devastated Oklahoma. These events were heartbreaking; they shook our communities to the core. But because of the resilience of the American people, these events could not come close to breaking us.

I think of Lauren Manning, the 9/11 survivor who had severe burns over 80 percent of her body, who said, "That's my reality. I put a Band-Aid on it, literally, and I move on."

I think of the New Yorkers who filled Times Square the day after an attempted car bomb as if nothing had happened.

I think of the proud Pakistani parents who, after their daughter was invited to the White House, wrote to us, "We have raised an American Muslim daughter to dream big and never give up because it does pay off."

I think of all the wounded warriors rebuilding their lives, and helping other vets to find jobs.

I think of the runner planning to do the 2014 Boston Marathon, who said, "Next year, you're going to have more people than ever. Determination is not something to be messed with."

That's who the American people are—determined, and not to be messed with. And now we need a strategy and a politics that reflects this resilient spirit.

Our victory against terrorism won't be measured in a surrender ceremony at a battleship or a statue being pulled to the ground. Victory will be measured in parents taking their kids to school; immigrants coming to our shores; fans taking in a ballgame; a veteran starting a business; a bustling city street; a citizen shouting her concerns at a president.

The quiet determination; that strength of character and bond of fellowship; that refutation of fear—that is both our sword and our shield. And long after the current messengers of hate have faded from the world's memory, alongside the brutal despots, and deranged madmen, and ruthless demagogues who litter history—the flag of the United States will still wave from small-town cemeteries to national monuments, to distant outposts abroad. And that flag will still stand for freedom.

Thank you very much, everybody. God bless you. May God bless the United States of America.

Addenda I

(To Remarks by the President at
National Defense University)

Fact Sheet:
US Policy Standards and Procedures for the
Use of Force in Counterterrorism Operations Outside
the United States and Areas of Active Hostilities
White House Office of the Press Secretary
May 23, 2013

Since his first day in office, President Obama has been clear that the United States will use all available tools of national power to protect the American people from the terrorist threat posed by Al Qaeda and its associated forces. The president has also made clear that, in carrying on this fight, we will uphold our laws and values and will share as much information as possible with the American people and the Congress, consistent with our national security needs and the proper functioning of the executive branch. To these ends, the president has approved, and senior members of the executive branch have briefed to the Congress, written policy standards and procedures that formalize and strengthen the administration's rigorous process for reviewing and approving operations to capture or employ lethal force against terrorist targets outside the United States and outside areas of active hostilities. Additionally, the president has decided to share, in this document, certain key elements of these standards and procedures with the American people so that they can make informed judgments and hold the executive branch accountable.

This document provides information regarding counterterrorism policy standards and procedures that are either already in place or will be transitioned into place over time. As administration officials have stated publicly on numerous occasions, we are continually working to refine, clarify, and strengthen our standards and processes for using force to keep the nation safe from the terrorist threat. One constant is our commitment to conducting counterterrorism operations lawfully. In addition, we consider the separate question of whether force should be used as a matter of policy. The most important policy consideration, particularly when the United States contemplates using lethal force, is whether our actions protect American lives.

Preference for Capture

The policy of the United States is not to use lethal force when it is feasible to capture a terrorist suspect, because capturing a terrorist offers the best opportunity to gather meaningful intelligence and to mitigate and disrupt terrorist plots. Capture operations are conducted only against suspects who may lawfully be captured or otherwise taken into custody by the United States and only when the operation can be conducted in accordance with all applicable laws and consistent with our obligations to other sovereign states.

Standards for the Use of Lethal Force

Any decision to use force abroad—even when our adversaries are terrorists dedicated to killing American citizens—is a significant one. Lethal force will not be proposed or pursued as punishment or as a substitute for prosecuting a terrorist suspect in a civilian court or a military commission. Lethal force will be used only to prevent or stop attacks against US persons and, even then, only when capture is not feasible and no other reasonable alternatives exist to address the threat effectively. In particular, lethal force will be used outside areas of active hostilities only when the following preconditions are met:

First, there must be a legal basis for using lethal force, whether it is against a senior operational leader of a terrorist organization or the forces that organization is using or intends to use to conduct terrorist attacks.

Second, the United States will use lethal force only against a target that poses a continuing, imminent threat to US persons. It is simply not the case that all terrorists pose a continuing, imminent threat to US persons; if a terrorist does not pose such a threat, the United States will not use lethal force.

Third, the following criteria must be met before lethal action may be taken:

1. Near certainty that the terrorist target is present
2. Near certainty that non-combatants[1] will not be injured or killed
3. An assessment that capture is not feasible at the time of the operation
4. An assessment that the relevant governmental authorities in the country where action is contemplated cannot or will not effectively address the threat to US persons
5. An assessment that no other reasonable alternatives exist to effectively address the threat to US persons

Finally, whenever the United States uses force in foreign territories, international legal principles, including respect for sovereignty and the law of armed conflict, impose important constraints on the

---

1. *Non-combatants are individuals who may not be made the object of attack under applicable international law. The term "non-combatant" does not include an individual who is part of a belligerent party to an armed conflict, an individual who is taking a direct part in hostilities, or an individual who is targetable in the exercise of national self-defense. Males of military age may be non-combatants; it is not the case that all military-aged males in the vicinity of a target are deemed to be combatants.*

ability of the United States to act unilaterally— and on the way in which the United States can use force. The United States respects national sovereignty and international law.

US Government Coordination and Review

Decisions to capture or otherwise use force against individual terrorists outside the United States and areas of active hostilities are made at the most senior levels of the US government, informed by departments and agencies with relevant expertise and institutional roles. Senior national security officials—including the deputies and heads of key departments and agencies—will consider proposals to make sure that our policy standards are met, and attorneys—including the senior lawyers of key departments and agencies—will review and determine the legality of proposals.

These decisions will be informed by a broad analysis of an intended target's current and past role in plots threatening US persons; relevant intelligence information the individual could provide; and the potential impact of the operation on ongoing terrorism plotting, on the capabilities of terrorist organizations, on US foreign relations, and on US intelligence collection. Such analysis will inform consideration of whether the individual meets both the legal and policy standards for the operation.

Other Key Elements

US Persons. If the United States considers an operation against a terrorist identified as a US person, the Department of Justice will conduct an additional legal analysis to ensure that such action may be conducted against the individual consistent with the Constitution and laws of the United States.

Reservation of Authority. These new standards and procedures do not limit the president's authority to take action in extraordinary circumstances when doing so is both lawful and necessary to protect the United States or its allies.

Congressional Notification. Since entering office, the president has made certain that the appropriate members of Congress have been kept fully informed about our counterterrorism operations. Consistent with this strong and continuing commitment to congressional oversight, appropriate members of the Congress will be regularly provided with updates identifying any individuals against whom lethal force has been approved. In addition, the appropriate committees of Congress will be notified whenever a counterterrorism operation covered by these standards and procedures has been conducted.

Addenda 2

(To Remarks by the President at National Defense University)

Letter from Eric H. Holder, Jr., Attorney General, to Sen. Patrick J. Leahy, Chairman, Senate Judiciary Committee
May 22, 2013
(Re: Drone Warfare and US Citizens)

May 22, 2013

The Honorable Patrick J. Leahy
Chairman
Committee on the Judiciary
United States Senate
Washington, DC 20530

Dear Mr. Chairman:

Since entering office, the President has made clear his commitment to providing Congress and the American people with as much information as possible about our sensitive counterterrorism operations, consistent with our national security and the proper functioning of the Executive Branch. Doing so is necessary, the President stated in his May 21, 2009 National Archives speech, because it enables the citizens of our democracy to "make informed judgments and hold [their Government] accountable."

In furtherance of this commitment, the Administration has provided an unprecedented level of transparency into how sensitive counterterrorism operations are conducted. Several senior Administration officials, including myself, have taken numerous steps to explain publicly the legal basis for the United States' actions to the American people and the Congress. For example, in March 2012, I delivered an address at Northwestern University Law School discussing certain aspects of the Administration's counterterrorism legal framework. And the Department of Justice and other departments and agencies have continually worked with the appropriate oversight committees in the Congress to ensure that those committees are fully informed of the legal basis for our actions.

The Administration is determined to continue these extensive outreach efforts to communicate with the American people. Indeed, the President reiterated in his State of the Union address earlier this year that he would continue to engage with the Congress about our counterterrorism efforts to ensure that they remain consistent with our laws and values, and become more transparent to the American people and to the world.

To this end, the President has directed me to disclose certain information that until now has been properly classified. You and other Members of your Committee have on numerous occasions expressed a particular interest in the Administration's use of lethal force against US citizens. In light of this fact, I am writing to disclose to you certain information about the number of US citizens who have been killed by US counterterrorism operations outside of areas of active hostilities. Since 2009, the United States, in the conduct of US counterterrorism operations against Al Qaeda and its associated forces outside of areas of active hostilities, has specifically targeted and killed one US citizen, Anwar al-Awlaki. The United States is further aware of three other US citizens who have been killed in such US counterterrorism operations over that same time period: Samir Khan, 'Abd al-Rahman Anwar al-Awlaki, and Jude Kenan Mohammed. These individuals were not specifically targeted by the United States.

As I noted in my speech at Northwestern, "it is an unfortunate but undeniable fact" that a "small number" of US citizens "have decided to commit violent attacks against their own country from abroad." Based on generations-old legal principles and Supreme Court decisions handed down during World War II, as well as during the current conflict, it is clear and logical that United States citizenship alone does not make such individuals immune from being targeted. Rather, it means that the government must take special care and take into account all relevant constitutional considerations, the laws of war, and other law with respect to US citizens—even those who are leading efforts to kill their fellow, innocent Americans. Such considerations allow for the use of lethal force *in a foreign country* against a US citizen who is a senior operational leader of Al Qaeda or its associated forces, and who is actively engaged in planning to kill Americans, in the following circumstances: (1) the US government has determined, after a thorough and careful review, that the individual poses an imminent threat of violent attack against the United States; (2) capture is not feasible; and (3) the operation would be conducted in a manner consistent with applicable law-of-war principles.

These conditions should not come as a surprise: the Administration's legal views on this weighty issue have been clear and consistent over time. The analysis in my speech at Northwestern University Law School is entirely consistent with not only the analysis found in the unclassified white paper the Department of Justice provided to your Committee soon after my speech, but also with the classified analysis the Department shared with other congressional committees in May 2011—months before the operation that resulted in the death of Anwar al-Awlaki. The analysis in my speech is also entirely consistent with the classified legal advice on this issue the Department of Justice has shared with your Committee more recently. In short, the Administration has demonstrated its commitment to discussing with the Congress and the American people the circumstances in which it could lawfully use lethal force in a foreign country against a US citizen who is a senior operational leader of Al Qaeda or its associated forces, and who is actively engaged in planning to kill Americans.

Anwar al-Awlaki plainly satisfied all of the conditions I outlined in my speech at Northwestern. Let me be more specific. Al-Awlaki was a senior operational leader of Al Qaeda in the Arabian Peninsula (AQAP), the most dangerous regional affiliate of Al Qaeda and a group that has committed numerous terrorist attacks overseas and attempted multiple times to conduct terrorist attacks against the US homeland. And al-Awlaki was not just a senior leader of AQAP—he was the group's chief of external operations, intimately involved in detailed planning and putting in place plots against US persons.

In this role, al-Awlaki repeatedly made clear his intent to attack US persons and his hope that these attacks would take American lives. For example, in a message to Muslims living in the United States, he noted that he had come "to the conclusion that jihad against America is binding upon myself just as it is binding upon every other able Muslim." But it was not al-Awlaki's *words* that led the United States to act against him: they only served to demonstrate his intentions and state of mind, that he "pray[ed] that Allah [would] destro[y] America and all its allies." Rather, it was al-Awlaki's *actions*—and, in particular, his direct personal involvement in the continued planning and execution of terrorist attacks against the US homeland—that made him a lawful target and led the United States to take action.

For example, when Umar Farouk Abdulmutallab—the individual who attempted to blow up an airplane bound for Detroit on Christmas Day 2009—went to Yemen in 2009, al-Awlaki arranged an introduction via text message. Abdulmutallab told US officials that he stayed at al-Awlaki's house for three days, and then spent two weeks at an AQAP training camp. Al-Awlaki planned a suicide operation for Abdulmutallab, helped Abdulmutallab draft a statement for a martyrdom video to be shown after the attack, and directed him to take down a US airliner. Al-Awlaki's last instructions were to blow up the airplane *when it was over American soil*. Al-Awlaki also played a key role in the October 2010 plot to detonate explosive devices on two US-bound cargo planes: he not only helped plan and oversee the plot, but was also directly involved in the details of its execution—to the point that he took part in the development and testing of the explosive devices that were placed on the planes. Moreover, information that remains classified to protect sensitive sources and methods evidences al-Awlaki's involvement in the planning of numerous *other* plots against US and Western interests and makes clear he was continuing to plot attacks when he was killed.

Based on this information, high-level US government officials appropriately concluded that al-Awlaki posed a continuing and imminent threat of violent attack against the United States. Before carrying out the operation that killed al-Awlaki, senior officials also determined, based on a careful evaluation of the circumstances at the time, that it was not feasible to capture al-Awlaki. In addition, senior officials determined that the operation would be conducted consistent with applicable law-of-war principles, including the cardinal principles of (1) necessity—the requirement that the target have definite military value; (2) distinction—the idea that only military objectives may be intentionally targeted and that civilians are protected from being intentionally targeted; (3) proportionality—the notion that the anticipated collateral damage of an action cannot be excessive in relation to the anticipated concrete and direct military advantage; and (4) humanity—a principle that requires us to use weapons that will not inflict unnecessary suffering. The operation was also undertaken consistent with Yemeni sovereignty.

While a substantial amount of information indicated that Anwar al-Awlaki was a senior AQAP leader actively plotting to kill Americans, the decision that he was a lawful target was not taken lightly. The decision to use lethal force is one of the gravest that our government, at every level, can face. The operation to target Anwar al-Awlaki was thus subjected to an exceptionally rigorous interagency legal review: not only did I and other Department of Justice lawyers conclude after a thorough and searching review that the operation was lawful, but so too did other departments and agencies within the US government.

The decision to target Anwar al-Awlaki was additionally subjected to extensive policy review at the highest levels of the US Government, and senior US officials also briefed the appropriate committees of Congress on the possibility of using lethal force against al-Awlaki. Indeed, the Administration informed the relevant congressional oversight committees that it had approved the use of lethal force against al-Awlaki in February 2010—well over a year before the operation in question—and the legal justification was subsequently explained in detail to those committees, well before action was taken against al-Awlaki. This extensive outreach is consistent with the Administration's strong and continuing commitment to congressional oversight of our counterterrorism operations—oversight which ensures, as the President stated during his State of the Union address, that our actions are "consistent with our laws and system of checks and balances."

The Supreme Court has long "made clear that a state of war is not a blank check for the President when it comes to the rights of the Nation's citizens." *Hamdi v. Rumsfeld*, 542 US 507, 536 (2004);

Youngstown Sheet & Tube Co. v. Sawyer, 343 US 578,587 (1952). But the Court's case law and longstanding practice and principle also make clear that the Constitution does not prohibit the Government it establishes from taking action to protect the American people from the threats posed by terrorists who hide in faraway countries and continually plan and launch plots against the US homeland. The decision to target Anwar al-Awlaki was lawful, it was considered, and it was just.

* * * * *

This letter is only one of a number of steps the Administration will be taking to fulfill the President's State of the Union commitment to engage with Congress and the American people on our counterterrorism efforts. This week the President approved and relevant congressional committees will be notified and briefed on a document that institutionalizes the Administration's exacting standards and processes for reviewing and approving operations to capture or use lethal force against terrorist targets outside the United States and areas of active hostilities; these standards and processes are either already in place or are to be transitioned into place. While that document remains classified, it makes clear that a cornerstone of the Administration's policy is one of the principles I noted in my speech at Northwestern: that lethal force should not be used when it is feasible to capture a terrorist suspect. For circumstances in which capture is feasible, the policy outlines standards and procedures to ensure that operations to take into custody a terrorist suspect are conducted in accordance with all applicable law, including the laws of war. When capture is not feasible, the policy provides that lethal force may be used only when a terrorist target poses a continuing, imminent threat to Americans, and when certain other preconditions, including a requirement that no other reasonable alternatives exist to effectively address the threat, are satisfied. And in all circumstances there must be a legal basis for using force against the target. Significantly, the

President will soon be speaking publicly in greater detail about our counterterrorism operations and the legal and policy framework that governs those actions.

I recognize that even after the Administration makes unprecedented disclosures like those contained in this letter, some unanswered questions will remain. I assure you that the President and his national security team are mindful of this Administration's pledge to public accountability for our counterterrorism efforts, and we will continue to give careful consideration to whether and how additional information may be declassified and disclosed to the American people without harming our national security.

Sincerely,

Eric H. Holder, Jr.
Attorney General

cc:

Ranking Member Charles
   Grassley
Chairman Dianne Feinstein
Vice Chairman Saxby Chambliss
Chairman Carl Levin
Ranking Member James Inhofe
Chairman Bob Goodlatte
Ranking Member John
   Conyers, Jr.
Chairman Mike Rogers
Ranking Member C.A. Dutch
   Ruppersberger
Chairman Howard P. McKeon

Ranking Member Adam Smith
Chairman Robert Menendez
Ranking Member Bob Corker
Chairman Ed Royce
Ranking Member Eliot Engel
Majority Leader Harry Reid
Minority Leader Mitch
   McConnell
Speaker John Boehner
Majority Leader Eric Cantor
Minority Leader Nancy Pelosi
Minority Whip Steny Hoyer

Appendix: Obama–D

President Barack Obama,
"Remarks by the President on Review of
Signals Intelligence," Department of Justice,
Washington, D.C., January 17, 2014

At the dawn of our republic, a small, secret surveillance committee borne out of "The Sons of Liberty" was established in Boston. And the group's members included Paul Revere. At night they would patrol the streets, reporting back any signs that the British were preparing raids against America's early patriots.

Throughout American history, intelligence has helped secure our country and our freedoms. In the Civil War, Union balloon reconnaissance tracked the size of Confederate armies by counting the number of campfires. In World War II, code-breakers gave us insights into Japanese war plans, and when Patton marched across Europe, intercepted communications helped save the lives of his troops. After the war, the rise of the Iron Curtain and nuclear weapons only increased the need for sustained intelligence gathering. And so, in the early days of the Cold War, President Truman created the National Security Agency, or NSA, to give us insights into the Soviet bloc and provide our leaders with information they needed to confront aggression and avert catastrophe.

Throughout this evolution, we benefited from both our Constitution and our traditions of limited government. US intelligence agencies were anchored in a system of checks and balances with oversight from elected leaders and protections for ordinary citizens. Meanwhile, totalitarian states like East Germany offered a cautionary tale of what could happen when vast, unchecked surveillance turned citizens into informers and persecuted people for what they said in the privacy of their own homes.

In fact, even the United States proved not to be immune to the abuse of surveillance. And in the 1960s, government spied on civil rights leaders and critics of the Vietnam War. And partly in response to these revelations, additional laws were established in the 1970s to ensure that our intelligence capabilities could not be misused against our citizens. In the long, twilight struggle against communism, we had been reminded that the very liberties that we sought to preserve could not be sacrificed at the altar of national security.

If the fall of the Soviet Union left America without a competing superpower, emerging threats from terrorist groups and the proliferation of weapons of mass destruction placed new and, in some ways, more complicated demands on our intelligence agencies. Globalization and the Internet made these threats more acute, as technology erased borders and empowered individuals to project great violence as well as great good. Moreover, these new threats raised new legal and new policy questions. For while few doubted the legitimacy of spying on hostile states, our framework of laws was not fully adapted to prevent terrorist attacks by individuals acting on their own, or acting in small, ideologically driven groups on behalf of a foreign power.

The horror of September 11 brought all these issues to the fore. Across the political spectrum, Americans recognized that we had to adapt to a world in which a bomb could be built in a basement and our electric grid could be shut down by operators an ocean away. We were shaken by the signs we had missed leading up to the attacks—how the hijackers had made phone calls to known extremists and traveled to suspicious places. So we demanded that our intelligence community improve its capabilities and that law enforcement change practices to focus more on preventing attacks before they happen than prosecuting terrorists after an attack.

It is hard to overstate the transformation America's intelligence community had to go through after 9/11. Our agencies suddenly needed to do far more than the traditional mission of monitoring hostile powers and gathering information for policymakers. Instead, they were now asked to identify and target plotters in some of the most remote parts of the world and to anticipate the actions of networks that, by their very nature, cannot be easily penetrated with spies or informants.

And it is a testimony to the hard work and dedication of the men and women of our intelligence community that over the past decade we've made enormous strides in fulfilling this mission. Today, new capabilities allow intelligence agencies to track who a terrorist is in contact with, and follow the trail of his travel or his funding. New laws allow information to be collected and shared more quickly and effectively between federal agencies, and state and local law enforcement. Relationships with foreign intelligence services have expanded and our capacity to repel cyber-attacks has been strengthened. And taken together, these efforts have prevented multiple attacks and saved innocent lives—not just here in the United States, but around the globe.

And yet, in our rush to respond to a very real and novel set of threats, the risk of government overreach—the possibility that we lose some of our core liberties in pursuit of security—also became more pronounced. We saw, in the immediate aftermath of 9/11, our government engaged in enhanced interrogation techniques that contradicted our values. As a senator, I was critical of several practices, such as warrantless wiretaps. And all too often new authorities were instituted without adequate public debate.

Through a combination of action by the courts, increased congressional oversight, and adjustments by the previous administration, some of the worst excesses that emerged after 9/11 were curbed by the time I took office. But a variety of factors have continued to complicate America's efforts to both defend our nation and uphold our civil liberties.

First, the same technological advances that allow US intelligence agencies to pinpoint an Al Qaeda cell in Yemen or an e-mail between two terrorists in the Sahel also mean that many routine communications around the world are within our reach. And at a time when more and more of our lives are digital, that prospect is disquieting for all of us.

Second, the combination of increased digital information and powerful supercomputers offers intelligence agencies the possibility of sifting through massive amounts of bulk data to identify patterns or pursue leads that may thwart impending threats. It's a powerful tool. But the government collection and storage of such bulk data also creates a potential for abuse.

Third, the legal safeguards that restrict surveillance against US persons without a warrant do not apply to foreign persons overseas. This is not unique to America; few, if any, spy agencies around the world constrain their activities beyond their own borders. And the whole point of intelligence is to obtain information that is not publicly available. But America's capabilities are unique, and the power of new technologies means that there are fewer and fewer technical constraints on what we can do. That places a special obligation on us to ask tough questions about what we should do.

And finally, intelligence agencies cannot function without secrecy, which makes their work less subject to public debate. Yet there is an inevitable bias not only within the intelligence community, but among all of us who are responsible for national security, to collect more information about the world, not less. So in the absence of institutional requirements for regular debate—and oversight that is public, as well as private or classified—the danger of government overreach becomes more acute. And this is particularly true when surveillance technology and our reliance on digital information are evolving much faster than our laws.

For all these reasons, I maintained a healthy skepticism toward our surveillance programs after I became president. I ordered that our programs be reviewed by my national security team and our lawyers, and in some cases I ordered changes in how we did business. We increased oversight and auditing, including new structures aimed at compliance. Improved rules were proposed by the government and approved by the Foreign Intelligence Surveillance Court. And we sought to keep Congress continually updated on these activities.

What I did not do is stop these programs wholesale—not only because I felt that they made us more secure, but also because nothing in that initial review, and nothing that I have learned since, indicated that our intelligence community has sought to violate the law or is cavalier about the civil liberties of their fellow citizens.

To the contrary, in an extraordinarily difficult job—one in which actions are second-guessed, success is unreported, and failure can be catastrophic—the men and women of the intelligence community, including the NSA, consistently follow protocols designed to protect the privacy of ordinary people. They're not abusing authorities in order to listen to your private phone calls or read your e-mails. When mistakes are made—which is inevitable in any large and complicated human enterprise—they correct those mistakes. Laboring in obscurity, often unable to discuss their work even with family and friends, the men and women at the NSA know that if another 9/11 or massive cyber-attack occurs they will be asked, by Congress and the media, why they failed to connect the dots. What sustains those who work at NSA and our other intelligence agencies through all these pressures is the knowledge that their professionalism and dedication play a central role in the defense of our nation.

Now, to say that our intelligence community follows the law, and is staffed by patriots, is not to suggest that I or others in my administration felt complacent about the potential impact of these programs. Those of us who hold office in America have a responsibility to our Constitution, and while I was confident in the integrity of those who lead our intelligence community, it was clear to me in observing our intelligence operations on a regular basis that changes in our technological capabilities were raising new questions about the privacy safeguards currently in place.

Moreover, after an extended review of our use of drones in the fight against terrorist networks, I believed a fresh examination of our surveillance programs was a necessary next step in our effort to get off the open-ended war footing that we've maintained since 9/11. And for these reasons, I indicated in a speech at the National Defense University last May that we needed a more robust public discussion about the balance between security and liberty. Of course, what I did not know at the time is that within weeks of my speech, an avalanche of unauthorized disclosures would spark controversies at home and abroad that have continued to this day.

And given the fact of an open investigation, I'm not going to dwell on Mr. (Edward) Snowden's actions or his motivations; I will say that our nation's defense depends in part on the fidelity of those entrusted with our nation's secrets. If any individual who objects to government policy can take it into their own hands to publicly disclose classified information, then we will not be able to keep our people safe or conduct foreign policy. Moreover, the sensational way in which these disclosures have come out has often shed more heat than light, while revealing methods to our adversaries that could impact our operations in ways that we may not fully understand for years to come.

Regardless of how we got here, though, the task before us now is greater than simply repairing the damage done to our operations or preventing more disclosures from taking place in the future. Instead, we have to make some important decisions about how to protect ourselves and sustain our leadership in the world, while upholding the civil liberties and privacy protections that our ideals and our Constitution require. We need to do so not only because it is right, but because the challenges posed by threats like terrorism and proliferation and cyber-attacks are not going away any time soon. They are going to continue to be a major problem. And for our intelligence community to be effective over the long haul, we must maintain the trust of the American people and people around the world.

This effort will not be completed overnight and, given the pace of technological change, we shouldn't expect this to be the last time America has this debate. But I want the American people to know that the work has begun. Over the last six months, I created an outside Review Group on Intelligence and Communications Technologies to make recommendations for reform. I consulted with the Privacy and Civil Liberties Oversight Board, created by Congress. I've listened to foreign partners, privacy advocates, and industry leaders. My administration has spent countless hours considering how to approach intelligence in this era of diffuse threats and technological revolution. So before outlining specific changes that I've ordered, let me make a few broad observations that have emerged from this process.

First, everyone who has looked at these problems, including skeptics of existing programs, recognizes that we have real enemies and threats and that intelligence serves a vital role in confronting them. We cannot prevent terrorist attacks or cyber-threats without some capability to penetrate digital communications—whether it's to unravel a terrorist plot; to intercept malware that targets a stock exchange; to make sure air traffic control systems are not compromised; or to ensure that hackers do not empty your bank accounts. We are expected to protect the American people; that requires us to have capabilities in this field.

Moreover, we cannot unilaterally disarm our intelligence agencies. There is a reason why BlackBerrys and iPhones are not allowed in the White House Situation Room. We know that the intelligence services of other countries—including some who feign surprise over the Snowden disclosures—are constantly probing our government and private sector networks, and accelerating programs to listen to our conversations, and intercept our e-mails, and compromise our systems. We know that.

Meanwhile, a number of countries, including some who have loudly criticized the NSA, privately acknowledge that America has special responsibilities as the world's only superpower; that our intelligence capabilities are critical to meeting these responsibilities; and that they themselves have relied on the information we obtain to protect their own people.

Second, just as ardent civil libertarians recognize the need for robust intelligence capabilities, those with responsibilities for our national security readily acknowledge the potential for abuse as intelligence capabilities advance and more and more private information is digitized. After all, the folks at NSA and other intelligence agencies are our neighbors. They're our friends and family. They've got electronic bank and medical records like everybody else. They have kids on Facebook and Instagram and they know, more than most of us, the vulnerabilities to privacy that exist in a world where transactions are recorded, and e-mails and text and messages are stored, and even our movements can increasingly be tracked through the GPS on our phones.

Third, there was a recognition by all who participated in these reviews that the challenges to our privacy do not come from government alone. Corporations of all shapes and sizes track what you buy, store and analyze our data, and use it for commercial purposes; that's how those targeted ads pop up on your computer and your smartphone periodically. But all of us understand that the standards for government surveillance must be higher. Given the unique power of the state, it is not enough for leaders to say: "Trust us, we won't abuse the data we collect." For history has too many examples when that trust has been breached. Our system of government is built on the premise that our liberty cannot depend on the good intentions of those in power; it depends on the law to constrain those in power.

I make these observations to underscore that the basic values of most Americans when it comes to questions of surveillance and privacy converge a lot more than the crude characterizations that have emerged over the last several months. Those who are troubled by our existing programs are not interested in repeating the tragedy of 9/11, and those who defend these programs are not dismissive of civil liberties.

The challenge is getting the details right, and that is not simple. In fact, during the course of our review, I have often reminded myself I would not be where I am today were it not for the courage of dissidents like Dr. King, who were spied upon by their own government. And as president, a president who looks at intelligence every morning, I also can't help but be reminded that America must be vigilant in the face of threats.

Fortunately, by focusing on facts and specifics rather than speculation and hypotheticals, this review process has given me—and hopefully the American people—some clear direction for change. And today, I can announce a series of concrete and substantial reforms that my administration intends to adopt administratively or will seek to codify with Congress.

First, I have approved a new presidential directive for our signals intelligence activities both at home and abroad. This guidance will strengthen executive branch oversight of our intelligence activities. It will ensure that we take into account our security requirements, but also our alliances; our trade and investment relationships, including the concerns of American companies; and our commitment to privacy and basic liberties. And we will review decisions about intelligence priorities and sensitive targets on an annual basis so that our actions are regularly scrutinized by my senior national security team.

Second, we will reform programs and procedures in place to provide greater transparency to our surveillance activities and fortify the safeguards that protect the privacy of US persons. Since we began this review, including information being released today, we have declassified over forty opinions and orders of the Foreign Intelligence Surveillance Court, which provides judicial review of some of our most sensitive intelligence activities—including the section 702 program targeting foreign individuals overseas and the section 215 telephone metadata program.

And going forward, I'm directing the director of national intelligence (DNI), in consultation with the attorney general, to annually review for the purposes of declassification any future opinions of the court with broad privacy implications and to report to me and to Congress on these efforts. To ensure that the court hears a broader range of privacy perspectives, I am also calling on Congress to authorize the establishment of a panel of advocates from outside government to provide an independent voice in significant cases before the Foreign Intelligence Surveillance Court.

Third, we will provide additional protections for activities conducted under section 702, which allows the government to intercept the communications of foreign targets overseas who have information that's important for our national security. Specifically, I am asking the attorney general and DNI to institute reforms that place additional restrictions on government's ability to retain, search, and use in criminal cases communications between Americans and foreign citizens incidentally collected under section 702.

Fourth, in investigating threats, the FBI also relies on what's called national security letters, which can require companies to provide specific and limited information to the government without disclosing the orders to the subject of the investigation. These are cases in which it's important that the subject of the investigation, such as a possible terrorist or spy, isn't tipped off. But we can and should be more transparent in how government uses this authority.

I have therefore directed the attorney general to amend how we use national security letters so that this secrecy will not be indefinite, so that it will terminate within a fixed time unless the government demonstrates a real need for further secrecy. We will also enable communications providers to make public more information than ever before about the orders that they have received to provide data to the government.

This brings me to the program that has generated the most controversy these past few months—the bulk collection of telephone records under section 215. Let me repeat what I said when this story first broke: this program does not involve the content of phone calls or the names of people making calls. Instead, it provides a record of phone numbers and the times and lengths of calls—metadata that can be queried if and when we have a reasonable suspicion that a particular number is linked to a terrorist organization.

Why is this necessary? The program grew out of a desire to address a gap identified after 9/11. One of the 9/11 hijackers—Khalid al-Mihdhar—made a phone call from San Diego to a known Al Qaeda safe house in Yemen. NSA saw that call, but it could not see that the call was coming from an individual already in the United States. The telephone metadata program under section 215 was designed to map the communications of terrorists so we can see who they may be in contact with as quickly as possible. And this capability could also prove valuable in a crisis. For example, if a bomb goes off in one of our cities and law enforcement is racing to determine whether a network is poised to conduct additional attacks, time is of the essence. Being able to quickly review phone connections to assess whether a network exists is critical to that effort.

In sum, the program does not involve the NSA examining the phone records of ordinary Americans. Rather, it consolidates these records into a database that the government can query if it has a specific lead—a consolidation of phone records that the companies already retained for business purposes. The review group turned up no indication that this database has been intentionally abused. And I believe it is important that the capability that this program is designed to meet is preserved.

Having said that, I believe critics are right to point out that without proper safeguards, this type of program could be used to yield more information about our private lives and open the door to more intrusive bulk collection programs in the future. They're also right to point out that although the telephone bulk collection program was subject to oversight by the Foreign Intelligence Surveillance Court and has been reauthorized repeatedly by Congress, it has never been subject to vigorous public debate.

For all these reasons, I believe we need a new approach. I am therefore ordering a transition that will end the section 215 bulk metadata program as it currently exists and establish a mechanism that preserves the capabilities we need without the government holding this bulk metadata.

This will not be simple. The review group recommended that our current approach be replaced by one in which the providers or a third party retain the bulk records, with government accessing information as needed. Both of these options pose difficult problems. Relying solely on the records of multiple providers, for example, could require companies to alter their procedures in ways that raise new privacy concerns. On the other hand, any third party maintaining a single, consolidated database would be carrying out what is essentially a government function but with more expense, more legal ambiguity, potentially less accountability—all of which would have a doubtful impact on increasing public confidence that their privacy is being protected.

During the review process, some suggested that we may also be able to preserve the capabilities we need through a combination of existing authorities, better information sharing, and recent technological advances. But more work needs to be done to determine exactly how this system might work.

Because of the challenges involved, I've ordered that the transition away from the existing program will proceed in two steps. Effective immediately, we will only pursue phone calls that are two steps removed from a number associated with a terrorist organization instead of the current three. And I have directed the attorney general to work with the Foreign Intelligence Surveillance Court so that during this transition period, the database can be queried only after a judicial finding or in the case of a true emergency.

Next, step two, I have instructed the intelligence community and the attorney general to use this transition period to develop options for a new approach that can match the capabilities and fill the gaps that the section 215 program was designed to address without the government holding this metadata itself. They will report back to me with options for alternative approaches before the program comes up for reauthorization on March 28. And during this period, I will consult with the relevant committees in Congress to seek their views and then seek congressional authorization for the new program as needed.

Now, the reforms I'm proposing today should give the American people greater confidence that their rights are being protected, even as our intelligence and law enforcement agencies maintain the tools they need to keep us safe. And I recognize that there are additional issues that require further debate. For example, some who participated in our review, as well as some members of Congress, would like to see more sweeping reforms to the use of national security letters so that we have to go to a judge each time before issuing these requests. Here, I have concerns that we should not set a standard for terrorism investigations that is higher than those involved in investigating an ordinary crime. But I agree that greater oversight on the use of these letters may be appropriate, and I'm prepared to work with Congress on this issue.

There are also those who would like to see different changes to the FISA Court than the ones I've proposed. On all these issues, I am open to working with Congress to ensure that we build a broad consensus for how to move forward and I'm confident that we can shape an approach that meets our security needs while upholding the civil liberties of every American.

Let me now turn to the separate set of concerns that have been raised overseas and focus on America's approach to intelligence collection abroad. As I've indicated, the United States has unique responsibilities when it comes to intelligence collection. Our capabilities help protect not only our nation, but our friends and our allies, as well. But our efforts will only be effective if ordinary citizens in other countries have confidence that the United States respects their privacy, too. And the leaders of our close friends and allies deserve to know that if I want to know what they think about an issue, I'll pick up the phone and call them, rather than turning to surveillance. In other words, just as we balance security and privacy at home, our global leadership demands that we balance our security requirements against our need to maintain the trust and cooperation among people and leaders around the world.

For that reason, the new presidential directive that I've issued today will clearly prescribe what we do, and do not do, when it comes to our overseas surveillance. To begin with, the directive makes clear that the United States only uses signals intelligence for legitimate national security purposes, and not for the purpose of indiscriminately reviewing the e-mails or phone calls of ordinary folks. I've also made it clear that the United States does not collect intelligence to suppress criticism or dissent, nor do we collect intelligence to disadvantage people on the basis of their ethnicity, or race, or gender, or sexual orientation, or religious beliefs. We do not collect intelligence to provide a competitive advantage to US companies or US commercial sectors.

And in terms of our bulk collection of signals intelligence, US intelligence agencies will only use such data to meet specific security requirements: counterintelligence, counterterrorism, counter-proliferation, cyber-security, force protection for our troops and our allies, and combating transnational crime, including sanctions evasion.

In this directive, I have taken the unprecedented step of extending certain protections that we have for the American people to people overseas. I've directed the DNI, in consultation with the attorney general, to develop these safeguards, which will limit the duration that we can hold personal information while also restricting the use of this information.

The bottom line is that people around the world, regardless of their nationality, should know that the United States is not spying on ordinary people who don't threaten our national security and that we take their privacy concerns into account in our policies and procedures. This applies to foreign leaders as well. Given the understandable attention that this issue has received, I have made clear to the intelligence community that unless there is a compelling national security purpose, we will not monitor the communications of heads of state and government of our close friends and allies. And I've instructed my national security team, as well as the intelligence community, to work with foreign counterparts to deepen our coordination and cooperation in ways that rebuild trust going forward.

Now let me be clear: our intelligence agencies will continue to gather information about the intentions of governments—as opposed to ordinary citizens—around the world, in the same way that the intelligence service of every other nation does. We will not apologize simply because our services may be more effective. But heads of state and government with whom we work closely, and on whose cooperation we depend, should feel confident that we are treating them as real partners. And the changes I've ordered do just that.

Finally, to make sure that we follow through on all these reforms, I am making some important changes to how our government is organized. The State Department will designate a senior officer to coordinate our diplomacy on issues related to technology and signals intelligence. We will appoint a senior official at the White House to implement the new privacy safeguards that I have announced today. I will devote the resources to centralize and improve the process we use to handle foreign requests for legal assistance, keeping our high standards for privacy while helping foreign partners fight crime and terrorism.

I have also asked my counselor, John Podesta, to lead a comprehensive review of big data and privacy. And this group will consist of government officials who, along with the President's Council of Advisors on Science and Technology, will reach out to privacy experts, technologists, and business leaders and look how the challenges inherent in big data are being confronted by both the public and private sectors; whether we can forge international norms on how to manage this data; and how we can continue to promote the free flow of information in ways that are consistent with both privacy and security.

For ultimately, what's at stake in this debate goes far beyond a few months of headlines or passing tensions in our foreign policy. When you cut through the noise, what's really at stake is how we remain true to who we are in a world that is remaking itself at dizzying speed. Whether it's the ability of individuals to communicate ideas; to access information that would have once filled every great library in every country in the world; or to forge bonds with people on other sides of the globe, technology is remaking what is possible for individuals, and for institutions, and for the international order. So while the reforms that I have announced will point us in a new direction, I am mindful that more work will be needed in the future.

One thing I'm certain of: this debate will make us stronger. And I also know that in this time of change, the United States of America will have to lead. It may seem sometimes that America is being held to a different standard. And I'll admit the readiness of some to assume the worst motives by our government can be frustrating. No one expects China to have an open debate about their surveillance programs, or Russia to take privacy concerns of citizens in other places into account. But let's remember: we are held to a different standard precisely because we have been at the forefront of defending personal privacy and human dignity.

As the nation that developed the Internet, the world expects us to ensure that the digital revolution works as a tool for individual empowerment, not government control. Having faced down the dangers of totalitarianism and fascism and communism, the world expects us to stand up for the principle that every person has the right to think and write and form relationships freely—because individual freedom is the wellspring of human progress.

Those values make us who we are. And because of the strength of our own democracy, we should not shy away from high expectations. For more than two centuries, our Constitution has weathered every type of change because we have been willing to defend it and because we have been willing to question the actions that have been taken in its defense. Today is no different. I believe we can meet high expectations. Together, let us chart a way forward that secures the life of our nation while preserving the liberties that make our nation worth fighting for.

Thank you. God bless you. May God bless the United States of America.

Appendix: Koh–A

Harold H. Koh, legal adviser to the
Department of State, address to the
American Society of International Law,
"The Obama Administration and International Law,"
March 25, 2010

. . .

II. The Strategic Vision

That brings me to my second topic: what strategic vision of international law are we trying to implement? How does obeying international law advance US foreign policy interests and strengthen America's position of global leadership? Or to put it another way, with respect to international law, is this administration really committed to what our president has famously called "change we can believe in"? Some, including a number of the panelists who have addressed this conference, have argued that there is really more continuity than change from the last administration to this one.

To them I would answer that, of course, in foreign policy, from administration to administration, there will always be more continuity than change; you simply cannot turn the ship of state 360 degrees from administration to administration every four to eight years, nor should you. But, I would argue—and these are the core of my remarks today—to say that is to understate the most important difference between this administration and the last. And that is with respect to its approach and attitude toward international law. The difference in that approach to international law, I would argue, is captured in an emerging "Obama-Clinton doctrine" which is based on four commitments to:

1. Principled engagement
2. Diplomacy as a critical element of smart power
3. Strategic multilateralism
4. The notion that living our values makes us stronger and safer, by following rules of domestic and international law and following universal standards, not double standards.

As articulated by the president and Secretary [of State Hillary] Clinton, I believe the Obama/Clinton doctrine reflects these four core commitments:

First, a commitment to principled engagement: a powerful belief in the interdependence of the global community is a major theme for our president, whose father came from a Kenyan family and who as a child spent several years in Indonesia.

Second, a commitment to what Secretary Clinton calls "smart power—a blend of principle and pragmatism" that makes "intelligent use of all means at our disposal," including promotion of democracy, development, technology, and human rights and international law to place diplomacy at the vanguard of our foreign policy.

Third, a commitment to what some have called strategic multilateralism: the notion acknowledged by President Obama at Cairo that the challenges of the twenty-first century "can't be met by any one leader or any one nation" and must therefore be addressed by open dialogue and partnership by the United States with peoples and nations across traditional regional divides "based on mutual interest and mutual respect" as well as acknowledgment of "the rights and responsibilities of [all] nations."

And fourth and finally, a commitment to living our values by respecting the rule of law. As I said, both the president and Secretary Clinton are outstanding lawyers, and they understand that by imposing constraints on government action, law legitimates and gives credibility to governmental action. As the president emphasized forcefully in his National Archives speech and elsewhere, the American political system was founded on a vision of common humanity, universal rights, and rule of law. Fidelity to [these] values makes us stronger and safer. This also means following universal standards, not double standards. In his Nobel lecture at Oslo, President Obama affirmed that "[a]dhering to standards, international standards, strengthens those who do, and isolates those who don't." And in her December speech on a twenty-first-century human rights agenda, and again two weeks ago in introducing our annual human rights reports, Secretary Clinton reiterated that "a commitment to human rights starts with universal standards and with holding everyone accountable to those standards, including ourselves."

. . .

III. The Law of 9/11

Let me focus the balance of my remarks on that aspect of my job that I call the Law of 9/11. In this area, as in the other areas of our work, we believe, in the president's words, that "living our values doesn't make us weaker, it makes us safer and it makes us stronger."

We live in a time when, as you know, the United States finds itself engaged in several armed conflicts. As the president has noted, one conflict, in Iraq, is winding down. He also reminded us that the conflict in Afghanistan is a "conflict that America did not seek, one in which we are joined by forty-three other countries . . . in an effort to defend ourselves and all nations from further attacks." In the conflict occurring in Afghanistan and elsewhere, we continue to fight the perpetrators of 9/11: a non-state actor, Al Qaeda (as well as the Taliban forces that harbored Al Qaeda).

Everyone here at this meeting is committed to international law. But as President Obama reminded us, "the world must remember that it was not simply international institutions—not just treaties and declarations—that brought stability to a post–World War II world. . . . [T]he instruments of war do have a role to play in preserving the peace."

With this background, let me address a question on many of your minds: how has this administration determined to conduct these armed conflicts and to defend our national security, consistent with its abiding commitment to international law? Let there be no doubt: the Obama administration is firmly committed to complying with all applicable law, including the laws of war, in all aspects of these ongoing armed conflicts. As the president reaffirmed in his Nobel Prize lecture, "Where force is necessary, we have a moral and strategic interest in binding ourselves to certain rules of conduct . . . [E]ven as we confront a vicious adversary that abides by no rules . . . the United States of America must remain a standard bearer in the conduct of war. That is what makes us different from those whom we fight. That is the source of our strength." We in the Obama administration have worked hard since we entered office to ensure that we conduct all aspects of these armed conflicts—in particular, detention operations, targeting, and prosecution of terrorist suspects—in a manner consistent not just with the applicable laws of war but also with the Constitution and laws of the United States.

Let me say a word about each: detention, targeting, and prosecution.

1. Detention

With respect to detention, as you know, the last administration's detention practices were widely criticized around the world and, as a private citizen, I was among the vocal critics of those practices. This administration and I personally have spent much of the last year seeking to revise those practices to ensure their full compliance with domestic and international law: first, by unequivocally guaranteeing humane treatment for all individuals in US custody as a result of armed conflict; and second, by ensuring that all detained individuals are being held pursuant to lawful authorities.

a. Treatment

To ensure humane treatment, on his second full day in office the president unequivocally banned the use of torture as an instrument of US policy, a commitment that he has repeatedly reaffirmed in the months since. He directed that executive officials could no longer rely upon the Justice Department OLC [Office of Legal Counsel] opinions that had permitted practices that I consider to be torture and cruel treatment—many of which he later disclosed publicly— and he instructed that, henceforth, all interrogations of detainees must be conducted in accordance with Common Article 3 of the Geneva Conventions and with the revised *Army Field Manual*. An interagency review of US interrogation practices later advised—and the president agreed—that no techniques beyond those in the *Army Field Manual* (and traditional non-coercive FBI techniques) are necessary to conduct effective interrogations. That Interrogation and Transfer Task Force also issued a set of recommendations to help ensure that the United States will not transfer individuals to face torture. The president also revoked Executive Order 13440, which had interpreted particular provisions of Common Article 3, and restored the meaning of those provisions to the way they have traditionally been understood in international law. The president ordered CIA "black sites" closed and directed the secretary of defense to conduct an immediate review—with two follow-up visits by a blue ribbon task force of former government officials—to ensure that the conditions of detention at Guantánamo fully comply with Common Article 3 of the Geneva Conventions. Last December, I visited Guantánamo, a place I had visited several times over the last two decades, and I believe that the conditions I observed are humane and meet Geneva Conventions standards.

As you all know, also on his second full day in office, the president ordered Guantánamo closed and his commitment to doing so has not wavered, even as closing Guantánamo has proven to be an arduous and painstaking process. Since the beginning of the administration, through the work of my colleague Ambassador Dan Fried, we have transferred approximately fifty-seven detainees to twenty-two different countries, of whom thirty-three were resettled in countries that are not the detainees' countries of origin. Our efforts continue on a daily basis. Just this week, five more detainees were transferred out of Guantánamo for resettlement. We are very grateful to those countries who have contributed to our efforts to close Guantánamo by resettling detainees; that list continues to grow as more and more countries see the positive changes we are making and wish to offer their support.

During the past year, we completed an exhaustive, rigorous, and collaborative interagency review of the status of the roughly 240 individuals detained at Guantánamo Bay when President Obama took office. The president's executive order placed responsibility for review of each Guantánamo detainee with six entities—the departments of Justice, State, Defense, and Homeland Security, the Office of the Director of National Intelligence (ODNI), and the Joint Chiefs of Staff—to collect and consolidate from across the government all information concerning the detainees and to ensure that diplomatic, military, intelligence, homeland security, and law enforcement viewpoints would all be fully considered in the review process. This interagency task force, on which several State Department attorneys participated, painstakingly considered each and every Guantánamo detainee's case to assess whether the detainee could be transferred or repatriated consistently with national security, the interests of justice, and our policy not to transfer individuals to countries where they would likely face torture or persecution. The six entities ultimately reached unanimous agreement on the proper disposition of all detainees subject to review. As the president has made clear, this is not a one-time review; there will be "a thorough process of periodic review, so that *any* prolonged detention is carefully evaluated and justified." Similarly, the Department of Defense has created new review procedures for individuals held at the detention facility in Parwan at Bagram Airfield, Afghanistan, with increased representation for detainees, greater opportunities to present evidence, and more transparent proceedings. Outside organizations have begun to monitor these proceedings, and even some of the toughest critics have acknowledged the positive changes that have been made.

b. Legal Authority to Detain

Some have asked what legal basis we have for continuing to detain those held on Guantánamo and at Bagram. But as a matter of both international and domestic law, the legal framework is well-established. As a matter of international law, our detention operations rest on three legal foundations. First, we continue to fight a war of self-defense against an enemy that attacked us on September 11, 2001, and before, and that continues to undertake armed attacks against the United States. Second, in Afghanistan, we work as partners with a consenting host government. And third, the United Nations Security Council has, through a series of successive resolutions, authorized the use of "all necessary measures" by the NATO countries constituting the International Security Assistance Force (ISAF) to fulfill their mandate in Afghanistan. As a nation at war, we must comply with the laws of war, but detention of enemy belligerents to prevent them from returning to hostilities is a well-recognized feature of the conduct of armed conflict, as the drafters of Common Article 3 and Additional Protocol II [of the Geneva Conventions] recognized and as our own Supreme Court recognized in *Hamdi v. Rumsfeld*.

The federal courts have confirmed our legal authority to detain in the Guantánamo habeas cases, but the administration is not asserting an unlimited detention authority. For example, with regard to individuals detained at Guantánamo, we explained in a March 13, 2009, habeas filing before the D.C. federal court—and repeatedly in habeas cases since—that we are resting our detention authority on a domestic statute, the 2001 Authorization for Use of Military Force (AUMF), as informed by the principles of the laws of war. Our detention authority in Afghanistan comes from the same source.

In explaining this approach, let me note two important differences from the legal approach of the last administration. First, as a matter of domestic law, the Obama administration has not based its claim of authority to detain those at Gitmo and Bagram on the president's Article II authority as commander-in-chief. Instead, we have relied on legislative authority expressly granted to the president by Congress in the 2001 AUMF.

Second, unlike the last administration, as a matter of international law, this administration has expressly acknowledged that international law informs the scope of our detention authority. Both in our internal decisions about specific Guantánamo detainees and before the courts in habeas cases, we have interpreted the scope of detention authority authorized by Congress in the AUMF as informed by the laws of war. Those laws of war were designed primarily for traditional armed conflicts among states, not conflicts against a diffuse, difficult-to-identify terrorist enemy. Therefore construing what is "necessary and appropriate" under the AUMF requires some "translation," or analogizing principles from the laws of war governing traditional *international* conflicts.

Some commentators have criticized our decision to detain certain individuals based on their membership in a non-state armed group. But as those of you who follow the Guantánamo habeas litigation know, we have defended this position based on the AUMF, as informed by the text, structure, and history of the Geneva Conventions and other sources of the laws of war. Moreover, while the various judges who have considered these arguments have taken issue with certain points, they have accepted the overall proposition that individuals who are part of an organized armed group like Al Qaeda can be subject to law-of-war detention for the duration of the current conflict. In sum, we have based our authority to detain not on conclusory labels, like "enemy combatant," but on whether the factual record in the particular case meets the legal standard. This includes, but is not limited to, whether an individual joined with or became part of Al Qaeda or Taliban forces or associated forces, which can be demonstrated by relevant evidence of formal or functional membership, which may include an oath of loyalty, training with Al Qaeda, or taking positions with enemy forces. Often these factors operate in combination. While we disagree with the International Committee of the Red Cross on some of the particulars, our general approach of looking at "functional" membership in an armed group has been endorsed not only by the federal courts, but also is consistent with the approach taken in the targeting context by the ICRC in its recent study on Direct Participation in Hostilities (DPH).

A final point: the Obama administration has made clear its goals not only of closing Guantánamo but also of moving to shift detention responsibilities to the local governments in Iraq and Afghanistan. Last July, I visited the detention facilities in Afghanistan at Bagram, as well as Afghan detention facilities near Kabul, and I discussed the conditions at those facilities with both Afghan and US military officials and representatives of the International Committee of the Red Cross. I was impressed by the efforts that the Department of Defense is making both to improve our ongoing operations and to prepare the Afghans for the day when we turn over responsibility for detention operations. This fall, DOD created a joint task force led by a three-star admiral, Robert Harward, to bring new energy and focus to these efforts, and you can see evidence of his work in the rigorous implementation of our new detainee review procedures at Bagram, the increased transparency of these proceedings, and closer coordination with our Afghan partners in our detention operations.

In sum, with respect to both treatment and detainability, we believe that our detention practices comport with both domestic and international law.

2. Targeting

In the same way, in all of our operations involving the use of force, including those in the armed conflict with Al Qaeda, the Taliban, and associated forces, the Obama administration is committed by word and deed to conducting ourselves in accordance with all applicable law. With respect to the subject of targeting, which has been much commented upon in the media and international legal circles, there are obviously limits to what I can say publicly. What I can say is that it is the considered view of this administration—and it has certainly been my experience during my time as legal adviser—that US targeting practices, including lethal operations conducted with the use of unmanned aerial vehicles, comply with all applicable law, including the laws of war.

The United States agrees that it must conform its actions to all applicable law. As I have explained, as a matter of international law the United States is in an armed conflict with Al Qaeda, as well as the Taliban and associated forces, in response to the horrific 9/11 attacks, and may use force consistent with its inherent right to self-defense under international law. As a matter of domestic law, Congress authorized the use of all necessary and appropriate force through the 2001 Authorization for Use of Military Force (AUMF). These domestic and international legal authorities continue to this day.

As recent events have shown, Al Qaeda has not abandoned its intent to attack the United States, and indeed continues to attack us. Thus, in this ongoing armed conflict the United States has the authority under international law, and the responsibility to its citizens, to use force, including lethal force, to defend itself, including by targeting persons such as high-level Al Qaeda leaders who are planning attacks. As you know, this is a conflict with an organized terrorist enemy that does not have conventional forces but that plans and executes its attacks against us and our allies while hiding among civilian populations. That behavior simultaneously makes the application of international law more difficult and more critical for the protection of innocent civilians. Of course, whether a particular individual will be targeted in a particular location will depend upon considerations specific to each case, including those related to the imminence of the threat, the sovereignty of the other states involved, and the willingness and ability of those states to suppress the threat the target poses. In particular, this administration has carefully reviewed the rules governing targeting operations to ensure that these operations are conducted consistently with law-of-war principles, including:

- First, the principle of *distinction*, which requires that attacks be limited to military objectives and that civilians or civilian objects shall not be the object of the attack.
- Second, the principle of *proportionality*, which prohibits attacks that may be expected to cause incidental loss of civilian life, injury to civilians, damage to civilian objects, or a combination thereof, that would be excessive in relation to the concrete and direct military advantage anticipated.

In US operations against Al Qaeda and its associated forces—including lethal operations conducted with the use of unmanned aerial vehicles—great care is taken to adhere to these principles in both planning and execution, to ensure that only legitimate objectives are targeted and that collateral damage is kept to a minimum.

Recently, a number of legal objections have been raised against US targeting practices. While today is obviously not the occasion for a detailed legal opinion responding to each of these objections, let me briefly address four.

First, some have suggested that the *very act of targeting* a particular leader of an enemy force in an armed conflict must violate the laws of war. But individuals who are part of such an armed group are belligerents and, therefore, lawful targets under international law. During World War II, for example, American aviators tracked and shot down the airplane carrying the architect of the Japanese attack on Pearl Harbor, who was also the leader of enemy forces in the Battle of Midway. This was a lawful operation then, and would be if conducted today. Indeed, targeting particular individuals serves to narrow the focus when force is employed and to avoid broader harm to civilians and civilian objects.

Second, some have challenged *the very use of advanced weapons systems*, such as unmanned aerial vehicles, for lethal operations. But the rules that govern targeting do not turn on the type of weapons system used, and there is no prohibition under the laws of war on the use of technologically advanced weapons systems in armed conflict—such as pilotless aircraft or so-called smart bombs—so long as they are employed in conformity with applicable laws of war. Indeed, using such advanced technologies can ensure both that the best intelligence is available for planning operations and that civilian casualties are minimized in carrying out such operations.

Third, some have argued that the use of lethal force against specific individuals fails to provide adequate process and thus constitutes *unlawful extrajudicial killing*. But a state that is engaged in an armed conflict or in legitimate self-defense is not required to provide targets with legal process before the state may use lethal force. Our procedures and practices for identifying lawful targets are extremely robust, and advanced technologies have helped to make our targeting even more precise. In my experience, the principles of distinction and proportionality that the United States applies are not just recited at meetings. They are implemented rigorously throughout the planning and execution of lethal operations to ensure that such operations are conducted in accordance with all applicable law.

Fourth, and finally, some have argued that our targeting practices violate *domestic law,* in particular, the long-standing *domestic ban on assassinations*. But under domestic law, the use of lawful weapons systems—consistent with the applicable laws of war—for precision targeting of specific high-level belligerent leaders when acting in self-defense or during an armed conflict is not unlawful, and hence does not constitute "assassination."

In sum, let me repeat: as in the area of detention operations, this administration is committed to ensuring that the targeting practices that I have described are lawful.

3. Prosecution

The same goes, third and finally, for our policy of prosecutions. As the president made clear in his May 2009 National Archives speech, we have a national security interest in trying terrorists, either before Article III courts or military commissions, and in keeping the number of individuals detained under the laws of war low.

Obviously, the choice between Article III courts and military commissions must be made on a case-by-case basis, depending on the facts of each particular case. Many acts of terrorism committed in the context of an armed conflict can constitute both war crimes and violations of our federal criminal law, and they can be prosecuted in either federal courts or military commissions. As the last administration found, those who have violated American criminal laws can be successfully tried in federal courts: for example, Richard Reid, Zacarias Moussaoui, and a number of others.

With respect to the criminal justice system, to reiterate what Attorney General Holder recently explained, Article III prosecutions have proven to be remarkably effective in incapacitating terrorists. In 2009, there were more defendants charged with terrorism violations in federal court than in any year since 9/11. In February 2010, for example, Najibullah Zazi pleaded guilty in the Eastern District of New York to a three-count information charging him with conspiracy to use weapons of mass destruction, specifically explosives, against persons or property in the United States; conspiracy to commit murder in a foreign country; and provision of material support to Al Qaeda. We have also effectively used the criminal justice system to pursue those who have sought to commit terrorist acts overseas. On March 18, 2010, for example, David Headley pleaded guilty to a dozen terrorism charges in US federal court in Chicago, admitting that he participated in planning the November 2008 terrorist attacks in Mumbai, India, as well as later planning to attack a Danish newspaper.

As the president noted in his National Archives speech, lawfully constituted military commissions are also appropriate venues for trying persons for violations of the laws of war. In 2009, with significant input from this administration, the Military Commissions Act was amended, with important changes to address the defects in the previous Military Commissions Act of 2006, including the addition of a provision that renders inadmissible any statements taken as a result of cruel, inhuman, or degrading treatment. The 2009 legislative reforms also require the government to disclose more potentially exculpatory information, restrict hearsay evidence, and generally require that statements of the accused be admitted only if they were provided voluntarily (with a carefully defined exception for battlefield statements).

. . .

Appendix: Koh–B

Harold H. Koh, legal adviser to the Department of State, address to the USCYBERCOM Inter-Agency Legal Conference, "International Law in Cyberspace," Fort Meade, Maryland, September 18, 2012

. . .

Everyone here knows that cyberspace presents new opportunities and new challenges for the United States in every foreign policy realm, including national defense. But for international lawyers, it also presents cutting-edge issues of international law, which go to a very fundamental question: how do we apply old laws of war to new cyber-circumstances, staying faithful to enduring principles while accounting for changing times and technologies?

Many, many international lawyers here in the US government and around the world have struggled with this question, so today I'd like to present an overview of how we in the US government have gone about meeting this challenge. At the outset, let me highlight that the entire endeavor of applying established international law to cyberspace is part of a broader international conversation. We are not alone in thinking about these questions; we are actively engaged with the rest of the international community, both bilaterally and multilaterally, on the subject of applying international law in cyberspace.

With your permission, I'd like to offer a series of questions and answers that illuminate where we are right now—in a place where we've made remarkable headway in a relatively short period of time, but are still finding new questions for each and every one we answer.

In fact, the US government has been regularly sharing these thoughts with our international partners. Most of the points that follow we have not just agreed upon internally, but made diplomatically, in our submissions to the UN Group of Governmental Experts (GGE) that deals with information technology issues.

I. International Law in Cyberspace: What We Know

So let me start with the most fundamental questions.

Question 1: Do established principles of international law apply to cyberspace?

Answer 1: Yes, international law principles do apply in cyberspace. Everyone here knows how cyberspace opens up a host of novel and extremely difficult legal issues. But on this key question, this answer has been apparent, at least as far as the US government has been concerned.

Significantly, this view has not necessarily been universal in the international community. At least one country has questioned whether existing bodies of international law apply to the cutting-edge issues presented by the Internet. Some have also said that existing international law is not up to the task and that we need entirely new treaties to impose a unique set of rules on cyberspace. But the United States has made clear our view that established principles of international law do apply in cyberspace.

Question 2: Is cyberspace a law-free zone, where anything goes?

Answer 2: Emphatically no. Cyberspace is not a "law-free" zone where anyone can conduct hostile activities without rules or restraint.

Think of it this way. This is not the first time that technology has changed and that international law has been asked to deal with those changes. In particular, because the tools of conflict are constantly evolving, one relevant body of law—international humanitarian law, or the law of armed conflict—affirmatively anticipates technological innovation and contemplates that its existing rules will apply to such innovation. To be sure, new technologies raise new issues and thus new questions. Many of us in this room have struggled with such questions, and we will continue to do so over many years. But to those who say that established law is not up to the task, we must articulate and build consensus around how it applies and reassess from there whether and what additional understandings are needed.

Developing common understandings about how these rules apply in the context of cyber-activities in armed conflict will promote stability in this area.

That consensus-building work brings me to some questions and answers we have offered to our international partners to explain how both the law of going to war (*jus ad bellum*) and the laws that apply in conducting war (*jus in bello*) apply to cyber-action:

Question 3: Do cyber-activities ever constitute a use of force?

Answer 3: Yes. Cyber-activities may in certain circumstances constitute uses of force within the meaning of Article 2(4) of the UN Charter and customary international law. In analyzing whether a cyber-operation would constitute a use of force, most commentators focus on whether the direct physical injury and property damage resulting from the cyber-event looks like that which would be considered a use of force if produced by kinetic weapons. *Cyber-activities that proximately result in death, injury, or significant destruction would likely be viewed as a use of force.* In assessing whether an event constituted a use of force in or through cyberspace, we must evaluate factors including the context of the event, the actor perpetrating the action (recognizing challenging issues of attribution in cyberspace), the target and location, effects, and intent, among other possible issues. Commonly cited examples of cyber-activity that would constitute a use of force include, for example: (1) operations that trigger a nuclear plant meltdown; (2) operations that open a dam above a populated area causing destruction; or (3) operations that disable air traffic control resulting in airplane crashes. Only a moment's reflection makes you realize that this is common sense: if the physical consequences of a cyber-attack work the kind of physical damage that dropping a bomb or firing a missile would, that cyber-attack should equally be considered a use of force.

Question 4: May a state ever respond to a computer network attack by exercising a right of national self-defense?
Answer 4: Yes. A state's national right of self-defense, recognized in Article 51 of the UN Charter, may be triggered by computer network activities that amount to an armed attack or imminent threat thereof. As the United States affirmed in its 2011 International Strategy for Cyberspace, "when warranted, the United States will respond to hostile acts in cyberspace as we would to any other threat to our country."

Question 5: Do *jus in bello* rules apply to computer network attacks?
Answer 5: Yes. In the context of an armed conflict, the law of armed conflict applies to regulate the use of cyber-tools in hostilities, just as it does other tools. The principles of necessity and proportionality limit uses of force in self-defense and would regulate what may constitute a lawful response under the circumstances. There is no legal requirement that the response to a cyber-armed attack take the form of a cyber-action, as long as the response meets the requirements of necessity and proportionality.

Question 6: Must attacks distinguish between military and non-military objectives?

Answer 6: Yes. The *jus in bello* **principle of** *distinction* **applies to computer network attacks undertaken in the context of an armed conflict.** The principle of distinction applies to cyber-activities that amount to an "attack"—as that term is understood in the law of war—in the context of an armed conflict. As in any form of armed conflict, the principle of distinction requires that the intended effect of the attack must be to harm a legitimate *military* target. We must distinguish military objectives—that is, objects that make an effective contribution to military action and whose destruction would offer a military advantage—from civilian objects, which under international law are generally protected from attack.

Question 7: Must attacks adhere to the principle of proportionality?

Answer 7: Yes. The *jus in bello* **principle of** *proportionality* **applies to computer network attacks undertaken in the context of an armed conflict.** The principle of proportionality prohibits attacks that may be expected to cause incidental loss to civilian life, injury to civilians, or damage to civilian objects that would be excessive in relation to the concrete and direct military advantage anticipated. Parties to an armed conflict must assess what the expected harm to civilians is likely to be and weigh the risk of such collateral damage against the importance of the expected military advantage to be gained. In the cyber-context, this rule requires parties to a conflict to assess: (1) the effects of cyber-weapons on both military and civilian infrastructure and users, including shared physical infrastructure (such as a dam or a power grid) that would affect civilians; (2) the potential physical damage that a cyber-attack may cause, such as death or injury that may result from effects on critical infrastructure; and (3) the potential effects of a cyber-attack on civilian objects that are not military objectives, such as private, civilian computers that hold no military significance but may be networked to computers that are military objectives.

Question 8: How should states assess their cyber-weapons?
Answer 8: States should undertake a legal review of weapons,
including those that employ a cyber-capability. Such a review
should entail an analysis, for example, of whether a particular capability would be *inherently indiscriminate*, i.e., that it could not be used
consistent with the principles of distinction and proportionality. The
US government undertakes at least two stages of legal review of the
use of weapons in the context of armed conflict—first, an evaluation
of new weapons to determine whether their use would be *per se* prohibited by the law of war; and second, specific operations employing
weapons are always reviewed to ensure that each particular operation
is also compliant with the law of war.

Question 9: In this analysis, what role does state
sovereignty play?
Answer 9: States conducting activities in cyberspace must take
into account the sovereignty of other states, including outside
the context of armed conflict. The physical infrastructure that supports the Internet and cyber-activities is generally located in sovereign
territory and subject to the jurisdiction of the territorial state. Because
of the interconnected, interoperable nature of cyberspace, operations
targeting networked information infrastructures in one country may
create effects in another country. Whenever a state contemplates conducting activities in cyberspace, the sovereignty of other states needs
to be considered.

Question 10: Are states responsible when cyber-acts are
undertaken through proxies?
Answer 10: Yes. States are legally responsible for activities
undertaken through "proxy actors" who act on the state's
instructions or under its direction or control. The ability to mask
one's identity and geography in cyberspace and the resulting difficulties of timely, high-confidence attribution can create significant chal-

lenges for states in identifying, evaluating, and accurately responding to threats. But putting attribution problems aside for a moment, established international law does address the question of proxy actors. States are legally responsible for activities undertaken through putatively private actors who act on the state's instructions or under its direction or control. If a state exercises a sufficient degree of control over an ostensibly private person or group of persons committing an internationally wrongful act, the state assumes responsibility for the act, just as if official agents of the state itself had committed it. These rules are designed to ensure that states cannot hide behind putatively private actors to engage in conduct that is internationally wrongful.

II. International Law in Cyberspace: Challenges and Uncertainties

These ten answers should give you a sense of how far we have come in doing what any good international lawyer does: applying established law to new facts and explaining our positions to other interested lawyers. At the same time, there are obviously many more issues where the questions remain under discussion. Let me identify three particularly difficult questions that I don't intend to answer here today. Instead, my hope is to shed some light on some of the cutting-edge legal issues that we'll all be facing together over the next few years.

Unresolved Question 1: How can a use-of-force regime take into account all of the novel kinds of *effects* that states can produce through the click of a button?

As I said above, the United States has affirmed that established *jus ad bellum* rules do apply to uses of force in cyberspace. I have also noted some clear-cut cases where the physical effects of a hostile cyber-action would be comparable to what a kinetic action could achieve: for example, a bomb might break a dam and flood a civilian population, but insertion of a line of malicious code from a distant computer might just as easily achieve that same result. As you all know, however, there are other types of cyber-actions that do not have a clear kinetic parallel, which raise profound questions about exactly what we mean by "force." At the same time, the difficulty of reaching a definitive legal conclusion or consensus among states on when and under what circumstances a hostile cyber-action would constitute an armed attack does not automatically suggest that we need an entirely new legal framework specific to cyberspace. Outside of the cyber-context, such ambiguities and differences of view have long existed among states.

To cite just one example of this, the United States has for a long time taken the position that the inherent right of self-defense potentially applies against *any* illegal use of force. In our view, there is no threshold for a use of deadly force to qualify as an "armed attack" that may warrant a forcible response. But that is not to say that any illegal use of force triggers the right to use any and all force in response— such responses must still be *necessary* and of course *proportionate*. We recognize, on the other hand, that some other countries and commentators have drawn a distinction between the "use of force" and an "armed attack," and view "armed attack"—triggering the right to self-defense—as a subset of uses of force, which passes a higher threshold of gravity. My point here is not to rehash old debates but to illustrate that states have long had to sort through complicated *jus ad bellum* questions. In this respect, the existence of complicated cyber-questions relating to *jus ad bellum* is not in itself a new development; it is just applying old questions to the latest developments in technology.

Unresolved Question 2: What do we do about "*dual-use* infrastructure" in cyberspace?

As you all know, information and communications infrastructure is often shared between state militaries and private, civilian communities. The law of war requires that civilian infrastructure not be used to seek to immunize military objectives from attack, including in the cyber-realm. But how, exactly, are the *jus in bello* rules to be implemented in cyberspace? Parties to an armed conflict will need to assess the potential effects of a cyber-attack on computers that are *not* military objectives, such as private, civilian computers that hold no military significance but may be networked to computers that are valid military objectives. Parties will also need to consider the harm to the civilian uses of such infrastructure in performing the necessary proportionality review. Any number of factual scenarios could arise, however, which will require a careful, fact-intensive legal analysis in each situation.

Unresolved Question 3: How do we address the problem of *attribution* in cyberspace?

As I mentioned earlier, cyberspace significantly increases an actor's ability to engage in attacks with "plausible deniability" by acting through proxies. I noted that legal tools exist to ensure that states are held accountable for those acts. What I want to highlight here is that many of these challenges—in particular, those concerning attribution—are as much questions of technical and policy nature rather than exclusively or even predominantly questions of law. Cyberspace remains a new and dynamic operating environment, and we cannot expect that all answers to the new and confounding questions we face will be *legal* ones.

These questions about effects, dual use, and attribution are difficult legal and policy questions that existed long before the development of cyber-tools, and that will continue to be a topic of discussion among our allies and partners as cybertools develop. Of course, there remain many other difficult and important questions about the application of international law to activities in cyberspace—for example, about the implications of sovereignty and neutrality law, enforcement mechanisms, and the obligations of states concerning "hacktivists" operating from within their territory. While these are not questions that I can address in this brief speech, they are critically important questions on which international lawyers will focus intensely in the years to come.

And just as cyberspace presents challenging new issues for lawyers, it presents challenging new technical and policy issues. Not all of the issues I've mentioned are susceptible to clear legal answers derived from existing precedents—in many cases, quite the contrary. Answering these tough questions within the framework of existing law, consistent with our values and accounting for the legitimate needs of national security, will require a constant dialogue between lawyers, operators, and policymakers. All that we as lawyers can do is to apply in the cyber-context the same rigorous approach to these hard questions that arise in the future, as we apply every day to what might be considered more traditional forms of conflict.

III. The Role of International Law in a "Smart Power" Approach to Cyberspace

This, in a nutshell, is where we are with regard to cyber-conflict: we have begun work to build consensus on a number of answers, but questions continue to arise that must be answered in the months and years ahead. Beyond these questions and answers and unresolved questions, though, lies a much bigger picture, one that we are very focused on at the State Department, which brings me to my final two questions.

Final Question 1: Is international humanitarian law the only body of international law that applies in cyberspace? Final Answer 1: No. As important as international humanitarian law is, it is not the only international law that applies in cyberspace.

Obviously, cyberspace has become pervasive in our lives, not just in the national defense arena, but also through social media, publishing and broadcasting, expressions of human rights, and expansion of international commerce, both through online markets and online commercial techniques. Many other bodies of international and national law address those activities, and how those different bodies of law overlap and apply with the laws of cyber-conflict is something we will all have to work out over time.

Take human rights. At the same time that cyber-activity can pose a threat, we all understand that cyber-communication is increasingly becoming a dominant mode of expression in the twenty-first century. More and more people express their views not by speaking on a soap box at Speakers' Corner but by blogging, tweeting, commenting, or posting videos and commentaries. The 1948 Universal Declaration of Human Rights (UDHR)—adopted more than seventy years ago—was remarkably forward-looking in anticipating these trends. It says: "Everyone has the right to freedom of opinion and expression; this right includes freedom to hold opinions without interference and to seek, receive, and impart information and ideas *through any media and regardless of frontiers*" (emphasis added). In short, all human beings are entitled to certain rights, whether they choose to exercise them in a city square or an Internet chat room. This principle is an important part of our global diplomacy and is encapsulated in the Internet freedom agenda about which my boss, Secretary Clinton, has spoken so passionately.

You all know of this administration's efforts not just in the areas of cyber-conflict but also in many other cyber areas: cyber-security, cyber-commerce, fighting child pornography and other forms of cyber-crime and stopping intellectual property piracy, as well as promoting free expression and human rights. So the cyber-conflict issues with which this group grapples do not constitute the whole of our approach to cyberspace; they are an important part—but only a part—of this administration's broader "smart power" approach to cyberspace.

What I have outlined today are a series of answers to cyberspace questions that the United States is on the record as supporting. I have also suggested a few of the challenging questions that remain before us and developments over the next decade will surely produce new questions. But you should not think of these questions and answers as just a box to check before deciding whether a particular proposed operation is lawful or not. Rather, these questions and answers are part of a much broader foreign policy agenda which transpires in a broader framework of respect for international law.

That leads to my final question for this group.

Final Question 2: Why should US government lawyers care about international law in cyberspace at all?
Final Answer 2: Because compliance with international law frees us to do more, and do more legitimately, in cyberspace, in a way that more fully promotes our national interests. Compliance with international law in cyberspace is part and parcel of our broader "smart power" approach to international law as part of US foreign policy.

It is worth noting a fundamental difference in philosophy about international law. One way to think about law, whether domestic or international, is as a straitjacket, a pure constraint. This approach posits that nations have serious, legitimate interests, and legal regimes restrict their ability to carry them out. One consequence of this view is that, since law is just something that constrains, it should be resisted whenever possible. Resisting so-called "extensions" of the law to new areas often seems attractive because, after all, the old laws weren't built for these new challenges anyway, some say, so we should tackle those challenges without the legal straitjacket, while leaving the old laws behind.

But that is *not* the US government's view of the law, domestic or international. We see law not as a straitjacket but as what one great university calls it when it confers its diplomas: a body of "wise restraints that make us free." International law is not purely constraint, it frees us and empowers us to do things we could never do without law's legitimacy. If we succeed in promoting a culture of compliance, we will reap the benefits. And if we earn a reputation for compliance, the actions we *do* take will earn enhanced legitimacy worldwide for their adherence to the rule of law.

These are not new themes, but I raise them here because they resonate squarely with the strategy we have been pursuing in cyberspace over the past few years. Of course, the United States has impressive cyber-capabilities; it should be clear from the bulk of my discussion that adherence to established principles of law does not prevent us from using those capabilities to achieve important ends. But we also know that we will be safer the more that we can rally other states to the view that these established principles *do* impose meaningful constraints and that there is already an existing set of laws that protects our security in cyberspace. And the more widespread the understanding that cyberspace follows established rules— and that we live by them—the stronger we can be in pushing back against those who would seek to introduce brand new rules that may be contrary to our interests.

That is why, in our diplomacy, we do not whisper about these issues. We talk about them *openly and bilaterally* with other countries— about the application of established international law to cyberspace. We talk about them *multilaterally*, at the UN Group of Governmental Experts and at other fora, in promoting this vision of compliance with international law in cyberspace. We talk about them *regionally*, as when we recently co-sponsored an ASEAN Regional Forum event to focus the international community's attention on the problem of proxy actors engaging in unlawful conduct in cyberspace. Preventing proxy attacks on us is an important interest, and as part of our discussions we have outlined the ways that existing international law addresses this problem.

The diplomacy I have described is not limited to the legal issues this group of lawyers is used to facing in the operational context. These issues are interconnected with countless other cyber-issues that we face daily in our foreign policy, such as cyber-security, cyber-commerce, human rights in cyberspace, and public diplomacy through cybertools. In all of these areas, let me repeat again, *compliance with international law in cyberspace is part and parcel of our broader smart power approach to international law as part of US foreign policy.* Compliance with international law—and thinking actively together about how best to promote that compliance—can only free us to do more, and to do more legitimately, in the emerging frontiers of cyberspace in a way that more fully promotes our US national interests.

. . .

Appendix: Kris–A

David Kris, assistant attorney general for national security, "Law Enforcement as a Counterterrorism Tool," address at the Brookings Institution, June 11, 2010

. . .

I've been asked to discuss the role of law enforcement as a counterterrorism tool. This is a timely subject; you may have noticed recently some talk about whether the federal courts should be used against international terrorists. I will discuss this issue in four main parts.

First, I'll review the recent history of our national counterterrorism strategy, focused in particular on the origins and evolution of the Justice Department's National Security Division (NSD), which I head. Knowing a little about NSD may be interesting to you anyway (I hope), but it's also an important part of how the country came to a consensus, at least until recently, about the appropriate role of law enforcement as a counterterrorism tool.

Second, I will try to sketch out a conceptual framework for thinking about the role of law enforcement in the current conflict. The idea here is to identify the right questions, the right way of approaching the policy debate that we are now engaged in as a country. Identifying the right questions, I think, is not as easy as it sounds, but it is, as always, critically important.

Third, I'll try to answer these questions that I have identified. To do this, I'll briefly describe some of the empirical evidence about how law enforcement has been used to combat terrorism. I'll also offer a comparison between civilian law enforcement and its two major alternatives: detention under the law of war and prosecution in a military commission. This comparison will not be nearly as detailed as you would need to make intelligent decisions about public policy, let alone about particular cases, but it will give you an idea of the major pros and cons of each system as I see them.

Fourth, and finally, I will conclude with some ideas on how to improve the effectiveness of law enforcement as a counterterrorism tool. Here I'll address, among other things, the idea of legislation on the public-safety exception to *Miranda* that has been discussed of late.

To begin with recent history, we often hear that before September 11, [2001], the United States took a "law enforcement approach" to counterterrorism. There is some truth in that, but I think it oversimplifies things. In fact, the 9/11 Commission found that before September 11, "the CIA was plainly the lead agency confronting Al Qaeda"; law enforcement played a "secondary" role; and military and diplomatic efforts were "episodic." I was involved in national security before September 11, and that seems about right to me.

After September 11, of course, all of our national security agencies ramped up their counterterrorism activities; as our troops deployed to foreign battlefields and the intelligence community expanded its operations, the Department of Justice (DOJ) and the FBI also evolved. We began with an important legal change, tearing down the so-called "FISA wall," under which law enforcement and intelligence were largely separate enterprises and law enforcement was correspondingly limited as a counterterrorism tool. For those of you who don't know what FISA is, it is a federal statute [Foreign Intelligence Surveillance Act], enacted by Congress in 1978, that governs electronic surveillance and physical searches of foreign intelligence targets in the United States. It is an extremely powerful investigative tool, and one that is vitally important to our national security. Until the wall came down, however, the price of using FISA—

or preserving the option to use FISA—was a requirement to keep law enforcement and intelligence at arm's length. Tearing down the wall permitted intelligence and law enforcement to work together more effectively.

I think this legal change reflected, and also reinforced, the conclusion that law enforcement helps protect national security. Not that law enforcement is the only way to protect national security, or even that it's the best way. But I do think we came to a national consensus, in the years immediately after 9/11, that law enforcement is one important way of protecting national security.

This consensus led to significant structural changes at DOJ and the FBI. The Bureau integrated intelligence and law enforcement functions with respect to counterterrorism and dramatically increased its resources and focus on intelligence collection and analysis. The FBI has long been the intelligence community element with primary responsibility for collecting and coordinating intelligence about terrorist threats in the United States, and since 9/11 it has made this mission its highest priority. It also led Congress to strengthen our counterterrorism criminal laws and to create NSD, which combines terrorism and espionage prosecutors with intelligence lawyers and other intelligence professionals. NSD personnel are all united by a single, shared mission: to protect against terrorism and other threats to national security using all lawful methods. At some level, NSD is indifferent to the particular lawful method used to neutralize a threat; we prefer the method that is most effective under the circumstances. This, I think, is the crystallized consensus of our federal government and the American people in the aftermath of 9/11.

Today, however, the consensus that developed in the aftermath of 9/11 shows some signs of unraveling. In particular, there are some who say that law enforcement can't—or shouldn't—be used for counterterrorism. They appear to believe that we should treat all terrorists exclusively as targets for other parts of the intelligence community or the Defense Department.

The argument, as I understand it, is basically the following:

(1) We are at war.
(2) Our enemies in this war are not common criminals.
(3) Therefore we should fight them using military and intelligence methods, not law enforcement methods.

This is a simple and rhetorically powerful argument and, precisely for that reason, it may be attractive.

In my view, however, and with all due respect, it is not correct. And it will, if adopted, make us less safe. Of course, it's not that law enforcement is always the right tool for combating terrorism. But it's also not the case that it's never the right tool. The reality, I think, is that it's sometimes the right tool. And whether it's the right tool in any given case depends on the specific facts of that case.

Here's my version of the argument:

(1) We're at war. The president has said this many times, as has the attorney general.
(2) In war you must try to win—no other goal is acceptable.
(3) To win the war, we need to use all available tools that are consistent with the law and our values, selecting in any case the tool that is best under the circumstances.

We must, in other words, be relentlessly pragmatic and empirical. We can't afford to limit our options artificially or yield to preconceived notions of suitability or "correctness." We have to look dispassionately at the facts, and then respond to those facts using whatever methods will best lead us to victory.

Put in more concrete terms, we should use the tool that's designed best for the problem we face. When the problem looks like a nail, we need to use a hammer. But when it looks like a bolt, we need to use a wrench. Hitting a bolt with a hammer makes a loud noise, and it can be satisfying in some visceral way, but it's not effective and it's not smart. If we want to win, we can't afford that.

If you take this idea seriously it complicates strategic planning, because it requires a detailed understanding of our various counterterrorism tools. If you're a pragmatist, focused relentlessly on winning, you can't make policy or operational decisions at 30,000 feet. You have to come down and get into the weeds, and understand the details of our counterterrorism tools at the operational level. And that leads me to this question: as compared to the viable alternatives, what is the value of law enforcement in this war? Does it in fact help us win? Or is it categorically the wrong tool for the job—at best a distraction, and at worst an affirmative impediment?

I think law enforcement helps us win this war. And I want to make clear, for the limited purpose of today's remarks and in light of the nature of our current national debate, that this is not primarily a values-based argument. That is, I am not saying law enforcement helps us win in the sense that it is a shining city on a hill that captures hearts and minds around the world (although I do think our criminal justice system is widely respected). Values are critically important, both in themselves and in their effect on us, our allies, and our adversaries, but I am talking now about something more direct and concrete.

When I say that law enforcement helps us win this war, I mean that it helps us disrupt, defeat, dismantle, and destroy our adversaries (without destroying ourselves or our way of life in the process). In particular, law enforcement helps us in at least three ways: it can disrupt terrorist plots through arrests, incapacitate terrorists through incarceration resulting from prosecution, and gather intelligence from interrogation and recruitment of terrorists or their supporters via cooperation agreements.

Here's some of the evidence for that argument. Between September 2001 and March 2010, DOJ convicted more than 400 defendants in terrorism-related cases. Some of these convictions involve per se terrorism offenses, while others do not—Al Capone was convicted of tax fraud rather than racketeering, but that doesn't make him any less of a gangster. Of course we have Najibullah Zazi and David Headley, both of whom have pleaded guilty and are awaiting sentencing, and now Faisal Shahzad, but there have been many others over the years, ranging from Ramzi Yousef (the first World Trade Center bomber) to the East Africa Embassy bombers, to Richard Reid, to Ahmed Omar Abu Ali, all of whom are now serving life sentences in federal prison. Just in the past year, among others, Wesam al-Delaema was sentenced to twenty-five years for planting IEDs in Iraq, Syed Harris and Ehsanul Sadequee were sentenced to thirteen and seventeen years for providing material support to Al Qaeda, and Oussama Kassir was sentenced to life in prison for attempting to establish a jihad training camp in the United States. Last year we also arrested two individuals in separate undercover operations after they allegedly tried to blow up buildings in Dallas, Texas, and Springfield, Illinois. And there are many others.

Not all of these cases make the headlines and not all of the defendants we've convicted were hard-core terrorists or key terrorist operatives. As in organized crime or traditional intelligence investigations, aggressive and wide-ranging counter-terrorism efforts may net a lot of smaller fish along with the big fish. That may mean we are disrupting plots before they're consummated, and it may give us a chance to deter or recruit the smaller fish before they're fully radicalized.

We've also used the criminal justice system to collect valuable intelligence. In effect, the criminal justice system has worked as what the intelligence community would call a HUMINT [HUMan INTelligence] collection platform. The fact is that when the government has a strong prosecution case, the defendant knows he will spend a long time in prison and this creates powerful incentives for him to cooperate with us.

There's a limit to what I can say publicly, of course, but I can say that terrorism suspects in the criminal justice system have provided information on all of the following:

- Telephone numbers and e-mail addresses used by Al Qaeda
- Al Qaeda recruiting techniques, finances, and geographical reach
- Terrorist tradecraft used to avoid detection in the West
- Experiences at, and the location of, Al Qaeda training camps
- Al Qaeda weapons programs and explosives training
- The location of Al Qaeda safe houses (including drawing maps)
- Residential locations of senior Al Qaeda figures
- Al Qaeda communications methods and security protocols
- Identification of operatives involved in past and planned attacks
- Information about plots to attack US targets

The intelligence community, including the National Counterterrorism Center (NCTC), believes that the criminal justice system has provided useful information. For example, NCTC has explained that it "regularly receives and regularly uses . . . valuable terrorism information obtained through the criminal justice system—and in particular federal criminal proceedings pursued by the FBI and Department of Justice. Increasingly close coordination between the Department of Justice and NCTC has resulted in an increase in both the intelligence value and quality of reporting related to terrorism."

Having explained the basic affirmative case for law enforcement as a counter-terrorism tool, let me address some of the arguments on the other side. The first argument is that there's an inherent tension between national security and law enforcement. I think this argument confuses ends with means. The criminal justice system is a tool—one of several—for promoting national security, for protecting our country against terrorism. Sometimes it's the right tool; sometimes it's the wrong tool. That is no different than saying sometimes the best way to protect national security is through diplomacy and sometimes it's through military action.

Another argument is that the criminal justice system is fundamentally incompatible with national security because it is focused on defendants' rights. But this argument suffers from two basic flaws. First, the criminal justice system is not focused solely on defendants' rights—it strikes a balance between defendants' rights and the interests of government, victims, and society. And whatever the balance that has been struck, the empirical fact is that when we prosecute terrorists we convict them around 90 percent of the time. To be sure, the criminal justice system has its limits, and in part because of those limits it is not always the right tool for the job. But when the executive branch concludes that it is the right tool—as it has more than 400 times since September 11—we in fact put steel on target almost every time.

The second flaw in the "fundamental incompatibility" argument is equally significant. The criminal justice system is not alone in facing legal constraints; all of the US government's activities must operate under the rule of law. For example, the US military operates under rules that require it to forego strikes against terrorists if they will inflict disproportionate harm on civilians. (It also has rules governing who may be detained, how detainees have to be treated, and how long they can be held.) These limits are real, and they are not trivial, but no one thinks they're a reason to abandon or forbid the use of military force against Al Qaeda. (By the way, the point of this argument is not to equate the legal constraints in the two systems; they are in fact very different. The point is only to emphasize that all of our counterterrorism tools have legal limits—this is the price of living under the rule of law—and those limits inform judgments about which tool is best in any given case.)

Ultimately, the worth of the criminal justice system is a relative thing. In other words, its value as a counterterrorism tool must be compared to the value of other tools. Comparing the criminal justice system to the use of military force or diplomacy is difficult because it shares so little in common with them. But as a tool for disrupting and incapacitating terrorists and gathering intelligence, the criminal justice system is readily comparable with two others—detention under the law of war and prosecution in a military commission. So I will turn to that comparison now.

Before I focus on the differences between these systems, however, I want to acknowledge the similarities of the two prosecution systems. Whether you're in civilian court or a military commission, there is the presumption of innocence; a requirement of proof beyond a reasonable doubt; the right to an impartial decision-maker; similar processes for selecting members of the jury or commission; the right to counsel and choice of counsel; the right to qualified self-representation; the right to be present during proceedings; the right against self-incrimination; the right to present evidence, cross-examine the government's witnesses, and compel attendance of witnesses; the right to exclude prejudicial evidence; the right to exculpatory evidence; protections against double jeopardy; protections against ex post facto laws; and the right to an appeal. Both systems afford the basic rights most Americans associate with a fair trial.

As to the differences, an exhaustive comparison would require a longer discussion, but I have identified five relative advantages of our military authorities and five of the civilian system, viewed solely from the perspective of the government and their effectiveness in combating terrorism. I need to emphasize, however, that this is not nearly as detailed a comparison as you would need to make informed policy or operational judgments. The comparisons that really matter are far more granular and nuanced than anything that I can offer in this setting. Also, the extent and significance of the differences between the systems often turn on the facts of a particular case. There is no substitute for immersion in the details. With those important caveats, here are five general advantages that using military authorities rather than civilian prosecution may offer to the government, depending on the facts.

1. Proof requirements. In military commissions, the burden of proof is the same as in civilian court—beyond a reasonable doubt—but in non-capital cases only two-thirds of the jurors (rather than all of them) are needed for conviction. Under the law of war, if it's tested through a habeas corpus petition, the government need only persuade the judge by a preponderance of the evidence that the petitioner is part of Al Qaeda or affiliated forces, though that is not always easy as our track record in the Guantánamo cases has shown.

2. Admissibility of confessions. In a military commission, unlike in federal court, *Miranda* warnings are not required to use the defendant's custodial statements against him. While the voluntariness test generally applies in the commissions as it does in federal court, there's an exception in the commissions for statements taken at the point of capture on or near a battlefield. For law-of-war detention, the test is reliability, which may in practical effect be pretty similar to a basic voluntariness requirement.

3. Closing the courtroom. While both federal trials and commission proceedings are generally open proceedings, compared to federal court, there may be some increased ability to close the courtroom in a military commission, and certain military commission trials have implemented a 45-second delay of the broadcast of statements to permit classified information to be blocked before it is aired in certain cases. There certainly is a greater ability to close the courtroom in a habeas corpus proceeding, and—unlike both military commission and civilian trials—the petitioner is not required to be present, which can help in dealing with classified information.

4. Admissibility of hearsay. The hearsay rules are somewhat more relaxed in military commissions than in federal prosecutions, and they are significantly more relaxed in habeas proceedings. This can be good for the government in some cases, particularly in protecting sensitive sources, but it can also help the defendant/petitioner in

some cases. In the Hamdan case [*Hamdan v. Rumsfeld*], for example, Hamdan used the hearsay rules more than the government did.

5. Classified evidence. The rules governing protection of classified information are very similar in the two prosecution forums—indeed, the military commission rules were modeled on the federal court rules. But the rules may be somewhat better in military commissions because they codify some of the federal case law and adopt lessons learned from litigating classified information issues in federal court. I would say the classified information rules in habeas proceedings over law-of-war detention are both more flexible and less certain.

Those are, in my view, the five main advantages that the government might enjoy in using military rather than civilian authorities. Now, here are the five main advantages of using federal courts rather than military commissions or law-of-war detention, subject to the same caveats as above.

1. Certainty and finality. The rules governing civilian prosecutions are more certain and well-established than those in the other two systems. This can speed the process, reduce litigation risk, promote cooperation and guilty pleas, and result in reliable long-term incapacitation. This is a very significant factor for now, but it will hopefully recede over time as we gain more experience in the commissions.

2. Scope. The civilian criminal justice system is much broader than the other two—it has far more crimes (covering everything from terrorism to tax evasion) and applies to everyone. Military commissions are not available for US citizens—folks like Anwar al-Awlaki and Faisal Shahzad—and neither commissions nor law-of-war detention apply to terrorists not related to Al Qaeda or the Taliban. Groups like Hamas, Hezbollah, or the FARC [Revolutionary Armed Forces of Colombia] are out of bounds, as are lone-wolf terrorists who may be inspired by Al Qaeda but are not part of it (like the two individuals I mentioned who allegedly tried to blow up buildings in Illinois and Texas last year).

3. Incentives for cooperation. The criminal justice system has more reliable and more extensive mechanisms to encourage cooperation. While the military commissions have borrowed a plea and sentencing agreement mechanism from the courts-martial system which could be used for cooperation—Rule 705—this system has not yet been tested in military commissions and its effectiveness is as yet unclear. In law-of-war detention, interrogators can offer detainees improvements in their conditions of confinement, but there is no "sentence" over which to negotiate and no judge to enforce an agreement. Detainees may have little incentive to provide information in those circumstances. On the other hand, in some circumstances law-of-war detainees may lawfully be held in conditions that many believe are helpful to effective interrogation.

4. Sentencing. In federal court, judges impose sentences based in large part on tough sentencing guidelines, while sentencing in the military commissions is basically done by the jury without any guidelines. What little experience we have with the commissions suggests that sentencing in that forum is less predictable—two of the three commission defendants convicted thus far (including Osama bin Laden's driver) received sentences of five to six years, with credit for time served, and were released within months of sentencing. Under the law of war, of course, there is no sentence; if their detention is lawful, detainees may be held until the end of the conflict. But the Supreme Court has warned that if the circumstances of the current conflict "are entirely unlike those of the conflicts that informed the development of the law of war," the authority to detain "may unravel." As circumstances change, or if active combat operations are concluded, it is not clear how long the detention authority will endure.

Without going into too much detail, I should also say that there may be some advantages to bringing a capital case in federal court rather than in a military commission, in light of the different rules. The military commissions, for example, may not permit a capital sentence to be imposed following a guilty plea, at least for now.

5. International cooperation. Finally, the criminal justice system may help us obtain important cooperation from other countries. Unfortunately, some countries won't provide us with evidence we may need to hold suspected terrorists in law-of-war detention or prosecute them in military commissions. In some cases, they have agreed to extradite terrorist suspects to us only on the condition that they not be tried in military commissions. In such cases, use of federal courts may mean the difference between holding a terrorist and having him go free. This is not, of course, a plea to subject our counterterrorism efforts to some kind of global test of legitimacy; it is simply a hard-headed, pragmatic recognition that in some cases, where we need help from abroad, we will have to rely on law enforcement rather than military detention or prosecution.

To conclude, I think we cannot and should not immunize terrorists from prosecution any more than we should immunize them from the use of military strikes or our other counterterrorism tools. Law enforcement is too effective a weapon to discard.

Having said that, we do need to educate ourselves about all of the tools in the president's national security toolbox. Within the government, people who use hammers for a living need to know something about wrenches, and vice versa. If they don't, there is a danger of myopia: to a person holding a hammer, every problem begins to look like a nail. More generally, the American people need to understand, and have confidence in, all of the tools in the toolbox. That's part of why I came here today.

We also need to consider improving and sharpening our tools. Our adversaries are smart and adaptable, and we must be the same. For example, there has been some discussion recently about *Miranda* warnings in terrorism cases and the possibility of legislation on that score. Now, obviously, *Miranda* is a constitutional rule—we know that from the Supreme Court's decision in *Dickerson*—and it can't be overruled or even changed by statute. But the Supreme Court has recognized an exception to the *Miranda* rule. In 1984, in a case called

Quarles [New York v. Quarles], it said that questioning prompted by concerns about public safety need not be preceded by *Miranda* warnings. In other words, you can use the person's answers to public-safety questions to support his conviction and resulting incarceration.

Now, *Quarles* really did involve a common criminal—a man who committed an armed robbery and ran into a supermarket to escape the police. The question today is how the public-safety exception would apply in a very different context—modern international terrorism. The threat posed by terrorism today is more complex, sophisticated, and serious than the threat posed by ordinary crime. Correspondingly, therefore, there are arguments that the public safety exception should, likewise, permit more questioning where it's in fact designed to mitigate that threat.

We want to work with Congress to see if we can develop something that could help us—give us some more flexibility and clarity—in these narrow circumstances involving operational terrorists. The goal, always, is to promote and protect national security, and this may be one way to help do that.

. . .

Appendix: Johnson–A

*Jeh C. Johnson, general counsel,
Department of Defense, "Jeh C. Johnson
Speech to the Heritage Foundation,"
Washington, D.C., October 18, 2011*

. . .

I am convinced that one of the other reasons our military is so revered and respected is that, for all its power, we place sharp limits on the military's ability to intrude into the civilian life and affairs of our democracy. This is a core American value that is part of our heritage, dating back to before the founding of our country.

The Declaration of Independence listed among our grievances against the king the fact that he had "kept among us, in times of peace, Standing Armies without the Consent of our legislatures," and had "quarter[ed] large bodies of armed troops among us." This value is reflected in the Federalist Papers and the father of our Constitution, James Madison, wrote: "A standing military force, with an overgrown Executive, will not long be safe companions to liberty. The means of defense against foreign danger have been always the instruments of tyranny at home."

This core value and this heritage are today reflected in such places as the Third Amendment, which prohibits the peacetime quartering of soldiers in private homes without consent, and in the 1878 federal criminal statute, still on the books today, which prohibits willfully using the military as a posse comitatus unless expressly authorized by Congress or the Constitution.

This brings me to the point of these remarks today.

There is danger in over-militarizing our approach to Al Qaeda and its affiliates. There is risk in permitting and expecting the US military to extend its powerful reach into areas traditionally reserved for civilian law enforcement in this country. Against an unconventional non-state actor that does not play by the rules, operates in secret, observes no geographic limits, constantly morphs and metastasizes, and continues to look for opportunities to export terrorism to our homeland, we must use every tool at our disposal. The military should not and cannot be the only answer.

Recent events remind us that broad assertions of military power can provoke controversy and invite challenge. Over-reaching with military power can result in litigation in which the courts intrude further and further into our affairs, and can result in national security setbacks, not gains—a point best illustrated by the question Donald Rumsfeld once asked my predecessor: "So I'm going to go down in history as the only secretary of defense to have lost a case to a terrorist?"

Particularly when we attempt to extend the reach of the military onto US soil, the courts resist, consistent with our core values and our heritage.

We have worked to make military detention, in particular, less controversial, not more. The overall goal should be to build a counterterrorism framework that is legally sustainable and credible and that preserves every lawful tool and authority at our disposal. This has meant, as the president's counterterrorism adviser John Brennan said recently, an approach that is "pragmatic, neither a wholesale overhaul nor a wholesale retention of past practices."

To build that less controversial, more credible and sustainable legal framework, we have in the last several years accomplished the following:

We have applied the standards of the Army Field Manual to all interrogations conducted by the federal government in the context of armed conflict.

Where appropriate, in the context of terrorist activity, we have invoked the "public safety" exception to the *Miranda* rule created by the Supreme Court in *New York v. Quarles*—ensuring that the opportunity to gather valuable intelligence is fully utilized and, at the same time, preserving the prosecution option.

We worked with the Congress to bring about a number of reforms reflected in the Military Commissions Act of 2009 and, following that, we issued a new *Manual for Military Commissions*. By law, use of statements obtained by cruel, inhuman, and degrading treatment—what was once the most controversial aspect of military commissions—is now prohibited.

We accomplished those reforms working with a bipartisan coalition in Congress and with the full support of the JAG [Judge Advocate General] leadership in the military.

We have appointed the highly respected former judge advocate general of the navy, retired Vice Admiral Bruce MacDonald, to be the convening authority for military commissions; appointed a recognized military justice expert, Marine Colonel Jeff Caldwell, to be chief defense counsel; and this month appointed Brigadier General Mark Martins, a West Point valedictorian, Harvard Law School graduate, and Rhodes Scholar to be the chief prosecutor. We are recruiting the "A team" for this system.

We have reformed the rules for press access to military commissions' proceedings, established a new public website for the commissions system, and, in general, built what I believe is a credible, sustainable, and more transparent system.

In the habeas litigation brought by Guantánamo detainees, lawyers in the Department of Justice and the Department of Defense have worked hard to build credibility with the courts by conducting a thorough scrub of the evidence and the intelligence before we put forward our case for detention in the courts.

We have refined existing systems for periodic review for the cases of detainees at Guantánamo and at Bagram in Afghanistan.

Overall, the hard work of many civilian and military counterterrorism professionals, spanning both this administration and the last, is producing results.

First and foremost, we have been aggressive and focused in the fight against Al Qaeda. Where necessary, we have not hesitated to use lawful, lethal force against Al Qaeda and its affiliates and we are literally taking the fight to them, where they plot, where they meet, where they plan, and where they train to export terrorism to the United States. Counterterrorism experts state publicly that Al Qaeda senior leadership is today severely crippled and degraded.

Second, just as we brought justice to the man who ordered the attacks on 9/11, we seek to bring to justice KSM [Khalid Shaikh Mohammed] and the other alleged planners of 9/11, in reformed military commissions. New charges have also been referred in the case of the alleged Cole bomber, Hussayn Muhammed Al-Nashiri.

Third, the government is seeing consistent success in the habeas cases brought by Guantánamo detainees. The courts have largely recognized and accepted our legal interpretation of our detention authority, and the government has now prevailed at the District Court level in more than ten consecutive habeas cases brought by Guantánamo detainees. We are seeing similar good results in the D.C. Circuit.

In the D.C. Circuit, the Department of Justice successfully defended against an effort to extend the habeas remedy to detainees held in Afghanistan.

Fourth, through the interrogation of those captured by the United States and our partners overseas, we continue to collect valuable intelligence about Al Qaeda, its plans, and its intentions.

Fifth, this administration, like its predecessors, continues to successfully prosecute terrorists in our federal civilian courts.

As a former federal prosecutor, I know firsthand the strength, security, and effectiveness of our federal court system. . . . Given the reforms since 9/11, the federal court system is even more effective.

And, as a result of lengthy and mandatory minimum prison sentences authorized by Congress and the Federal Sentencing Guidelines, those convicted of terrorism-related offenses often face decades, if not life, in prison.

The results speak for themselves. Since 9/11, numerous individuals have been convicted of terrorism-related offenses. In the last two years alone, we have seen in our federal courts a guilty plea from the man who admitted plotting to bomb the New York subway system, a guilty plea from the man who tried to bomb the commercial aircraft over Detroit on Christmas Day 2009, a life sentence imposed on the individual who attempted to detonate a bomb in Times Square, and a life sentence imposed for participation in the 1998 bombing of our embassies in Kenya and Tanzania. Going back decades, the Department of Justice has successfully prosecuted hundreds of terrorism-related cases.

Despite our successes, we know that the fight is not over. We know there is still great danger. Though degraded and on the run, we know that, in this post–bin Laden period, Al Qaeda and its affiliates still remain determined to conduct terrorist attacks against the United States. We know also that while Al Qaeda's core is degraded, it is a far more decentralized organization than it was ten years ago and relies on affiliates to carry out its terrorist aims. We know that Al Qaeda is likely to continue to metastasize and try to recruit affiliates to its cause.

These terrorist threats are increasingly complex and multifaceted, and defy easy labeling and categorization. Just within the last several months, we have seen terrorists who in my judgment:

- claim affiliations to more than one terrorist organization.
- belong to one terrorist organization and serve as the conduit to another.
- fit within our military detention authority but not our military commissions' jurisdiction.

- fit within our military commissions' jurisdiction but not the military detention authority stemming from the 2001 Authorization for the Use of Military Force.
- fit within neither our military detention authority nor our commissions' jurisdiction, but can be prosecuted in our federal civilian courts.

On top of this are Al Qaeda's concerted efforts to recruit via the Internet, with a reach into the United States. Over and over again, we see individuals within the United States who self-radicalize and who find vindication for their hatred toward America in Al Qaeda's ideology and propaganda. In dealing with this category of people who are here in the United States—who have never trained at an Al Qaeda camp in Afghanistan or never sworn *bayat* [allegiance] to an Al Qaeda leader—we must guard against any impulse to label that person part of the congressionally declared enemy, to be dealt with by military force. There is no jurisdiction to try US citizens in military commissions, and our prior efforts in this conflict to put into military detention those arrested on US soil led to protracted litigation in which the government narrowly prevailed in the federal appellate courts.

As I said before, the military cannot always be the first and only answer. This is contrary to our heritage and, in the long run, will undermine our overall counterterrorism efforts.

In responding to threats and acts of terrorism, we must build a legally sustainable arsenal and have all the legally available tools in the arsenal—whether it is lethal force against a valid military objective, military detention, interrogation, supporting the counterterrorism efforts of other nations, or prosecution in federal court or by military commissions.

Against this backdrop, we confront a series of laws and pending legislation concerning detainees that limit the executive branch's and the military's counterterrorism options, complicate our efforts to achieve continued success, and will make military detention more controversial, not less. Here are some specific examples:

Section 1032 of the 2011 Defense Authorization Act prohibits the use of Defense Department funds to transfer any Guantánamo detainee to the United States for any conceivable purpose, no waivers or exceptions, including federal prosecution or to be a cooperating witness in a federal prosecution. Given the lengthy prison sentences mandated by Title 18 and the sentencing guidelines and the range of offenses available for prosecution under Title 18, there are some instances in which it is simply preferable and more effective to prosecute an individual in our federal civilian courts.

Section 1033 of the same law requires that, before the government can transfer a Guantánamo detainee to a foreign country, my client, the secretary of defense, must personally certify to the Congress certain things about the detainee and the transferee country, unless there is a court order directing the detainee's release. After living with this provision now for almost a year, I will tell you that it is onerous and nearly impossible to satisfy. Not one Guantánamo detainee has been certified for transfer since this legal restriction has been imposed.

Rigid certification requirements reduce our ability to pursue the best options for national security in an evolving world situation and intrude upon the executive branch's traditional ability to conduct foreign policy—in this case, to determine when sending a detainee to another country for prosecution or reintegration would better serve our national security and foreign policy interests. Our nation is not the only one on Earth that can deal effectively with this issue. The other potential consequence of such a rigid certification requirement is that it incentivizes the executive branch to leave to the courts the hard work of determining who can and should remain at Guantánamo. We want the courts less involved in this business, not more.

Certain legislative proposals for the 2012 Defense Authorization Act are equally problematic.

Section 1039 of the House version of the bill prohibits the use of Department of Defense funds to transfer to the United States any non-US citizen the military captures anywhere in the world as part of the conflict against Al Qaeda and its affiliates—no waivers or exceptions. Within the national security community of the executive branch, we have determined that such an unqualified, across-the-board ban is not in the best interests of national security. Suppose the military captures a dangerous terrorist and doubts arise about our detention authority overseas? Suppose the military captures an individual who, it turns out, would be vital as a cooperating witness in a terrorist prosecution in the United States? Must the option to bring these individuals to a civilian courtroom in the United States be prohibited by law?

Likewise, Section 1046 of the House bill imposes an across-the-board requirement that, if military commissions' jurisdiction exists to prosecute an individual, we must use commissions, not the federal courts, for the prosecution of a broad range of terrorist acts. Decisions about the most appropriate forum in which to prosecute a terrorist should be left, case-by-case, to prosecutors and national security professionals. The considerations that go into those decisions include the offenses available in both systems for prosecuting a particular course of conduct, the weight and nature of the evidence, and the likely prison sentence that would result if there is a conviction. A flat legislative ban on the use of one system—whether it is commissions or the civilian courts—in favor of the other is not the answer.

Section 1036 of the House bill rewrites the periodic review process the president's national security team carefully crafted for Guantánamo detainees designated for continued law-of-war detention. The proposed congressional rewrite mandates the use of "military review panels," contrary to our best judgment. Our experience shows that interagency review is valuable and preferred, to take advantage of the expertise and perspectives across the national security community in our government.

Finally, Section 1032 of the Senate version of the 2012 Defense Authorization bill includes what has come to be known as the "mandatory military custody" provision. Basically, it requires that certain members of Al Qaeda or its affiliates "be held in military custody pending disposition under the law of war" unless the secretary of defense, in writing, agrees to give them up.

For starters, the trigger for this requirement is unclear. Some of my friends on the Hill say that the provision is intended to apply only to those who have been "captured in the course of hostilities." Read literally, the provision extends to individuals wherever they are taken into custody or brought under the control of the United States, who fit within our definition of an enemy combatant in the conflict against Al Qaeda and its affiliates—including those arrested in the United States by first responders in law enforcement. This would include an individual who, in the midst of an interrogation by an FBI or TSA officer at an airport, admits he is part of Al Qaeda. Must the agent stop a very revealing and productive interrogation and go call the Army to take the suspect away?

On top of all that, the provision adds that the individual must be a member or part of Al Qaeda or an "affiliated entity." While we use the phrase "Al Qaeda and its affiliates" publicly to describe the contours of the conflict in non-legal terms, the term "affiliated entity" has no accepted legal meaning and has never been tested in court. Likewise, the phrase in the bill "a participant in the course of planning or carrying out an attack against the United States" has never been tested in court.

For this and future administrations, we will oppose efforts to make military detention more controversial and restrict the executive branch's flexibility to pursue our counterterrorism mission. The executive branch, regardless of the administration in power, needs the flexibility, case-by-case, to make well-informed decisions about the best way to capture, detain, and bring to justice suspected terrorists.

The conflict against Al Qaeda is complex and multifaceted. Congress must be careful not to micromanage, complicate, and impose across-the-board limits on our options. Both the Congress and the executive branch must be careful not to impose rules that make military detention more controversial, not less.

. . .

Appendix: Johnson–B

Jeh C. Johnson, general counsel,
Department of Defense, "National Security Law,
Lawyers, and Lawyering in the Obama Administration,"
address at Yale Law School, February 22, 2012

. . .

Involvement in the Obama administration has been the highlight of my professional life. Day to day, the job I occupy is all at once interesting, challenging, and frustrating. But when I take a step back and look at the larger picture, I realize that I have witnessed many transformative events in national security over the last three years.

We have focused our efforts on Al Qaeda and put that group on a path to defeat. We found bin Laden. Scores of other senior members of Al Qaeda have been killed or captured. We have taken the fight to Al Qaeda: where they plot, where they meet, where they plan, and where they train to export terrorism to the United States. Though the fight against Al Qaeda is not over, and multiple arms of our government remain vigilant in the effort to hunt down those who want to do harm to Americans, counterterrorism experts state publicly that Al Qaeda senior leadership is today severely crippled and degraded.

Thanks to the extraordinary sacrifices of our men and women in uniform, we have responsibly ended the combat mission in Iraq.

We are making significant progress in Afghanistan and have begun a transition to Afghan-led responsibility for security there.

We have applied the standards of the Army Field Manual to all interrogations conducted by the federal government in the context of armed conflict.

We worked with the Congress to bring about a number of reforms to military commissions, reflected in the Military Commissions Act of 2009 and the new Manual for Military Commissions. By law, use of statements obtained by cruel, inhuman, and degrading treatment—what was once the most controversial aspect of military commissions—is now prohibited.

We are working to make that system a more transparent one by reforming the rules for press access to military commissions' proceedings [and by] establishing closed-circuit TV and a new public website for the commissions system.

We have ended "don't ask, don't tell," which I discussed last time I was here.

Finally, we have, in these times of fiscal austerity, embarked upon a plan to transform the military to a more agile, flexible, rapidly deployable, and technologically advanced force that involves reducing the size of the active duty Army and Marine Corps, and the defense budget by $487 billion over ten years.

Perhaps the best part of my job is I work in the national security field with, truly, some of the best and brightest lawyers in the country. In this illustrious and credentialed group, I often ask myself, "How did I get here?"

Many in this group are graduates of this law school: my special assistant and Navy reservist Brodi Kemp, who is here with me today (class of '04); Caroline Krass at OLC [Office of Legal Counsel] (class of '93); Dan Koffsky at OLC (class of '78); Marty Lederman, formerly of OLC (class of '88); Greg Craig, the former White House counsel (class of '72); Bob Litt, general counsel of ODNI [Office of the Director of National Intelligence] (class of '76); retired Marine Colonel Bill Lietzau (class of '89); Beth Brinkman at DOJ (class of '85);

Sarah Cleveland, formerly at State Legal (class of '92); David Pozen at State Legal (class of '08); Steve Pomper (class of '93); and my deputy, Bob Easton (class of '90). I also benefit from working with a number of Yale law students as part of my office's internship and externship programs.

Last but not least: your former dean. Like many in this room, I count myself a student of Harold Koh's. Within the administration, Harold often reminds us of many of the things Barack Obama campaigned on in 2007–08. As I wrote these remarks, I asked myself to settle on the one theme from the 2008 campaign that best represents what Harold has carried forward in his position as lawyer for the State Department. The answer was easy: "The United States must lead by the power of our example and not by the example of our power."

There have been press reports that, occasionally, Harold and I, and other lawyers within the Obama administration, disagree from time to time on national security legal issues. I confess this is true, but it is also true that we actually agree on issues most of the time.

The public should be reassured, not alarmed, to learn there is occasional disagreement and debate among lawyers within the executive branch of government.

From 2001 to 2004, while I was in private practice in New York City, I also chaired the Judiciary Committee of the New York City Bar Association, which rates all the nominees and candidates for federal, state, and local judicial office in New York City. In June 2002, our bar committee was in the awkward position of rejecting the very first candidate the new mayor's judicial screening committee had put forth to the mayor for the Family Court in New York City. On very short notice, I was summoned to City Hall for a meeting with Mayor Michael Bloomberg and the chair of his judicial screening committee, who was called on to defend his committee's recommendation of the judge. The mayor wanted to know why our committees had come out differently. The meeting was extremely awkward, but I'll never forget what Mayor Bloomberg said to us: "If you guys always agree, somebody's not doing their job."

Knowing that we must subject our national security legal positions to other very smart lawyers who will scrutinize and challenge them has made us all work a lot harder to develop and refine those positions. On top of that, our clients are sophisticated consumers of legal advice. The president, the vice president, the national security adviser, the vice president's national security adviser, the secretary of state, the secretary of defense, the secretary of homeland security are themselves all lawyers. They are not engaged in the practice of law but, in the presentation to them of our legal advice, any weakness in the logic chain will be seized upon and questioned immediately, usually with a statement that begins with the ominous preface: "I know I'm not supposed to play lawyer here, but . . ."

By contrast, "group think" among lawyers is dangerous because it makes us lazy and complacent in our thinking and can lead to bad results. Likewise, shutting your eyes and ears to the legal dissent and concerns of others can also lead to disastrous consequences.

Before I was confirmed by the Senate for this job, Senator Carl Levin, the chairman of the Armed Services Committee, made sure that I read the committee's November 2008 report on the treatment and interrogation of detainees at Guantánamo.

The report chronicles the failure of my predecessor in the Bush administration to listen to the objections of the JAG leadership about enhanced interrogation techniques, the result of which was that the legal opinion of one lieutenant colonel, without more, carried the day as the legal endorsement for stress positions, removal of clothing, and use of phobias to interrogate detainees at Guantánamo Bay.

Just before becoming president, Barack Obama told his transition team that the rule of law should be one of the cornerstones of national security in his administration. In retrospect, I believe that President Obama made a conscious decision three years ago to bring in to his administration a group of strong lawyers who would reflect differing points of view. And, though it has made us all work a lot harder, I believe that over the last three years the president has benefited from healthy and robust debate among the lawyers on his national security team, which has resulted in carefully delineated, pragmatic, credible, and sustainable judgments on some very difficult legal issues in the counterterrorism realm—judgments that, for the most part, are being accepted within the mainstream legal community and the courts.

Tonight I want to summarize for you, in this one speech, some of the basic legal principles that form the basis for the US military's counterterrorism efforts against Al Qaeda and its associated forces. These are principles with which the top national security lawyers in our administration broadly agree. My comments are general in nature about the US military's legal authority, and I do not comment on any operation in particular.

First: in the conflict against an *unconventional* enemy such as Al Qaeda, we must consistently apply *conventional* legal principles. We must apply, and we have applied, the law of armed conflict, including applicable provisions of the Geneva Conventions and customary international law, core principles of distinction and proportionality, historic precedent, and traditional principles of statutory construction. Put another way, we must not make it up to suit the moment.

Against an unconventional enemy that observes no borders and does not play by the rules, we must guard against aggressive interpretations of our authorities that will discredit our efforts, provoke controversy, and invite challenge. As I told the Heritage Foundation last October, over-reaching with military power can result in national security setbacks, not gains. Particularly when we attempt to extend the reach of the military onto US soil, the courts resist, consistent with our core values and our American heritage—reflected, no less, in places such as the Declaration of Independence, the Federalist Papers, the Third Amendment, and in the 1878 federal criminal statute, still on the books today, which prohibits willfully using the military as a posse comitatus unless expressly authorized by Congress or the Constitution.

Second: in the conflict against Al Qaeda and associated forces, the bedrock of the military's domestic legal authority continues to be the Authorization for the Use of Military Force passed by the Congress one week after 9/11. The AUMF, as it is often called, is Congress's authorization to the president to ". . . use all necessary and appropriate force against those nations, organizations, or persons he determines planned, authorized, committed, or aided the terrorist attacks that occurred on September 11, 2001, or harbored such organizations or persons, in order to prevent any future acts of international terrorism against the United States by such nations, organizations, or persons."

Ten years later, the AUMF remains on the books, and it is still a viable authorization today. In the detention context, we in the Obama administration have interpreted this authority to include ". . . those persons who were part of, or substantially supported, Taliban or Al Qaeda forces or associated forces that are engaged in hostilities against the United States or its coalition partners."

This interpretation of our statutory authority has been adopted by the courts in the habeas cases brought by Guantánamo detainees, and in 2011 Congress joined the executive and judicial branches of government in embracing this interpretation when it codified it almost word-for-word in Section 1021 of this year's National Defense Authorization Act, ten years after enactment of the original AUMF. (A point worth noting here: contrary to some reports, neither Section 1021 nor any other detainee-related provision in this year's Defense Authorization Act creates or expands upon the authority for the military to detain a US citizen.)

But, the AUMF, the statutory authorization from 2001, is not open-ended. It does not authorize military force against anyone the executive labels a "terrorist." Rather, it encompasses only those groups or people with a link to the terrorist attacks on 9/11, or associated forces.

Nor is the concept of an "associated force" an open-ended one, as some suggest. This concept, too, has been upheld by the courts in the detention context, and it is based on the well-established concept of co-belligerency in the law of war. The concept has become more relevant over time, as Al Qaeda has, over the last ten years, become more decentralized, and relies more on associates to carry out its terrorist aims.

An "associated force," as we interpret the phrase, has two characteristics to it: (1) an organized, armed group that has entered the fight alongside Al Qaeda and (2) is a co-belligerent with Al Qaeda in hostilities against the United States or its coalition partners. In other words, the group must not only be aligned with Al Qaeda; it must have also entered the fight against the United States or its coalition partners. Thus, an "associated force" is not any terrorist group in the world that merely embraces the Al Qaeda ideology. More is required before we draw the legal conclusion that the group fits within the statutory authorization for the use of military force passed by the Congress in 2001.

Third: there is nothing in the wording of the 2001 AUMF or its legislative history that restricts this statutory authority to the "hot" battlefields of Afghanistan. Afghanistan was plainly the focus when the authorization was enacted in September 2001, but the AUMF authorized the use of necessary and appropriate force against the organizations and persons connected to the September 11 attacks—Al Qaeda and the Taliban—without a geographic limitation.

The legal point is important because, in fact, over the last ten years Al Qaeda has not only become more decentralized, it has also, for the most part, migrated away from Afghanistan to other places where it can find safe haven.

However, this legal conclusion too has its limits. It should not be interpreted to mean that we believe we are in any "global war on terror" or that we can use military force whenever we want, wherever we want. International legal principles, including respect for a state's sovereignty and the laws of war, impose important limits on our ability to act unilaterally and on the way in which we can use force in foreign territories.

Fourth: I want to spend a moment on what some people refer to as "targeted killing." Here I will largely repeat Harold's much-quoted address to the American Society of International Law in March 2010. In an armed conflict, lethal force against known, individual members of the enemy is a long-standing and long-legal practice. What is new is that, with advances in technology, we are able to target military objectives with much more precision, to the point where we can identify, target, and strike a single military objective from great distances.

Should the legal assessment of targeting a single identifiable military objective be any different in 2012 than it was in 1943, when the US Navy targeted and shot down over the Pacific the aircraft flying Admiral Yamamoto, the commander of the Japanese navy during World War II, with the specific intent of killing him? Should we take a dimmer view of the legality of lethal force directed against individual members of the enemy, because modern technology makes our weapons more precise? As Harold stated two years ago, the rules that govern targeting do not turn on the type of weapon system used, and there is no prohibition under the law of war on the use of technologically advanced weapons systems in armed conflict, so long as they are employed in conformity with the law of war. Advanced technology can ensure both that the best intelligence is available for planning operations and that civilian casualties are minimized in carrying out such operations.

On occasion, I read or hear a commentator loosely refer to lethal force against a valid military objective with the pejorative term "assassination." Like any American shaped by national events in 1963 and 1968, the term is to me one of the most repugnant in our vocabulary, and it should be rejected in this context. Under well-settled legal principles, lethal force against a valid *military* objective in an armed conflict is consistent with the law of war and does not, by definition, constitute an "assassination."

Fifth: as I stated at the public meeting of the ABA Standing Committee on Law and National Security, belligerents who also happen to be US citizens do not enjoy immunity where non-citizen belligerents are valid military objectives. Reiterating principles from *Ex parte Quirin* in 1942, the Supreme Court in 2004, in *Hamdi v. Rumsfeld*, stated that "[a] citizen, no less than an alien, can be 'part of or supporting forces hostile to the United States or coalition partners' and 'engaged in an armed conflict against the United States.'"

Sixth: contrary to the view of some, targeting decisions are not appropriate for submission to a court. In my view, they are core functions of the executive branch and often require real-time decisions based on an evolving intelligence picture that only the executive branch may timely possess. I agree with Judge [John D.] Bates of the federal district court in Washington, who ruled in 2010 that the judicial branch of government is simply not equipped to become involved in targeting decisions.

As I stated earlier in this address, within the executive branch the views and opinions of the lawyers on the president's national security team are debated and heavily scrutinized, and a legal review of the application of lethal force is the weightiest judgment a lawyer can make. (And, when these judgments start to become easy, it is time for me to return to private law practice.)

Finally: as a student of history I believe that those who govern today must ask ourselves how we will be judged ten, twenty, or fifty years from now. Our applications of law must stand the test of time because, over the passage of time, what we find tolerable today may be condemned in the permanent pages of history tomorrow.

Appendix: Johnson–C

Jeh C. Johnson, general counsel,
Department of Defense, "The Conflict against
Al Qaeda and Its Affiliates: How Will It End?"
Oxford Union, Oxford University, November 30, 2012

. . .

It is the US military's efforts against Al Qaeda and associated forces that has demanded most of my time, generated much public legal commentary, and presented for us what are perhaps the weightiest legal issues in national security. It is the topic I will spend the balance of my remarks on tonight.

The US government is in an armed conflict against Al Qaeda and associated forces, to which the laws of armed conflict apply. One week after 9/11, our Congress authorized our president "to use all necessary and appropriate force" against those nations, organizations, and individuals responsible for 9/11. President Obama, like President Bush before him, as commander-in-chief of our armed forces, has acted militarily based on that authorization. In 2006, our Supreme Court also endorsed the view that the United States is in an armed conflict with Al Qaeda. Therefore, all three branches of the United States government—including the two political branches elected by the people and the judicial branch appointed for life (and therefore not subject to the whims and political pressures of the voters)—have endorsed the view that our efforts against Al Qaeda may properly be viewed as an armed conflict.

But, for the United States, this is a new kind of war. It is an unconventional war against an unconventional enemy. And, given its unconventional nature, President Obama—himself a lawyer and a good one—has insisted that our efforts in pursuit of this enemy stay firmly rooted in *conventional* legal principles. For, in our efforts to destroy and dismantle Al Qaeda, we cannot dismantle our laws and our values, too.

The danger of Al Qaeda is well known. It is a terrorist organization determined to commit acts of violence against innocent civilians. The danger of *the conflict* against Al Qaeda is that it lacks conventional boundaries, against an enemy that does not observe the rules of armed conflict, does not wear a uniform, and can resemble a civilian.

But we refuse to allow this enemy, with its contemptible tactics, to define the way in which we wage war. Our efforts remain grounded in the rule of law. In this *unconventional* conflict, therefore, we apply *conventional* legal principles—conventional legal principles found in treaties and customary international law.

As in armed conflict, we have been clear in defining the enemy and defining our objective against that enemy.

We have made clear that we are not at war with an idea, a religion, or a tactic. We are at war with an organized, armed group—a group determined to kill innocent civilians.

We have publicly stated that our enemy consists of those persons who are part of the Taliban, Al Qaeda, or associated forces, a declaration that has been embraced by two US presidents, accepted by our courts, and affirmed by our Congress.

We have publicly defined an "associated force" as having two characteristics: (1) an organized, armed group that has entered the fight alongside Al Qaeda, and (2) is a co-belligerent with Al Qaeda in hostilities against the United States or its coalition partners.

Our enemy does not include anyone solely in the category of activist, journalist, or propagandist.

Nor does our enemy in this armed conflict include a "lone wolf" who, inspired by Al Qaeda's ideology, *self-radicalizes* in the basement of his own home, without ever actually becoming part of Al Qaeda. Such persons are dangerous, but are a matter for civilian law enforcement, not the military, because they are not part of the enemy force.

And we have publicly stated that our goal in this conflict is to "disrupt, dismantle, and ensure a lasting defeat of Al Qaeda and violent extremist affiliates."

Some legal scholars and commentators in our country brand the detention by the military of members of Al Qaeda as "indefinite detention without charges." Some refer to targeted lethal force against known, identified individual members of Al Qaeda as "extrajudicial killing."

Viewed within the context of law enforcement or criminal justice, where no person is sentenced to death or prison without an indictment, an arraignment, and a trial before an impartial judge or jury, these characterizations might be understandable.

Viewed within the context of conventional armed conflict—as they should be—capture, detention, and lethal force are traditional practices as old as armies. Capture and detention by the military are part and parcel of armed conflict. We employ weapons of war against Al Qaeda, but in a manner consistent with the law of war. We employ lethal force, but in a manner consistent with the law-of-war principles of proportionality, necessity, and distinction. We detain those who are part of Al Qaeda, but in a manner consistent with Common Article 3 of the Geneva Conventions and all other applicable law.

But, now that efforts by the US military against Al Qaeda are in their twelfth year, we must also ask ourselves: how will this conflict end? It is an unconventional conflict, against an unconventional enemy, and will not end in conventional terms.

Conventional conflicts in history tend to have had conventional endings.

Two hundred years ago, our two nations fought the War of 1812. The United States lost many battles, Washington, D.C., was captured, and the White House was set ablaze. By the winter of 1814 British and American forces had strengthened their forts and fleets and assumed that fighting would resume between them in the spring. But the war ended when British and American diplomats in Belgium came to a peace agreement on December 24, 1814. Diplomats from both sides then joined together in a Christmas celebration at Ghent Cathedral. Less than eight weeks later, the US Senate provided advice and consent to that peace treaty, which for the United States legally and formally terminated the conflict.

In the American Civil War, the Battle of Appomattox was the final engagement of Confederate General Robert E. Lee's great Army of Northern Virginia, and one of the last battles of that war. After four years of war, General Lee recognized that "[i]t would be useless and therefore cruel to provoke the further effusion of blood." Three days later the Army of Northern Virginia surrendered. Lee's army then marched to the field in front of Appomattox Court House and, division by division, deployed into line, stacked their arms, folded their colors, and walked home empty-handed.

The last day of the First World War was November 11, 1918, when an armistice was signed at 5:00 a.m. in a railroad carriage in France, and a cease-fire took effect on the eleventh hour of the eleventh day of the eleventh month of 1918.

The Second World War concluded in the Pacific theater in August 1945 with a ceremony that took place on the deck of the *USS Missouri*.

During the Gulf War of 1991, one week after Saddam Hussein's forces set fire to oil wells as they were driven out of Kuwait, US General [Norman] Schwarzkopf sat down with Iraqi military leaders under a tent in a stretch of the occupied Iraqi desert a few miles from the Kuwaiti border. General Schwarzkopf wanted to keep discussions simple; he told his advisers: "I just want to get my soldiers home as fast as possible . . . I want no ceremonies, no handshakes." In the space of two hours they had negotiated the terms of a permanent cease-fire to end the First Gulf War.

We cannot and should not expect Al Qaeda and its associated forces to all surrender, to all lay down their weapons in an open field, or to sign a peace treaty with us. They are terrorist organizations. Nor can we capture or kill every last terrorist who claims an affiliation with Al Qaeda.

I am aware of studies that suggest that many "terrorist" organizations eventually denounce terrorism and violence, and seek to address their grievances through some form of reconciliation or participation in a political process.

Al Qaeda is *not* in that category.

Al Qaeda's radical and absurd goals have included global domination through a violent Islamic caliphate, terrorizing the United States and other Western nations [into] retreating from the world stage, and the destruction of Israel. There is no compromise or political bargain that can be struck with those who pursue such aims.

In the current conflict with Al Qaeda, I can offer no prediction about *when* this conflict will end or whether we are, as Winston Churchill described it, near the "beginning of the end."

I do believe that on the present course, there will come a tipping point—a tipping point at which so many of the leaders and operatives of Al Qaeda and its affiliates have been killed or captured, and the group is no longer able to attempt or launch a strategic attack against the United States, such that Al Qaeda as we know it, the organization that our Congress authorized the military to pursue in 2001, has been effectively destroyed.

At that point, we must be able to say to ourselves that our efforts should no longer be considered an "armed conflict" against Al Qaeda and its associated forces. Rather, [we have] a counterterrorism effort against *individuals* who are the scattered remnants of Al Qaeda, or are parts of groups unaffiliated with Al Qaeda, for which the law enforcement and intelligence resources of our government are principally responsible, in cooperation with the international community—with our military assets available in reserve to address continuing and imminent terrorist threats.

At that point we will also need to face the question of what to do with any members of Al Qaeda who still remain in US military detention without a criminal conviction and sentence. In general, the military's authority to detain ends with the "cessation of active hostilities." For this particular conflict, all I can say today is that we should look to conventional legal principles to supply the answer and that both our nations faced similar challenging questions after the cessation of hostilities in World War II and our governments delayed the release of some Nazi German prisoners of war.

For now, we must continue our efforts to disrupt, dismantle, and ensure a lasting defeat of Al Qaeda. Though severely degraded, Al Qaeda remains a threat to the citizens of the United States, the United Kingdom, and other nations. We must disrupt Al Qaeda's terrorist attack planning before it gets anywhere near our homeland or our citizens. We must counter Al Qaeda in the places where it seeks to establish safe haven and prevent it from reconstituting in others. To do this we must utilize every national security element of our government and work closely with our friends and allies like the United Kingdom and others.

Finally, it was a war-fighting four-star general who reminded me, as I previewed these remarks for him, that none of this will ever be possible if we fail to understand and address what attracts a young man to an organization like Al Qaeda in the first place. Al Qaeda claims to represent the interests of all Muslims. By word and deed, we must stand with the millions of people within the Muslim world who reject Al Qaeda as a marginalized, extreme, and violent organization that does *not* represent the Muslim values of peace and brotherhood. For, if Al Qaeda can recruit new terrorists to its cause faster than we can kill or capture them, we fight an endless, hopeless battle that only perpetuates a downward spiral of hate, recrimination, violence, and fear.

"War" must be regarded as a finite, extraordinary, and unnatural state of affairs. War permits one man—if he is a "privileged belligerent," consistent with the laws of war—to kill another. War violates the natural order of things, in which children bury their parents; in war, parents bury their children. In its twelfth year, we must not accept the current conflict, and all that it entails, as the "new normal." Peace must be regarded as the norm toward which the human race continually strives.

Right here at Oxford you have the excellent work of the Changing Character of War program: leading scholars committed to the study of war, who have observed that analyzing war in terms of a continuum of armed conflict—where military force is used at various points without a distinct break between war and peace—is counterproductive. Such an approach, they argue, results in an erosion of "any demarcation between war and peace," the very effect of which is to create uncertainty about how to define war itself.

I did not go to Oxford. I am a graduate of a small, all-male historically black college in the southern part of the United States, Morehouse College. The guiding light for every Morehouse man is our most famous alumnus, Martin Luther King, who preached the inherent insanity of all wars. I am therefore a student and disciple of Dr. King—though I became an imperfect one the first time I gave legal approval for the use of military force. I accepted this conundrum when I took this job. But I still carry with me the words from Dr. King: "Returning hate for hate multiplies hate, adding deeper darkness to a night already devoid of stars . . . violence multiplies violence, and toughness multiplies toughness in a descending spiral of destruction . . . The chain reaction of evil—hate begetting hate, wars producing more wars—must be broken, or we shall be plunged into the dark abyss of annihilation."

. . .

Appendix: Holder–A

Eric Holder, Attorney General, Department of Justice, Address at Northwestern University School of Law, March 5, 2012

. . .

Since this country's earliest days, the American people have risen to this challenge—and all that it demands. But, as we have seen—and as President John F. Kennedy may have described best—"In the long history of the world, only a few generations have been granted the role of defending freedom in its hour of maximum danger."

Half a century has passed since those words were spoken, but our nation today confronts grave national security threats that demand our constant attention and steadfast commitment. It is clear that, once again, we have reached an "hour of danger."

We are a nation at war. And, in this war, we face a nimble and determined enemy that cannot be underestimated.

Like President Obama—and my fellow members of his national security team—I begin each day with a briefing on the latest and most urgent threats made against us in the preceding twenty-four hours. And, like scores of attorneys and agents at the Justice Department, I go to sleep each night thinking of how best to keep our people safe.

I know that—more than a decade after the September 11 attacks and despite our recent national security successes, including the operation that brought to justice Osama bin Laden last year—there are people currently plotting to murder Americans, who reside in distant countries as well as within our own borders. Disrupting and preventing these plots—and using every available and appropriate tool to keep the American people safe—has been, and will remain, this administration's top priority.

But just as surely as we are a nation at war, we also are a nation of laws and values. Even when under attack, our actions must always be grounded on the bedrock of the Constitution—and must always be consistent with statutes, court precedent, the rule of law, and our founding ideals. Not only is this the right thing to do—history has shown that it is also the most effective approach we can take in combating those who seek to do us harm.

This is not just my view. My judgment is shared by senior national security officials across the government. As the president reminded us in 2009 at the National Archives where our founding documents are housed, "We uphold our most cherished values not only because doing so is right, but because it strengthens our country and it keeps us safe. Time and again, our values have been our best national security asset . . ." Our history proves this. We do not have to choose between security and liberty—and we will not.

Today, I want to tell you about the collaboration across the government that defines and distinguishes this administration's national security efforts. I also want to discuss some of the legal principles that guide—and strengthen—this work as well as the special role of the Department of Justice in protecting the American people and upholding the Constitution.

Before 9/11, today's level of interagency cooperation was not commonplace. In many ways, government lacked the infrastructure—as well as the imperative—to share national security information quickly and effectively. Domestic law enforcement and foreign intelligence operated in largely independent spheres. But those who attacked us on September 11 chose both military and civilian targets. They crossed borders and jurisdictional lines. And it immediately became clear that no single agency could address these threats because no single agency has all of the necessary tools.

To counter this enemy aggressively and intelligently, the government had to draw on all of its resources and radically update its operations. As a result, today, government agencies are better postured to work together to address a range of emerging national security threats. Now, the lawyers, agents, and analysts at the Department of Justice work closely with our colleagues across the national security community to detect and disrupt terrorist plots, to prosecute suspected terrorists, and to identify and implement the legal tools necessary to keep the American people safe. Unfortunately, the fact and extent of this cooperation are often overlooked in the public debate—but it's something that this administration, and the previous one, can be proud of.

As part of this coordinated effort, the Justice Department plays a key role in conducting oversight to ensure that the intelligence community's activities remain in compliance with the law and with the Foreign Intelligence Surveillance Court, in authorizing surveillance to investigate suspected terrorists. We must—and will continue to—use the intelligence-gathering capabilities that Congress has provided to collect information that can save and protect American lives. At the same time, these tools must be subject to appropriate checks and balances—including oversight by Congress and the courts, as well as within the Executive Branch—to protect the privacy and civil rights of innocent individuals. This administration is committed to making sure that our surveillance programs appropriately reflect all of these interests.

Let me give you an example. Under section 702 of the Foreign Intelligence Surveillance Act, the attorney general and the director of national intelligence may authorize annually, with the approval of the Foreign Intelligence Surveillance Court, collection directed at identified categories of foreign intelligence targets, without the need for a court order for each individual subject. This ensures that the government has the flexibility and agility it needs to identify and to respond to terrorist and other foreign threats to our security. But the government may not use this authority intentionally to target a US person, here or abroad, or anyone known to be in the United States.

The law requires special procedures, reviewed and approved by the Foreign Intelligence Surveillance Court, to make sure that these restrictions are followed and to protect the privacy of any US persons whose non-public information may be incidentally acquired through this program. The Department of Justice and the Office of the Director of National Intelligence conduct extensive oversight reviews of section 702 activities at least once every sixty days, and we report to Congress on implementation and compliance twice a year. This law therefore establishes a comprehensive regime of oversight by all three branches of government. Reauthorizing this authority before it expires at the end of this year is the top legislative priority of the intelligence community.

But surveillance is only the first of many complex issues we must navigate. Once a suspected terrorist is captured, a decision must be made as to how to proceed with that individual in order to identify the disposition that best serves the interests of the American people and the security of this nation.

Much has been made of the distinction between our federal civilian courts and revised military commissions. The reality is that both incorporate fundamental due process and other protections that are essential to the effective administration of justice—and we should not deprive ourselves of any tool in our fight against Al Qaeda.

Our criminal justice system is renowned not only for its fair process; it is respected for its results. We are not the first administration to rely on federal courts to prosecute terrorists, nor will we be the last. Although far too many choose to ignore this fact, the previous administration consistently relied on criminal prosecutions in federal court to bring terrorists to justice. John Walker Lindh, attempted shoe bomber Richard Reid, and 9/11 conspirator Zacarias

Moussaoui were among the hundreds of defendants convicted of terrorism-related offenses—without political controversy—during the last administration.

Over the past three years, we've built a remarkable record of success in terror prosecutions. For example, in October we secured a conviction against Umar Farouk Abdulmutallab for his role in the attempted bombing of an airplane traveling from Amsterdam to Detroit on Christmas Day 2009. He was sentenced last month to life in prison without the possibility of parole. While in custody, he provided significant intelligence during debriefing sessions with the FBI. He described in detail how he became inspired to carry out an act of jihad and how he traveled to Yemen and made contact with Anwar al-Awlaki, a US citizen and a leader of Al Qaeda in the Arabian Peninsula. Abdulmutallab also detailed the training he received as well as Awlaki's specific instructions to wait until the airplane was over the United States before detonating his bomb.

In addition to Abdulmutallab, Faizal Shahzad, the attempted Times Square bomber; Ahmed Ghailani, a conspirator in the 1998 US embassy bombings in Kenya and Tanzania; and three individuals who plotted an attack against John F. Kennedy Airport in 2007 have also recently begun serving life sentences. And convictions have been obtained in the cases of several homegrown extremists, as well. For example, last year, United States citizen and North Carolina resident Daniel Boyd pleaded guilty to conspiracy to provide material support to terrorists and conspiracy to murder, kidnap, maim, and injure persons abroad; and US citizen and Illinois resident Michael Finton pleaded guilty to attempted use of a weapon of mass destruction in connection with his efforts to detonate a truck bomb outside of a federal courthouse.

I could go on—which is why the calls that I've heard to ban the use of civilian courts in prosecutions of terrorism-related activity are so baffling and, ultimately, are so dangerous. These calls ignore reality. And if heeded, they would significantly weaken—in fact, they would cripple—our ability to incapacitate and punish those who attempt to do us harm.

Simply put, since 9/11, hundreds of individuals have been convicted of terrorism or terrorism-related offenses in Article III courts and are now serving long sentences in federal prison. Not one has ever escaped custody. No judicial district has suffered any kind of retaliatory attack. These are facts, not opinions. There are not two sides to this story. Those who claim that our federal courts are incapable of handling terrorism cases are not registering a dissenting opinion—they are simply wrong.

But federal courts are not our only option. Military commissions are also appropriate in proper circumstances, and we can use them as well to convict terrorists and disrupt their plots. This administration's approach has been to ensure that the military commissions system is as effective as possible, in part by strengthening the procedural protections on which the commissions are based. With the president's leadership and the bipartisan backing of Congress, the Military Commissions Act of 2009 was enacted into law. And, since then, meaningful improvements have been implemented.

It's important to note that the reformed commissions draw from the same fundamental protections of a fair trial that underlie our civilian courts. They provide a presumption of innocence and require proof of guilt beyond a reasonable doubt. They afford the accused the right to counsel as well as the right to present evidence and cross-examine witnesses. They prohibit the use of statements obtained through torture or cruel, inhuman, or degrading treatment. And they secure the right to appeal to Article III judges—all the way to the United States Supreme Court. In addition, like our federal civilian courts, reformed commissions allow for the protection of sensitive sources and methods of intelligence gathering and for the safety and security of participants.

A key difference is that, in military commissions, evidentiary rules reflect the realities of the battlefield and of conducting investigations in a war zone. For example, statements may be admissible even in the absence of *Miranda* warnings, because we cannot expect military personnel to administer warnings to an enemy captured in battle. But instead, a military judge must make other findings—for instance, that the statement is reliable and that it was made voluntarily.

I have faith in the framework and promise of our military commissions, which is why I've sent several cases to the reformed commissions for prosecution. There is, quite simply, no inherent contradiction between using military commissions in appropriate cases while still prosecuting other terrorists in civilian courts. Without question, there are differences between these systems that must be—and will continue to be—weighed carefully. Such decisions about how to prosecute suspected terrorists are core executive branch functions. In each case, prosecutors and counterterrorism professionals across the government conduct an intensive review of case-specific facts designed to determine which avenue of prosecution to pursue.

Several practical considerations affect the choice of forum.

First of all, the commissions only have jurisdiction to prosecute individuals who are a part of Al Qaeda, [who] have engaged in hostilities against the United States or its coalition partners, or have purposefully and materially supported such hostilities. This means that there may be members of certain terrorist groups who fall outside the jurisdiction of military commissions because, for example, they lack ties to Al Qaeda and their conduct does not otherwise make them subject to prosecution in this forum. Additionally, by statute, military commissions cannot be used to try US citizens.

Second, our civilian courts cover a much broader set of offenses than the military commissions, which can only prosecute specified offenses, including violations of the laws of war and other offenses traditionally triable by military commission. This means federal prosecutors have a wider range of tools that can be used to incapacitate suspected terrorists. Those charges, and the sentences they carry upon successful conviction, can provide important incentives to reach plea agreements and convince defendants to cooperate with federal authorities.

Third, there is the issue of international cooperation. A number of countries have indicated that they will not cooperate with the United States in certain counterterrorism efforts—for instance, in providing evidence or extraditing suspects—if we intend to use that cooperation in pursuit of a military commission prosecution. Although the use of military commissions in the United States can be traced back to the early days of our nation, in their present form they are less familiar to the international community than our time-tested criminal justice system and Article III courts. However, it is my hope that, with time and experience, the reformed commissions will attain similar respect in the eyes of the world.

Where cases are selected for prosecution in military commissions, Justice Department investigators and prosecutors work closely to support our Department of Defense colleagues. Today, the alleged mastermind of the bombing of the *USS Cole* is being prosecuted before a military commission. I am proud to say that trial attorneys from the Department of Justice are working with military prosecutors on that case as well as others.

And we will continue to reject the false idea that we must choose between federal courts and military commissions, instead of using them both. If we were to fail to use all necessary and available tools at our disposal, we would undoubtedly fail in our fundamental duty to protect the nation and its people. That is simply not an outcome we can accept.

This administration has worked in other areas as well to ensure that counterterrorism professionals have the flexibility that they need to fulfill their critical responsibilities without diverging from our laws and our values. Last week brought the most recent step, when the president issued procedures under the National Defense Authorization Act. This legislation, which Congress passed in December, mandated that a narrow category of Al Qaeda terrorist suspects be placed in temporary military custody.

Last Tuesday, the president exercised his authority under the statute to issue procedures to make sure that military custody will not disrupt ongoing law enforcement and intelligence operations—and that an individual will be transferred from civilian to military custody only after a thorough evaluation of his or her case, based on the considered judgment of the president's senior national security team. As authorized by the statute, the president waived the requirements for several categories of individuals where he found that the waivers were in our national security interest. These procedures implement not only the language of the statute but also the expressed intent of the lead sponsors of this legislation. And they address the concerns the president expressed when he signed this bill into law at the end of last year.

Now, I realize I have gone into considerable detail about tools we use to identify suspected terrorists and to bring captured terrorists to justice. It is preferable to capture suspected terrorists where feasible—among other reasons, so that we can gather valuable intelligence from them. But we must also recognize that there are instances where our government has the clear authority—and, I would argue, the responsibility—to defend the United States through the appropriate and lawful use of lethal force.

This principle has long been established under both US and international law. In response to the attacks perpetrated—and the continuing threat posed—by Al Qaeda, the Taliban, and associated forces, Congress has authorized the president to use all necessary and appropriate force against those groups. Because the United States is in an armed conflict, we are authorized to take action against enemy belligerents under international law. The Constitution empowers the president to protect the nation from any imminent threat of violent attack. And international law recognizes the inherent right of national self-defense. None of this is changed by the fact that we are not in a conventional war.

Our legal authority is not limited to the battlefields in Afghanistan. Indeed, neither Congress nor our federal courts have limited the geographic scope of our ability to use force to the current conflict in Afghanistan. We are at war with a stateless enemy, prone to shifting operations from country to country. Over the last three years alone, Al Qaeda and its associates have directed several attacks—fortunately, unsuccessful—against us from countries other than Afghanistan. Our government has both a responsibility and a right to protect this nation and its people from such threats.

This does not mean that we can use military force whenever or wherever we want. International legal principles, including respect for another nation's sovereignty, constrain our ability to act unilaterally. But the use of force in foreign territory would be consistent with these international legal principles if conducted, for example, with the consent of the nation involved—or after a determination that the nation is unable or unwilling to deal effectively with a threat to the United States.

Furthermore, it is entirely lawful—under both United States law and applicable law-of-war principles—to target specific senior operational leaders of Al Qaeda and associated forces. This is not a novel concept. In fact, during World War II, the United States tracked the plane flying Admiral Isoroku Yamamoto—the commander of Japanese forces in the attack on Pearl Harbor and the Battle of Midway—and shot it down specifically because he was on board. As I explained to the Senate Judiciary Committee following the operation that killed Osama bin Laden, the same rules apply today.

Some have called such operations "assassinations." They are not, and the use of that loaded term is misplaced. Assassinations are unlawful killings. Here, for the reasons I have given, the US government's use of lethal force in self-defense against a leader of Al Qaeda or an associated force who presents an imminent threat of violent attack would not be unlawful—and therefore would not violate the executive order banning assassination or criminal statutes.

Now, it is an unfortunate but undeniable fact that some of the threats we face come from a small number of US citizens who have decided to commit violent attacks against their own country from abroad. Based on generations-old legal principles and Supreme Court decisions handed down during World War II, as well as during this current conflict, it's clear that US citizenship alone does not make such individuals immune from being targeted. But it does mean that the government must take into account all relevant constitutional considerations with respect to US citizens—even those who are leading efforts to kill innocent Americans. Of these, the most relevant is the Fifth Amendment's due process clause, which says that the government may not deprive a citizen of his or her life without due process of law.

The Supreme Court has made clear that the due process clause does not impose one-size-fits-all requirements, but instead mandates procedural safeguards that depend on specific circumstances. In cases arising under the due process clause—including in a case involving a US citizen captured in the conflict against Al Qaeda—the court has applied a balancing approach, weighing the private interest that will be affected against the interest the government is trying to protect and the burdens the government would face in providing additional process. Where national security operations are at stake, due process takes into account the realities of combat.

Here, the interests on both sides of the scale are extraordinarily weighty. An individual's interest in making sure that the government does not target him erroneously could not be more significant. Yet it is imperative for the government to counter threats posed by senior operational leaders of Al Qaeda and to protect the innocent people whose lives could be lost in their attacks.

Any decision to use lethal force against a US citizen—even one intent on murdering Americans and who has become an operational leader of Al Qaeda in a foreign land—is among the gravest that government leaders can face. The American people can be—and deserve to be—assured that actions taken in their defense are consistent with their values and their laws. So, although I cannot discuss or confirm any particular program or operation, I believe it is important to explain these legal principles publicly.

Let me be clear. An operation using lethal force in a foreign country, targeted against a US citizen who is a senior operational leader of Al Qaeda or associated forces, and who is actively engaged in planning to kill Americans, would be lawful at least in the following circumstances: First, the US government has determined, after a thorough and careful review, that the individual poses an imminent threat of violent attack against the United States; second, capture is not feasible; and third, the operation would be conducted in a manner consistent with applicable law-of-war principles.

The evaluation of whether an individual presents an "imminent threat" incorporates considerations of the relevant window of opportunity to act, the possible harm that missing the window would cause to civilians, and the likelihood of heading off future disastrous attacks against the United States. As we learned on 9/11, Al Qaeda has demonstrated the ability to strike with little or no notice and to cause devastating casualties. Its leaders are continually planning attacks against the United States, and they do not behave like a traditional military—wearing uniforms, carrying arms openly, or massing forces in preparation for an attack. Given these facts, the Constitution does not require the president to delay action until some theoretical end-stage of planning when the precise time, place, and manner of an attack become clear. Such a requirement would create an unacceptably high risk that our efforts would fail and that Americans would be killed.

Whether the capture of a US citizen-terrorist is feasible is a fact-specific and, potentially, time-sensitive question. It may depend on, among other things, whether capture can be accomplished in the window of time available to prevent an attack and without undue risk to civilians or to US personnel. Given the nature of how terrorists act and where they tend to hide, it may not always be feasible to capture a United States citizen-terrorist who presents an imminent threat of violent attack. In that case, our government has the clear authority to defend the United States with lethal force.

Of course, any such use of lethal force by the United States will comply with the four fundamental laws-of-war principles governing the use of force. The principle of necessity requires that the target have definite military value. The principle of distinction requires that only lawful targets—such as combatants, civilians directly participating in hostilities, and military objectives—may be targeted intentionally. Under the principle of proportionality, the anticipated collateral damage must not be excessive in relation to the anticipated military advantage. Finally, the principle of humanity requires us to use weapons that will not inflict unnecessary suffering.

These principles do not forbid the use of stealth or technologically advanced weapons. In fact, the use of advanced weapons may help to ensure that the best intelligence is available for planning and carrying out operations and that the risk of civilian casualties can be minimized or avoided altogether.

Some have argued that the president is required to get permission from a federal court before taking action against a US citizen who is a senior operational leader of Al Qaeda or associated forces. This is simply not accurate. "Due process" and "judicial process" are not one and the same, particularly when it comes to national security. The Constitution guarantees due process, not judicial process.

The conduct and management of national security operations are core functions of the executive branch, as courts have recognized throughout our history. Military and civilian officials must often make real-time decisions that balance the need to act, the existence of alternative options, the possibility of collateral damage, and other judgments—all of which depend on expertise and immediate access to information that only the executive branch may possess in real time. The Constitution's guarantee of due process is ironclad, and it is essential. But, as a recent court decision makes clear, it does not require judicial approval before the president may use force abroad against a senior operational leader of a foreign terrorist organization with which the United States is at war—even if that individual happens to be a US citizen.

That is not to say that the executive branch has—or should ever have—the ability to target any such individuals without robust oversight. Which is why, in keeping with the law and our constitutional system of checks and balances, the executive branch regularly informs the appropriate members of Congress about our counterterrorism activities, including the legal framework, and would of course follow the same practice where lethal force is used against US citizens.

Now, these circumstances are sufficient under the Constitution for the United States to use lethal force against a US citizen abroad. But it is important to note that the legal requirements I have described may not apply in every situation—such as operations that take place on traditional battlefields.

The unfortunate reality is that our nation will likely continue to face terrorist threats that—at times—originate with our own citizens. When such individuals take up arms against this country and join Al Qaeda in plotting attacks designed to kill their fellow Americans, there may be only one realistic and appropriate response. We must take steps to stop them—in full accordance with the Constitution. In this hour of danger, we simply cannot afford to wait until deadly plans are carried out—and we will not.

This is an indicator of our times—not a departure from our laws and our values. For this administration—and for this nation—our values are clear. We must always look to them for answers when we face difficult questions, like the ones I have discussed today. As the president reminded us at the National Archives, "our Constitution has endured through secession and civil rights, through world war and cold war, because it provides a foundation of principles that can be applied pragmatically; it provides a compass that can help us find our way."

Our most sacred principles and values—of security, justice, and liberty for all citizens—must continue to unite us, to guide us forward, and to help us build a future that honors our founding documents and advances our ongoing—uniquely American—pursuit of a safer, more just, and more perfect union. In the continuing effort to keep our people secure, this administration will remain true to those values that inspired our nation's founding and, over the course of two centuries, have made America an example of strength and a beacon of justice for all the world. This is our pledge.

. . .

Appendix: Preston–A

*Stephen W. Preston, general counsel,
Central Intelligence Agency, "CIA and the Rule of Law,"
address at Harvard Law School, April 10, 2012*

For those working at the confluence of law and national security, the president has made clear that ours is a nation of laws and that an abiding respect for the rule of law is one of our country's greatest strengths, even against an enemy with only contempt for the law. This is so for the Central Intelligence Agency no less than any other instrument of national power engaged in the fight against Al Qaeda and its militant allies or otherwise seeking to protect the United States from foreign adversaries. And that is the central point of my remarks this afternoon: just as ours is a nation of laws, the CIA is an institution of laws and the rule of law is integral to agency operations.

Before we get to the rule of law, I want to spend a moment on the business of the CIA.

I will start off with two observations that I think are telling.

First, the number of significant national security issues facing our country may be as great today as it has ever been. Just think of what the president and his national security team confront every day: the ongoing threat of terrorist attack against the homeland and US interests abroad; war in Afghanistan and, until recently, Iraq; complex relations with countries like Pakistan and India; the challenges presented by Iran and North Korea; the emergence of China and its growing economic and military power; the growing number of computer network attacks originating outside the United States; profound change in the most volatile area of the world, the greater Middle East, with new regimes in Tunisia, Egypt, and Libya, and continuing violence in Syria; the financial challenges faced by countries in the euro zone; and the violence associated with drug trafficking in this hemisphere. And the list could go on.

Second, the national security issues facing our country today tend to be intelligence-intensive. Intelligence is fundamental to the efforts of policymakers to come to grips with nearly all of the issues I have just listed—whether international terrorism, the proliferation of weapons of mass destruction, the conduct of non-state actors and rogue states outside the community of nations, cyber-security, or the rise of new powers. The nation's leaders cannot fully understand these issues or make informed policy on these issues without first-rate intelligence.

Putting these two dynamics together—the multitude of different national security issues and the fact that intelligence is critical to almost all of them—it may be that intelligence has never been more important than it is today. At the very least, the intel business is booming.

So what does the CIA do? Our work boils down to three jobs. To quote from the National Security Act of 1947:

- Agency operators "collect intelligence through human sources and by other appropriate means." This is also referred to as foreign intelligence collection or, at times, espionage.
- Agency analysts "correlate and evaluate intelligence related to the national security and provide appropriate dissemination of such intelligence." This is also referred to as all-source analysis and national intelligence reporting, and it requires that the products of all intelligence disciplines be integrated.
- And the agency performs such other functions and duties as the president may direct, which may include activities to influence conditions abroad, "where it is intended that the role of

the US government will not be apparent or acknowledged publicly." In other words, covert action.

If that is, in essence, the business of the CIA, what about the rule of law? And, in particular, why do I say that the rule of law is integral to agency operations? The answer is that all intelligence activities of the agency must be properly authorized pursuant to, and must be conducted in accordance with, the full body of national security law that has been put in place over the six-plus decades since the creation of the CIA. And all such activities are subject to strict internal and external scrutiny. This breaks down into three propositions.

First, all intelligence activities of the agency must be properly authorized pursuant to the law. In this respect, the constraints on the agency exceed those on virtually any organization in the private sector. A business enterprise is free to do whatever it wants in pursuit of profit, shareholder value, or what have you, provided it does not violate the proscriptions of positive law. By contrast, the CIA cannot do anything without an affirmative grant of legal authority to engage in that activity. In some cases, such as foreign intelligence collection, the grant may be broad; in others, such as covert action, the grant of authority might be quite narrow and specific, and subject to numerous conditions. In any event, before any step is taken, the threshold question asked when considering a contemplated activity is, do we have the legal authority to act?

Second, all intelligence activities of the agency must be conducted in accordance with the law. Assuming there is legal authority to act in the first place, all steps taken must comply with applicable prohibitions and limitations embodied in the United States Constitution, federal statutes, executive orders and other presidential directives, and agency regulations. To single out some of them:

- The First, Fourth, and Fifth amendments to the Constitution, which protect the rights of American citizens and certain others.

- The National Security Act of 1947 and the Central Intelligence Agency Act of 1949, which establish the CIA, define its missions, and delineate its role within the intelligence community—including the so-called law enforcement proviso, which bars the agency from exercising law enforcement powers or performing internal security functions.
- Executive Order 12333, attorney general–approved guidelines, and internal agency regulations, which contain a host of restrictions on intelligence activities in general and those of the CIA in particular, including the assassination ban in Executive Order 12333. These directives include numerous provisions intended to protect privacy and civil liberties, including a prohibition against collection in the United States for the purpose of acquiring information on the domestic activities of US persons; limitations on acquisition, retention, and use of information about US persons; conditions on arrangements with US institutions of higher learning; and conditions on unwitting use of US persons in intelligence activities and undisclosed participation in organizations in the United States.
- And, finally, the Foreign Intelligence Surveillance Act and the FISA Amendments Act, which govern certain activities in the nature of electronic surveillance and physical searches.

Beyond all these, international law principles may be applicable, as well, and I will come back to this later.

Third, all intelligence activities of the agency are subject to strict internal and external scrutiny.

It is true that a lot of what the CIA does is shielded from public view, and for good reason: much of what the CIA does is a secret! Secrecy is absolutely essential to a functioning intelligence service, and a functioning intelligence service is absolutely essential to national security, today no less than in the past. This is not lost on the federal judiciary. The courts have long recognized the state secrets privilege and have consistently upheld its proper invocation to protect intelligence sources and methods from disclosure. Moreover, federal judges have dismissed cases on justiciability or political question grounds, acknowledging that the courts are, at times, institutionally ill-equipped and constitutionally incapable of reviewing national security decisions committed to the president and the political branches.

While public and judicial scrutiny may be limited in some respects, it simply does not follow that agency activities are immune from meaningful oversight. First, there is direct supervision by the National Security Council and the president, who, after all, not only is constitutionally responsible for keeping the American people safe but also "shall take Care that the Laws be faithfully executed." Beyond that, consider this catalog of agency overseers:

- The intelligence oversight committees of the Senate and House of Representatives. We are bound by statute to ensure that these two committees are kept "fully and currently informed" with respect to the entire range of intelligence activities, including covert action. They are afforded visibility into agency operations that far exceeds the usual scope of congressional oversight of federal agencies. Think about this: during the last Congress, the agency made, on average, more than two written submissions and two live appearances per day, 365 days a year.
- The Foreign Intelligence Surveillance Court, comprised of Article III judges, provides judicial supervision with respect to certain activities in the nature of electronic surveillance and physical searches.
- The President's Intelligence Advisory Board, an independent component of the Executive Office of the President, reviews and assesses the performance of the CIA and other elements of the intelligence community.

- The Intelligence Oversight Board is a committee of the President's Intelligence Advisory Board to which the CIA reports apparent legal violations and other significant or highly sensitive matters that could impugn the integrity of the intelligence community.
- The Office of the Director of National Intelligence and, new within the past year, the inspector general for the intelligence community.
- And the agency's own statutorily independent inspector general—the only other agency official, after the director and the general counsel, nominated by the president and confirmed by the Senate.
- Last, but by no means least, there is the US Department of Justice, to which the CIA is required to report all possible violations of federal criminal laws by employees, agents, liaison, or anyone else.

OK, I have described the legal regime in which CIA operates. Now I would like to illustrate how the law is applied in practice, by reference to a hypothetical case.

Suppose that the CIA is directed to engage in activities to influence conditions abroad, in which the hand of the US government is to remain hidden—in other words, covert action—and suppose that those activities may include the use of force, including lethal force. How would such a program be structured so as to ensure that it is entirely lawful? Approaches will, of course, vary depending on the circumstances—there is no single, cookie-cutter approach—but I conceive of the task in terms of a very simple matrix. First is the issue of whether there is legal authority to act in the first place. Second, there is the issue of compliance with the law in carrying out the action. For each of these issues, we would look first and foremost to US law. But we would also look to international law principles. So envision a four-box matrix with "US law" and "international law" across the top and "authority to act" and "compliance in execution" down the side. With a thorough legal review directed at each of the four boxes, we would make certain that all potentially relevant law is properly considered in a systematic and comprehensive fashion.

Now, when I say "we," I don't mean to suggest that these judgments are confined to the agency. To the contrary, as the authority for covert action is ultimately the president's, and covert action programs are carried out by the director and the agency at and subject to the president's direction, agency counsel share their responsibilities with respect to any covert action with their counterparts at the National Security Council. When warranted by circumstances, we— CIA and NSC—may refer a legal issue to the Department of Justice. Or we may solicit input from our colleagues at the Office of the Director of National Intelligence, the Department of State, or the Department of Defense, as appropriate.

Getting back to my simple matrix . . .

(1) Let's start with the first box: authority to act under US law.

First, we would confirm that the contemplated activity is authorized by the president in the exercise of his powers under Article II of the US Constitution, for example, the president's responsibility as chief executive and commander-in-chief to protect the country from an imminent threat of violent attack. This would not be just a one-time check for legal authority at the outset. Our hypothetical program would be engineered so as to ensure that, through careful review and senior-level decision-making, each individual action is linked to the imminent threat justification.

A specific congressional authorization might also provide an independent basis for the use of force under US law.

In addition, we would make sure that the contemplated activity is authorized by the president in accordance with the covert action procedures of the National Security Act of 1947, such that Congress is properly notified by means of a presidential finding.

(2) Next we look at authority to act with reference to international law principles.

Here we need look no further than the inherent right of national self-defense, which is recognized by customary international law and, specifically, in Article 51 of the United Nations Charter. Where, for example, the United States has already been attacked, and its adversary has repeatedly sought to attack since then and is actively plotting to attack again, then the United States is entitled as a matter of national self-defense to use force to disrupt and prevent future attacks.

The existence of an armed conflict might also provide an additional justification for the use of force under international law.

(3) Let's move on to compliance in execution under US law.

First, we would make sure all actions taken comply with the terms dictated by the president in the applicable finding, which would likely contain specific limitations and conditions governing the use of force. We would also make sure all actions taken comply with any applicable executive order provisions, such as the prohibition against assassination in 12333. Beyond presidential directives, the National Security Act of 1947 provides, quote, "[a] Finding may not authorize any action that would violate the Constitution or any statute of the United States." This crucial provision would be strictly applied in carrying out our hypothetical program.

In addition, the agency would have to discharge its obligation under the congressional notification provisions of the National Security Act to keep the intelligence oversight committees of Congress "fully and currently informed" of its activities. Picture a system of notifications and briefings—some verbal, others written; some periodic, others event-specific; some at a staff level, others for members.

(4) That leaves compliance in execution with reference to international law principles.

Here, the agency would implement its authorities in a manner consistent with the four basic principles in the law of armed conflict governing the use of force: necessity, distinction, proportionality, and humanity. Great care would be taken in the planning and execution of actions to satisfy these four principles and, in the process, to minimize civilian casualties.

So there you have it: four boxes, each carefully considered with reference to the contemplated activity. That is how an agency program involving the use of lethal force would be structured so as to ensure that it satisfies applicable US and international law.

Switching gears, let us consider a real world case in point: the operation against Osama bin Laden in Abbottabad, Pakistan, on May 2 [local time]. My purpose is not to illustrate our hypothetical program, but to show that the rule of law reaches the most sensitive activities in which the agency is engaged.

The bin Laden operation was, of course, a critically important event in the fight against Al Qaeda. Much has been said and written about the operation in this regard, and I won't dwell on it now. Rather, I want to focus on the legal aspect of the operation. But if you will indulge me, there are a few other aspects of this historic event that warrant mention up front.

First, finding bin Laden was truly a triumph of intelligence. It's a long story—too long to tell here—but it begins nine years earlier, with the nom de guerre of an Al Qaeda courier. Through painstaking collection and analysis over several years, the agency and its partners in the intelligence community determined his true name. Finding the courier and then his residence in Abbottabad took another year of hard work. Instead of a small house from which the agency hoped to follow him to bin Laden, the Abbottabad compound suggested immediately the possibility that bin Laden was living there. Extraordinarily high walls, barbed wire, no telephone or Internet service, trash burned instead of put out for collection like everybody else's, children not going to school. Then we learned that an additional family matching the expected profile of bin Laden's family in flight was living at the compound, never left it, and was unknown to the neighbors. And we learned that the courier was, nine years later, still working for Al Qaeda.

It all added up—the only conclusion that made sense of it all was that bin Laden was there. But there was no positive ID.

Which leads to the next point: this was also an example of difficult and momentous presidential decision-making. There was strong circumstantial evidence that bin Laden was there, but not one iota of direct evidence. No eyes-on identification. And the risks and potential consequences of conducting an operation deep inside Pakistan were enormous, particularly if the operation failed. The president made a sound decision and, in my mind, a gutsy decision.

And, finally, the operation itself was a great triumph for our military. More dramatic than any work of fiction: the tension at the outset, the sickening feeling when one of the helos went down, the seeming eternity waiting to find out if the objective was achieved, and the relief when the last helo lifted off with the force unharmed. My hat's off to these Special Unit operators—incredibly professional. When the helo went down, they didn't skip a beat. They had trained for all contingencies and slipped right into Plan B. Then there's the guy first in the room with bin Laden. Charged by two young women. Trained to expect suicide bombers in these circumstances. He grabbed them, shoved them into a corner and threw himself on top of them, shielding them from the shooting and shielding the guys behind him from the blast if they detonated. His quick thinking, and raw bravery, saved two lives that did not have to end that night.

I am sure the role of the lawyers is not the first thought to come to mind when you think of the bin Laden operation. Admittedly, it may not be the most fascinating aspect, but it is illustrative of the careful attention to the law brought to bear on our country's most sensitive counterterrorism operations.

Because of the paramount importance of keeping the possibility that bin Laden had been located a secret and then of maintaining operational security as the Abbottabad raid was being planned, there were initially very few people in under the tent. So I cannot say the operation was heavily lawyered, but I can tell you it was thoroughly lawyered. From a legal perspective, this was like other counterterrorism operations in some respects. In other respects, of course, it was extraordinary. What counsel concentrated on were the law-related issues that the decision-makers would have to decide, legal issues of which the decision-makers needed to be aware, and lesser issues that needed to be resolved. By the time the force was launched, the US government had determined with confidence that there was clear and ample authority for the use of force, including lethal force, under US and international law and that the operation would be conducted in complete accordance with applicable US and international legal restrictions and principles.

As a result, the operation against bin Laden was not only militarily successful and strategically important, but also fully consistent with all applicable law.

. . .

When I talk about CIA and the rule of law, I speak of the business of the agency and sometimes draw an analogy between the agency and a regulated business—a rule-bound and closely watched business at that. But I have to admit that the analogy is seriously flawed in at least one respect: the CIA is not a business enterprise. It is, of course, a secret intelligence service charged with protecting the United States against foreign adversaries. It operates at the very tip of the spear in the fight against Al Qaeda and its affiliates and adherents. The work of the CIA is not measured in dollars. Too often the measure is taken in lives lost—like the seven officers killed a little more than a year ago at a forward operating base in eastern Afghanistan and others whose stars consecrate our Memorial Wall. But the measure is also taken in lives saved, which are countless. As I stand before you, I am deeply grateful for what the good men and women who are the CIA do every day—literally, the sacrifices they make—to keep you and me, and our families, safe and secure. All of us should be.

. . .

Appendix: Brennan–A

John O. Brennan, assistant to the president for homeland security and counterterrorism, "Strengthening Our Security by Adhering to Our Values and Laws," address at Harvard Law School, September 16, 2011

. . .

Now, I am not a lawyer, despite Dan's best efforts. I am the president's senior adviser on counterterrorism and homeland security. And in this capacity—and during more than thirty years working in intelligence and on behalf of our nation's security—I've developed a profound appreciation for the role that our values, especially the rule of law, play in keeping our country safe. It's an appreciation, of course, understood by President Obama, who, as you may know, once spent a little time here. That's what I want to talk about this evening—how we have strengthened, and continue to strengthen, our national security by adhering to our values and our laws.

Obviously, the death of Osama bin Laden marked a strategic milestone in our effort to defeat Al Qaeda. Unfortunately, bin Laden's death and the death and capture of many other Al Qaeda leaders and operatives do not mark the end of that terrorist organization or its efforts to attack the United States and other countries. Indeed, Al Qaeda, its affiliates, and its adherents remain the preeminent security threat to our nation.

The core of Al Qaeda—its leadership based in Pakistan—though severely crippled, still retains the intent and capability to attack the

United States and our allies. Al Qaeda's affiliates—in places like Pakistan, Yemen, and countries throughout Africa—carry out its murderous agenda. And Al Qaeda adherents—individuals, sometimes with little or no contact with the group itself—have succumbed to its hateful ideology and work to facilitate or conduct attacks here in the United States, as we saw in the tragedy at Fort Hood.

Guiding principles

In the face of this ongoing and evolving threat, the Obama administration has worked to establish a counterterrorism framework that has been effective in enhancing the security of our nation. This framework is guided by several core principles.

First, our highest priority is—and always will be—the safety and security of the American people. As President Obama has said, we have no greater responsibility as a government.

Second, we will use every lawful tool and authority at our disposal. No single agency or department has sole responsibility for this fight because no single department or agency possesses all the capabilities needed for this fight.

Third, we are pragmatic, not rigid or ideological—making decisions not based on preconceived notions about which action seems "stronger," but based on what will actually enhance the security of this country and the safety of the American people. We address each threat and each circumstance in a way that best serves our national security interests, which includes building partnerships with countries around the world.

Fourth—and the principle that guides all our actions, foreign and domestic—we will uphold the core values that define us as Americans, and that includes adhering to the rule of law. And when I say "all our actions," that includes covert actions, which we undertake under the authorities provided to us by Congress. President Obama has directed that all our actions—even when conducted out of public view—remain consistent with our laws and values.

For when we uphold the rule of law, governments around the globe are more likely to provide us with intelligence we need to disrupt ongoing plots, they're more likely to join us in taking swift and decisive action against terrorists, and they're more likely to turn over suspected terrorists who are plotting to attack us, along with the evidence needed to prosecute them.

When we uphold the rule of law, our counterterrorism tools are more likely to withstand the scrutiny of our courts, our allies, and the American people. And when we uphold the rule of law it provides a powerful alternative to the twisted worldview offered by Al Qaeda. Where terrorists offer injustice, disorder, and destruction, the United States and its allies stand for freedom, fairness, equality, hope, and opportunity.

In short, we must not cut corners by setting aside our values and flouting our laws, treating them like luxuries we cannot afford. Indeed, President Obama has made it clear: we must reject the false choice between our values and our security. We are constantly working to optimize both. Over the past two and a half years, we have put in place an approach—both here at home and abroad—that will enable this administration and its successors, in cooperation with key partners overseas, to deal with the threat from Al Qaeda, its affiliates, and its adherents in a forceful, effective, and lasting way.

In keeping with our guiding principles, the president's approach has been pragmatic—neither a wholesale overhaul nor a wholesale retention of past practices. Where the methods and tactics of the previous administration have proven effective and enhanced our security, we have maintained them. Where they did not, we have taken concrete steps to get us back on course.

Unfortunately, much of the debate around our counterterrorism policies has tended to obscure the extraordinary progress of the past few years. So with the time I have left, I want to touch on a few specific topics that illustrate how our adherence to the rule of law advances our national security.

Nature and geographic scope of the conflict

First, our definition of the conflict. As the president has said many times, we are at war with Al Qaeda. In an indisputable act of aggression, Al Qaeda attacked our nation and killed nearly 3,000 innocent people. And as we were reminded just last weekend, Al Qaeda seeks to attack us again. Our ongoing armed conflict with Al Qaeda stems from our right—recognized under international law—to self-defense.

An area in which there is some disagreement is the geographic scope of the conflict. The United States does not view our authority to use military force against Al Qaeda as being restricted solely to "hot" battlefields like Afghanistan. Because we are engaged in an armed conflict with Al Qaeda, the United States takes the legal position that—in accordance with international law—we have the authority to take action against Al Qaeda and its associated forces without doing a separate self-defense analysis each time. And as President Obama has stated on numerous occasions, we reserve the right to take unilateral action if or when other governments are unwilling or unable to take the necessary actions themselves.

That does not mean we can use military force whenever we want, wherever we want. International legal principles, including respect for a state's sovereignty and the laws of war, impose important constraints on our ability to act unilaterally—and on the way in which we can use force—in foreign territories.

Others in the international community—including some of our closest allies and partners—take a different view of the geographic scope of the conflict, limiting it only to the "hot" battlefields. As such, they argue that, outside of these two active theaters, the United States can only act in self-defense against [members of] Al Qaeda when they are planning, engaging in, or threatening an armed attack against US interests if it amounts to an "imminent" threat.

In practice, the US approach to targeting in the conflict with Al Qaeda is far more aligned with our allies' approach than many assume.

This administration's counterterrorism efforts outside of Afghanistan and Iraq are focused on those individuals who are a threat to the United States, whose removal would cause a significant—even if only temporary—disruption of the plans and capabilities of Al Qaeda and its associated forces. Practically speaking, then, the question turns principally on how you define "imminence."

We are finding increasing recognition in the international community that a more flexible understanding of "imminence" may be appropriate when dealing with terrorist groups, in part because threats posed by non-state actors do not present themselves in the ways that evidenced imminence in more traditional conflicts. After all, Al Qaeda does not follow a traditional command structure, wear uniforms, carry its arms openly, or mass its troops at the borders of the nations it attacks. Nonetheless, it possesses the demonstrated capability to strike with little notice and cause significant civilian or military casualties. Over time, an increasing number of our international counterterrorism partners have begun to recognize that the traditional conception of what constitutes an "imminent" attack should be broadened in light of the modern-day capabilities, techniques, and technological innovations of terrorist organizations.

The convergence of our legal views with those of our international partners matters. The effectiveness of our counterterrorism activities depends on the assistance and cooperation of our allies—who, in ways public and private, take great risks to aid us in this fight. But their participation must be consistent with their laws, including their interpretation of international law. Again, we will never abdicate the security of the United States to a foreign country or refrain from taking action when appropriate. But we cannot ignore the reality that cooperative counterterrorism activities are a key to our national defense. The more our views and our allies' views on these questions converge, without constraining our flexibility, the safer we will be as a country.

Privacy and transparency at home

We've also worked to uphold our values and the rule of law in a second area: our policies and practices here at home. As I said, we will use all lawful tools at our disposal, and that includes authorities under the renewed Patriot Act. We firmly believe that our intelligence-gathering tools must enable us to collect the information we need to protect the American people. At the same time, these tools must be subject to appropriate oversight and rigorous checks and balances that protect the privacy of innocent individuals.

As such, we have ensured that investigative techniques in the United States are conducted in a manner that is consistent with our laws and subject to the supervision of our courts. We have also taken administrative steps to institute additional checks and balances, above and beyond what is required by law, in order to better safeguard the privacy rights of innocent Americans.

Our democratic values also include—and our national security demands—open and transparent government. Some information obviously needs to be protected. And since his first days in office, President Obama has worked to strike the proper balance between the security the American people deserve and the openness our democratic society expects.

In one of his first acts, the president issued a new executive order on classified information that, among other things, reestablished the principle that all classified information will ultimately be declassified. The president also issued a Freedom of Information Act Directive mandating that agencies adopt a presumption of disclosure when processing requests for information.

The president signed into law the first intelligence authorization act in over five years to ensure better oversight of intelligence activities. Among other things, the legislation revised the process for reporting sensitive intelligence activities to Congress and created an inspector general for the intelligence community.

For the first time, President Obama released the combined budget of the intelligence community and reconstituted the Intelligence Oversight Board, an important check on the government's intelligence activities. The president declassified and released legal memos that authorized the use, in early times, of enhanced interrogation techniques. Understanding that the reasons to keep those memos secret had evaporated, the president felt it was important for the American people to understand how those methods came to be authorized and used.

The president, through the attorney general, instituted a new process to consider invocation of the so-called "state secrets privilege," where the government can protect information in civil lawsuits. This process ensures that this privilege is never used simply to hide embarrassing or unlawful government activities. But it also recognizes that its use is absolutely necessary in certain cases for the protection of national security. I know there has been some criticism of the administration on this. But by applying a stricter internal review process, including a requirement of personal approval by the attorney general, we are working to ensure that this extraordinary power is asserted only when there is a strong justification to do so.

Detention and interrogation

We've worked to uphold our values and the rule of law in a third area—the question of how to deal with terrorist suspects, including the significant challenge of how to handle suspected terrorists who were already in our custody when this administration took office. There are few places where the intersection of our counterterrorism efforts, our laws, and our values come together as starkly as they do at the prison at Guantánamo. By the time President Obama took office, Guantánamo was viewed internationally as a symbol of a counterterrorism approach that flouted our laws and strayed from our values, undercutting the perceived legitimacy—and therefore the effectiveness—of our efforts.

Aside from the false promises of enhanced security, the purported legality of depriving detainees of their rights was soundly and repeatedly rejected by our courts. It came as no surprise, then, that before 2009 few counterterrorism proposals generated as much bipartisan support as those to close Guantánamo. It was widely recognized that the costs associated with Guantánamo ran high, and the promised benefits never materialized.

That was why—as Dan knows so well—on one of his first days in office, President Obama issued the executive order to close the prison at Guantánamo. Yet, almost immediately, political support for closure waned. Over the last two years Congress has placed unprecedented restrictions on the discretion of our experienced counterterrorism professionals to prosecute and transfer individuals held at the prison. These restrictions prevent these professionals—who have carefully studied all of the available information in a particular situation—from exercising their best judgment as to what the most appropriate disposition is for each individual held there.

The Obama administration has made its views on this clear. The prison at Guantánamo Bay undermines our national security, and our nation will be more secure the day when that prison is finally and responsibly closed. For all of the reasons mentioned above, we will not send more individuals to the prison at Guantánamo. And we continue to urge Congress to repeal these restrictions and allow our experienced counterterrorism professionals to have the flexibility they need to make individualized, informed decisions about where to bring terrorists to justice and when and where to transfer those whom it is no longer in our interest to detain.

This administration also undertook an unprecedented review of our detention and interrogation practices and their evolution since 2001, and we have confronted squarely the question of how we will deal with those we arrest or capture in the future, including those we take custody of overseas. Nevertheless, some have suggested that we do not have a detention policy; that we prefer to kill suspected terrorists, rather than capture them. This is absurd, and I want to take this opportunity to set the record straight.

As a former career intelligence professional, I have a profound appreciation for the value of intelligence. Intelligence disrupts terrorist plots and thwarts attacks. Intelligence saves lives. And one of our greatest sources of intelligence about Al Qaeda, its plans, and its intentions has been the members of its network who have been taken into custody by the United States and our partners overseas.

So I want to be very clear—whenever it is possible to capture a suspected terrorist, it is the unqualified preference of the administration to take custody of that individual so we can obtain information that is vital to the safety and security of the American people. This is how our soldiers and counterterrorism professionals have been trained. It is reflected in our rules of engagement. And it is the clear and unambiguous policy of this administration.

Now, there has been a great deal of debate about the best way to interrogate individuals in our custody. It's been suggested that getting terrorists to talk can be accomplished simply by withholding Miranda warnings or subjecting prisoners to so-called "enhanced interrogation techniques." It's also been suggested that prosecuting terrorists in our federal courts somehow impedes the collection of intelligence. A long record of experience, however, proves otherwise.

Consistent with our laws and our values, the president unequivocally banned torture and other abusive interrogation techniques, rejecting the claim that these are effective means of interrogation. Instead, we have focused on what works. The president approved the creation of a High-Value Detainee Interrogation Group, or HIG, to bring together resources from across the government—experienced interrogators, subject-matter experts, intelligence analysts, and linguists—to conduct or assist in the interrogation of those terrorists with the greatest intelligence value both at home and overseas. Through the HIG, we have brought together the capabilities that are essential to effective interrogation and ensured they can be mobilized quickly and in a coordinated fashion.

Claims that Miranda warnings undermine intelligence collection ignore decades of experience to the contrary. Yes, some terrorism suspects have refused to provide information in the criminal justice system, but so have many individuals held in military custody, from Afghanistan to Guantánamo, where Miranda warnings were not given. What is undeniable is that many individuals in the criminal justice system have provided a great deal of information and intelligence—even after being given their Miranda warnings. The real danger is failing to give a *Miranda* warning in those circumstances where it's appropriate, which could well determine whether a terrorist is convicted and spends the rest of his life behind bars or is set free.

Moreover, the Supreme Court has recognized a limited exception to Miranda, allowing statements to be admitted if the unwarned interrogation was "reasonably prompted by a concern for public safety." Applying this public safety exception to the more complex and diverse threat of international terrorism can be complicated, so our law enforcement officers require clarity.

Therefore, at the end of 2010, the FBI clarified its guidance to agents on use of the public safety exception to Miranda, explaining how it should apply to terrorism cases. The FBI has acknowledged that this exception was utilized last year, including during the questioning of Faisal Shahzad, accused of attempting to detonate a car bomb in Times Square. Just this week in a major terrorism case, a federal judge ruled that statements obtained under the public safety exception before the defendant was read his Miranda rights are, in fact, admissible at trial.

Some have argued that the United States should simply hold suspected terrorists in law-of-war detention indefinitely. It is worth remembering, however, that, for a variety of reasons, reliance upon military detention for individuals apprehended outside of Afghanistan and Iraq actually began to decline precipitously years before the Obama administration came into office.

In the years following the 9/11 attacks, our knowledge of the Al Qaeda network increased and our tools with which to bring them to justice in federal courts or reformed military commissions were strengthened, thus reducing the need for long-term law-of-war detention. In fact, from 2006 to the end of 2008, when the previous administration apprehended terrorists overseas and outside of Iraq and Afghanistan, it brought more of those individuals to the United States to be prosecuted in our federal courts than it placed in long-term military detention at Guantánamo.

Article III courts and reformed military commissions
When we succeed in capturing suspected terrorists who pose a threat to the American people, our other critical national security objective is to maintain a viable authority to keep those individuals behind bars. The strong preference of this administration is to accomplish that through prosecution, either in an Article III court or a reformed military commission. Our decisions on which system to use in a given case must be guided by the factual and legal complexities of each case, and relative strengths and weaknesses of each system. Otherwise, terrorists could be set free, intelligence lost, and lives put at risk.

That said, it is the firm position of the Obama administration that suspected terrorists arrested inside the United States will, in keeping with long-standing tradition, be processed through our Article III courts—as they should be. Our military does not patrol our streets or enforce our laws—nor should it.

This is not a radical idea, nor is the idea of prosecuting terrorists captured overseas in our Article III courts. Indeed, terrorists captured beyond our borders have been successfully prosecuted in our federal courts on many occasions. Our federal courts are time-tested, have unquestioned legitimacy, and, at least for the foreseeable future, are capable of producing a more predictable and sustainable result than military commissions. The previous administration successfully prosecuted hundreds of suspected terrorists in our federal courts, gathering valuable intelligence from several of them that helped our counterterrorism professionals protect the American people. In fact, every single suspected terrorist taken into custody on American soil—before and after the September 11 attacks—has first been taken into custody by law enforcement.

In the past two years alone, we have successfully interrogated several terrorism suspects who were taken into law enforcement custody and prosecuted, including Faisal Shahzad, Najibullah Zazi, David Headley, and many others. In fact, faced with the firm but fair hand of the American justice system, some of the most hardened terrorists have agreed to cooperate with the FBI, providing valuable information about Al Qaeda's network, safe houses, recruitment methods, and even their plots and plans. That is the outcome that all Americans should not only want but demand from their government.

Similarly, when it comes to US citizens involved in terrorist-related activity, whether they are captured overseas or at home, we will prosecute them in our criminal justice system. There is bipartisan agreement that US citizens should not be tried by military commissions. Since 2001, two US citizens were held in military custody and, after years of controversy and extensive litigation, one was released; the other was prosecuted in federal court. Even as the number of US citizens arrested for terrorist-related activity has increased, our civilian courts have proven they are more than up to the job.

In short, our Article III courts are not only our single most effective tool for prosecuting, convicting, and sentencing suspected terrorists—they are a proven tool for gathering intelligence and preventing attacks. For these reasons, credible experts from across the political spectrum continue to demand that our Article III courts remain an unrestrained tool in our counterterrorism toolbox. And where our counterterrorism professionals believe prosecution in our federal courts would best protect the full range of US security interests and the safety of the American people, we will not hesitate to use them. The alternative—a wholesale refusal to utilize our federal courts—would undermine our values and our security.

At the same time, reformed military commissions also have their place in our counterterrorism arsenal. Because of bipartisan efforts to ensure that military commissions provide all of the core protections that are necessary to ensure a fair trial, we have restored the credibility of that system and brought it into line with our principles and our values. Where our counterterrorism professionals believe trying a suspected terrorist in our reformed military commissions would best protect the full range of US security interests and the safety of the American people, we will not hesitate to utilize them to try such individuals. In other words, rather than a rigid reliance on just one or the other, we will use both our federal courts and reformed military commissions as options for incapacitating terrorists.

As a result of recent reforms, there are indeed many similarities between the two systems, and at times, these reformed military commissions offer certain advantages. But important differences remain—differences that can determine whether a prosecution is more likely to succeed or fail.

For example, after Ahmed Warsame—a member of al-Shabaab with close ties to Al Qaeda in the Arabian Peninsula—was captured this year by US military personnel, the president's national security team unanimously agreed that the best option for prosecuting him was our federal courts where, among other advantages, we could avoid significant risks associated with, and pursue additional charges not available in, a military commission. And, if convicted of certain charges, he faces a mandatory life sentence.

In choosing between our federal courts and military commissions in any given case, this administration will remain focused on one thing—the most effective way to keep that terrorist behind bars. The only way to do that is to let our experienced counterterrorism professionals determine, based on the facts and circumstances of each case, which system will best serve our national security interests.

In the end, the Obama administration's approach to detention, inter-rogation, and trial is simple. We have established a practical, flexible, results-driven approach that maximizes our intelligence collection and preserves our ability to prosecute dangerous individuals. Anything less—particularly a rigid, inflexible approach—would be disastrous. It would tie the hands of our counterterrorism professionals by eliminating tools and authorities that have been absolutely essential to their success.

Capacity building abroad
This brings me to a final area where upholding the rule of law strength-ens our security: our work with other nations. As we have seen from Afghanistan in the 1990s to Yemen, Somalia, and the tribal areas of Pakistan today, Al Qaeda and its affiliates often thrive where there is disorder or where central governments lack the ability to effectively govern their own territory.

In contrast, helping such countries build a robust legal frame-work, coupled with effective institutions to enforce them and the transparency and fairness to sustain them, can serve as one of our most effective weapons against groups like Al Qaeda by eliminating the very chaos that organization needs to survive. That is why a key element of this administration's counterterrorism strategy is to help governments build their capacity, including a robust and balanced legal framework, to provide for their own security.

Though tailored to the unique circumstances of each country, we are working with countries in key locations to help them enact robust counterterrorism laws and establish the institutions and mechanisms to effectively enforce them. The establishment of a functioning criminal justice system and institutions has played a key role in the security gains that have been achieved in Iraq. We are working to achieve similar results in places like Afghanistan, Iraq, Yemen, Pakistan, and elsewhere.

These efforts are not a blank check. As a condition of our funding, training, and cooperation, we require that our partners comply with certain legal and humanitarian standards. At times, we have curtailed or suspended security assistance when these standards were not met. We encourage these countries to build a more just, more transparent system that can gain the respect and support of their own people.

As we are seeing across the Middle East and North Africa today, courageous people will continue to demand one of the most basic universal rights—the right to live in a society that respects the rule of law. Any security gains will be short-lived if these countries fail to provide just that. So where we see countries falling short of these basic standards, we will continue to support efforts of people to build institutions that both protect the rights of their own people and enhance our collective security.

Flexibility—critical to our success

In conclusion, I want to say again that the paramount responsibility of President Obama, and of those of us who serve with him, is to protect the American people, to save lives. Each of the tools I have discussed today, and the flexibility to apply them to the unique and complicated circumstances we face, are critical to our success.

This president's counterterrorism framework provides a sustainable foundation upon which this administration and its successors, in close cooperation with our allies and partners overseas, can effectively deal with the threat posed by Al Qaeda and its affiliates and adherents. It is, as I have said, a practical, flexible, result-driven approach to counterterrorism that is consistent with our laws and in line with the very values upon which this nation was founded. And the results we have been able to achieve under this approach are undeniable. We diverge from this path at our own peril.

Yet, despite the successes that this approach has brought, some—including some legislative proposals in Congress—are demanding that we pursue a radically different strategy. Under that approach, we would never be able to turn the page on Guantánamo. Our counterterrorism professionals would be compelled to hold all captured terrorists in military custody, casting aside our most effective and time-tested tool for bringing suspected terrorists to justice: our federal courts. Miranda warnings would be prohibited, even though they are at times essential to our ability to convict a terrorist and ensure that individual remains behind bars. In sum, this approach would impose unprecedented restrictions on the ability of experienced professionals to combat terrorism, injecting legal and operational uncertainty into what is already enormously complicated work.

I am deeply concerned that the alternative approach to counter-terrorism being advocated in some quarters would represent a drastic departure from our values and the body of laws and principles that have always made this country a force for positive change in the world. Such a departure would not only risk rejection by our courts and the American public, it would undermine the international cooperation that has been critical to the national security gains we have made.

Doing so would not make us safer, and would do far more harm than good. Simply put, it is not an approach we should pursue. Not when we have Al Qaeda on the ropes. Our counterterrorism professionals—regardless of the administration in power—need the flexibility to make well-informed decisions about where to prosecute terrorist suspects.

To achieve and maintain the appropriate balance, Congress and the executive branch must continue to work together. There have been and will continue to be many opportunities to do so in a way that strengthens our ability to defeat Al Qaeda and its adherents. As we do so, we must not tie the hands of our counterterrorism professionals by eliminating tools that are critical to their ability to keep our country safe.

As a people, as a nation, we cannot—and we must not—succumb to the temptation to set aside our laws and our values when we face threats to our security, including and especially from groups as depraved as Al Qaeda. We're better than that. We're better than them. We're Americans.

. . .

Appendix: Brennan–B

John O. Brennan, assistant to the president for homeland security and counterterrorism, "The Ethics and Efficacy of the President's Counterterrorism Strategy," Woodrow Wilson International Center for Scholars, Washington, D.C., April 30, 2012

. . .

The death of bin Laden was our most strategic blow yet against Al Qaeda. Credit for that success belongs to the courageous forces who carried out that mission, at extraordinary risk to their lives; to the many intelligence professionals who pieced together the clues that led to bin Laden's hideout; and to President Obama, who gave the order to go in.

One year later, it's appropriate to assess where we stand in this fight. We've always been clear that the end of bin Laden would neither mark the end of Al Qaeda nor our resolve to destroy it. So along with allies and partners, we've been unrelenting. And when we assess the Al Qaeda of 2012, I think it is fair to say that, as a result of our efforts, the United States is more secure and the American people are safer. Here's why.

In Pakistan, Al Qaeda's leadership ranks have continued to suffer heavy losses. This includes Ilyas Kashmiri, one of Al Qaeda's top operational planners, killed a month after bin Laden. It includes Atiyah Abd al-Rahman, killed when he succeeded Ayman al-Zawahiri as Al Qaeda's deputy leader. It includes Younis al-Mauritani, a planner of attacks against the United States and Europe—until he was captured by Pakistani forces.

With its most skilled and experienced commanders being lost so quickly, Al Qaeda has had trouble replacing them. This is one of the many conclusions we have been able to draw from documents seized at bin Laden's compound, some of which will be published online for the first time this week by West Point's Combating Terrorism Center. For example, bin Laden worried about—and I quote—"the rise of lower leaders who are not as experienced and this would lead to the repeat of mistakes."

Al Qaeda leaders continue to struggle to communicate with subordinates and affiliates. Under intense pressure in the tribal regions of Pakistan, they have fewer places to train and groom the next generation of operatives. They're struggling to attract new recruits. Morale is low, with intelligence indicating that some members are giving up and returning home, no doubt aware that this is a fight they will never win. In short, Al Qaeda is losing badly. And bin Laden knew it. In documents we seized, he confessed to "disaster after disaster." He even urged his leaders to flee the tribal regions and go to places "away from aircraft photography and bombardment."

For all these reasons, it is harder than ever for the Al Qaeda core in Pakistan to plan and execute large-scale, potentially catastrophic attacks against our homeland. Today, it is increasingly clear that—compared to 9/11—the core Al Qaeda leadership is a shadow of its former self. Al Qaeda has been left with just a handful of capable leaders and operatives, and with continued pressure is on the path to its destruction. And for the first time since this fight began, we can look ahead and envision a world in which the Al Qaeda core is simply no longer relevant.

Nevertheless, the dangerous threat from Al Qaeda has not disappeared. As the Al Qaeda core falters, it continues to look to its affiliates and adherents to carry on its murderous cause. Yet these affiliates continue to lose key commanders and capabilities as well. In Somalia, it is indeed worrying to witness Al Qaeda's merger with al-Shabaab, whose ranks include foreign fighters, some with US passports. At the same time, al-Shabaab continues to focus primarily on launching regional attacks, and ultimately this is a merger between two organizations in decline.

In Yemen, Al Qaeda in the Arabian Peninsula, or AQAP, continues to feel the effects of the death last year of Anwar al-Awlaki, its leader of external operations who was responsible for planning and directing terrorist attacks against the United States. Nevertheless, AQAP continues to be Al Qaeda's most active affiliate and it continues to seek the opportunity to strike our homeland. We therefore continue to support the government of Yemen in its efforts against AQAP, which is being forced to fight for the territory it needs to plan attacks beyond Yemen.

In north and west Africa, another Al Qaeda affiliate, Al Qaeda in the Islamic Maghreb, or AQIM, continues its efforts to destabilize regional governments and engages in kidnapping of Western citizens for ransom activities designed to fund its terrorist agenda. And in Nigeria, we are monitoring closely the emergence of Boko Haram, a group that appears to be aligning itself with Al Qaeda's violent agenda and is increasingly looking to attack Western interests in Nigeria in addition to Nigerian government targets.

More broadly, Al Qaeda's killing of innocents—mostly Muslim men, women, and children—has badly tarnished its image and appeal in the eyes of Muslims around the world. Even bin Laden and his lieutenants knew this. His propagandist, Adam Gadahn, admitted that they were now seen "as a group that does not hesitate to take people's money by falsehood, detonating mosques, [and] spilling the blood of scores of people." Bin Laden agreed that "a large portion" of Muslims around the world "have lost their trust" in Al Qaeda.

So damaged is Al Qaeda's image that bin Laden even considered changing its name. And one of the reasons? As bin Laden said himself, US officials "have largely stopped using the phrase 'the war on terror' in the context of not wanting to provoke Muslims." Simply calling them Al Qaeda, bin Laden said, "reduces the feeling of Muslims that we belong to them." To which I would add, that is because Al Qaeda does not belong to Muslims. Al Qaeda is the antithesis of the peace, tolerance, and humanity that is at the heart of Islam.

Despite the great progress we've made against Al Qaeda, it would be a mistake to believe this threat has passed. Al Qaeda and its associated forces still have the intent to attack the United States. And we have seen lone individuals, including American citizens—often inspired by Al Qaeda's murderous ideology—kill innocent Americans and seek to do us harm.

Still, the damage that has been inflicted on the leadership core in Pakistan, combined with how Al Qaeda has alienated itself from so much of the world, allows us to look forward. Indeed, if the decade before 9/11 was the time of Al Qaeda's rise, and the decade after 9/11 was the time of its decline, then I believe this decade will be the one that sees its demise.

This progress is no accident. It is a direct result of intense efforts over more than a decade, across two administrations, across the US government, and in concert with allies and partners. This includes the comprehensive counterterrorism strategy being directed by President Obama, a strategy guided by the president's highest responsibility: to protect the safety and security of the American people.

In this fight, we are harnessing every element of American power—intelligence, military, diplomatic, development, economic, financial, law enforcement, homeland security, and the power of our values, including our commitment to the rule of law. That's why, for instance, in his first days in office, President Obama banned the use of enhanced interrogation techniques, which are not needed to keep our country safe.

Staying true to our values as a nation also includes upholding the transparency upon which our democracy depends. A few months after taking office, the president travelled to the National Archives, where he discussed how national security requires a delicate balance between secrecy and transparency. He pledged to share as much information as possible with the American people "so that they can make informed judgments and hold us accountable." He has consistently encouraged those of us on his national security team to be as open and candid as possible as well.

Earlier this year, Attorney General Holder discussed how our counterterrorism efforts are rooted in, and are strengthened by, adherence to the law, including the legal authorities that allow us to pursue members of Al Qaeda—including US citizens—and to do so using "technologically advanced weapons."

In addition, Jeh Johnson, the general counsel at the Department of Defense, has addressed the legal basis for our military efforts against Al Qaeda. Stephen Preston, the general counsel at the CIA, has discussed how the agency operates under US law. These speeches build on a lecture two years ago by Harold Koh, the State Department legal adviser, who noted that "US targeting practices, including lethal operations conducted with the use of unmanned aerial vehicles, comply with all applicable law, including the laws of war."

Given these efforts, I venture to say that the United States government has never been so open regarding its counterterrorism policies and their legal justification. Still, there continues to be considerable public and legal debate surrounding these technologies and how they are sometimes used in our fight against Al Qaeda.

Now, I want to be very clear. In the course of the war in Afghanistan and the fight against Al Qaeda, I think the American people expect us to use advanced technologies, for example, to prevent attacks on US forces and to remove terrorists from the battlefield. We do, and it has saved the lives of our men and women in uniform.

What has clearly captured the attention of many, however, is a different practice, beyond hot battlefields like Afghanistan: identifying specific members of Al Qaeda and then targeting them with lethal force, often using aircraft remotely operated by pilots who can be hundreds if not thousands of miles away. This is what I want to focus on today.

Jack Goldsmith—a former assistant attorney general in the administration of George W. Bush and now a professor at Harvard Law School—captured the situation well. He wrote:

The government needs a way to credibly convey to the public that its decisions about who is being targeted—especially when the target is a US citizen—are sound. . . . First, the government can and should tell us more about the process by which it reaches its high-value targeting decisions . . . The more the government tells us about the eyeballs on the issue and the robustness of the process, the more credible will be its claims about the accuracy of its factual determinations and the soundness of its legal ones. All of this information can be disclosed in some form without endangering critical intelligence.

Well, President Obama agrees. And that is why I am here today.

I stand here as someone who has been involved with our nation's security for more than thirty years. I have a profound appreciation for the truly remarkable capabilities of our counterterrorism professionals—and our relationships with other nations—and we must never compromise them. I will not discuss the sensitive details of any specific operation today. I will not, nor will I ever, publicly divulge sensitive intelligence sources and methods. For when that happens, our national security is endangered and lives can be lost.

At the same time, we reject the notion that any discussion of these matters is to step onto a slippery slope that inevitably endangers our national security. Too often, that fear can become an excuse for saying nothing at all—which creates a void that is then filled with myths and falsehoods. That, in turn, can erode our credibility with the American people and with foreign partners, and it can undermine the public's understanding and support for our efforts. In contrast, President Obama believes that—done carefully, deliberately, and responsibly— we can be more transparent and still ensure our nation's security.

So let me say it as simply as I can. Yes, in full accordance with the law—and in order to prevent terrorist attacks on the United States and to save American lives—the US government conducts targeted strikes against specific Al Qaeda terrorists, sometimes using remotely piloted aircraft, often referred to publicly as drones. And I'm here today because President Obama has instructed us to be more open with the American people about these efforts.

Broadly speaking, the debate over strikes targeted at individual members of Al Qaeda has centered on their legality, their ethics, the wisdom of using them, and the standards by which they are approved. With the remainder of my time today, I would like to address each of these in turn.

First, these targeted strikes are legal. Attorney General Holder, Harold Koh, and Jeh Johnson have all addressed this question at length. To briefly recap, as a matter of domestic law, the Constitution empowers the president to protect the nation from any imminent threat of attack. The Authorization for Use of Military Force—the AUMF—passed by Congress after the September 11 attacks authorizes the president "to use all necessary and appropriate force" against those nations, organizations, and individuals responsible for 9/11. There is nothing in the AUMF that restricts the use of military force against Al Qaeda to Afghanistan.

As a matter of international law, the United States is in an armed conflict with Al Qaeda, the Taliban, and associated forces, in response to the 9/11 attacks, and we may also use force consistent with our inherent right of national self-defense. There is nothing in international law that bans the use of remotely piloted aircraft for this purpose or that prohibits us from using lethal force against our enemies outside of an active battlefield, at least when the country involved consents or is unable or unwilling to take action against the threat.

Second, targeted strikes are ethical. Without question, the ability to target a specific individual—from hundreds or thousands of miles away—raises profound questions. Here, I think it's useful to consider such strikes against the basic principles of the laws of war that govern the use of force.

Targeted strikes conform to the principle of necessity—the requirement that the target have definite military value. In this armed conflict, individuals who are part of Al Qaeda or its associated forces are legitimate military targets. We have the authority to target them with lethal force just as we targeted enemy leaders in past conflicts, such as German and Japanese commanders during World War II.

Targeted strikes conform to the principle of distinction—the idea that only military objectives may be intentionally targeted and that civilians are protected from being intentionally targeted. With the unprecedented ability of remotely piloted aircraft to precisely target a military objective while minimizing collateral damage, one could argue that never before has there been a weapon that allows us to distinguish more effectively between an Al Qaeda terrorist and innocent civilians.

Targeted strikes conform to the principle of proportionality—the notion that the anticipated collateral damage of an action cannot be excessive in relation to the anticipated military advantage. By targeting an individual terrorist or small numbers of terrorists with ordnance that can be adapted to avoid harming others in the immediate vicinity, it is hard to imagine a tool that can better minimize the risk to civilians than remotely piloted aircraft.

For the same reason, targeted strikes conform to the principle of humanity, which requires us to use weapons that will not inflict unnecessary suffering. For all these reasons, I suggest to you that these targeted strikes against Al Qaeda terrorists are indeed ethical and just.

Of course, even if a tool is legal and ethical, that doesn't necessarily make it appropriate or advisable in a given circumstance. This brings me to my next point.

Targeted strikes are wise. Remotely piloted aircraft in particular can be a wise choice because of geography, with their ability to fly hundreds of miles over the most treacherous terrain, strike their targets with astonishing precision, and then return to base. They can be a wise choice because of time, when windows of opportunity can close quickly and there may be just minutes to act.

They can be a wise choice because they dramatically reduce the danger to US personnel, even eliminating the danger altogether. Yet they are also a wise choice because they dramatically reduce the danger to innocent civilians, especially considered against massive ordnance that can cause injury and death far beyond its intended target.

In addition, compared against other options, a pilot operating this aircraft remotely—with the benefit of technology and with the safety of distance—might actually have a clearer picture of the target and its surroundings, including the presence of innocent civilians. It's this surgical precision—the ability, with laser-like focus, to eliminate the cancerous tumor called an Al Qaeda terrorist while limiting damage to the tissue around it—that makes this counterterrorism tool so essential.

There's another reason that targeted strikes can be a wise choice: the strategic consequences that inevitably come with the use of force. As we've seen, deploying large armies abroad won't always be our best offense. Countries typically don't want foreign soldiers in their cities and towns. In fact, large, intrusive military deployments risk playing into Al Qaeda's strategy of trying to draw us into long, costly wars that drain us financially, inflame anti-American resentment, and inspire the next generation of terrorists. In comparison, there is the precision of targeted strikes.

I acknowledge that we—as a government—along with our foreign partners, can and must do a better job of addressing the mistaken belief among some foreign publics that we engage in these strikes casually, as if we are simply unwilling to expose U.S forces to the dangers faced every day by people in those regions. For, as I'll describe today, there is absolutely nothing casual about the extraordinary care we take in making the decision to pursue an Al Qaeda terrorist, and the lengths to which we go to ensure precision and avoid the loss of innocent life.

Still, there is no more consequential a decision than deciding whether to use lethal force against another human being—even a terrorist dedicated to killing American citizens. So in order to ensure that our counterterrorism operations involving the use of lethal force are legal, ethical, and wise, President Obama has demanded that we hold ourselves to the highest possible standards and processes.

This reflects his approach to broader questions regarding the use of force. In his speech in Oslo accepting the Nobel Peace Prize, the president said that "all nations, strong and weak alike, must adhere to standards that govern the use of force." And he added:

"Where force is necessary, we have a moral and strategic interest in binding ourselves to certain rules of conduct. And even as we confront a vicious adversary that abides by no rules, I believe the United States of America must remain a standard bearer in the conduct of war. That is what makes us different from those whom we fight. That is a source of our strength."

The United States is the first nation to regularly conduct strikes using remotely piloted aircraft in an armed conflict. Other nations also possess this technology. Many more nations are seeking it, and more will succeed in acquiring it. President Obama and those of us on his national security team are very mindful that as our nation uses this technology, we are establishing precedents that other nations may follow, and not all of them will be nations that share our interests or the premium we put on protecting human life, including innocent civilians.

If we want other nations to use these technologies responsibly, we must use them responsibly. If we want other nations to adhere to high and rigorous standards for their use, then we must do so as well. We cannot expect of others what we will not do ourselves. President

Obama has therefore demanded that we hold ourselves to the highest possible standards—that, at every step, we be as thorough and deliberate as possible.

This leads me to the final point I want to discuss today: the rigorous standards and process of review to which we hold ourselves today when considering and authorizing strikes against a specific member of Al Qaeda outside the "hot" battlefield of Afghanistan. What I hope to do is to give you a general sense, in broad terms, of the high bar we require ourselves to meet when making these profound decisions today. That includes not only whether a specific member of Al Qaeda can legally be pursued with lethal force, but also whether he should be.

Over time, we've worked to refine, clarify, and strengthen this process and our standards, and we continue to do so. If our counterterrorism professionals assess, for example, that a suspected member of Al Qaeda poses such a threat to the United States as to warrant lethal action, they may raise that individual's name for consideration. The proposal will go through a careful review and, as appropriate, will be evaluated by the very most senior officials in our government for decision.

First and foremost, the individual must be a legitimate target under the law. Earlier, I described how the use of force against members of Al Qaeda is authorized under both international and US law, including both the inherent right of national self-defense and the 2001 Authorization for Use of Military Force, which courts have held extends to those who are part of Al Qaeda, the Taliban, and associated forces. If, after a legal review, we determine that the individual is not a lawful target, end of discussion. We are a nation of laws, and we will always act within the bounds of the law.

Of course, the law only establishes the outer limits of the authority in which counterterrorism professionals can operate. Even if we determine that it is lawful to pursue the terrorist in question with lethal force, it doesn't necessarily mean we should. There are, after all, literally thousands of individuals who are part of Al Qaeda, the Taliban, or associated forces—thousands. Even if it were possible, going after every single one of these individuals with lethal force would neither be wise nor an effective use of our intelligence and counterterrorism resources.

As a result, we have to be strategic. Even if it is lawful to pursue a specific member of Al Qaeda, we ask ourselves whether that individual's activities rise to a certain threshold for action and whether taking action will, in fact, enhance our security.

For example, when considering lethal force we ask ourselves whether the individual poses a significant threat to US interests. This is absolutely critical, and it goes to the very essence of why we take this kind of exceptional action. We do not engage in lethal action in order to eliminate every single member of Al Qaeda in the world. Most times, and as we have done for more than a decade, we rely on cooperation with other countries that are also interested in removing these terrorists with their own capabilities and within their own laws. Nor is lethal action about punishing terrorists for past crimes; we are not seeking vengeance. Rather, we conduct targeted strikes because they are necessary to mitigate an actual ongoing threat—to stop plots, prevent future attacks, and save American lives.

And what do we mean by a significant threat? I am not referring to some hypothetical threat—the mere possibility that a member of Al Qaeda might try to attack us at some point in the future. A significant threat might be posed by an individual who is an operational leader of Al Qaeda or one of its associated forces. Or perhaps the individual is himself an operative—in the midst of actually training for or planning to carry out attacks against US interests. Or perhaps the individual possesses unique operational skills that are being leveraged in a planned attack. The purpose of a strike against a particular individual is to stop him before he can carry out his attack and kill innocents. The purpose is to disrupt his plots and plans before they come to fruition.

In addition, our unqualified preference is to only undertake lethal force when we believe that capturing the individual is not feasible. I have heard it suggested that the Obama administration somehow prefers killing Al Qaeda members rather than capturing them. Nothing could be further from the truth. It is our preference to capture suspected terrorists whenever feasible.

For one reason, this allows us to gather valuable intelligence that we might not be able to obtain any other way. In fact, the members of Al Qaeda that we or other nations have captured have been one of our greatest sources of information about Al Qaeda, its plans, and its intentions. And once in US custody, we often can prosecute them in our federal courts or reformed military commissions—both of which are used for gathering intelligence and preventing terrorist attacks.

You see our preference for capture in the case of Ahmed Warsame, a member of al-Shabaab who had significant ties to Al Qaeda in the Arabian Peninsula. Last year, when we learned that he would be traveling from Yemen to Somalia, US forces captured him en route and we subsequently charged him in federal court.

The reality, however, is that since 2001 such unilateral captures by US forces outside of "hot" battlefields, like Afghanistan, have been exceedingly rare. This is due in part to the fact that in many parts of the world our counterterrorism partners have been able to capture or kill dangerous individuals themselves.

Moreover, after being subjected to more than a decade of relentless pressure, Al Qaeda's ranks have dwindled and scattered. These terrorists are skilled at seeking remote, inhospitable terrain—places where the United States and our partners simply do not have the ability to arrest or capture them. At other times, our forces might have the ability to attempt capture, but only by putting the lives of our personnel at too great a risk. Oftentimes, attempting capture could subject civilians to unacceptable risks. There are many reasons why capture might not be feasible, in which case lethal force might be the only remaining option to address the threat and prevent an attack.

Finally, when considering lethal force we are of course mindful that there are important checks on our ability to act unilaterally in foreign territories. We do not use force whenever we want, wherever we want. International legal principles, including respect for a state's sovereignty and the laws of war, impose constraints. The United States of America respects national sovereignty and international law.

Those are some of the questions we consider—the high standards we strive to meet. And in the end, we make a decision—we decide whether a particular member of Al Qaeda warrants being pursued in this manner. Given the stakes involved and the consequence of our decision, we consider all the information available to us, carefully, responsibly.

We review the most up-to-date intelligence, drawing on the full range of our intelligence capabilities. And we do what sound intelligence demands—we challenge it, we question it, including any assumptions on which it might be based. If we want to know more, we may ask the intelligence community to go back and collect additional intelligence or refine its analysis so that a more informed decision can be made.

We listen to departments and agencies across our national security team. We don't just hear out differing views, we ask for them and encourage them. We discuss. We debate. We disagree. We consider the advantages and disadvantages of taking action. We also carefully consider the costs of inaction and whether a decision not to carry out a strike could allow a terrorist attack to proceed and potentially kill scores of innocents.

Nor do we limit ourselves narrowly to counterterrorism considerations. We consider the broader strategic implications of any action, including what effect, if any, an action might have on our relationships with other countries. And we don't simply make a decision and never revisit it again. Quite the opposite. Over time, we refresh the intelligence and continue to consider whether lethal force is still warranted.

In some cases—such as senior Al Qaeda leaders who are directing and planning attacks against the United States—the individual clearly meets our standards for taking action. In other cases, individuals have not met our standards. Indeed, there have been numerous occasions where, after careful review, we have, working on a consensus basis, concluded that lethal force was not justified in a given case.

Finally, as the president's counterterrorism adviser, I feel that it is important for the American people to know that these efforts are overseen with extraordinary care and thoughtfulness. The president expects us to address all of the tough questions I have discussed today. Is capture really not feasible? Is this individual a significant threat to US interests? Is this really the best option? Have we thought through the consequences, especially any unintended ones? Is this really going to help protect our country from further attacks? Is it going to save lives?

Our commitment to upholding the ethics and efficacy of this counterterrorism tool continues even after we decide to pursue a specific terrorist in this way. For example, we only authorize a particular operation against a specific individual if we have a high degree of confidence that the individual being targeted is indeed the terrorist we are pursuing. This is a very high bar. Of course, how we identify an individual naturally involves intelligence sources and methods which I will not discuss. Suffice it to say, our intelligence community has multiple ways to determine, with a high degree of confidence that the individual being targeted is indeed the Al Qaeda terrorist we are seeking.

In addition, we only authorize a strike if we have a high degree of confidence that innocent civilians will not be injured or killed, except in the rarest of circumstances. The unprecedented advances we have made in technology provide us greater proximity to targets for a longer period of time, and as a result allow us to better understand what is happening in real time on the ground in ways that were previously impossible. We can be much more discriminating and we can make more informed judgments about factors that might contribute to collateral damage.

I can tell you today that there have indeed been occasions when we have decided against conducting a strike in order to avoid the injury or death of innocent civilians. This reflects our commitment to doing everything in our power to avoid civilian casualties—even if it means having to come back another day to take out that terrorist, as we have done. And I would note that these standards—for identifying a target and avoiding the loss of innocent civilians—exceed what is required as a matter of international law on a typical battlefield. That's another example of the high standards to which we hold ourselves.

Our commitment to ensuring accuracy and effectiveness continues even after a strike. In the wake of a strike, we harness the full range of our intelligence capabilities to assess whether the mission in fact achieved its objective. We try to determine whether there was any collateral damage, including civilian deaths. There is, of course, no such thing as a perfect weapon, and remotely piloted aircraft are no exception.

As the president and others have acknowledged, there have indeed been instances when—despite the extraordinary precautions we take—civilians have been accidentally injured or, worse, killed in these strikes. It is exceedingly rare, but it has happened. When it does, it pains us and we regret it deeply, as we do any time innocents are killed in war. And when this happens we take it seriously. We go back and review our actions. We examine our practices. And we constantly work to improve and refine our efforts so that we are doing everything in our power to prevent the loss of innocent life. This too is a reflection of our values as Americans.

Ensuring the ethics and efficacy of these strikes also includes regularly informing appropriate members of Congress and the committees who have oversight of our counterterrorism programs. Indeed, our counterterrorism programs—including the use of lethal force—have grown more effective over time because of congressional oversight and our ongoing dialogue with members and staff.

This is the seriousness, the extraordinary care, that President Obama and those of us on his national security team bring to this weightiest of questions—whether to pursue lethal force against a terrorist who is plotting to attack our country.

When that person is a US citizen, we ask ourselves additional questions. Attorney General Holder has already described the legal authorities that clearly allow us to use lethal force against an American citizen who is a senior operational leader of Al Qaeda. He has discussed the thorough and careful review, including all relevant constitutional considerations, that is to be undertaken by the US government when determining whether the individual poses an imminent threat of violent attack against the United States.

To recap, the standards and processes I've described today—which we have refined and strengthened over time—reflect our commitment to ensuring the individual is a legitimate target under the law; determining whether the individual poses a significant threat to US interests; determining that capture is not feasible; being mindful of the important checks on our ability to act unilaterally in foreign territories; having that high degree of confidence, both in the identity of the target and that innocent civilians will not be harmed; and, of course, engaging in additional review if the Al Qaeda terrorist is a US citizen.

Going forward, we'll continue to strengthen and refine these standards and processes. As we do, we'll look to institutionalize our approach more formally so that the high standards we set for ourselves endure over time, including as an example for other nations that pursue these capabilities. As the president said at Oslo, in the conduct of war America must be the standard bearer.

This includes our continuing commitment to greater transparency. With that in mind, I have made a sincere effort today to address some of the main questions that citizens and scholars have raised regarding the use of targeted lethal force against Al Qaeda. I suspect there are those, perhaps some in this audience, who feel we have not been transparent enough. I suspect there are those—both inside and outside our government—who feel I have been perhaps too open. If both groups feel a little unsatisfied, then I've probably struck the right balance.

Again, there are some lines we simply will not and cannot cross because, at times, our national security demands secrecy. But we are a democracy. The people are sovereign. And our counterterrorism tools do not exist in a vacuum. They are stronger and more sustainable when the American people understand and support them. They are weaker and less sustainable when the American people do not. As a result of my remarks today, I hope the American people have a better understanding of this critical tool—why we use it, what we do, how carefully we use it, and why it is absolutely essential to protecting our country and our citizens.

I would just like to close on a personal note. I know that for many people—in our government and across the country—the issue of targeted strikes raises profound moral questions. It forces us to confront deeply held personal beliefs and our values as a nation. If anyone in government who works in this area tells you they haven't struggled with this, then they haven't spent much time thinking about it. I know I have, and I will continue to struggle with it as long as I remain involved in counterterrorism.

But I am certain about one thing. We are at war. We are at war against a terrorist organization called Al Qaeda that has brutally murdered thousands of Americans—men, women, and children—as well as thousands of other innocent people around the world. In recent years, with the help of targeted strikes we have turned Al Qaeda into a shadow of what it once was. They are on the road to destruction.

Until that finally happens, however, there are still terrorists in hard-to-reach places who are actively planning attacks against us. If given the chance, they will gladly strike again and kill more of our citizens. And the president has a constitutional and solemn obligation to do everything in his power to protect the safety and security of the American people.

Yes, war is hell. It is awful. It involves human beings killing other human beings, sometimes innocent civilians. That is why we despise war. That is why we want this war against Al Qaeda to be over as soon as possible, and not a moment longer. And over time, as Al Qaeda fades into history and as our partners grow stronger, I'd hope that the United States would have to rely less on lethal force to keep our country safe.

Until that happens, as President Obama said here five years ago, if another nation cannot or will not take action, we will. And it is an unfortunate fact that to save many innocent lives we are sometimes obliged to take lives—the lives of terrorists who seek to murder our fellow citizens.

. . .

Appendix: Brennan–C

*John O. Brennan, assistant to the president for
homeland security and counterterrorism,
"US Policy toward Yemen," Council on Foreign
Relations, New York City, August 8, 2012*

. . .

When the subject of Yemen comes up, it's often through the
prism of the terrorist threat that is emanating from within its borders.
And for good reason: Al Qaeda in the Arabian Peninsula, or AQAP,
is Al Qaeda's most active affiliate. It has assassinated Yemeni leaders,
murdered Yemeni citizens, kidnapped and killed aid workers, targeted American interests, encouraged attacks in the United States
and attempted repeated attacks against US aviation. Likewise, discussion of Yemeni and American counterterrorism efforts tends to
focus almost exclusively on the use of one counterterrorism tool in
particular: targeted strikes.

At the White House, we have always taken a broader view, both
of Yemen's challenges and of US policy. Two months ago, however,
a number of experts on Yemen wrote an open letter to President
Obama arguing that there is a perception that the United States is
singularly focused on AQAP to the exclusion of Yemen's broader
political, economic, and social ills. Among their recommendations:
that US officials publicly convey that the United States is making a
sustained commitment to Yemen's political transition, economic
development, and stability. And it is in that spirit that I join you here

today, both in my official capacity and as someone who has come to know and admire Yemen and its people over the last three decades.

I want to begin with a snapshot of where Yemen is today. Since assuming office, President [Abdu Rabbu Mansour] Hadi and his administration have made progress toward implementing two key elements of the Gulf Cooperation Council [GCC] agreement that ended the rule of Ali Abdullah Saleh and provided a road map for political transition and reform.

As part of a military reorganization, powerful commanders, including some of the former president's family and supporters, have been dismissed or reassigned, and discussions are under way to bring the military under unified civilian command. And just two days ago President Hadi took the important step of issuing a decree that reassigns several brigades from under the command of Saleh's son as well as leading Saleh rival Ali Mohsen al-Ahmar.

In addition, to organize the national dialogue, President Hadi has appointed a committee with representatives from political parties, youth groups, women's organizations, the southern movement, and Houthi oppositionists in the north. And that committee met for the first time this week.

On the security front, government forces have achieved important gains against AQAP. Today AQAP's black flag no longer flies over the city centers of Ja'ar, Loudur, or Zinjibar. As one resident said, after AQAP's departure from these areas in June, "it is like seeing darkness lifted from our lives after a year."

Elsewhere in Yemen, checkpoints are being removed, businesses are reopening, public services have resumed in major cities, and public servants are getting paid. The energy infrastructure is slowly but surely being restored, including the Marib pipeline, which supplies half of Yemen's domestic oil.

At the same time, Yemen continues to face extraordinary challenges. Violence remains a tragic reality for many Yemenis. We saw this again in last week's clashes at the Ministry of Interior in Sana'a and in an outrageous suicide attack in Ja'ar on Saturday that killed dozens of innocent Yemenis.

Moreover, Yemen remains one of the poorest countries on earth, and conditions have only been compounded by last year's upheaval. Most Yemenis still lack access to basic services, including electricity and functioning water systems. Unemployment is as high as 40 percent. Chronic poverty is now estimated at 54 percent. Ten million people, nearly half of Yemen's population, go to bed hungry every night. One in ten children does not live to the age of five.

President Obama understands that Yemen's challenges are grave and intertwined. He has insisted that our policy emphasize governance and development as much as security and focus on a clear goal to facilitate a democratic transition while helping Yemen advance political, economic, and security reforms so it can support its citizens and counter AQAP.

You see our comprehensive approach in the numbers. This year alone, US assistance to Yemen is more than $337 million. Over half this money, $178 million, is for political transition, humanitarian assistance, and development. Let me repeat that. More than half of the assistance we provide to Yemen is for political transition, humanitarian assistance, and development. In fact, this is the largest amount of civilian assistance the United States has ever provided to Yemen. So any suggestion that our policy toward Yemen is dominated by our security and counterterrorism efforts is simply not true.

Today I want to walk through the key pillars of our approach.

First, the United States has been and will remain a strong and active supporter of the political transition in Yemen. That's why President Obama called on then-President Saleh to step down shortly after unrest erupted last year. Having consistently advocated for an orderly, peaceful transfer of power, despite claims by some that doing so would jeopardize counterterrorism operations, we've worked hard to help sustain the transition, facilitate elections, and promote an inclusive national dialogue. This past May President Obama issued an executive order authorizing sanctions against those who threaten the transition.

Going forward, we'll continue to push for the timely, effective, and full implementation of the GCC agreement. During this delicate transition, we call on all Yemenis, especially Ali Abdullah Saleh, Ali Mohsen al-Ahmar, Hamid al-Ahmar, and Ahmed Ali Saleh, to show that they will put Yemen's national interests ahead of parochial concerns and abide by the letter and the spirit of the GCC agreement so that Yemen can move toward a more inclusive democracy.

As we support the transition, our comprehensive approach has a second pillar: helping to strengthen governance and institutions upon which Yemen's long-term progress depends. Despite decades of rule by one man, Yemen has a foundation on which it is building. The country has a tradition of opposition political parties, a vibrant civil society, independent media, and leaders who place the larger national interests above politics, religion, sect, or tribe.

President Hadi is one such leader. This year I've met with him twice in Yemen and spoken to him numerous times. I've been impressed with his commitment to his nation, his integrity, and his willingness to make difficult decisions to move his country forward, even at great risk to himself. The Yemeni people are indeed very fortunate to have President Hadi as their leader. We are helping to strengthen Yemeni government institutions so that they become more responsive, effective, and accountable to the people. We are partnering with ministries to expand essential services, improve efficiency, combat corruption, and enhance transparency. We will support the reform of law enforcement and judicial institutions to strengthen the rule of law.

Beyond government, we're proud to continue our long tradition of helping to strengthen the role of civil society to conduct parliamentary oversight, raise public awareness on electoral reforms and Yemen's transition, empower women, provide leadership and advocacy training, and build the capacity of political parties to engage in peaceful democratic discourse.

Of course lasting political and economic progress is impossible so long as half of Yemenis are malnourished and struggling to survive another day. That is why the third pillar of our approach is immediate humanitarian relief. This year the United States is providing nearly $110 million in humanitarian assistance to Yemen, most of it through the UN's Humanitarian Response Plan. This makes the United States the single largest provider of humanitarian assistance to Yemen.

These funds are allowing our UN and NGO partners to provide food and food vouchers, improved sanitation, safe drinking water, and basic health services to help meet other urgent needs. USAID is providing more than $74 million for food security and nutrition programs, enabling UNICEF to rapidly scale up its assistance for starving children. With US support, UNICEF and the World Health Organization completed a large-scale immunization campaign, which may have successfully halted a polio outbreak that began last year.

Yet even with these efforts, so many Yemenis remain in desperate need. We commend the European Union for doubling its humanitarian aid to Yemen and urge other donors to follow suit by contributing more to the UN Humanitarian Response Plan, which is less than 50 percent funded. This will provide critical and lifesaving relief to millions of Yemenis.

As we help address immediate humanitarian needs, we're partnering with Yemen in a fourth area, the economic reforms and development necessary for long-term progress. In fact, the $68 million in transition assistance and economic development that we are providing this year includes vital assistance to improve the delivery of basic services, including health, education, and water.

We are helping Yemen address its staggering health gaps by renovating health clinics, providing medical equipment, training midwives and doctors in maternal and child health, and supporting community health education.

We are helping to introduce farmers to more productive techniques and provide youth with skills training, job placement, and entrepreneurial programs.

We are helping Yemen rebuild infrastructure and promote microfinance and small businesses. We are encouraging efforts to stabilize the economy and undertake reforms that will help raise living standards and promote a more diversified economy.

And following Yemen's success against AQAP in the south, USAID is supporting the Yemeni government's efforts to repair wartorn infrastructure and to rehabilitate communities.

For its part, Yemen must have a plan to address unemployment and poverty, as well as develop, diversify, and reform its economy, including by combating corruption so that government revenues and donor funds are not diverted to private interests at the expense of the Yemeni people.

International donors want to know that their contributions aren't misappropriated and that the projects they fund are part of a comprehensive plan. Providing a vision of where Yemen's leaders plan to take the country will help its friends invest wisely.

This brings me to the final pillar of our comprehensive approach to Yemen: improving security and combating the threat of AQAP. Put simply, Yemen cannot succeed politically, economically, socially so long as the cancerous growth of AQAP remains.

Ultimately, the long-term battle against AQAP in Yemen must be fought and won by Yemenis. To their great credit, President Hadi and his government, including Defense Minister [Muhammad Nasir Ahmad] Ali, Chief of Army Staff [Ahmed Ali] Ashwal, and Interior Minister [Abd al-Qadir] Qahtan, have made combating AQAP a top priority and have forced AQAP out of its stronghold in southern Yemen.

So long as AQAP seeks to implement its murderous agenda, we will be a close partner with Yemen in meeting this common threat. And just as our approach to Yemen is multidimensional, our counter-terrorism approach involves many different tools—diplomatic, intelligence, military, homeland security, law enforcement, and justice. With our Yemeni and international partners, we have put unprecedented pressure on AQAP. Recruits seeking to travel to Yemen have been disrupted. Operatives deployed from Yemen have been detained. Plots have been thwarted. And key AQAP leaders who have targeted US and Yemeni interests have met their demise, including Anwar al-Awlaki, AQAP's chief of external operations.

Of course, the tension has often focused on one counterterrorism tool in particular, targeted strikes, sometimes using remotely piloted aircraft, often referred to publicly as drones. In June the Obama administration declassified the fact that in Yemen, our joint efforts have resulted in direct action against AQAP operatives and senior leaders. This spring, I addressed the subject of targeted strikes at length and why such strikes are legal, ethical, wise, and highly effective.

Today I'd simply say that all our CT efforts in Yemen are conducted in concert with the Yemeni government. When direct action is taken, every effort is made to avoid any civilian casualty. And contrary to conventional wisdom, we see little evidence that these actions are generating widespread anti-American sentiment or recruits for AQAP. In fact, we see the opposite: our Yemeni partners are more eager to work with us. Yemenese citizens who have been freed from the hellish grip of AQAP are more eager, not less, to work with the Yemeni government. In short, targeted strikes against the most senior and most dangerous AQAP terrorists are not the problem, they are part of the solution.

Even as we partner against the immediate threat posed by AQAP, we're helping Yemen build its capacity for its own security. We are spearheading the international effort to help reform and restructure Yemen's military into a professional, unified force under civilian control. In fact, of the $159 million in security assistance we are providing to Yemen this year, almost all of it is for training and equipment to build capacity. We are empowering the Yemenese with the tools they need to conduct precise intelligence-driven operations to locate operatives and disrupt plots and the training they need to ensure counterterrorism operations are conducted lawfully in a manner that respects human rights and makes every effort to avoid civilian casualties.

Finally, I'd note that our approach to Yemen is reinforced by broad support from the international community. Throughout the last year, the Gulf Cooperation Council, especially Saudi Arabia, the G-10, the Friends of Yemen, the United Nations, and the diplomatic community in Sana'a have come together to push for a peaceful solution of the crisis and to facilitate a successful transition. The international community has threatened UN sanctions against those who would undermine the transition, provided humanitarian relief, and offered assistance for the national dialogue and electoral reform. International partners, including the UK, Germany, China, Russia, India, the EU, and the UAE have pledged aid. Saudi Arabia alone offered $3.25 billion on top of the significant fuel grants it gave Yemen to offset the losses caused by attacks against oil infrastructure. As such, close coordination with our international partners will be critical in the years ahead.

These are the pillars of our comprehensive approach to Yemen: supporting the transition, strengthening governance and institutions, providing humanitarian relief, encouraging economic reform and development, and improving security and combatting AQAP. Taken together, our efforts send an unmistakable message to the Yemeni people: the United States is committed to your success. We share the vision that guides so many Yemenese, a Yemen where all its citizens— Shia and Sunni, northerner and southerner, man and woman, rural villager and city dweller, old and young—have a government that is democratic, responsive, and just.

But we are under no illusions. Given the tremendous challenges that Yemen continues to face, progress toward such a future will take many, many years. Yet, if we've learned anything in the past two years, it's that we should not underestimate the will of the Yemeni people. Despite the seemingly insurmountable obstacles in front of them, hundreds of thousands of men and women took to the streets and engaged in political and social movements for the first time in their lives, and in so doing helped pave the way for change that just a few years ago would have seemed unimaginable.

That Yemen did not devolve into an all-out civil war is a testament to the courage, determination, and resilience of the Yemeni people. It showed that Yemen's future need not be determined by violence. The people of Yemen have a very long and hard road ahead of them. But they've shown that they are willing to make the journey, even with all the risk that it entails. As they go forward in pursuit of the security, prosperity, and dignity they so richly deserve, they will continue to have a partner in the United States of America.

Appendix: Litt—A

Robert S. Litt, general counsel with the
Office of the Director of National Intelligence,
"Privacy, Technology, and National Security:
An Overview of Intelligence Collection,"
address at the Brookings Institution,
Washington, D.C., July 19, 2013

I. Introduction

I wish that I was here in happier times for the intelligence community. The last several weeks have seen a series of reckless disclosures of classified information about intelligence activities. These disclosures threaten to cause long-lasting and irreversible harm to our ability to identify and respond to the many threats facing our nation. And because the disclosures were made by people who did not fully understand what they were talking about, they were sensationalized and led to mistaken and misleading impressions. I hope to be able to correct some of these misimpressions today.

My speech today is prompted by disclosures about two programs that collect valuable foreign intelligence that has protected our nation and its allies: the bulk collection of telephony metadata and the so-called PRISM program. Some people claim that these disclosures were a form of whistle-blowing. But let's be clear. These programs are not illegal. They are authorized by Congress and are carefully overseen by the congressional intelligence and judiciary committees. They are conducted with the approval of the Foreign Intelligence Surveillance Court and under its supervision. And they are subject to extensive, court-ordered oversight by the executive branch. In short, all three branches of government knew about these programs, approved them, and helped to ensure that they complied with the law. Only time will tell the full extent of the damage caused by the unlawful disclosures of these lawful programs.

Nevertheless, I fully appreciate that it's not enough for us simply to assert that our activities are consistent with the letter of the law. Our government's activities must always reflect and reinforce our core democratic values. Those of us who work in the intelligence profession share these values, including the importance of privacy. But security and privacy are not zero-sum. We have an obligation to give full meaning to both: to protect security while at the same time protecting privacy and other constitutional rights. But although our values are enduring, the manner in which our activities reflect those values must necessarily adapt to changing societal expectations and norms. Thus, the intelligence community continually evaluates and improves the safeguards we have in place to protect privacy, while at the same time ensuring that we can carry out our mission of protecting national security.

So I'd like to do three things today. First, I'd like to discuss very briefly the laws that govern intelligence collection activities. Second, I want to talk about the effect of changing technology, and the corresponding need to adapt how we protect privacy, on those collection activities. And third, I want to bring these two strands together, to talk about how some of these laws play out in practice—how we structure the intelligence community's collection activities under FISA (Foreign Intelligence Surveillance Act) to respond to these changes in a way that remains faithful to our democratic values.

II. Legal framework

Let me begin by discussing in general terms the legal framework that governs intelligence collection activities. And it is a bedrock concept that those activities are bound by the rule of law. This is a topic that has been well addressed by others, including the general counsels of the CIA and NSA (National Security Agency), so I will make this brief. We begin, of course, with the Constitution. Article II makes the president the commander in chief and gives him extensive responsibility for the conduct of foreign affairs. The ability to collect foreign intelligence derives from that constitutional source. The First Amendment protects freedom of speech. And the Fourth Amendment prohibits unreasonable searches and seizures.

I want to make a few points about the Fourth Amendment. First, under established Supreme Court rulings a person has no legally recognized expectation of privacy in information that he or she gives to a third party. So obtaining those records from the third party is not a search as to that person. I'll return to this point in a moment. Second, the Fourth Amendment doesn't apply to foreigners outside of the United States. Third, the Supreme Court has said that the "reasonableness" of a warrantless search depends on balancing the "intrusion on the individual's Fourth Amendment interests against" the search's "promotion of legitimate governmental interests."[1]

In addition to the Constitution, a variety of statutes govern our collection activities. First, the National Security Act and a number of laws relating to specific agencies, such as the CIA Act and the NSA Act, limit what agencies can do, so that, for example, the CIA cannot engage in domestic law enforcement. We are also governed by laws such as the Electronic Communications Privacy Act, the Privacy Act, and, in particular, the Foreign Intelligence Surveillance Act, or FISA. FISA was passed by Congress in 1978 and significantly amended in 2001 and 2008. It regulates electronic surveillance and certain other activities carried out for foreign intelligence purposes. I'll have much more to say about FISA later.

A final important source of legal restrictions is Executive Order 12333. This order provides additional limits on what intelligence agencies can do, defining each agency's authorities and responsibilities. In particular, section 2.3 of EO 12333 provides that elements of

---

1. *Vernonia School Dist. v. Acton*, 515 US 646, 652-3 (1995).

the intelligence community "are authorized to collect, retain, or disseminate information concerning United States persons only in accordance with procedures . . . approved by the attorney general . . . after
consultation with" the director of national intelligence. These procedures must be consistent with the agencies' authorities. They must
also establish strict limits on collecting, retaining or disseminating
information about US persons, unless that information is actually of
foreign intelligence value, or in certain other limited circumstances
spelled out in the order, such as to protect against a threat to life.
These so-called US person rules are basic to the operation of the
intelligence community. They are among the first things that our
employees are trained in, and they are at the core of our institutional
culture.

It's not surprising that our legal regime provides special rules for
activities directed at US persons. So far as I know, every nation recognizes legal distinctions between citizens and noncitizens. But as I
hope to make clear, our intelligence collection procedures also provide protection for the privacy rights of noncitizens.

III. Impact of changing societal norms

Let me turn now to the impact of changing technology on privacy.
Prior to the end of the nineteenth century there was little discussion
about a "right to privacy." In the absence of mass media, photography, and other technologies of the industrial age, the most serious
invasions of privacy were the result of gossip or Peeping Toms.
Indeed, in the 1890 article that first articulated the idea of a legal
right to privacy, Louis Brandeis and Samuel Warren explicitly
grounded that idea on changing technologies:

*Recent inventions and business methods call attention to the next
step which must be taken for the protection of the person, and for secur-
ing to the individual what Judge Cooley calls the right "to be let alone."
Instantaneous photographs and newspaper enterprise have invaded the
sacred precincts of private and domestic life; and numerous mechanical*

devices threaten to make good the prediction that "what is whispered in the closet shall be proclaimed from the house-top."[2]

Today, as a result of the way digital technology has developed, each of us shares massive amounts of information about ourselves with third parties. Sometimes this is obvious, as when we post pictures on social media or transmit our credit card numbers to buy products online. Other times it is less obvious, as when telephone companies store records listing every call we make. All in all, there's little doubt that the amount of data that each of us provides to strangers every day would astonish Brandeis and Warren—let alone Jefferson and Madison.

And this leads me to what I consider to be the key question. Why is it that people are willing to expose large quantities of information to private parties but don't want the government to have the same information? Why, for example, don't we care if the telephone company keeps records of all of our phone calls on its servers, but we feel very differently about the prospect of the same information being on NSA servers? This does not seem to me to be a difficult question: we care because of what the government could do with the information.

Unlike a phone company, the government has the power to audit our tax returns, to prosecute and imprison us, to grant or deny licenses to do business, and many other things. And there is an entirely understandable concern that the government may abuse this power. I don't mean to say that private companies don't have a lot of power over us. Indeed, the growth of corporate privacy policies, and the strong public reaction to the inadvertent release or commercial use of personal information, reinforces my belief that our primary privacy concern today is less with who has information than with what they do with it. But there is no question that the government, because of its powers, is properly viewed in a different light.

---

2. Samuel D. Warren & Louis D. Brandeis, "The Right to Privacy," *Harvard Law Review* 4 (5) (1890) 193, 195.

On the other hand, just as consumers around the world make extensive use of modern technology, so too do potentially hostile foreign governments and foreign terrorist organizations. Indeed, we know that terrorists and weapons proliferators are using global information networks to conduct research, to communicate, and to plan attacks. Information that can help us identify and prevent terrorist attacks or other threats to our security is often hiding in plain sight among the vast amounts of information flowing around the globe. New technology means that the intelligence community must continue to find new ways to locate and analyze foreign intelligence. We need to be able to do more than connect the dots when we happen to find them; we need to be able to find the right dots in the first place.

One approach to protecting privacy would be to limit the intelligence community to a targeted, focused query looking for specific information about an identified individual based on probable cause. But from the national security perspective, that would not be sufficient. The business of foreign intelligence has always been fundamentally different from the business of criminal investigation. Rather than attempting to solve crimes that have happened already, we are trying to find out what is going to happen before it happens. We may have only fragmentary information about someone who is plotting a terrorist attack, and need to find him and stop him. We may get information that is useless to us without a store of data to match it against, such as when we get the telephone number of a terrorist and want to find out who he has been in touch with. Or we may learn about a plot that we were previously unaware of, causing us to revisit old information and find connections that we didn't notice before—and that we would never know about if we hadn't collected the information and kept it for some period of time. We worry all the time about what we are missing in our daily effort to protect the nation and our allies.

So on the one hand there are vast amounts of data that contain intelligence needed to protect us not only from terrorism, but from cyber-attacks, weapons of mass destruction, and good old-fashioned espionage. And on the other hand, giving the intelligence community access to this data has obvious privacy implications. We achieve both security and privacy protection in this context in large part by a framework that establishes appropriate controls on what the government can do with the information it lawfully collects, and appropriate oversight to ensure that it respects those controls. The protections depend on such factors as the type of information we collect, where we collect it, the scope of the collection, and the use the government intends to make of the information. In this way we can allow the intelligence community to acquire necessary foreign intelligence while providing privacy protections that take account of modern technology.

IV. FISA collection

In showing that this approach is in fact the way our system deals with intelligence collection, I'll use FISA as an example for a couple of reasons. First, because FISA is an important mechanism through which Congress has legislated in the area of foreign intelligence collection. Second, because it covers a wide range of activities and involves all three sources of law I mentioned earlier: constitutional, statutory, and executive. And third, because several previously classified examples of what we do under FISA have recently been declassified, and I know people want to hear more about them.

I don't mean to suggest that FISA is the only way we collect foreign intelligence. But it's important to know that, by virtue of Executive Order 12333, all of the collection activities of our intelligence agencies have to be directed at the acquisition of foreign intelligence or counterintelligence. Our intelligence priorities are set annually through an interagency process. The leaders of our nation tell the intelligence community what information they need in the service of the nation, its citizens, and its interests, and we collect information in support of those priorities.

I want to emphasize that the United States, as a democratic nation, takes seriously this requirement that collection activities have a valid foreign intelligence purpose. We do not use our foreign intelligence collection capabilities to steal the trade secrets of foreign companies in order to give American companies a competitive advantage. We do not indiscriminately sweep up and store the contents of the communications of Americans, or of the citizenry of any country.

We do not use our intelligence collection for the purpose of repressing the citizens of any country because of their political, religious, or other beliefs. We collect metadata—information about communications—more broadly than we collect the actual content of communications, because it is less intrusive than collecting content and in fact can provide us information that helps us more narrowly focus our collection of content on appropriate targets. But it simply is not true that the United States government is listening to everything said by every citizen of any country.

Let me turn now to FISA. I'm going to talk about three provisions of that law: traditional FISA orders, the FISA business records provision, and section 702. These provisions impose limits on what kind of information can be collected and how it can be collected, require procedures restricting what we can do with the information we collect and how long we can keep it, and impose oversight to ensure that the rules are followed. This sets up a coherent regime in which protections are afforded at the front end, when information is collected; in the middle, when information is reviewed and used; and at the back end, through oversight, all working together to protect both national security and privacy. The rules vary depending on factors such as the type of information being collected (and in particular whether or not we are collecting the content of communications), the nature of the person or persons being targeted, and how narrowly or broadly focused the collection is. They aren't identical in every respect to the rules that apply to criminal investigations, but I hope to persuade you that they are reasonable and appropriate in the very different context of foreign intelligence.

So let's begin by talking about traditional FISA collection. Prior to the passage of FISA in 1978, the collection of foreign intelligence was essentially unregulated by statutory law. It was viewed as a core function of the executive branch. In fact, when the criminal wiretap provisions were originally enacted, Congress expressly provided that they did not "limit the constitutional power of the president . . . to obtain foreign intelligence information . . . deemed essential to the national security of the United States."[3] However, ten years later, as a result of abuses revealed by the Church and Pike committees, Congress imposed a judicial check on some aspects of electronic surveillance for foreign intelligence purposes. This is what is now codified in Title I of FISA, sometimes referred to as "traditional FISA."

FISA established a special court, the Foreign Intelligence Surveillance Court, to hear applications by the government to conduct electronic surveillance for foreign intelligence purposes. Because traditional FISA surveillance involves acquiring the content of communications, it is intrusive, implicating recognized privacy interests; and because it can be directed at individuals inside the United States, including American citizens, it implicates the Fourth Amendment. In FISA, Congress required that to get a "traditional" FISA electronic surveillance order, the government must establish probable cause to believe that the target of surveillance is a foreign power or an agent of a foreign power, a probable cause standard derived from the standard used for wiretaps in criminal cases. And if the target is a US person, he or she cannot be deemed an agent of a foreign power based solely on activity protected by the First Amendment—you cannot be the subject of surveillance merely because of what you believe or think.

Moreover, by law the use of information collected under traditional FISA must be subject to minimization procedures, a concept

---

3. 82 Stat. 214, formerly codified at 18 US C. § 2511(3).

that is key throughout FISA. Minimization procedures are procedures, approved by the FISA Court, that must be "reasonably designed in light of the purpose and technique of the particular surveillance, to minimize the acquisition and retention, and prohibit the dissemination, of nonpublicly available information concerning unconsenting United States persons consistent with the need of the United States to obtain, produce, and disseminate foreign intelligence information."[4] For example, they generally prohibit disseminating the identity of a US person unless the identity itself is necessary to understand the foreign intelligence or is evidence of a crime. The reference to the purpose and technique of the particular surveillance is important. Minimization procedures can and do differ depending on the purpose of the surveillance and the technique used to implement it. These tailored minimization procedures are an important way in which we provide appropriate protections for privacy.

So let me explain in general terms how traditional FISA surveillance works in practice. Let's say that the FBI suspects someone inside the United States of being a spy or a terrorist, and they want to conduct electronic surveillance. While there are some exceptions spelled out in the law, such as in the case of an emergency, as a general rule they have to present an application to the FISA Court establishing probable cause to believe that the person is an agent of a foreign power, according to the statutory definition. That application, by the way, is reviewed at several levels within both the FBI and Department of Justice before it is submitted to the court. Now, the target may have a conversation with a US person that has nothing to do with the foreign intelligence purpose of the surveillance, such as talking to a neighbor about a dinner party.

Under the minimization procedures, an analyst who listens to a conversation involving a US person that has no foreign intelligence value cannot generally share it or disseminate it unless it is evidence

---

4. See, e.g., 50 US C. §§ 1801(h)(1) & 1821(4)(A).

504 | Appendix: Litt—A

of a crime. Even if a conversation has foreign intelligence value—let's say a terrorist is talking to a confederate—that information may only be disseminated to someone with an appropriate need to know the information pursuant to his or her mission.

In other words, electronic surveillance under FISA's Title I implicates the well-recognized privacy interest in the contents of communications, and is subject to corresponding protections for that privacy interest—in terms of the requirements that it be narrowly targeted and that it have a substantial factual basis approved by the court, and in terms of the limitations imposed on use of the information.

Now let me turn to the second activity, the collection of business records. After FISA was passed, it became apparent that it left some significant gaps in our intelligence collection authority. In particular, while the government had the power in a criminal investigation to compel the production of records with a grand jury subpoena, it lacked similar authority in a foreign intelligence investigation. So a provision was added in 1998 to provide such authority and was amended by section 215 of the USA-PATRIOT Act passed shortly after 9/11. This provision, which is generally referred to as section 215, allows us to apply to the FISA Court for an order requiring production of documents or other tangible things when they are relevant to an authorized national security investigation. Records can be produced only if they are the type of records that could be obtained pursuant to a grand jury subpoena or other court process—in other words, where there is no statutory or other protection that would prevent use of a grand jury subpoena. In some respects this process is more restrictive than a grand jury subpoena. A grand jury subpoena is issued by a prosecutor without any prior judicial review, whereas under the FISA business records provision we have to get court approval. Moreover, as with traditional FISA, records obtained pursuant to the FISA business records provision are subject to court-approved minimization procedures that limit the retention and dissemination of information about US persons—another requirement that does not apply to grand jury subpoenas.

Now, of course, the FISA business records provision has been in the news because of one particular use of that provision. The FISA Court has repeatedly approved orders directing several telecommunications companies to produce certain categories of telephone metadata, such as the number calling, the number being called, and the date, time, and duration of the call. It's important to emphasize that under this program we do not get the content of any conversation; we do not get the identity of any party to the conversation; and we do not get any cell site or GPS locational information.

The limited scope of what we collect has important legal consequences. As I mentioned earlier, the Supreme Court has held that if you have voluntarily provided this kind of information to third parties, you have no reasonable expectation of privacy in that information. All of the metadata we get under this program is information that the telecommunications companies obtain and keep for their own business purposes. As a result, the government can get this information without a warrant, consistent with the Fourth Amendment.

Nonetheless, I recognize that there is a difference between getting metadata about one telephone number and getting it in bulk. From a legal point of view. section 215 only allows us to get records if they are "relevant" to a national security investigation, and from a privacy perspective people worry that, for example, the government could apply data mining techniques to a bulk data set and learn new personal facts about them—even though the underlying set of records is not subject to a reasonable expectation of privacy for Fourth Amendment purposes.

On the other hand, this information is clearly useful from an intelligence perspective: it can help identify links between terrorists overseas and their potential confederates in the United States. It's important to understand the problem this program was intended to solve. Many will recall that one of the criticisms made by the 9/11 Commission was that we were unable to find the connection between a hijacker who was in California and an Al Qaeda safe house in Yemen. Although NSA had collected the conversations from the Yemen safe house, they had no way to determine that the person at the other end of the conversation was in the United States, and hence to identify the homeland connection. This collection program is designed to help us find those connections.

In order to do so, however, we need to be able to access the records of telephone calls, possibly going back many years. However, telephone companies have no legal obligation to keep this kind of information, and they generally destroy it after a period of time determined solely by their own business purposes. And the different telephone companies have separate datasets in different formats, which makes analysis of possible terrorist calls involving several providers considerably slower and more cumbersome. That could be a significant problem in a fast-moving investigation where speed and agility are critical, such as the plot to bomb the New York City subways in 2009.

The way we fill this intelligence gap while protecting privacy illustrates the analytical approach I outlined earlier. From a subscriber's point of view, as I said before, the difference between a telephone company keeping records of his phone calls and the intelligence community keeping the same information is what the government could do with the records. That's an entirely legitimate concern. We deal with it by limiting what the intelligence community is allowed do with the information we get under this program—limitations that are approved by the FISA Court:

- First, we put this information in secure databases.
- Second, the only intelligence purpose for which this information can be used is counterterrorism.

- Third, we allow only a limited number of specially trained analysts to search these databases.
- Fourth, even those trained analysts are allowed to search the database only when they have a reasonable and articulable suspicion that a particular telephone number is associated with particular foreign terrorist organizations that have been identified to the court. The basis for that suspicion has to be documented in writing and approved by a supervisor.
- Fifth, they're allowed to use this information only in a limited way, to map a network of telephone numbers calling other telephone numbers.
- Sixth, because the database contains only metadata, even if the analyst finds a previously unknown telephone number that warrants further investigation, all she can do is disseminate the telephone number. She doesn't even know whose number it is. Any further investigation of that number has to be done pursuant to other lawful means and, in particular, any collection of the contents of communications would have to be done using another valid legal authority, such as a traditional FISA.
- Finally, the information is destroyed after five years.

The net result is that although we collect large volumes of metadata under this program, we only look at a tiny fraction of it, and only for a carefully circumscribed purpose—to help us find links between foreign terrorists and people in the United States. The collection has to be broad to be operationally effective, but it is limited to non-content data that has a low privacy value and is not protected by the Fourth Amendment. It doesn't even identify any individual. Only the narrowest, most important use of this data is permitted; other uses are prohibited. In this way, we protect both privacy and national security.

Some have questioned how collection of a large volume of tele-phone metadata could comply with the statutory requirement that business records obtained pursuant to section 215 be "relevant to an authorized investigation." While the government is working to deter-mine what additional information about the program can be declassi-fied and disclosed, including the actual court papers, I can give a broad summary of the legal basis. First, remember that the "autho-rized investigation" is an intelligence investigation, not a criminal one. The statute requires that an authorized investigation be conducted in accordance with guidelines approved by the attorney general, and those guidelines allow the FBI to conduct an investigation into a foreign terrorist entity if there is an "articulable factual basis . . . that reasonably indicates that the [entity] may have engaged in . . . inter-national terrorism or other threat to the national security," or may be planning or supporting such conduct.[5] In other words, we can inves-tigate an organization, not merely an individual or a particular act, if there is a factual basis to believe the organization is involved in terror-ism. And in this case, the government's applications to collect the telephony metadata have identified the particular terrorist entities that are the subject of the investigations.

Second, the standard of "relevance" required by this statute is not the standard that we think of in a civil or criminal trial under the rules of evidence. The courts have recognized in other contexts that "relevance" can be an extremely broad standard. For example, in the grand jury context, the Supreme Court has held that a grand jury subpoena is proper unless "there is no reasonable possibility that the category of materials the government seeks will produce information relevant to the general subject of the grand jury's investigation."[6] And in civil discovery, relevance is "construed broadly to encompass any

---

5. Attorney General's Guidelines for Domestic FBI Operations (2008), 23.
6. *United States v. R. Enterprises, Inc.*, 498 US 292, 301 (1991).

matter that bears on, or that reasonably could lead to other matter that could bear on, any issue that is or may be in the case."[7]

In each of these contexts, the meaning of "relevance" is sufficiently broad to allow for subpoenas or requests that encompass large volumes of records in order to locate within them a smaller subset of material that will be directly pertinent to, or actually be used in, furtherance of the investigation or proceedings. In other words, the requester is not limited to obtaining only those records that actually are potentially incriminating or pertinent to establishing liability, because to identify such records it is often necessary to collect a much broader set of the records that might potentially bear fruit by leading to specific material that could bear on the issue.

When it passed the business records provision, Congress made clear that it had in mind such broad concepts of relevance. The telephony metadata collection program meets this relevance standard because, as I explained earlier, the effectiveness of the queries allowed under the strict limitations imposed by the court—the queries based on "reasonable and articulable suspicion"—depends on collecting and maintaining the data from which the narrowly focused queries can be made. As in the grand jury and civil discovery contexts, the concept of "relevance" is broad enough to allow for the collection of information beyond that which ultimately turns out to be important to a terrorist-related investigation. While the scope of the collection at issue here is broader than typically might be acquired through a grand jury subpoena or civil discovery request, the basic principle is similar: the information is relevant because you need to have the broader set of records in order to identify within them the information that is actually important to a terrorism investigation. And the reasonableness of this method of collection is reinforced by all of the stringent limitations imposed by the court to ensure that the data is used only for the approved purpose.

---

7. *Oppenheimer Fund, Inc. v. Sanders*, 437 US 340, 351 (1978).

I want to repeat that the conclusion that the bulk metadata collection is authorized under section 215 is not that of the intelligence community alone. Applications to obtain this data have been repeatedly approved by numerous judges of the FISA Court, each of whom has determined that the application complies with all legal requirements. And Congress reauthorized section 215 in 2011, after the intelligence and judiciary committees of both houses had been briefed on the program and after information describing the program had been made available to all members. In short, all three branches of government have determined that this collection is lawful and reasonable—in large part because of the substantial protections we provide for the privacy of every person whose telephone number is collected.

The third program I want to talk about is section 702, part of the FISA Amendments Act of 2008. Again, a little history is in order. Generally speaking, as I said before, Title I of FISA, or traditional FISA, governs electronic surveillance conducted within the United States for foreign intelligence purposes. When FISA was first passed in 1978, Congress did not intend it to regulate the targeting of foreigners outside of the United States for foreign intelligence purposes.

This kind of surveillance was generally carved out of coverage under FISA by the way Congress defined "electronic surveillance." Most international communications in 1978 took place via satellite, so Congress excluded international radio communications from the definition of electronic surveillance covered by FISA, even when the radio waves were intercepted in the United States, unless the target of the collection was a US person in the United States.

Over time, that technology-based differentiation fell apart. By the early twenty-first century, most international communications travelled over fiber optic cables and thus were no longer "radio communications" outside of FISA's reach. At the same time, there was a dramatic increase in the use of the Internet for communications purposes, including by terrorists. As a result, Congress's original intention was frustrated; we were increasingly forced to go to the FISA Court to get individual warrants to conduct electronic surveillance of foreigners overseas for foreign intelligence purposes.

After 9/11, this burden began to degrade our ability to collect the communications of foreign terrorists. Section 702 created a new, more streamlined procedure to accomplish this surveillance. So section 702 was not, as some have called it, a "defanging" of the FISA Court's traditional authority. Rather, it extended the FISA Court's oversight to a kind of surveillance that Congress had originally placed outside of that oversight: the surveillance, for foreign intelligence purposes, of foreigners overseas. This American regime imposing judicial supervision of a kind of foreign intelligence collection directed at citizens of other countries is a unique limitation that, so far as I am aware, goes beyond what other countries require of their intelligence services when they collect against persons who are not their own citizens.

The privacy and constitutional interests implicated by this program fall between traditional FISA and metadata collection. On the one hand we are collecting the full content of communications; on the other hand we are not collecting information in bulk and we are only targeting non-US persons for valid foreign intelligence purposes. And the information involved is unquestionably of great importance for national security: collection under section 702 is one of the most valuable sources of foreign intelligence we have. Again, the statutory scheme and the means by which we implement it are designed to allow us to collect this intelligence while providing appropriate protections for privacy. Collection under section 702 does not require individual judicial orders authorizing collection against each target. Instead, the FISA Court approves annual certifications submitted by the attorney general and the director of national intelligence that identify categories of foreign intelligence that may be collected, subject to court-approved targeting procedures and minimization procedures.

The targeting procedures are designed to ensure that we target someone only if we have a valid foreign intelligence purpose; that we target only non-US persons reasonably believed to be outside of the United States; that we do not intercept wholly domestic communications; and that we do not target any person outside the United States as a backdoor means of targeting someone inside the United States. The procedures must be reviewed by the court to ensure that they are consistent with the statute and the Fourth Amendment. In other words, the targeting procedures are a way of minimizing the privacy impact of this collection both as to Americans and as to non-Americans by limiting the collection to its intended purpose.

The concept of minimization procedures should be familiar to you by now: they are the procedures that limit the retention and dissemination of information about US persons. We may incidentally acquire the communications of Americans even though we are not targeting them—for example, if they talk to non-US persons outside of the United States who are properly targeted for foreign intelligence collection. Some of these communications may be pertinent; some may not be. But the incidental acquisition of non-pertinent information is not unique to section 702. It is common whenever you lawfully collect information, whether it's by a criminal wiretap (where the target's conversations with his friends or family may be intercepted) or when we seize a terrorist's computer or address book, either of which is likely to contain non-pertinent information. In passing section 702, Congress recognized this reality and required us to establish procedures to minimize the impact of this incidental collection on privacy.

How does section 702 work in practice? As of today, there are certifications for several different categories of foreign intelligence information. Let's say that the intelligence community gets information that a terrorist is using a particular e-mail address. NSA analysts look at available data to assess whether that e-mail address would be a valid target under the statute—whether the e-mail address belongs to someone who is not a US person, whether the person with the e-mail address is outside the United States, and whether targeting that e-mail address is likely to lead to the collection of foreign intelligence relevant to one of the certifications. Only if all three requirements of the statute are met and validated by supervisors will the e-mail address be approved for targeting. We don't randomly target e-mail addresses or collect all foreign individuals' e-mails under section 702; we target specific accounts because we are looking for foreign intelligence information. And even after a target is approved, the court-approved procedures require NSA to continue to verify that its targeting decision is valid based on any new information.

Any communications that we collect under section 702 are placed in secure databases, again with limited access. Trained analysts are allowed to use this data for legitimate foreign intelligence purposes, but the minimization procedures require that if they review a communication that they determine involves a US person or information about a US person, and they further determine that it has no intelligence value and is not evidence of a crime, it must be destroyed. In any case, conversations that are not relevant are destroyed after a maximum of five years. So under section 702, we have a regime that involves judicial approval of procedures that are designed to narrow the focus of the surveillance and limit its impact on privacy. I've outlined three different collection programs, under different provisions of FISA, which all reflect the framework I described. In each case, we protect privacy by a multilayered system of controls on what we collect and how we use what we collect, controls that are based on the nature and intrusiveness of the collection, but that take into account the ways in which that collection can be useful to protect national security. But we don't simply set out a bunch of rules and trust people to follow them. There are substantial safeguards in place that help ensure that the rules are followed.

These safeguards operate at several levels. The first is technological. The same technological revolution that has enabled this kind of intelligence collection and made it so valuable also allows us to place relatively stringent controls on it. For one thing, intelligence agencies can work with providers so that they provide the information we are allowed to acquire under the relevant order, and not additional information. Second, we have secure databases to hold this data, to which only trained personnel have access. Finally, modern information security techniques allow us to create an audit trail tracking who uses these databases and how, so that we have a record that can enable us to identify any possible misuse. And I want to emphasize that there's no indication so far that anyone has defeated those technological controls and improperly gained access to the databases containing people's communications. Documents such as the leaked secondary order are kept on other NSA databases that do not contain this kind of information, to which many more NSA personnel have access.

We don't rely solely on technology. NSA has an internal compliance officer, whose job includes developing processes that all NSA personnel must follow to ensure that NSA is complying with the law. In addition, decisions about what telephone numbers we use as a basis for searching the telephone metadata are reviewed first within NSA and then by the Department of Justice. Decisions about targeting under section 702 are reviewed first within NSA and then by the Department of Justice and by my agency, the Office of the Director of National Intelligence, which has a dedicated civil liberties protection officer who actively oversees these programs. For Title I collection, the Department of Justice regularly conducts reviews to ensure that information collected is used and disseminated in accordance with the court-approved minimization procedures. Finally, independent inspectors general also review the operation of these programs. The point is not that these individuals are perfect; it's that as you have more and more people from more and more organizations overseeing the operation of the programs, it becomes less and less likely that unintentional errors will go unnoticed or that anyone will be able to misuse the information.

But wait, there's more. In addition to this oversight by the executive branch, there is considerable oversight by both the FISA Court and the Congress. As I've said, the FISA Court has to review and approve the procedures by which we collect intelligence under FISA to ensure that those procedures comply with the statute and the Fourth Amendment. In addition, any compliance matter, large or small, has to be reported to the court. Improperly collected information generally must be deleted, subject only to some exceptions set out in the court's orders, and corrective measures are taken and reported to the court until it is satisfied.

And I want to correct the erroneous claim that the FISA Court is a rubber stamp. Some people assume that because the FISA Court approves almost every application, it does not give these applications careful scrutiny. In fact, the exact opposite is true. The judges and their professional staff review every application carefully and often ask extensive and probing questions, seek additional information, or request changes before the application is ultimately approved. Yes, the court approves the great majority of applications at the end of this process; but before it does so, its questions and comments ensure that the application complies with the law.

Finally, there is the Congress. By law, we are required to keep the intelligence and judiciary committees informed about these programs, including detailed reports about their operation and compliance matters. We regularly engage with them and discuss these authorities, as we did this week, to provide them information to further their oversight responsibilities. For example, when Congress reauthorized section 215 in 2009 and 2011 and section 702 in 2012, information was made available to every member of Congress, by briefings and written material, describing these programs in detail.

* * *

In short, the procedures by which we implement collection under FISA are a sensible means of accounting for the changing nature of privacy in the information age. They allow the intelligence community to collect information that is important to protect our nation and its allies while protecting privacy by imposing appropriate limits on the use of that information. Much is collected, but access, analysis, and dissemination are subject to stringent controls and oversight. This same approach—making the extent and nature of controls over the use of information vary depending on the nature and sensitivity of the collection—is applied throughout our intelligence collection.

And make no mistake, our intelligence collection has helped to protect our nation from a variety of threats—and not only our nation, but the rest of the world. We have robust intelligence relationships with many other countries. These relationships go in both directions, but it is important to understand that we cannot use foreign intelligence to get around the limitations in our laws, and we assume that other countries similarly expect their intelligence services to operate in compliance with their own laws. By working closely with other countries, we have helped ensure our common security. For example, while many of the details remain classified, we have provided the Congress a list of fifty-four cases in which the bulk metadata and section 702 authorities have given us information that helped us understand potential terrorist activity and even disrupt it, from potential bomb attacks to material support for foreign terrorist organizations. Forty-one of these cases involved threats in other countries, including twenty-five in Europe. We were able to alert officials in these countries to these events, and help them fulfill their mission of protecting their nations, because of these capabilities.

I believe that our approach to achieving both security and privacy is effective and appropriate. It has been reviewed and approved by all three branches of government as consistent with the law and the Constitution. It is not the only way we could regulate intelligence collection, however. Even before the recent disclosures, the president said that we welcomed a discussion about privacy and national security, and we are working to declassify more information about our activities to inform that discussion. In addition, the Privacy and Civil Liberties Oversight Board—an independent body charged by law with overseeing our counterterrorism activities—has announced that it intends to provide the president and Congress a public report on the section 215 and 702 programs, including the collection of bulk metadata. The board met recently with the president, who welcomed their review and committed to providing them access to all materials they will need to fulfill their oversight and advisory functions. We look forward to working with the board on this important project.

This discussion can, and should, have taken place without the recent disclosures, which have brought into public view the details of sensitive operations that were previously discussed on a classified basis with the Congress and in particular with the committees that were set up precisely to oversee intelligence operations. The level of detail in the current public debate certainly reflects a departure from the historic understanding that the sensitive nature of intelligence operations demanded a more limited discussion. Whether or not the value of the exposure of these details outweighs the cost to national security is now a moot point. As the debate about our surveillance programs goes forward, I hope that my remarks today have helped provide an appreciation of the efforts that have been made—and will continue to be made—to ensure that our intelligence activities comply with our laws and reflect our values.

Thank you.

About the Authors

Kenneth Anderson is a professor of international law at Washington College of Law, American University, Washington, D.C., and a visiting fellow at the Hoover Institution, where he is also a member of its Task Force on National Security and Law. He specializes in international law, human rights and the laws of war, as well as international business law, international development, and not-for-profit law. Before joining the American University law faculty, he was founding director of the Human Rights Watch Arms Division and later general counsel to the Open Society Institute/Soros Foundations. He is author of *Living with the U.N.: American Responsibilities and International Order* (published by Hoover Institution Press, 2012).

Benjamin Wittes is a senior fellow in governance studies at the Brookings Institution and is a member of the Hoover Institution Task Force on National Security and Law. He is editor-in-chief of *Lawfare* (http://www.lawfareblog.com/), which is devoted to nonideological discussions of hard national security choices. He is the co-author most recently of *The Future of Violence: Robots and Germs, Hackers and Drones—Confronting a New Age of Threat* (Basic Books, 2015).

About the Hoover Institution's
JEAN PERKINS TASK FORCE ON
NATIONAL SECURITY AND LAW

The JEAN PERKINS TASK FORCE ON NATIONAL SECURITY AND LAW examines the rule of law, the laws of war, and American constitutional law with a view to making proposals that strike an optimal balance between individual freedom and the vigorous defense of the nation against terrorists both abroad and at home.

The task force's focus is the rule of law and its role in Western civilization, as well as the roles of international law and organizations, the laws of war, and US criminal law. Those goals will be accomplished by systematically studying the constellation of issues—social, economic, and political—on which striking a balance depends.

Peter Berkowitz serves as chair of the National Security and Law Task Force. Current members of this task force are: Kenneth Anderson, Peter Berkowitz, Philip Bobbitt, Jack Goldsmith, Stephen D. Krasner, Shavit Matias, Jessica Stern, Matthew Waxman, Ruth Wedgwood, Benjamin Wittes, and Amy Zegart.

Index

government branches, speeches and. *See* speeches in interaction with branches of government

"gradual evolution of human institutions," 302–3

Graham, Lindsey, 117–18, 247, 249, 290

Grassley, Charles, 339

Greenwald, Glenn, 220, 220n2

group think, 411

Guantánamo Bay detention facility
Abu Zubaydah, 180, 195, 229
Atta, M., 180
AUMF and, 56
Bergdahl and, 258
British detainees, 198
Detention and Denial: The Case for Candor after Guantánamo, 120–21, 121n26, 203n15
"The Emerging Law of Detention 2.0: The Guantanamo Habeas Cases as Lawmaking," 205n18
Executive Order 13492, 64n7, 66, 361, 457
future of, Obama's NDU speech, 175–81
Hambali (Riduan Isamuddin), 229
hunger strike, 141–42, 178, 322, 324
Johnson's speech, 93n8, 404
legacy detainees, 265–66
legal framework, 56
Miranda warnings, 62
Obama on, 52–53, 54, 55, 287–93
Qatani, M., 180
review of cases, 288
Uighur detainees, 288
See also detention

Hambali (Riduan Isamuddin), 229

Hamdan v. Rumsfeld, 205–6, 205n19, 394

Hamdi v. Rumsfeld, 57, 194n5, 337, 362, 416

Harris, Syed, 389

Harvard Law School professor. *See* Goldsmith, Jack

Harvard Law School speeches. *See* Brennan-A; Preston-A

Hasan, Nidal, 110, 110n22
See also Fort Hood shooting

Headley, David, 369, 389, 461

heckler interruption, Obama's NDU speech, 322–25

Heritage Foundation speech. *See* Johnson-A

Heyns, Christof, 195–96

Hezb-i Islami Gulbuddin, 95n10, 195

Hezbollah, 129, 308, 394

High-Value Detainee Interrogation Group (HIG), 62, 458–59

Holder, Eric
letter (from Attorney General Eric Holder to Senator Patrick Leahy), 145, 156, 169, 332–39
testimony to Senate Judiciary Committee, drone strikes, 84–85, 433

Holder-A (Northwestern University School of Law address)
capture of terrorists, 432
criticism of, 85
lethal force, against American citizens, 434–35
lethal force, lawful use, 432–33
military commissions, 429–31
targeted killing of US citizens, 48–51, 434–36
terrorist prosecutions, 428–29
text of speech, 424–38

Hoover Task Force on National Security and the Law, 16

hostage situation, targeted killing, 105–6

hot battlefields
Afghanistan, 191, 194, 414, 453, 470, 476, 478
armed conflict's limit, 32, 33
first-term speeches, 37, 95
Mauritania detainee, 97n11, 195

Hoyer, Steny, 339

H.R. 1904, 212n25

human rights
cyber-operations and, 75
Universal Declaration of Human Rights, 380
See also international humanitarian law

Human Rights First, 189

Human Rights Watch, 189, 232, 236, 237n10

humanity (law-of-war principle)
Brennan on, 43, 473
first-term speeches, 101–2

military commissions, advantages,
387–90
overview of speech, 384–85
recent history of counterterrorism strategy, 385–87
text of speech, 384–97

law articulation, through speeches, 8,
84–90
See also speeches
law enforcement approach. *See* criminal-
justice approach
"Law Enforcement as a Counterterrorism
Tool." *See* Kris-A
Law of 9/11, 358–59
law of armed conflict (law of war)
Bush administration, detention and
interrogations, 96, 98
cyber-operations and, 72–75, 373
drone strikes, 42–43, 101–2
international humanitarian law and, 32,
195, 221
jus ad bellum rules, 74, 372, 376, 377
jus in bello rules, 74, 372, 373, 374, 378
principles of, 25–26
targeted killings, 101–2
See also armed conflict; distinction;
humanity; necessity; proportionality
law-free zone, cyberspace, 371–72
"Lawfulness of a Lethal Operation
Directed Against a U.S. Citizen Who
is a Senior Operational Leader of
Al-Qa'ida or An Associated Force,"
51, 108n19
Leahy, Patrick J., 332–39
See also Obama-C (NDU speech)
legacy detainees, Guantánamo, 265–66
legal briefs filed in court cases, 87–88
legal policy framework. *See* speeches
*Legislating the War on Terror: An Agenda
for Reform*, 3n1
"Lethal Force Under Law," 6n4
letter (from Attorney General Eric Holder
to Senator Patrick Leahy)
al-Awlaki killing, 169
summary of, 145, 156
text of letter, 332–39
See also Obama-C (NDU speech)
Levin, Carl, 339
libertarian wing of Republican Party

Obama administration's speeches, criticism of, 217, 243–46
Paul, R., 143, 211, 217, 243–44
Libyan militant, Abu Khattala, 258–59,
264, 264n2
Litt-A ("Privacy, Technology, and National
Security: An Overview of Intelligence
Collection"), 494–517
changing societal norms, impact of,
497–500
FISA collection, 500–517
introduction, 494–95
legal framework, 495–97
section 215, PATRIOT ACT, 504, 505,
508, 510, 515, 517
section 702, FISA Amendments Act,
501, 510–14, 515, 516
"The Longest Battle," 227n4

MacDonald, Bruce, 400
Madison, James, 148, 307
Maghreb. *See* Al Qaeda in the Islamic
Maghreb
Manes, Jonathan, 4n3
Manning, Lauren, 325
Manual for Military Commissions, 69,
400, 409
al-Marri, 290
Martins, Mark, 400
Mathews v. Eldridge, 270, 270n7
McCain, John, 247, 249, 287, 322
McConnell, Mitch, 339
McKeon, Buck, 114n24, 339
McMahon, Colleen, 85
McRaven, William, 117–19, 119n25, 120,
121
media shield law, 182, 320
"Memorandum For The Attorney General
Re: Applicability of Federal Criminal
Laws and the Constitution to Con-
templated Lethal Operations Against
Shaykh Anwar al-Aulaqi," 266–70,
267n3
"Memorandum Opinion on the Geo-
graphic Scope of the International
Covenant on Civil and Political
Rights," 237, 237n11
Menendez, Robert, 339
"MEPs concerned about EU drone pro-
gramme," 234n6

RD UNIVERSITY